RENEWALS 458-4574
DATE DUE

**WITHDRAWN
UTSA Libraries**

PROGRESS IN TOURISM MARKETING

ADVANCES IN TOURISM RESEARCH

Series Editor: **Professor Stephen J. Page**
University of Stirling, UK
s.j.page@stir.ac.uk

Advances in Tourism Research series publishes monographs and edited volumes that comprise state-of-the-art research findings, written and edited by leading researchers working in the wider field of tourism studies. The series has been designed to provide a cutting edge focus for researchers interested in tourism, particularly the management issues now facing decision-makers, policy analysts and the public sector. The audience is much wider than just academics and each book seeks to make a significant contribution to the literature in the field of study by not only reviewing the state of knowledge relating to each topic but also questioning some of the prevailing assumptions and research paradigms which currently exist in tourism research. The series also aims to provide a platform for further studies in each area by highlighting key research agendas, which will stimulate further debate and interest in the expanding area of tourism research. The series is always willing to consider new ideas for innovative and scholarly books, inquiries should be made directly to the Series Editor.

Published:

Destination Marketing Organisations
PIKE

Small Firms in Tourism: International Perspectives
THOMAS

Tourism and Transport
LUMSDON & PAGE

Tourism Public Policy and the Strategic Management of Failure
KERR

Managing Tourist Health and Safety in the New Millennium
WILKS & PAGE

Indigenous Tourism
RYAN AND AICKEN

Taking Tourism to the Limits
RYAN, PAGE & AICKEN

An International. Handbook on Tourism Education
AIREY & TRIBE

Tourism in Turbulent Times
WILKS, PENDERGAST & LEGGAT

Benchmarking National Tourism Organisations and Agencies
LENNON, SMITH, COCKEREL & TREW

Extreme Tourism: Lessons from the World's Coldwater Islands
BALDACCHINO

Forthcoming titles include:

Tourism and Small Businesses in the New Europe
THOMAS & AUGUSTYN

Tourism Micro-clusters & Networks: The Growth of Tourism
MICHAEL

Related Elsevier Journals — sample copies available on request
Annals of Tourism Research
International Journal of Hospitality Management
Tourism Management
World Development

PROGRESS IN TOURISM MARKETING

METIN KOZAK
University of Namur, Belgium

LUISA ANDREU
University of Valencia, Spain

Amsterdam • Boston • Heidelberg • London • New York • Oxford
Paris • San Diego • San Francisco • Singapore • Sydney • Tokyo

Elsevier
The Boulevard, Langford Lane, Kidlington, Oxford OX5 1GB, UK
Radarweg 29, PO Box 211, 1000 AE Amsterdam, The Netherlands

First edition 2006

Copyright © 2006 Elsevier Ltd. All rights reserved

No part of this publication may be reproduced, stored in a retrieval system
or transmitted in any form or by any means electronic, mechanical, photocopying,
recording or otherwise without the prior written permission of the publisher

Permissions may be sought directly from Elsevier's Science & Technology Rights
Department in Oxford, UK: phone (+44) (0) 1865 843830; fax (+44) (0) 1865 853333;
email: permissions@elsevier.com. Alternatively you can submit your request online by
visiting the Elsevier web site at http://elsevier.com/locate/permissions, and selecting
Obtaining permission to use Elsevier material

Notice
No responsibility is assumed by the publisher for any injury and/or damage to persons
or property *as* a matter of products liability, negligence or otherwise, or from any use
or operation of any methods, products, instructions or ideas contained in the material
herein, Because of rapid advances in the medical sciences, in particular, independent
verification of diagnoses and drug dosages should be made

British Library Cataloguing in Publication Data
A catalogue record for this book is available from the British Library

Library of Congress Cataloging-in-Publication Data
A catalog record for this book is available from the Library of Congress

ISBN-13: 978-0-08-045040-7
ISBN-10: 0-08-045040-7

For information on all Elsevier publications
visit our website at books.elsevier.com

Printed and bound in The Netherlands
06 07 08 09 10 10 9 8 7 6 5 4 3 2 1

Contents

List of Figures	ix
List of Tables	xi
Contributors	xv
About the Authors	xix
Preface *Metin Kozak and Luisa Andreu*	xxv
1. Introduction: Tourism and Hospitality Marketing Research — Update and Suggestions *Haemoon Oh, Byeong-Yong Kim and Jee Hye Shin*	1

Part I: "IT" Marketing

Introduction *Metin Kozak and Luisa Andreu*	31
2. A Historical Development of "IT" in Tourism Marketing *Yasar Sari, Metin Kozak and Teoman Duman*	33
3. Use of Electronic Documents and Brochures for Sustainable Tourism Marketing *Yasar Sari, Ismail Cinar and Dogan Kutukiz*	45
4 Online Travel Purchases from Third-Party Travel Web Sites *Cihan Cobanoglu, Jonathan H. Powley, Ali Şukru Cetinkaya and Pamela R. Cummings*	55

Part II: Destination Marketing and Competitiveness

Introduction *Metin Kozak and Luisa Andreu*	73

vi Contents

5. Destination Marketing: A Framework for Future Research 75
   Alan Fyall, Brian Garrod and Cevat Tosun

6. A Reclassification of Tourism Industries to Identify the Focal Actors 87
   David Ermen and Juergen Gnoth

7. A Comparative Analysis of Competition Models for Tourism Destinations 101
   Norbert Vanhove

8. Media Strategies for Improving National Images during Tourism Crises 115
   Eli Avraham and Eran Ketter

Part III: Market Segmentation

Introduction 129
Metin Kozak and Luisa Andreu

9. Using the Experientially based Approach to Segment Heritage Site Visitors 133
   Avital Biran, Yaniv Poria and Arie Reichel

10. Motivations and Lifestyle: Segmentation Using the Construct A.I.O 147
    *Ana M. González Fernández, Miguel Cervantes Blanco and
    Carmen Rodríguez Santos*

11. Correlates of Destination Risk Perception and Risk Reduction Strategies 161
    Galia Fuchs and Arie Reichel

12. Segmented (Differential or Discriminatory) Pricing and Its Consequences 171
    Asli D. A. Tasci, Ali Kemal Gurbuz and William C. Gartner

Part IV: Consumer Behavior

Introduction 187
Metin Kozak and Luisa Andreu

13. Seeking to Escape: Sights over Approach-Avoidance Dialectics 191
    Carlos Peixeira Marques

14. Cultural Approximation and Tourist Satisfaction 207
    Muammer Tuna

15. The Role of Non-Monetary Costs in a Model of Leisure Travel Value 221
    Teoman Duman, Goknil Nur Kocak and Ozkan Tutuncu

16. Studying Visitor Loyalty to Rural Tourist Destinations 239
    Elisabeth Kastenholz, Maria João Carneiro and Celeste Eusébio

17. Waiting Time Effects on the Leisure Experience and Visitor Emotions 255
    Juergen Gnoth, J. Enrique Bigné and Luisa Andreu

18. Effects of Price Promotions on Consumer Loyalty towards Travel Agencies 269
    S. Campo Martínez and M. J. Yagüe Guillén

Author Index 281

Subject Index 291

List of Figures

Figure 2.1:	Developments in IT and its use in tourism.	38
Figure 10.1:	Hipotesis.	154
Figure 12.1:	Marketing exchange model.	176
Figure 13.1:	Estimated means of motivation scores by age and employment status.	201
Figure 14.1:	The tourist satisfaction process.	208
Figure 15.1:	Proposed cost-based model of leisure travel value.	222
Figure 15.2:	Tested cost-based model of leisure travel value.	232
Figure 16.1:	Model specification.	245
Figure 16.2:	Global Model of likelihood to come back.	247
Figure 16.3:	Separate models of likelihood to come back for Portuguese and foreign tourists.	250
Figure 17.1:	A model of visitors' experience in LTS.	259
Figure 18.1:	Theoretical model of price promotions on consumer loyalty towards a commercial establishment.	271
Figure 18.2:	A model of the effect of promotions on consumer loyalty towards a travel agency.	276

List of Tables

Table 1.1:	Hospitality and tourism marketing research by subjet.	4
Table 1.2:	Hospitality and tourism marketing research by industry application.	6
Table 1.3:	Hospitality and tourism marketing research by method employed.	7
Table 1.4:	Industry trends and current research issues.	18
Table 2.1:	E-marketing applications in tourism.	41
Table 3.1:	Services offered in the websites of the organizations.	49
Table 3.2:	Advertisement and promotion items used in electronic documents and brochures in the websites of the organizations.	49
Table 3.3:	Opinions of the organizations about their own paper consumption in the years following a website possession.	50
Table 4.1:	Demographic information of sample.	59
Table 4.2:	Internet behavior.	60
Table 4.3:	Purchasing behavior online.	61
Table 4.4:	Online travel expenditures per year.	62
Table 4.5:	Summary of factor analysis Web site quality.	63
Table 4.6:	Summary of factor analysis purchasing motivators.	64
Table 4.7:	Summary of factor analysis Travel information source.	65
Table 6.1:	All industry groups and subgroups included in the TSA analysis (Statistics New Zealand, 2002).	91
Table 6.2:	Industries excluded from the new classification.	96
Table 6.3:	Industries reclassified as TRIs in the new classification.	97
Table 7.1:	The determinants of competitive advantage in tourism.	104

Table 7.2:	Strengths with respect to competitiveness — the case of Bruges.	105
Table 7.3:	Weaknesses or points for improvement with respect to competitiveness — the case of Bruges.	106
Table 7.4:	Factors conditioning the competitive position.	108
Table 7.5:	The major competition variables by model.	112
Table 9.1:	Timothy's classification of heritage sites.	135
Table 9.2:	Perception of the site in relation to visitors' personal heritage.	137
Table 9.3:	Perception of the site as world, national and local heritage.	138
Table 9.4:	Tourists' expectations of on-site interpretation.	139
Table 9.5:	Factor analysis of visitor's expectations of on-site interpretation.	140
Table 9.6:	Expectations of the interpretation in relation to perceptions of the site.	142
Table 10.1:	Applications of AIO in tourism.	150
Table 10.2:	Technical specifications.	152
Table 10.3:	Breakdown of population by segments.	154
Table 10.4:	Lifestyles and tourist motivations.	156
Table 10.5:	Comparison of the relationship between lifestyle and social motivation of the travel Whole sample/segments.	158
Table 11.1:	Age distribution of interviewees.	164
Table 11.2:	Perceived average income.	164
Table 11.3:	Validation results: Factor analysis results (Varimax rotation).	165
Table 11.4:	Discriminate analysis results FIT vs. groups travelers risk dimensions.	168
Table 11.5:	Discriminate analysis FIT vs. groups, travelers, risk reduction strategies.	169
Table 12.1:	The reasons and number of managers mentioning these reasons.	177
Table 12.2:	Potential results of equal pricing for domestic and foreign markets.	178
Table 13.1:	Factor analysis solution of pleasure travel motives.	195
Table 13.2:	MANOVA results for the fixed effects of age and employment on motivation dimensions.	198

Table 13.3:	Estimates of the fixed effects of age and employment on motivation dimensions.	200
Table 14.1:	Demographic distribution of the sample.	210
Table 14.2:	Descriptive statistics.	212
Table 14.3:	Factor analysis (rotated component matrix) internal reliability.	214
Table 14.4:	Comparison of tourist satisfaction by nationalities.	215
Table 15.1:	Principal component analysis of perceived non-monetary price scale items.	226
Table 15.2:	Final measurement items.	228
Table 15.3:	Correlations between constructs in the research model.	229
Table 15.4:	Multiple regression analysis on perceived overall value.	229
Table 15.5:	Multiple regression analysis on behavioural intentions.	230
Table 15.6:	Demographic and travelling profile of the respondents.	231
Table 15.7:	Path estimates for the proposed links in the research model.	233
Table 16.1:	PCA of cognitive images.	244
Table 16.2:	Determinants of the likelihood to come back to North Portugal.	246
Table 16.3:	Determinants of the likelihood to come back to North Portugal.	249
Table 17.1:	Socio-demographic characteristics.	261
Table 17.2:	Final multi-group structural equation model results with partial metric invariance constraints.	263
Table 18.1:	Reliability and validity of "perceived quality" and "travel agency loyalty".	272
Table 18.2:	The effect of price promotions on the formation of brand loyalty.	274

Contributors

Luisa Andreu
University of Valencia, Spain

Eli Avraham
University of Haifa, Israel

J. Enrique Bigné
University of Valencia, Spain

Avital Biran
Ben-Gurion University of the Negev, Israel

Miguel Cervantes Blanco
University of Leon, Spain

Maria João Carneiro
University of Aveiro, Portugal

Ali Şukru Cetinkaya
Selcuk University, Turkey

Ismail Cinar
Mugla University, Turkey

Cihan Cobanoglu
University of Delaware, USA

Pamela R. Cummings
University of Delaware, USA

Teoman Duman
Gaziosmanpaşa University, Turkey

David Ermen
University of Otago, New Zealand

Celeste Eusébio
University of Aveiro, Portugal

Ana M. González Fernández
University of Leon, Spain

Galia Fuchs
College of Management, Israel

Alan Fyall
Bournemouth University, UK

Brian Garrod
University of Wales, Aberystwyth, UK

William C. Gartner
University of Minnesota, USA

Juergen Gnoth
University of Otago, New Zealand

M. J. Yagüe Guillén
Autónoma University of Madrid, Spain

Ali Kemal Gurbuz
Balikesir University, Turkey

Elisabeth Kastenholz
University of Aveiro, Portugal

Eran Ketter
University of Haifa, Israel

Byeong-Yong Kim
The University of Suwon, Korea

Goknil Nur Kocak
Dokuz Eylul University, Turkey

Metin Kozak
University of Namur, Belgium

Dogan Kutukiz
Mugla University, Turkey

Carlos Peixeira Marques
CETRAD, Portugal

S. Campo Martínez
Autónoma University of Madrid, Spain

Haemoon Oh
Iowa State University, IA, USA

Yaniv Poria
Ben-Gurion University of the Negev, Israel

Jonathan H. Powley
Trump International Hotel & Tower, USA

Arie Reichel
University of the Negev, Israel

Carmen Rodríguez Santos
University of Leon, Spain

Yasar Sari
Mugla University, Turkey

Jee Hye Shin
Iowa State University, USA

Asli D. A. Tasci
Mugla University, Turkey

Cevat Tosun
Mustafa Kemal University, Turkey

Muammer Tuna
Mugla University, Turkey

Ozkan Tutuncu
Dokuz Eylul University, Turkey

Norbert Vanhove
University Leuven, Belgium

About the Authors

Luisa Andreu is a lecturer in marketing at the University of Valencia, Spain. She obtained her Master's degree in Tourism from the International Centre for Tourism at Bournemouth University, UK, and a Ph.D. in Business Administration from the University of Valencia. She is a member of the Spanish Association of Scientifics in Tourism. Her research interests include consumer behaviour, destination marketing, and cross-cultural issues in service marketing.

Eli Avraham is a senior lecturer in the Department of Communication, the University of Haifa, Israel. He obtained a Ph.D. from Hebrew University, Israel. His research interests include, among others, images of social groups and places in the media, marketing places, advertising, and public relations. He has published numerous articles and books on these subjects.

J. Enrique Bigné is a professor of marketing at the University of Valencia, Spain. He obtained his Ph.D. in Business Administration and Economics from the University of Valencia, Spain. He is a member of the Spanish Association of Scientifics in Tourism, European Marketing Academy, Academy of Marketing Science, and American Marketing Association, among others. His research interests include consumer behaviour, strategic marketing, services marketing, and advertising.

Avital Biran is a Ph.D. student at the School of Management, Ben Gurion University, Israel. Her Ph.D. focuses on tourists' experiences at heritage settings.

Miguel Cervantes Blanco is an assistant professor of marketing and trade research in the Department of Management and Business Economy, at the University of Leon, Spain. He obtained his Ph.D. in Business Sciences. He is the author of a number of papers and contributions to publications dealing with market research and marketing. His research lines include marketing, brands, and city marketing.

Maria João Carneiro is a lecturer of tourism and marketing at the University of Aveiro, Portugal. She has a five-year degree in Tourism Management and Planning, an MBA, and is now doing a Ph.D. in Tourism. Her research focuses on consumer behaviour in tourism, namely on decision-making processes, and information search. Another area of research is the development of new products in tourism.

Ali Şukru Cetinkaya is an instructor in the Department of Tourism and Hospitality Management, Selcuk University, Turkey. He has over 10 years of industry experience. He is the co-author of a textbook entitled *Management in Hospitality and Tourism Organizations Under the Light of Information Technologies: An Informatics Viewpoint*.

Ismail Cinar is a lecturer in the Department of Landscape, Mugla University, Turkey. He obtained his Master's degree in Landscape Architecture and his Ph.D. degree in Landscape Planning related with bioclimate, from Ege University, Turkey. His research interest is in the field of natural environmental parameters especially bioclimate in relation to physical planning in order to construct comfortable residences as in tourism activity.

Cihan Cobanoglu is an assistant professor of Hospitality Information Technology, the University of Delaware. He is a Certified Hospitality Technology Professional (CHTP) commissioned by Hospitality Financial and Technology Professionals, and Educational Institute of American Hotel and Lodging Association.

Pamela R. Cummings is an associate professor of Hotel, Restaurant, and Institutional Management, the University of Delaware, USA. She has completed industry internships with Marriott, Red Lobster, Hyatt, ARAMARK, and Watson Foods (a wholesale food distributor). The courses she currently teaches include Introduction to Hospitality, Cross-Cultural Etiquette and Protocol, and Meeting and Conference Management.

Teoman Duman is the lecturer and director of School of Tourism and Hotel Management, Gaziosmanpasa University, Turkey. He completed his Master's degree in Tourism and Hotel Management, the University of South Carolina, USA and obtained his Ph.D. degree in Leisure Studies from Penn State University, USA. He specializes in different areas of tourism marketing such as destination marketing, consumer behaviour, service value, and special interest tourism.

David Ermen is a Ph.D. candidate in the Department of Marketing at the University of Otago, New Zealand. His thesis addresses issues of reputation management in tourism destinations with a focus on collective action that occurs in destination networks.

Celeste Eusébio is a lecturer of tourism at the University of Aveiro, Portugal. She holds a BA degree in Tourism Management and Planning, a Master's degree in Economics, and is about to complete her Ph.D. in Tourism. Her research interests are in consumer behaviour, economic impacts of tourism, forecasting tourism demand, and destination development.

Ana M. González Fernández is an assistant professor of marketing and trade research in the Department of Management and Business Economy, the University of Leon, Spain. She gained her Ph.D. degree in Business Sciences from the same university. She is the author of a number of papers and has contributions to international and national publications specialized in marketing. Her research lines entail marketing, consumer behaviour, market segmentation, and lifestyles.

Galia Fuchs is a lecturer of marketing management in the College of Management and Ben-Gurion University, Israel. An industrial engineer by training, Galia specializes in service and product marketing. During the last three years she studied extensively the destination risk perceptions of tourists of various segments: from mass tourists to backpackers.

Alan Fyall is a reader in tourism management in the International Centre for Tourism and Hospitality Research, and Head of Research within the School of Services Management, Bournemouth University, UK. He has published widely in the areas of tourism and marketing. Alan has recently co-authored *Tourism Principles and Practice* and *Tourism Marketing: A Collaborative Approach*. He has also presented numerous conference papers across the world.

Brian Garrod is a senior lecturer in tourism management at the Institute of Rural Sciences, the University of Wales, Aberystwyth, UK. He holds an honours degree in Economics from Portsmouth Polytechnic, a Master's degree in Agricultural Economics from the University of East Anglia and a Ph.D. from the University of Portsmouth, all in the UK. His main interests are in sustainable tourism, ecotourism, heritage tourism, and visitor attractions.

William C. Gartner is a professor of applied economics at the University of Minnesota, USA. He has a Ph.D. in Resource Development with an emphasis in Resource Economics from Michigan State University, USA. Gartner has conducted numerous research studies in the area of tourism image development, seasonal home impacts, tourism marketing, and methods for tourism research.

Juergen Gnoth is a senior lecturer at the University of Otago, New Zealand. He obtained his Ph.D. in Tourism from University of Otago. His interests lie in consumer behaviour, tourism services marketing, and marketing ethics. Juergen is a leading member of the Tourism Research Group and is involved in researching the constructs of intentions, expectations, image, and satisfaction of international tourists. Other research deals with understanding and measuring the influence of emotions on consumption behaviour.

M. J. Yagüe Guillén is a professor of marketing at the Faculty of Economics, the Autónoma University of Madrid, Spain. She obtained her Ph.D. in Business Administration from the University of Zaragoza, Spain. She is a member of the European Marketing Academy and the European Association for Education and Research in Commercial Distribution. She is specialized in the study of prices, promotions, distribution, and tourism marketing and has published in these and related areas.

A. Kemal Gurbuz is a professor of economics in the School of Tourism and Hospitality Management, Balikesir University, Turkey. He has a Ph.D. in Economic Policy from

Uludag University, Turkey. His area of research includes several subjects related to economics of tourism and travel operations.

Elisabeth Kastenholz is an assistant professor of marketing in the University of Aveiro, Portugal. She also coordinates the undergraduate degree course of Tourism Management and Planning at the University of Aveiro. Holding a degree in Tourism Management and Planning, an MBA, and a Ph.D. in Tourism Studies, her research focuses on consumer behaviour in tourism, destination marketing, and sustainable destination development.

Eran Ketter is an undergraduate student in the Department of Communication, the University of Haifa, Israel, and works as a teaching and research assistant in the department. His research interests include crisis communication, branding, marketing, and advertising.

Byeong-Yong Kim is a lecturer of hospitality and tourism management, the University of Suwon, Korea. He received a Ph.D. degree in Foodservice and Lodging Management from Iowa State University, USA. His teaching areas include hospitality and tourism management and marketing research. His research interests are in the areas of relationship marketing, strategic management, and customer relationship management.

Goknil Nur Kocak completed her Master's degree in Tourism and Hotel Management, Mersin University, Turkey. She continues her Ph.D. in Tourism Management at Dokuz Eylul University, Turkey. She has over 10 years industry experience at sales and marketing departments. Her research interests include customer sacrifices to obtain a service, customer behaviour in tourism, and customer perceptions.

Metin Kozak is a lecturer in the School of Tourism and Hotel Management, Mugla University, Turkey. He obtained his Master's degree in Tourism from Dokuz Eylul University, Turkey and a Ph.D. in Tourism from Sheffield Hallam University, UK. His main research interests focus on consumer behaviour, repeat travel, benchmarking, performance measurement, competitiveness, destination management and marketing, and Mediterranean tourism.

Dogan Kutukiz is an assistant professor in the Department of Tourism Management, Mugla University, Turkey. He obtained both his Master's and Ph.D. degrees in Finance Management from Inonu University, Turkey. His research interest encompasses accounting.

Carlos Peixeira Marques obtained MBA and MSc degrees in Marketing from Catholic University of Lisbon, Portugal. He is a researcher in consumer behaviour and quantitative market research at the Centre for Transdisciplinary Development Studies (CETRAD) and lecturer at the Department of Business, Economics, and Sociology, UTAD, Portugal.

S. Campo Martínez is a lecturer in marketing at the Faculty of Economics at the Autónoma University of Madrid, Spain. She obtained her Ph.D. in Business Administration from the Autónoma University of Madrid. Her research interests focus on sales promotions, pricing, distribution, and tourism marketing.

Haemoon Oh is an associate professor at Iowa State University, USA, where he teaches hospitality marketing and law and directs hospitality graduate education. His current research is focused on customers' (travellers') experiential perceptions and related scale development. His work appears in a number of hospitality and tourism journals, several of which have resulted in awards.

Yaniv Poria is a lecturer in the Department of Hotel and Tourism Management, Ben Gurion University of the Negev, Israel. His main research interest is the management of heritage in tourism.

Jonathan H. Powley, currently works as a Junior Concierge at the Trump International Hotel and Tower, USA. He is a graduate of Hotel, Restaurant, and Institutional Management programme at the University of Delaware, USA.

Arie Reichel is the Dean of the School of Management, Ben-Gurion University, Israel. He has founded the Eilat Campus and the Department of Hotel and Tourism Management. He published numerous articles in tourism journals such as the *Annals of Tourism Research* and *Tourism Management* and serves on the editorial boards of several refereed journals.

Carmen Rodríguez Santos is an assistant professor of marketing and trade research in the Department of Management and Business Economy, the University of Leon, Spain. He holds a Ph.D. in Economics and Business Sciences, and has papers presented at conferences and published in national and international journals. He is specialized in consumer behaviour, advertising, and strategy and brand image.

Yasar Sari is a lecturer in the Department of Informatics, Mugla University, Turkey. He obtained his Master's degree in Information Technology from Karadeniz Teknik University, Turkey and his Ph.D. degree in Economics from Mugla University, Turkey. His research interest is in the field of information technologies related to finance management and tourism marketing.

Jee Hye Shin is a doctoral candidate in Foodservice and Lodging Management at Iowa State University, USA. She received her Master's degree from the University of Nevada, Las Vegas, USA, and her current research interests include customer perceptions of psychophysical benefits of food consumptions and fine dining experiences.

Asli D. A. Tasci is an assistant professor of marketing in the School of Tourism and Hospitality Management, Mugla University, Turkey. Her BA is from the Middle East Technical University, Turkey and her MS and Ph.D. degrees are from Michigan State University, USA. Her interests entail a range of subjects in the general area of travel and destination marketing.

Cevat Tosun is an associate professor of the School of Tourism and Hospitality Management, Mustafa Kemal University, Turkey. He gained a BA from Cukurova

University, Turkey; MSc from Erciyes University, Turkey; MPhil and Ph.D. in Tourism from Strathclyde University, UK. He works on tourism development, regional planning, destination marketing, sustainable tourism, and impacts of tourism development.

Muammer Tuna is an associate professor in the Department of Sociology, Mugla University, Turkey. He has a Ph.D. degree in Environmental Sociology from the Mississippi State University, USA. His main areas of interests are environmental sociology, environmental attitudes, modernization, tourism, and environment. He has published some books and articles on these subjects.

Ozkan Tutuncu is an associate professor in the Department of Tourism and Hotel Management, Dokuz Eylul University, Turkey. He completed his Master's and Ph.D. degrees in the same department and at the same university. He has several papers published in national and international journals, four books, and many research projects in the field of quality management.

Norbert Vanhove studied at the University of Gent and obtained his Ph.D. in Economics at the Erasmus University in Rotterdam, The Netherlands. He is a professor at the University of Leuven, Belgium. He is vice president of the International Association of Scientific Experts in Tourism and has been the Secretary General of the Tourist Research Centre since 1965. He has published several books about regional economics and the economics of tourism.

Preface

The development of research in tourism marketing should first be analysed by situating the appearance and evolution of the discipline of marketing in time (Bigné, 1996). The academic conceptualization of marketing has gradually evolved during the course of the 20th century (Bartels, 1988). Marketing was initially conceived as a set of activities concerned with the distribution of products from producer to consumer. Since then several conceptions of marketing have appeared (AMA, 1960) resulting in the intense debate of the 1970s, which led to an identity crisis in marketing (Bartels, 1988) and the subsequent consideration of the application of marketing to non-profit organizations. A large number of these ideas crystallized in the definition of the American Marketing Association in 1985, which emphasized the role of marketing by extending its sphere of action to create exchange and satisfy individual and organizational objectives, both in goods and services and idea.

In the 1980s, the emergence of services marketing as a sub-discipline becomes a notable extension of marketing (Brown, Fisk, & Bitner, 1994; Vargo & Lusch, 2004). In the US, service firms such as airlines, financial services, health services and telecommunications started a stage of great competition during the 1980s (Brown et al., 1994), with encouraging academics and practitioners to better understand service marketing. During the 1980s, Berry (1983), a service marketing researcher, was the pioneer in introducing the "relationship marketing" term which, together with a higher customer orientation via the added-value concept, has evolved to the new definition of marketing (Keefe, 2004). Kotler, Bower, and Makens (1996) define marketing as "a social and managerial process by which individuals and groups obtain what they need and want through creating and exchanging products and value with other" (p. 8). Nowadays, the American Marketing Association (AMA, 2004) defines marketing as "an organizational function and a set of processes for creating, communicating and delivering value to customers and for managing customer relationships in ways that benefit the organization and its stakeholders".

In a similar vein, the importance of marketing was becoming widely recognized within the tourism industry and academics in the late 1980s (i.e., Coltman, 1989; Middleton, 1988; Witt & Moutinho, 1989). The more demanding customers and global competition need to know the specific characteristics of their clientele and reach them in the most effective ways (Witt & Moutinho, 1989). Tourism products as services are traditionally featured as intangible, heterogeneous, with temporary ownership, perishable and inseparable. Additionally, tourism differs from other services in the following terms (Seaton & Bennet, 1996): tourism is more supply-led than other services, frequently a multiple product involving cooperation between several suppliers, extended product experience with no predictable critical evaluation point, a high-involvement product to its customers, a product partly formed by the dreams and fantasies of its customers and a fragile industry susceptible to external forces beyond the control of its suppliers. Marketing within tourism becomes "the application of the marketing process to the specific characteristics which apply to tourism industry and its products" (Gilbert, 1989, p. 78). Tourism organizers and marketers need to understand these features in order to commercialize its products. These issues are discussed in this book, emphasizing the importance of marketing in tourism. Quoting Jefferson and Lickorish (1988), one may emphasize that "the marketing concept can and must be embraced by all organizations engaged in tourism, whether they are commercial or governmental" (p. 35).

Previous studies have analysed the evolution of research and recent developments in tourism marketing. From an international point of view, we would like to refer to a study, which reviews all tourism marketing articles in two international tourism journals — *Annals of Tourism Research* (ATR) and *Tourism Management* (TM) — during the period 1995–2003. Taking into account this sample, Bigné (2005) identified key research topics of tourism marketing publications using the categorization used in the *Journal of Marketing* (i.e., marketing environment, marketing functions and research in marketing). Research in the marketing environment, which includes market and demand analysis, consumer behaviour, macro environmental issues, as well as social responsibility, has attracted profuse attention by tourism researchers. Particularly, consumer behaviour becomes the more relevant topic in both international journals, with 59.3% and 37.5% of the marketing papers published in ATR and TM, respectively. Additionally, the study of marketing functions is, after marketing environment, the second research area with highest attention of tourism marketing publications, especially in TM. Within this category, during the 1995–2003 period, research in management and planning, product and marketing strategy have been the main topics published in the mentioned journal. Until 2003, less research has been applied to the influence of new technologies in marketing, pricing and sales promotion, among others.

A recent study focused on papers published in selected hospitality and tourism journals for the period of 2002–2003 reinforces the conclusion of the key role of understanding consumer behaviour in tourism marketing research (Oh, Kim, & Shin, 2004). Although the mentioned study is included in this book, we would like to highlight their main findings to better understand the content of this book. Together with consumer behaviour, notable is also the studies of marketing management, planning and/or strategy functions. Based on the review studies, these authors underline that new technologies in tourism marketing are emerging as viable research topics in the discipline. Findings show that studies of marketing theories, philosophies and research methods were under-researched across the journals than topics related to marketing environment and functions. Taking into account previous papers, which analyse the developments in tourism marketing research (Bigné, 2005; Oh et al., 2004), the pattern of fundamental issues undertaken in tourism marketing can be reflected in the contents of this book as it is explained below.

The papers presented in this book focused on issues both well-established in tourism marketing research (i.e., consumer behaviour) as well as other growing topics in tourism marketing literature (i.e., information technology in tourism, sustainable tourism marketing). In Akyaka, Turkey, during 20–22 May 2005, a successful *International Tourism*

Marketing Conference (ITMC), first edition, focused on "Perspectives in Tourism Marketing" was held. This new academic event was jointly co-ordinated by Mugla University, Turkey and the Universitat de Valencia, Spain. The novelty of the ITMC represents an important contribution for the tourism marketing research arena, which will be biennially organized. The aim of this ITMC represents an attempt to explore, analyse and evaluate the state of the art in tourism marketing from an international perspective. As such, the first edition of this conference brought together researchers, PhD candidates, policy makers and practitioners, providing a forum for the discussion and dissemination of themes related to perspectives in marketing of travel and tourism.

In the ITMC, 17 papers, selected on the basis of a reviews process by the scientific committee, were presented spanning a broad four main themes in Tourism Marketing. Based upon the discussion that took place in Akyaka and co-chairs' comments, authors revised their papers before submitting them for a strict review one further time prior to the publication in this book. The structure of the book is based upon the inclusion of an introduction and four main parts, namely IT marketing, destination competitiveness, image measurement and consumer behaviour. There is a brief introduction for each part prior to the discussion of specific chapters just to make the readers familiar with their content.

- In recent years, tourism marketing has gone through strategic changes with the advances in new technologies, the pursuit of a relationship approach with customers and suppliers, as well as the importance of sustainability issues in marketing. Societal orientation in tourism marketing considers the needs and wants of the tourists but does not ignore the long-term economic, environmental, social and cultural interests of the local population (Coltman, 1989). This part examines, in the first part, several applications of the *information technologies* and changes shaping tourism marketing (i.e., IT in tourism marketing and sustainable tourism marketing).
- Because most tourism activities take place at destinations and they form a mainstay in the tourism product, this topic has played an active role in the international tourism marketing literature (Ashworth & Goodall, 1990; Heath & Wall, 1992; Pike, 2004). The prominent place of destinations in the tourism system has attracted attention at the ITMC. As such, the second part of this book explores in greater detail *destination marketing and competitiveness,* with four interesting contributions (i.e., competition models for tourism destinations, and crisis management).
- The third part comprises a comprehensive analysis of *market segmentation*, with four chapters stressing current applications of this relevant topic in tourism marketing. As a result of increasing fragmentation of international mass markets into hundreds of micromarkets, each with different needs and life styles, target marketing is increasingly taking the form of micromarketing (Kotler et al., 1996). The fundamental attention towards segmentation can be justified, as it is a prerequisite for selective market operation. When targeting marketing efforts to selected segments, "one can reduce the competitive pressure that would prevail if all products and services were indiscriminately offered to the same market" (Teare, Mazanec, Crawford-Welch, & Calver, 1994, p. 99).
- Finally, the fourth part, which concludes this book, demonstrates the special attention of *consumer behaviour* in tourism marketing. Consumer behaviour is an eclectic field involving dynamic interactions of affect, cognition, behaviour and the environment by

which human beings conduct the exchange aspect of their lives (Mattila, 2004). Earlier studies have emphasized the indispensable concern of consumer behaviour in marketing (Moutinho, 1987; Witt & Moutinho, 1989). A recent review of consumer behaviour across tourism journals in the period 2002–2003 underlines that the topics seem to fall in the general categories of destination choice/image, segmentation and decision-making or choice (Mattila, 2004). In this book, segmentation has been dealt in a special section due to the interest for tourism marketing research. Applied to different settings (i.e., theme parks, destinations and travel agencies), the consumer behaviour section analyses specific topics referring to cognitive and affective variables, taking into account cultural issues. Particularly, the chapters of this part cover key related aspects of consumer behaviour (i.e., motivations, emotions, loyalty, satisfaction and value).

The book starts with the presentation of an introductory part on an overview of 223 marketing-oriented articles published in tourism and hospitality journals within the period of 2002–2003. Oh, Kim and Shin, as the authors of this timely and well-deserved study, attempt to identify contemporary marketing issues and practices which are emerging in the industry whereas they are missing in the academic studies or not addressed at a greater extent. The review includes summaries of research topics, industry applications and methods of study design and data analysis. Significant research trends are identified and discussed to raise issues for future research. Included are also the industry-specific current trends and issues that dictate immediate research attention. The gaps between tourism and hospitality marketing research and the industry's research needs are addressed to encourage additional research on neglected topics. As the authors already note, "… as a result, a number of marketing issues were found to be worth noting and to warrant systematic inquiries".

The findings of the research indicate that one-third of the reviewed articles focus primarily on marketing management, planning and strategy functions. It is also apparent that research on market segmentation, positioning and targeting gained a greater interest in the journals than any other marketing topics. Nevertheless, such topics as advertising, personal selling, empowerment and training did not get much attention. Topics dealing with marketing theories, philosophies and research methods are also among the other issues which need to be taken into consideration in the future studies of tourism and hospitality marketing. In its conclusion, the authors confess that the tourism and hospitality marketing research is still in its infancy to meet the practitioners' demand with regard to the topical diversity although one may see a growing number of studies carried out and published in the academic journals.

From the academic point of view, such studies are missing to make a strong contribution to the development of theories in respect to the field of tourism and hospitality marketing despite the fact that this field of discipline borrows theories heavily from those on pure marketing or psychology. Theory development is also important as is drawing implications for the practice. Success in the former brings success in the latter. The authors further suggest that future research needs to make a substantial contribution to the literature as well as to the successful development of the industry for the sake of resources that we invest in conducting a study. Therefore, the researchers could take a more questioning and critical role on taking the marketing research to a further stage. An improvement in the theoretical background on practical papers would be a top priority of the tourism researchers of the future. The text concludes with further general suggestions for future tourism and hospitality marketing research.

We hope that you will enjoy reading this book and using it in developing the scope of tourism marketing to make further progress.

Metin Kozak and Luisa Andreu
The Co-Editors

References

AMA. (1960). *Marketing definitions: A glossary of marketing terms*. Chicago: American Marketing Association Committee on Terms.
AMA. (2004). http://www.marketingpower.com/content4620.php (16.09.2005).
Ashworth, G., & Goodall, B. (1990). *Marketing tourism places*. London: Routlege.
Bartels, R. (1988). *The history of marketing thought*. Columbus: Publishing Horizons.
Berry, L. L. (1983). Relationship marketing. In: L. L. Berry, G. L. Shostack, & G. Upah (Eds), *Emerging perspectives on services marketing* (pp. 25–28). Chicago, IL: American Marketing Association.
Bigné, J. E. (1996). Tourism and marketing in Spain: Analysis of the situation and future perspectives. *The Tourist Review, 1*, 34–40.
Bigné, J. E. (2005). Nuevas orientaciones del marketing turístico: de la imagen de destinos a la fidelización de los turistas. *Papeles de Economía, 102*, 221–235.
Brown, S. W., Fisk, R. P., & Bitner, M. J. (1994). The development and emergence of services marketing thought. *International Journal of Service Industry Management, 5*(1), 21–48.
Coltman, M. M. (1989). *Tourism marketing*. New York: Van Nostrand Reinhold.
Gilbert, D. C. (1989). Tourism marketing — its emergence and establishment. *Progress in Hospitality and Tourism Research, 1*, 77–90.
Heath, W., & Wall, G. (1992). *Marketing tourism destinations. A strategic planning approach*. Canada: Wiley.
Jefferson, A., & Lickorish, L. (1988). *Marketing tourism. A practical guide*. London: Longman.
Keefe, L. M. (2004). What is the meaning of 'marketing'? *Marketing News*, September 15, 17–18.
Kotler, P., Bowen, J., & Makens, J. (1996). *Marketing for hospitality and tourism*. Englewood Cliffs, NJ: Prentice-Hall.
Mattila, A. S. (2004). Consumer behaviour research in hospitality and tourism journals. *International Journal of Hospitality Management, 23*, 449–457.
Middleton, V. T. C. (1988). *Marketing in travel and tourism*. Oxford: Butterworth Heinemann.
Moutinho, L. (1987). Consumer behaviour in tourism. *European Journal of Marketing, 21*(10), 5–44.
Oh, H., Kim, B., & Shin, J. (2004). Hospitality and tourism marketing recent developments in research and future directions. *International Journal of Hospitality Management, 23*, 425–447.
Pike, S. (2004). *Destination marketing organisations*. Advances in Tourism Research Series. Oxford: Elsevier.
Seaton, A. V., & Bennett, M. M. (1996). *Marketing tourism products*. Oxford: International Thomson Business Press.
Teare, R., Mazanec, J. A., Crawford-Welch, S., & Calver, S. (1994). *Marketing in hospitality and tourism. A consumer focus*. London: Cassell.
Vargo, S. L., & Lusch, R. F. (2004). Evolving to a new dominant logic for marketing. *Journal of Marketing, 68*(1), 1–17.
Witt, S. F., & Moutinho, L. (1989). *Tourism marketing and management handbook*. Cambridge: Prentice-Hall.

Chapter 1

Introduction: Tourism and Hospitality Marketing Research — Update and Suggestions[1]

Haemoon Oh, Byeong-Yong Kim and Jee Hye Shin

Introduction

This part aims to review recent significant developments in hospitality and tourism marketing research and practices. To this end, we first reviewed 223 marketing-focused articles published in eight journals in 2002–2003, four of the journals being rather "hospitality-oriented" (hereafter, "hospitality" journals) and the other four rather "tourism-oriented" ("tourism" journals). The hospitality journals included *Cornell Hotel and Restaurant Administration Quarterly*, *International Journal of Hospitality Management*, *Journal of Hospitality & Leisure Marketing*, and *Journal of Hospitality & Tourism Research*. The tourism journals were *Annals of Tourism Research*, *Journal of Travel Research*, *Journal of Travel & Tourism Marketing*, and *Tourism Management*. While the journals were selected rather subjectively according to the purpose of this study, they were in line, if not the same, with the "major" journals reviewed by Bowen and Sparks (1998, p. 125) for similar review purposes. Thus, this study could serve as an extended update on Bowen and Sparks' (1998) review that focused on nine topical areas of "hospitality" marketing. The review results are presented by study subjects investigated and research methods employed and several significant research trends are identified for additional discussions in later sections.

Second, the study attempts to identify contemporary marketing issues and practices that were active or emerging in the hospitality and tourism industries but that have not yet been systematically addressed in the reviewed journals. A variety of trade magazines and Websites was scanned and reviewed the research issues and priorities put forward by relevant organizations such as the American Hotel & Lodging Foundation, Hospitality Sales & Marketing

---

[1]This part was also published in the *International Journal of Hospitality Management*, 2004, 23(5), 425–447.

Association, and Marketing Science Institute. This review effort emphasized sources from non-profit organizations more than those from private marketing research companies, with a particular attention given to generalized industry-wide issues. As a result, a number of marketing issues were found to be worth noting and to warrant systematic inquiries.

Finally, the part summarizes and contrast academic research with industry marketing trends to highlight the marketing issues to be tackled in upcoming hospitality and tourism research. The significant trends appearing in the reviewed marketing studies also are critically considered to develop general suggestions for future research. Throughout this study, the term "significant trend" is defined as a general tendency or inclination in both the content and frequency of hospitality/tourism marketing research that is likely to have a major effect on or meaning for subsequent hospitality/tourism marketing research and practices. The part concludes with a general call for domain-specific marketing theory development and knowledge accumulation through growing hospitality and tourism research.

Literature Review

A total of 223 marketing articles (97 from the four hospitality and 126 from the four tourism journals) were reviewed and classified into topical areas and the results appear in Table 1.1.[2] The scope of marketing is broad and still evolving (see Day & Montgomery, 1999; Kerin, 1996), which challenged the task of selecting marketing-focused articles from all studies published in the eight journals. We relied on the classification scheme that had been used by *Journal of Marketing* for its published studies and added relevant sub-categories to several subject areas so as to improve clarity and applications. For example, in Table 1.1, all the sub-categories of consumer/traveler behavior and management, planning, and strategy were newly added based on topical focus and relatedness. Similar to Bowen and Sparks (1998), the sub-categories and articles were sorted according to the deemed major focus of the category and article in case of possible cross-classifications. As such, the category and article classification of this study is to be viewed rather flexibly.

Table 1.1 reveals that more than a third of the marketing articles (34.4%) were devoted to studying consumer/traveler behavior, evidencing a vibrant growth of research on consumer behavior in the discipline when compared to about 20% reported by Bowen and Sparks (1998). Of these, studies examining satisfaction, complaint behaviors, and service failure-recovery had the strongest representation, followed somewhat distantly by those investigating target product/service/destination perceptions and evaluations. These patterns were consistent between the hospitality and tourism journals. Note that the category of perceptions/performance evaluations did not include studies of service quality and delivery, which was classified into a marketing function category, as they were believed to focus on service design and offerings rather than consumers' behavioral processes. Both journal sets were absent of the studies that treated marketing ethics and social responsibility as the main theme. They further show some minor area-specific differences in the other topics examined.

---

[2]Owing to space limitation, a complete list of the 223 articles is not provided in this study, but it is available from the authors upon request.

Approximately another third of the reviewed studies (35.3%) dealt with marketing's management, planning, and/or strategy functions, with the remaining third examining other marketing functions such as understanding specific marketing mix elements and issues in basic marketing research. Notable from both the hospitality and tourism journals was the substantial appearance of research on market segmentation, positioning, and targeting. In fact, the studies of this category were more frequently reported in the journals than any other topics. Electronic marketing issues such as online transactions, Website development, and online distribution strategies also emerged as viable research topics in the discipline. Topics relating to an organization's external and internal relations such as advertising, personal selling, and empowerment and training did not take much space in the tourism journals. Fundamental issues of marketing theories, philosophies, and research methods were pursued less enthusiastically across the journals than topics related to marketing environment and functions during the 2002–2003 period.

Industry Applications

Table 1.2 summarizes the target hospitality and tourism industries where the reviewed studies were conducted or from which the main study samples were drawn. Overall, more than a half of the studies took place with tourist destinations or destination marketing organizations and, expectedly, the studies reported in the tourism journals contributed to the dominance of such applications. Diversity in industry applications tended to be stronger with the hospitality journals than with the tourism journals. Both the hotel/lodging and restaurant/foodservice industries received equivalent research attention, while other hospitality and tourism industries were relatively under-represented in the journals. Perhaps the nature of the reviewed journals affected such disproportionate industry applications.

Methodological Review

A summary of research designs and methods reviewed for the marketing studies appears in Table 1.3. In general, hospitality and tourism marketing research was predominantly empirical in its approach (91%). Reviewing slightly different journals, Bowen and Sparks (1998) once reported that about 66% of the selected marketing studies were empirical. The most frequently employed study design was primary field survey, followed by the use of secondary data that frequented more in the tourism than hospitality journals. Experiment, case study, and Delphi methods were employed relatively infrequently. The "other" study design category includes the use of various illustrations, examples, and episodic observations to build arguments as well as to draw conclusions. As suggested in industry applications above, general or potential travelers were the dominant source of data and information, especially for tourism journal publications. Some "rare" samples included organizational employees, organizational properties, skiers, and tourist destinations.

The most typical sample size used in the empirical studies was small to medium ($n = 100–350$). Use of both small (i.e., <100) and large samples, however, was not uncommon, either. In particular, larger data (i.e., >850) were the second most frequently used sample size, frequent enough (27.5%) to attest as a main mode of sample size for hospitality and

Table 1.1: Hospitality and tourism marketing research by subject ($N = 223$).

Subject	Hospitality ($N = 97$)		Tourism ($N = 126$)		Total ($N = 223$)	
	n	%	N	%	n	%
Marketing environment						
Consumer/traveler behavior[a]						
Satisfaction/complaining behavior/recovery	13	13.4	13	10.3	26	11.7
Perceptions/performance evaluations	6	6.2	6	4.8	12	5.4
General consumer/traveler characteristics	3	3.1	4	3.2	7	3.1
Information search and processing	1	1.0	4	3.2	5	2.2
Attitude/motivation/pull-push factors	0	0.0	4	3.2	4	1.8
Choice theory and utility models	2	2.1	2	1.6	4	1.8
Tipping	4	4.1	0	0.0	4	1.8
Image/symbolization	1	1.0	3	2.4	4	1.8
Perceived risk/terrorism/safety/security	0	0.0	3	2.4	3	1.3
Sensation/novelty/variety seeking	1	1.0	2	1.6	3	1.3
Perceived value	0	0.0	2	1.6	2	0.9
Persuasion	1	1.0	0	0.0	1	0.4
Legal, political, and economic issues	2	2.1	0	0.0	2	0.9
Ethics and social responsibility	0	0.0	0	0.0	0	0.0
Marketing functions[a]						
Management, planning, and strategy[a]						
Market segmentation/positioning/targeting	15	15.5	27	21.4	42	18.8
Consumer relationship marketing/CRM/loyalty	10	10.3	7	5.6	17	7.6
Service quality and delivery	5	5.2	7	5.6	12	5.4

Category	n	%	n	%	n	%
General marketing strategies	0	0.0	3	2.4	3	1.3
Business relationship management	1	1.0	2	1.6	3	1.3
Branding/brand extensions	1	1.0	1	0.8	2	0.9
Electronic marketing/Website/Internet/distribution	8	8.2	8	6.3	16	7.2
Sales, demand, and capacity management/forecasting	4	4.1	8	6.3	12	5.4
Pricing/revenue/yield management	2	2.1	5	4.0	7	3.1
Products, services, and destinations in general	4	4.1	1	0.8	5	2.2
PR and crisis management	2	2.1	3	2.4	5	2.2
Sales promotion	2	2.1	0	0.0	2	0.9
Advertising	3	3.1	1	0.8	4	1.8
Internal marketing/empowerment/training	3	3.1	0	0.0	3	1.3
Personal Selling	1	1.0	0	0.0	1	0.4
Physical distribution	0	0.0	0	0.0	0	0.0
Marketing research						
Research methodology	1	1.0	5	4.0	6	2.7
Information technology	1	1.0	3	2.4	4	1.8
Theory and philosophy of science	0	0.0	0	0.0	0	0.0
Special marketing applications						
International and comparative	0	0.0	2	1.6	2	0.9
Nonprofit, political, and social causes	0	0.0	0	0.0	0	0.0

[a]Their sub-categories were added as deemed necessary to classify the reviewed studies and they do not necessarily represent the classification scheme used by the *Journal of Marketing* (see the text for additional explanations)

Table 1.2: Hospitality and tourism marketing research by industry application (N = 223).

Target industry	Hospitality (N = 97)		Tourism (N = 126)		Total (N = 223)	
	n	%	N	%	n	%
Marketing environment						
General tourism destinations/organizations	23	23.7	99	78.6	122	54.7
Hotel/lodging	28	28.9	5	4.0	33	14.8
Restaurant/foodservice	22	22.7	8	6.3	30	13.5
General/multiple industries	12	12.4	1	0.8	13	5.8
Resort/convention/conference/timeshare	6	6.2	6	4.8	12	5.4
Casino/gaming	6	6.2	3	2.4	9	4.0
Airline	0	0.0	4	3.2	4	1.8

Table 1.3: Hospitality and tourism marketing research by method employed ($N = 223$).

Study method[a]	Hospitality ($N = 97$)		Tourism ($N = 126$)		Total ($N = 223$)	
	n	%	N	%	n	%
Type of study						
Empirical	88	90.7	115	91.3	203	91.0
Conceptual	9	9.3	11	8.7	20	9.0
Study design	62	63.9	80	63.5	142	63.7
Primary field survey	4	4.1	25	19.8	29	13.0
Secondary data	6	6.2	2	1.6	8	3.6
Experiment	2	2.1	5	4.0	7	3.1
Case study	3	3.1	1	0.8	4	1.8
Delphi	20	20.6	13	10.3	33	14.7
Other						
Sample type for main study[b]						
General/potential travelers	22	23.4	69	63.9	91	45.0
Hotel/lodging guests	16	17.0	1	0.9	17	8.4
Restaurant customers	10	10.6	4	3.7	14	6.9
Tour organizers/meeting planners	5	5.3	8	7.4	13	6.4
Students	5	5.3	5	4.6	10	5.0
Hotel owners/managers	5	5.3	3	2.8	8	4.0
Restaurants/dining facilities	4	4.3	0	0.0	4	2.0
Casino visitors/players	2	2.1	2	1.9	4	2.0

(Continued)

Table 1.3 (Continued)

Study method[a]	Hospitality (N = 97)		Tourism (N = 126)		Total (N = 223)	
	n	%	N	%	n	%
Golfers	1	1.1	3	2.8	4	2.0
Experts	3	3.2	1	0.9	4	2.0
Destinations/Provinces/Parks	0	0.0	3	2.8	3	1.5
Skiers	1	1.1	2	1.9	3	1.5
Hotels/lodging properties	2	2.1	0	0.0	2	1.0
Food/beverage owners/managers	2	2.1	0	0.0	2	1.0
Restaurant/foodservice employees	2	2.1	0	0.0	2	1.0
General/cross-industries/other	14	14.9	7	6.5	21	10.4
Sample size (property and qualitative research samples tended to be smaller than consumer survey samples)[b]						
Less than 100	10	12.5	16	16.3	26	14.6
100–350	32	40.0	31	31.6	63	35.4
351–600	11	13.8	17	17.3	28	15.7
601–850	5	6.3	7	7.1	12	6.7
Greater than 850	22	27.5	27	27.6	49	27.5

Response rate[b,c]				
Less than 10%	2		2	
10–20%	3		5	
21–30%	2		4	
31–40%	3		6	
41–50%	4		7	
Greater than 50%	5		22	
Main analysis methods (multiple counts of the same study allowed)[b]				
Descriptive	30	29.1	41	28.1	71	28.5
Factor/cluster/discriminant analyses	17	16.5	36	24.7	53	21.3
Regression/logit-logistic regression	28	27.2	19	13.0	47	18.9
Analysis of (co)variance (ANOVA/MANOVA)	13	12.6	27	18.5	40	16.1
Structural equation modeling/path	9	8.7	11	7.5	20	8.0
Time series	0	0.0	4	2.7	4	1.6
Other	6	5.8	8	5.5	14	5.6

[a]The first sub-categories (i.e., type of study, study design, etc.) are exclusive each other.
[b]The entries may not sum to the total as some studies were not counted in due to the nature of the study and/or lack of information.
[c]The percentages were not calculated due to too small a sample size overall.

tourism marketing research. Corporate databases and nation-wide study sampling often contributed to the large sample size. Although empirical hospitality and tourism marketing research tended to be conducted based on high-response rates, the general lack of reports on exact response rates in many studies prohibits detecting significant trends.

Researchers most frequently used descriptive data analysis methods including, for example, content analysis, correlation, t-test, frequency and cross-tabulation, and importance-performance analysis. Multivariate techniques such as factor, cluster, and discriminant analyses also showed high-usage rates, especially coupled with the methods of the analysis-of-variance family in market segmentation studies. Causal modeling using regression, logit, and structural equation analyses shared strong popularity, when compared to techniques such as time series, conjoint, and artificial neural networks. Used in a much lesser frequency were special analysis methods such as the analytical hierarchical process, repertory grid analysis, cohort analysis, data envelopment analysis, and discrete choice analysis. Overall, applications of statistical data analysis methods converged on their type and frequency to those reported earlier by Bowen and Sparks (1998).

Synthesized Reviews of Topical Significant Trends and Comments

In this section, we summarize topical research trends and provide critical comments in an effort to identify mainstream issues associated with the research topics. The reviewed studies were conveniently categorized into eight thematic topics based on their conceptual and practical linkages; the studies that could not be grouped into one of the eight categories are summarized under "other topics." We begin with the most frequently reported topic, consumer (traveler) satisfaction, during the review period.

Consumer Satisfaction, Complaining Behavior, and Service Failure and Recovery

Consumer satisfaction, coupled with service failure and recovery, was by far the most examined topic in the consumer behavior category and several attempts are worth noting. Based on satisfaction research with client hotels, Schall (2003) discusses best methodological practices for measuring guest satisfaction; the discussed issues include proper sequence and face validity of question items, choice of measurement scales, and appropriate sample sizes for drawing reliable conclusions. Namasivayam and Hinkin (2003) experimented with the degrees of control and fairness perceived by the hotel and restaurant customers in a transaction process and found that the two boundary conditions had both main and interaction effects on customer satisfaction. Barsky and Nash (2003) and Zins (2002) emphasize emotional dominance in satisfaction in an attempt to tie up experience-based satisfaction feelings with attitudinal loyalty. Satisfaction benchmarking between destinations was attempted in the work of Kozak (2002a), while an international comparison of traveler satisfaction was the focus of Wong and Law (2003). Measuring tourist satisfaction via participant observation seems to merit a new approach to tapping the underlying process of satisfaction (Bowen, 2002). Other researchers tended to apply the existing satisfaction research framework, which is based mostly on the expectancy disconfirmation model (see Oh & Parks, 1997), to different markets such as senior travelers (Wei & Milman, 2002), Kenyan safari goers (Akama & Kieti, 2003), motor coach travelers (Hsu, 2003), and vacation golfers (Petrick & Backman, 2002). In general, although these studies provide good application examples for the existing satisfaction theory, they fall short of making a significant breakthrough in satisfaction theory beyond the widely adopted expectancy model.

Despite its close link to satisfaction research, complaining behavior received limited attention. According to Jones, McCleary, and Lepisto (2002), about 20% of baby boomers are active complainers, if necessary, and chronic verbal complainers tend to be younger, employed, with children, less price-conscious, and self-assertive. Satisfaction as a result of online complaints was affected by how fast the company responded to the complaint and technology enthusiasts seemed to be less tolerant about delayed complaint handling (Mount & Mattila, 2002). Financial implications of timely problem handling are well documented in Miller and Grazer (2003). Lam and Tang (2003) applied equity theory to understand complaining behaviors and reported demographic characteristics of typical restaurant complainers. Most studies of complaining behavior tended to focus somewhat narrowly on episodic problem situations and the resulting satisfaction and, hence, the negative effect of the problem could be exaggerated; marketers need to understand customer complaints as a part of a more general consumption and evaluation process.

The main and dyadic effects of service failure and recovery efforts by companies received recurrent research attention since their relatively recent debut in the hospitality and tourism research. Using a corporate database, Oh (2003) reexamines a fundamental assumption of service failure-recovery research, called the recovery paradox, and reports that the concept could not be empirically supported. Mattila and Mount (2003) newly apply justice theory and find significant effects of distributive, interactional, and procedural justices or fairness on satisfaction with recovery efforts. Service failures seem to be common in both the United States and Ireland, but recovery efforts appeared to be more extensive in the former due to high-customer expectations (Mueller, Palmer, Mack, & McMullan, 2003). Research design on these topics is challenging because many known moderating variables come into play in actual situations (e.g., Mattila, 1999; Sundaram, Jurowski, & Webster, 1997) and, thus, reported results tend to be highly case sensitive, thereby impeding development of a general theory.

Market Segmentation, Targeting, and Positioning

Market segmentation research alone took more space than any other single research topic in the hospitality and tourism journals. A predominant segmentation approach was the combinational use of factor analysis for data reduction, cluster analysis for classification, analysis of variance and discriminant analysis for cross-method validations of the classification results, descriptive profiling of each cluster, and other subsequent analyses depending on the study objectives (see also Dolnicar, 2002 for an illustration). Minor variations, however, existed in the target sample or market to be segmented, the focus of segmentation variables, and method-specific segmentation results. A segmentation grounded in an existing arousal theory is interesting in that an *a priori* specified theory was used to expect cluster results (Sirakaya, Uysal, & Yoshioka, 2003). Several researchers applied non-traditional segmentation methods such as a gerontographic approach combining the aging process and life circumstance (Moschis, Curasi, & Bellenger, 2003), a chi-square automatic interaction detection model (Chen, 2003), and artificial neural networks (Kim, Wei, & Ruys, 2003b).

In contrast to the quantity of market segmentation research, the knowledge generated is somewhat fragmentary and local. Use of different segmentation criteria or variables, narrowly targeted products or destinations, and pervasive convenience sampling seem to have caused such divergent outcomes without contributing much to the mainstream progress in segmentation research. Moreover, most segmentation studies were driven by data *post hoc*, thereby inhibiting theoretical predictions and testing of the segmentation outcomes. Combined with the highly subjective nature of the decision on the number of clusters, these data-driven segmentation approaches could have produced chance outcomes in most cases. Another critical issue in segmentation research is that most researchers failed to advance beyond securing only high internal reliability of the segmented market structures; seriously lacking were the efforts to justify externally the value of the resulting market structure by satisfying, for example, Kotler, Bowen, and Makens' (2003) assessment criteria — accessibility, measurability, substantiality, and actionability. Testing and discussing the stability of the method-dependent cluster solution was largely ignored as well (Dolnicar, 2002).

Despite their strategic importance and logical connection to market segmentation, targeting and positioning were relatively neglected research topics. Brown and Ragsdale (2002) applied data envelopment analysis to assess brand positioning and market efficiency of hotel brands and found that inefficient brands tended to result in lower customer satisfaction and value perceptions. Relying on correspondence analysis and logit modeling, Chen and Uysal (2002) attempted to determine an ideal positioning of Virginia against seven other eastern states. In the future, targeting and positioning research as a natural byproduct of market segmentation studies deserves serious considerations. Linking targeting and positioning issues to image research is also likely to prove an interesting line of inquiry.

Consumer Relationship Marketing/Management and Loyalty

Although consumer relationship marketing and loyalty had established distinct research traditions, with the former having evolved around the concepts of trust and commitment and the latter relating to repeat purchases, recent studies on both topics tended to gradually converge to a comprehensive research framework for retaining markets. One catalyst for such a movement seems to be a recent, general shift in the focus of marketing research from consumers' rational to emotional decision-making processes. Emphasis on emotional commitment for creating strong customer relationships and loyalty is well reflected in industry practices (Shoemaker & Bowen, 2003), national consumer opinions about segment-specific lodging offerings (Barsky & Nash, 2002), and casino club members' continued patronage (Baloglu, 2002; Sui & Baloglu, 2003). Potential common antecedents to customer loyalty and business-to-customer (B2C) relationships include satisfaction (Back & Parks, 2003; Oh, 2002), the firm's market orientation characteristics (Kim, McCahon, & Miller, 2003a), corporate image (Christou, 2003; Kandampully & Suhartanto, 2003), and the firm's dependability and familiarity (Macintosh, 2002).

Several researchers applied new methodological frameworks to relationship marketing and loyalty. Morais and Zillifro (2003) use resource exchange theory to understand the relationship between nature-based tourism providers and their customers, while Au and Law (2002) examine relationships in tourism dining by means of mathematical rough set theory. A new analytic approach to loyalty in application of artificial neural networks appears in Tsaur et al.'s (2002b) study and the Markov process was adopted to model relationships and loyalty in Kozak, Huan, and Beaman's (2002).

With active research programs still unfolding in this area, some challenges remain to be resolved. First, given the nature of the focal concepts, longitudinal investigations into how B2C relationships and emotional loyalty develop and evolve over time are needed, perhaps by means of analytical tools like survival analysis. Second, applicability of the relationship and loyalty concepts to tourism destinations and destination marketing organizations is questionable, calling for illustrations and guidelines (see Fyall, Callod, & Edwards, 2003). The same issue pertains to hotels and resorts located in remote tourist destinations whose major markets are mostly novice leisure travelers. Third, ways of efficiently and competitively managing relationship and loyalty programs await further research, especially with regard to emotional and affective aspects. Additional research efforts that can build on Brownell and Reynolds (2002) and Pan (2003) are needed to enrich marketers' understanding of not only "backward" business-to-business (B2B) relationships with suppliers but also "forward" B2B relationships with eMediaries and other distribution channels.

Electronic Marketing and E-Commerce Research

Effective Website designs seem to be a significant issue, as the largest number of e-marketing studies concentrated on understanding how to elicit favorable product/service perceptions and generate actual sales transactions via change of Website features. Researchers stressed that effective Websites could be built with features of social interaction and emotion (Dubs, Bel, & Sears, 2003), transactional security (Law & Wong, 2003), informational integrity and navigational ease (Jeong, Oh, & Gregoire, 2003), and multimedia and virtual footages (Cho, Wang, & Fesenmaier, 2002; Kasavana, 2002). E-distribution issues examined include selection of hotel distribution channels by travelers and continued growth of dotcom companies (Carroll & Siguaw, 2003), upcoming competition of traditional eMediaries with Digital TV and mCommerce (Buhalis & Licata, 2002), necessary cooperation among e-channels (Pearce, 2002), and determinants of e-shopping intention (Christou & Kassianidis, 2002). Finally, general Internet marketing strategies and some guidelines for developing competitive online strategies are discussed in the work of Murphy and Tan (2003), Sigala (2003), and Wang, Yu, and Fesenmaier (2002).

Research on electronic marketing is in its inception stage, mostly addressing how industry and customers adopt the constantly updated technology for marketing exchanges. As such, it is common that many studies reported a year or so ago become obsolete today; hence, research programs that focus on the current developments of e-commerce are likely to be short-lived in their contribution to marketing knowledge. Researchers will have to reevaluate most existing marketing theories for creative applications in e-commerce and, more importantly, it is the time to think about cyberspace as a primary place for testing as well as developing new marketing theories.

Motivation, Choice, Perceptions, and Performance Evaluations

Travel motivations, typically separated into *push* and *pull* factors, continue to be a frequent concern to researchers. Motivations and pull factors affecting destination choice and evaluations were examined for different destinations as well as different groups of travelers in Caldwell and Coshall (2003), Kim and Jogaratnam (2002), and Kozak (2002b). The underlying process of embodying travel motivations was insightfully analyzed via a means-end framework (Klenosky, 2002). In a similar vein, hospitality and destination choice scenarios are modeled in application of new theories and approaches such as random utility theory and discrete choice analysis (Verma, Plaschka, & Louviere, 2002; Verma & Plaschka, 2003), the Lancasterian product characteristics framework (Seddighi & Theocharous, 2002), and a rule-based heuristic process based on the chi-square automatic interaction detection algorithm (Middelkoop, Borgers, & Timmermans, 2003).

Experiential perceptions and performance evaluations also were recurring topics in recent years. Hardine, Wooldridge, and Jones (2003) analyzed how customers perceive performance of hotel staff, while other researchers examined specific destination perceptions of tourists and their consequences (Rittichainuwat, Qu, & Mongknonvanit, 2002; Pike, 2003; Vogt & Andereck, 2003). Restaurant crowding and patrons' attribution-dependent satisfaction were the focus of Heung, Wong, and Qu's (2002) study. In general, most studies in this area produced results that were highly specific to the target product or destination evaluated and, thus, limited generality in obtained knowledge. The main reason for this was perhaps the lack of standardized theoretical approaches to studying perceptions and performance evaluations.

Service Quality and Delivery

The vehemently debated model, SERVQUAL, of Parasuraman, Zeithaml, and Berry (1988) continued to receive attention in hospitality and tourism research, although the topic has become a bit "cold" in recent years. Yoon and Ekinci (2003) reexamine the SERVQUAL dimensions of hotel services by using an alternative Guttman scaling procedure, while Gilbert and Wong (2003) study a similar issue for airline passenger services. Khan (2003) develops an ECOSERV version to tap ecotourists' service quality expectations and Walsh (2002) distinguishes expert-based versus service-oriented delivery strategies of services. Service frequency seems to differ across firms and service delivery designs tend to be biased toward particular customer characteristics (Harris, Bojanic, & Cannon, 2003). New approaches used to assess firms' service quality and delivery include fuzzy multiple criteria decision theory in the airline industry (Tsaur et al., 2002a) and critical incident techniques in the gaming environment (Johnson, 2002). Organizational efforts to improve service quality and delivery process are reflected in some internal marketing studies such as Hancer and George (2003) and Kim et al. (2003a).

Service quality and delivery is another area awaiting a major theoretical breakthrough. Most studies have addressed issues related to definition of service quality, its measurement, and its empirical dimensions. Seriously lacking has been an endeavor to advance its theoretical status beyond Parasuraman et al.'s (1988) method-oriented conception of service quality. Discovering unique consequences of service quality may be one beginning step toward a theoretical progress (e.g., Dean, Morgan, & Tan, 2002), while clarifying the relative role of service quality against other similar concepts like performance, satisfaction, and value may lead to conceptual enrichment (see Oliver, 1997). Furthermore, additional research is needed to probe more elaborate and interactional aspects of service delivery processes and strategies.

Sales, Demand, and Capacity Management

The hospitality and tourism industries face unique supply and demand problems, which greatly influence companies' sales strategies. General factors affecting tourism demands are explored in the works of Hiemstra and Wong (2002), Tan, McCahon, and Miller (2002), and Kim and Qu (2002); Higham and Hinch (2002) discuss ways to overcome seasonality in sport and tourism. Formica and McCleary (2003) illustrate seven steps for estimating demands for a conference center, while other researchers used rough set theory and a time-varying parameter model, or a Kalman filter, to analyze and forecast tourism demands (Goh & Law, 2003; Song & Wong, 2003). Pullman and Thompson (2002) explore management strategies for maximizing capacity in the resort service system by applying queuing theory and simulation. Given the relatively weak emphasis placed on management science concepts in hospitality and tourism curricula, these studies provide strong impetus for future research and education in the discipline.

Comparatively less research attention was given to sales-oriented organizational issues like sales promotions and personal selling. Taylor and Long-Tolbert (2002) examined the influence of coupons on consumers' quick service restaurant purchases and Lucas and Bowen (2002) assessed the effectiveness of large-scale casino promotions. Corporate travel managers' and salespeople's personal selling techniques are empirically identified in Weilbaker and Crocker's (2002) study. Research on sales promotions and personal selling needs to be conducted at the level of not only the firm's organized efforts but also individual service employees' interactions with customers, because service encounters are known as "moments of truth" or sources of "critical incidents" for both current and future sales.

Pricing and Revenue/Yield Management

Pricing-related research covered fairly diverse issues, with general modeling efforts to be noticed. Pellinen (2003) describes pricing decision models and processes employed by tourism enterprises and Dwyer, Forsyth, and Rao (2002) attempt to develop international indices of tourism price competitiveness and discuss the factors that may affect the indices over time across destinations. Another modeling effort appears in Tyrrell and Johnston's (2003) study in which a standardized method of assessing changes in tourists' expenditure across state welcome centers and the method's effectiveness are discussed in an empirical application. Using conjoint analysis, Mazanec (2002) investigates tourists' perceptions of travel packages and of the companies selling them to determine the influence of Euro pricing and pricing in local currency. Additional unique, interesting attempts include hedonic pricing based on product and service characteristics at bed and breakfast facilities (Monty & Skidmore, 2003) and pricing models for online auctions in the lodging industry (Kasavana & Singh, 2002). It is surprising that current price competition and erosion occurring in online transactions was not addressed in pricing research.

Other Topics

Besides the major trends discussed above, several lines of research are notable. Hospitality customers' tipping behaviors were examined in relation to the essential reasons and antecedents of tipping (Dewald, 2003), expectancy disconfirmation of services (Tse, 2003), and the magnitude and measurement scale effects of tipping (Lynn, 2003; Lynn & Sturman, 2003). Image research addressed the roles of famous individuals and icons in developing tourist attractions (Kim & Richardson, 2003; Pearce, Morrison, & Moscardo, 2003), selection of appropriate research methods (Gallarza, Saura, & García, 2002), and tests of different measurement models (Kim & Yoon, 2003; Litvin & Goh, 2002).

Proposed factors affecting tourists' information search behavior include travel purpose and tourist characteristics (Lo, Cheung, & Law, 2002), culture (Money & Crotts, 2003), and prior knowledge (Gursoy, 2003). Tourists' product and destination choices were understood in light of their sensation seeking (Pizam, Reichel, & Uriely, 2002), novelty seeking (Petrick, 2002), and variety seeking (Andsager & Drzewiecka, 2002). Stimulated perhaps by the September 11 incident and Iraqi war situations, several researchers studied issues associated with crisis management and recovery for businesses (Blake & Sinclair, 2003; Henderson, 2003; Israeli & Reichel, 2003; Stafford, Yu, & Armoo, 2002), safety of Americans' overseas travel (Lepp & Gibson, 2003), and tourists' perceptions of safety and security (George, 2003). Topics not specifically reviewed in this and earlier sections tended to appear relatively infrequently and in divergent themes in the reviewed journals.

Industry Trends and Current Research Issues

This section summarizes significant research issues associated with industry trends to see whether the reviewed hospitality and tourism journals reflect industry's research demands. Various sources were reviewed for the period from 2000 (about the time the reviewed studies were conducted or written) to the present and only enduring issues were selected for mention in this study. Although a large number of trade magazines, newsletters, and Websites were scanned for this purpose, we rely heavily on sources from non-profit organizations as they tend to cover industry issues more broadly in a structured manner and as they could reflect both directly and indirectly industry-wide marketing practices and research problems. While numerous sources suggested specific research issues and marketing practices that could be locally important, we attempted to arrange the issues at the same topical level as we organized academic research in Table 1.1 for easier comparisons. In addition, the issues were grouped conveniently by industry to enhance industry-specific topical representation: "hospitality" mainly covers issues in the lodging and related industries and marketing in general; "tourism" relates to destination marketing organizations and tourist behavior; and "foodservice" broadly represents restaurant/foodservice businesses and eating behavior. The results appear in Table 1.4 and the issue items are in a rough order of recurrence across the sources cited.

Although Table 1.4 provides various industry-specific research issues, several converging themes are noticeable. First, regardless of industries, research on consumer behavior seems to be a generally significant priority. Understanding guests, travelers, and patrons in terms of their needs, demographic changes, and shifting preferences is a pervasive concern to all industries. Customer satisfaction, along with longer-term relationship and loyalty management, remains an important area of research as well. Second, technological innovations and their replacement of traditional business concepts and tools are on top of marketers' mind across the board. In particular, the Internet technology has led the industries to rethink the traditionally downplayed role of distribution channels. Abundance of alternative choices and product information for customers via the Internet is one source of escalating marketing challenges and firms' direct versus indirect, via eMediaries, control of the market is another. Third, attributed mainly to the 9/11 incident and Iraqi war, safety and security of consumers became a salient issue in hospitality and tourism marketing. While the safety and security issues are rather environmental in the lodging and tourism industries, they are fundamentally product-related in the foodservice and restaurant industries. Branding is another critical issue demanding increased research investments. Research needs on branding and brand extensions have been stimulated by the recent frenzy of mergers and consolidations in the lodging industry (see Matovic & McCleary, 2003), while branding is an emerging research issue in the tourism and foodservice industries.

Compared to the industry trends and research issues in Table 1.4, hospitality and tourism marketing research needs to diversify greatly in its scope and depth of examinations. Although several issues like satisfaction, relationship management, and electronic marketing had a fairly good representation, other issues like branding, safety and security, and information processing fell short of the industry needs. Additional diversification within the consumer behavior topics is also highly desirable so that topics like perceived value, choice behavior, and image can share stronger research interests. Studies addressing current economic and political environments and providing specific marketing guidelines in relation to crisis management will serve current industry concerns. Industry also awaits invigorated research efforts on marketing functions of pricing, demand generation, and product development and innovations through reintroduced business concepts like mass customization and experiential consumption.

At the industry level, a few significant trends are worth mentions. As the role and contribution of marketing is increasingly important to society as well as business organizations (see Wilkie & Moore, 1999), metrics to measure the value of marketing activities and performance have drawn strong research attention in recent years. Such an issue, however, is not specially covered in the hospitality and tourism journals. Destination branding and image, a traditionally important research topic in tourism, received relatively little space in the journals during the years and research on destination development using such marketing concepts as experiential tourism is yet to be reported. The foodservice/restaurant industry continues to grapple with issues like healthy eating and regulatory efforts, technology adaptation, menu engineering and product development, and labor management.

Conclusions and Implications

This study reviewed eight hospitality and tourism journals for the period of 2002–2003 in an effort to summarize significant trends in marketing research. The review included classifications of 223 reported studies based on research topics, industry applications, and design and analysis methods employed. Selected significant research trends were reviewed in further detail, followed by succinct comments on the general aspect of the topical progress. Significant industry trends that either appeared or not appeared in the reviewed journals were additionally summarized specifically into three industry groups and they

Table 1.4: Industry trends and current research issues.

Hospitality[a]	Tourism[b]	Foodservice[c]
• Technology and new business methods	• Technology for travel planning and buying	• Healthier lifestyle (obesity, blood alcohol level, low carbohydrate, low fat, and health care)
• Branding and brand extensions	• Website evaluations	
• Public safety and security	• Destination branding	• Multibranding/brand styles
• Pricing, bundles, and promotions	• Safety and security, risk, terrorism, and personal comfort	• Food Safety; general and special (e.g., Mad Cow)
• Growth, innovation, and new products	• Building sustainable travel demand	• Technology (integrated food production information systems)
• Managing customer relationships and loyalty	• Barriers to travel	
• Finding, training, motivating, and retaining capable employees	• Travel motivation	• Nutrition and menu labeling
	• Vacation choice/decision making process	• Customer satisfaction and relationship
• Understanding customers	• Customer relationship marketing	
• Management employees' service	• Factors affecting international travels	• Food power (dining out and market growth)
• Assessing marketing productivity and marketing Management and conservation of natural resources metrics/ development of better key indicators and analysis tools	• Image/awareness	
	• Special events in destination branding	Menu planning and menu evolution
	• Minority traveler	
	• Heritage and cultural tourism	
• Distribution channels and channel conflicts	• Experiential tourism	

- Current economic situation and impacts
- Value drivers
- Quality and satisfaction
- Marketing information system: collecting, interpreting, and using information
- Consolidation and alliances
- Culinary tourism
- Impacts of child nutrition programs on eating behavior and educational performance
- Human resources (turnover, training, workforce diversity, etc.)
- Competition and food sales
- Food quality program
- Natural/fresh foods/locally grown foods
- Ethnic splintering in market bases
- Benchmarking
- Entertainment (e.g., fun foods and interactive restaurants)
- Affluenza (luxury foods, driven boomers)

Sources (in the alphabetical order; some information was obtained through the authors' direct contact with the cited organizations and the Website homepage of the organizations are provided in the reference list).
[a]American Hotel & Lodging Educational Foundation; Benchmark Hospitality; Earnst & Young's Hospitality Advisory Services; Hospitality Sales & Marketing Association International's (HSMAI); International Society of Hospitality Consultants (ISHC); Marketing Science Institute (MSI); and Matovic & McCleary (2003).
[b]Travel Industry Association of America (TIA); Travel and Tourism Research Association (TTRA); and Randal travel marketing, Inc.
[c]American School FoodService Association (ASFSA); Food Marketing Institute (FMI); National Food Service Management Institute (NFSMI); National Restaurant Association Educational Foundation (NRAEF); and U.S. Department of Agriculture (USDA).

were compared to the research topics covered by the journals. In conclusion, while hospitality and tourism research is growing in its scope and rigor, it still does not seem to fully meet the industry's research demands with regard to topical diversity.

While specific comments and suggestions for different research topics were already provided, there still are several fundamental issues for hospitality and tourism research that were detected during our review. We briefly discuss them below in a critical manner for the sake of stimulating additional scientific marketing research on diverse hospitality and tourism topics and improving general research practices toward a sounder tradition of domain research.

(a) *Not only applications but also theory development.* The reviewed journals generally lack reports on theory development efforts. The majority of the reviewed studies were exploratory or application-minded simply "trying out" some research questions or testing some borrowed theories in a different segment of the hospitality and tourism industry. These studies were typically absent of testable formal hypotheses and they tended to be driven by data or methods; frequented market segmentation studies are good examples. While it is hardly arguable that the hospitality and tourism discipline is an applied science, the discipline still needs its own domain-specific theories as its knowledge infrastructure to strengthen its scientific identity and status. Applications are not a wrong effort to make; what is needed is stronger conceptual rigor and meaningful contribution back to the mainstream theoretical thought through creative applications and domain-specific theory development activities.

(b) *Lack of ground theories and substantive knowledge accumulation.* Few research topics are tightly hinged upon one or two central theories in a pedagogical structure showing conspicuous progresses in knowledge generation. As mentioned above, perhaps theory development efforts are tepid in this discipline, which is believed to have hampered subsequent accumulation of knowledge about domain theories. Most exploratory studies produced fragmentary local knowledge without embodying a sustained connectedness to existing theories. What are topically representative theories and what significant progresses have we seen over time for the theories? Hospitality and tourism transactions, which usually involve exchanges of both products and services simultaneously, offer ample processing and evaluation cues and, thus, can serve as excellent breeding grounds for theory building.

(c) *Let's experiment more.* Primary cross-sectional field surveys were the dominant study design for data gathering. While such field surveys could provide valuable reality information, they are seriously limited for testing various marketing phenomena that are often structured in dynamic processes or causal relationships between two or more variables. Experiment has been the major vehicle for developing and testing theories in other disciplines such as psychology. The tourism and hospitality discipline has underutilized experiments, which reflects in a way the application-dominant research tradition as discussed above. Qualitative research methods, which are also infrequently employed in hospitality and tourism research, are likely to advance along with the progress in experimental sophistication as well.

(d) *Methods are just means.* Many studies give an impression that the data were gathered to serve application of chosen statistical analysis techniques. Such method-driven studies typically lacked both compelling problem statements and strong conceptual footholds. Data and methods are just selected ways or means to achieve the (conceptual) goals of a study. Only with solid conceptual research goals can competent analyses merit generation of meaningful knowledge and substantive contributions to the literature.

(e) *What's new?* Valuable resources are invested in conducting a study. However, findings often grossly fail to justify the investments, because they often end up confirming what is already known and reported in the cited studies. In contrast, some findings are new, but highly case-specific as well as incoherent with the mainstream background theory used for the study. In such cases, a substantive contribution to the literature has not occurred and valuable resources wasted. Mere application studies contribute little to the scientific progress. At the end of every study, we must ask a question, what's new to the theory as well as the key stakeholders?

No single study is without flaws, to a certain degree. No one will argue about the importance of understanding limitations, and their implications for the results, inherent in published studies. Hence, it has become a norm for a manuscript to include a section to discuss study limitations. Anecdotal editorial evidence is that many gatekeepers (i.e., editors and reviewers) require such a discussion. However, this section often records the researcher's most uncommitted efforts, aimed primarily to defend or excuse the study. What is necessary is the view that each study is a building block of the research tradition for the specific theory examined and for the discipline as a whole. Thus, discussions on limitations should be directed to seeding new ideas and bettering thoughts and ways in future inquiries. This is one-way science progresses.

References

AHLEF. (2004). American hotel and lodging educational foundation. http://www.ahlef.org

Akama, J.S., & Kieti, D.M. (2003). Measuring tourist satisfaction with Kenya's wildlife safari: A case study of Tsavo West National Park. *Tourism Management, 24*(1), 73–81.

Andsager, J.L., & Drzewiecka, J.A. (2002). Desirability of differences in destinations. *Annals of Tourism Research, 29*(20), 401–421.

ASFSA. (2004). American School FoodService Association. http://www.asfsa.org

Au, N., & Law, R. (2002). Categorical classification of tourism dining. *Annals of Tourism Research, 29*(3), 819–833.

Back, K., & Parks, S.C. (2003). A brand loyalty model involving cognitive, affective, and conative brand loyalty and customer satisfaction. *Journal of Hospitality and Tourism Research, 27*(4), 419–435.

Baloglu, S. (2002). Dimensions of customer loyalty: Separating friends from well wishers. *Cornell Hotel and Restaurant Administration Quarterly, 43*(1), 47–59.

Barsky, J., & Nash, L. (2002). Evoking emotion: Affective keys to hotel loyalty. *Cornell Hotel and Restaurant Administration Quarterly, 43*(1), 39–46.

Barsky, J., & Nash, L. (2003). Customer satisfaction: Applying concepts to industry-wide measures. *Cornell Hotel and Restaurant Administration Quarterly, 44*(5/6), 173–183.

Blake, A., & Sinclair, M.T. (2003). Tourism crisis management: US response to September 11. *Annals of Tourism Research, 30*(4), 813–832.

Bowen, D. (2002). Research through participant observation in tourism: A creative solution to the measurement of consumer satisfaction/dissatisfaction (CS/D) among tourists. *Journal of Travel Research*, *41*(1), 4–14.

Bowen, J.T., & Sparks, B.A. (1998). Hospitality marketing research: A content analysis and implications for future research. *International Journal of Hospitality Management*, 17(2), 125–144.

Brown, J.R., & Ragsdale, C.T. (2002). The competitive market efficiency of hotel brands: An application of data envelopment analysis. *Journal of Hospitality and Tourism Research*, *26*(4), 332–360.

Brownell, J., & Reynolds, D. (2002). Strengthening the F&B purchaser–supplier partnership: Actions that make a difference. *Cornell Hotel and Restaurant Administration Quarterly*, *43*(6), 49–61.

Buhalis, D., & Licata, M.C. (2002). The future of tourism intermediaries. *Tourism Management*, *23*(3), 207–220.

Caldwell, N., & Coshall, J. (2003). Tourists' preference structures for London's Tate Modern Gallery: The implications for strategic marketing. *Journal of Travel and Tourism Marketing*, *14*(2), 23–45.

Carroll, B., & Siguaw, J. (2003). The evolution of electronic distribution: Effects on hotels and intermediaries. *Cornell Hotel and Restaurant Administration Quarterly*, *44*(4), 38–50.

Chen, J.S. (2003). Developing a travel segmentation methodology: A criterion-based approach. *Journal of Hospitality and Tourism Research*, *27*(3), 310–327.

Chen, J.S., & Uysal, M. (2002). Market positioning analysis: A hybrid approach. *Annals of Tourism Research*, *29*(4), 987–1003.

Cho, Y., Wang, Y., & Fesenmaier, D.R. (2002). Searching for experiences: The Web-based virtual tour in tourism marketing. *Journal of Travel and Tourism Marketing*, *12*(4), 1–17.

Christou, E. (2003). Guest loyalty likelihood in relation to hotels' corporate image and reputation: A study of three countries in Europe. *Journal of Hospitality and Leisure Marketing*, *10*(3/4), 85–99.

Christou, E., & Kassianidis, P. (2002). Consumer's perceptions and adoption of online buying for travel products. *Journal of Travel and Tourism Marketing*, *12*(4), 93–107.

Day, G.S., & Mongomery, D.B. (1999). Charting new directions for marketing. *Journal of Marketing*, 63(special issue), 3–13.

Dean, A., Morgan, D., & Tan, T.E. (2002). Service quality and customers' willingness to pay more for travel services. *Journal of Travel and Tourism Marketing*, *12*(2/3), 95–110.

Dewald, B. (2003). Tipping in Hong Kong restaurants. *International Journal of Hospitality Management*, *22*(3), 307–319.

Dolnicar, S. (2002). A review of data-driven market segmentation in tourism. *Journal of Travel and Tourism Marketing*, *12*(1), 1–22.

Dubs, L., Bel, J.L., & Sears, D. (2003). From customer value to engineering pleasurable experiences in real life and online. *Cornell Hotel and Restaurant Administration Quarterly*, *44*(5/6), 124–130.

Dwyer, L., Forsyth, P., & Rao, P. (2002). Destination price competitiveness: Exchange rate changes versus domestic inflation. *Journal of Travel Research*, *40*(3), 328–336.

FMI. (2004). Food Marketing Institute. http://www.fmi.org

Formica, S., & McCleary, K. (2003). Estimating demand for a conference center in a rural community. *Journal of Hospitality and Leisure Marketing*, *10*(1/2), 123–136.

Fyall, A., Callod, C., & Edwards, B. (2003). Relationship marketing: The challenge for destinations. *Annals of Tourism Research*, *30*(3), 644–659.

Gallarza, M.G., Saura, I.G., & García, H.C. (2002). Destination image: Towards a conceptual framework. *Annals of Tourism Research*, *29*(1), 56–78.

George, R. (2003). Tourist's perceptions of safety and security while visiting Cape Town. *Tourism Management*, *24*(5), 575–585.

Gilbert, D., & Wong, R.K.C. (2003). Passenger expectations and airline services: A Hong Kong based study. *Tourism Management*, *24*(5), 519–532.

Goh, C., & Law, R. (2003). Incorporating the rough sets theory into travel demand analysis. *Tourism Management*, *24*(5), 511–517.

Gursoy, D. (2003). Prior product knowledge and its influence on the traveler's information search behavior. *Journal of Hospitality and Leisure Marketing*, *10*(3/4), 113–130.

Hancer, M., & George, R.T. (2003). Psychological empowerment of non-supervisory employees working in full-service restaurants. *International Journal of Hospitality Management*, *22*(1), 3–16.

Hardine, M.D., Wooldridge, B.R., & Jones, K.C. (2003). Guest perceptions of hotel quality: Determining which employee groups count most. *Cornell Hotel and Restaurant Administration Quarterly*, *44*(1), 43–52.

Harris, K.J., Bojanic, D., & Cannon, D.F. (2003). Service encounters and service bias: A preliminary investigation. *Journal of Hospitality and Tourism Research*, *27*(3), 272–290.

Henderson, J.C. (2003). Communicating in a crisis: Flight SQ 006. *Tourism Management*, *24*(3), 279–287.

Heung, V.C.S., Wong, M.Y., & Qu, H. (2002). A study of tourists' satisfaction and post-experience behavioral intentions in relation to airport restaurant services in the Hong Kong SAR. *Journal of Travel and Tourism Marketing*, *12*(2/3), 111–135.

Hiemstra, S., & Wong, K.K.F. (2002). Factors affecting demand for tourism in Hong Kong. *Journal of Travel and Tourism Marketing*, *12*(1/2), 43–62.

Higham, J., & Hinch, T. (2002). Tourism, sport and seasons: The challenges and potential of overcoming seasonality in the sport and tourism sectors. *Tourism Management*, *23*(2), 175–185.

Hotel-online.com. (2004). Benchmark's top ten meeting industry trends for 2004. Retrieved July 14, from http://www.hotel-online.com/News/PR2004_1st/Jan04_ BenchmarkMeetingTrends.html

Hotel-online.com. (2004). Hospitality industry top 10 thoughts for 2004. Retrieved July 14, from http://www.hotel-online.com/News/PR2004_1st/Jan04_TenKeyIssues.html

Hotel-online.com. (2004). HSMAI survey of 7,000 members reveals the "top 10 issues of concern" facing sales and marketing executives in 2004. Retrieved July 14, from http://www.hotel-online.com/News/PR2004_1st/Feb04_HSMAIIssues.html

Hsu, C.H.C. (2003). Mature motorcoach travelers' satisfaction: A preliminary step toward measurement development. *Journal of Hospitality and Tourism Research*, *27*(3), 291–309.

ISHC. (2004). International Society of Hospitality Consultants. http://www.ishc.com

Israeli, A.A., & Reichel, A. (2003). Hospitality crisis management practices: The Israeli case. *International Journal of Hospitality Management*, *22*(4), 353–372.

Jeong, M., Oh, H., & Gregoire, M. (2003). Conceptualizing web site quality and its consequences in the lodging industry. *International Journal of Hospitality Management*, *22*(2), 161–175.

Johnson, L. (2002). An application of the critical incident technique in gaming research. *Journal of Travel and Tourism Marketing*, *12*(2/3), 45–63.

Jones, D.L., McCleary, K.W., & Lepisto, L.R. (2002). Consumer complaint behavior manifestations for table service restaurants: Identifying socio-demographic characteristics, personality, and behavioral factors. *Journal of Hospitality and Tourism Research*, *26*(2), 105–123.

Kandampully, J., & Suhartanto, D. (2003). The role of customer satisfaction and image in gaining customer loyalty in the hotel industry. *Journal of Hospitality and Leisure Marketing*, *10*(1/2), 3–25.

Kasavana, M.L. (2002). EMarketing: Restaurant websites that click. *Journal of Hospitality and Leisure Marketing*, *9*(3/4), 161–178.

Kasavana, M.L., & Singh, A.J. (2002). Online auctions: Dynamic pricing and the lodging industry. *Journal of Hospitality and Leisure Marketing*, *9*(3/4), 127–140.

Kerin, R.A. (1996). In pursuit of an ideal: The editorial and literary history of the *Journal of Marketing*. *Journal of Marketing*, *60*(1), 1–13.

Khan, M. (2003). ECOSERV: Ecotourists' quality expectations. *Annals of Tourism Research*, *30*(1), 109–124.

Kim, H., & Richardson, S.L. (2003). Motion picture impacts on destination images. *Annals of Tourism Research*, *30*(1), 216–237.

Kim, H.J., McCahon, C., & Miller, J. (2003a). Service orientation for contact employees in Korean casual-dining restaurants. *International Journal of Hospitality Management*, *22*(1), 67–83.

Kim, J., Wei, S., & Ruys, H. (2003b). Segmenting the market of West Australian senior tourists using an artificial neural network. *Tourism Management*, *24*(1), 25–34.

Kim, K., & Jogaratnam, G. (2002). Travel Motivations: A comparative study of Asian international and domestic American college students. *Journal of Travel and Tourism Marketing*, *12*(4), 61–82.

Kim, S., & Yoon, Y. (2003). The hierarchical effects of affective and cognitive components on tourism destination image. *Journal of Travel and Tourism Marketing*, *14*(2), 1–22.

Kim, W.G., & Qu, H. (2002). Determinants of domestic travel expenditure in South Korea. *Journal of Travel and Tourism Marketing*, *12*(1/2), 85–97.

Klenosky, D.B. (2002). The "pull" of tourism destinations: A means-end investigation. *Journal of Travel Research*, *40*(4), 385–395.

Kotler, P., Bowen, J.T., & Makens, J. (2003). *Marketing for hospitality and tourism* (3rd ed.). Upper Saddle River, NJ: Prentice-Hall.

Kozak, M. (2002a). Measuring comparative destination performance: A study in Spain and Turkey. *Journal of Travel and Tourism Marketing*, *12*(3), 83–110.

Kozak, M. (2002b). Comparative analysis of tourist motivations by nationality and destinations. *Tourism Management*, *23*(3), 221–232.

Kozak, M., Huan, T.C., & Beaman, J. (2002). A systematic approach to non-repeat and repeat travel: With measurement and destination loyalty concept implications. *Journal of Travel and Tourism Marketing*, *12*(4), 19–38.

Lam, T., & Tang, V. (2003). Recognizing customer complaint behavior: The case of Hong Kong hotel restaurants. *Journal of Travel and Tourism Marketing*, *14*(1), 69–86.

Law, R., & Wong, J. (2003). Successful factors for a travel web site: Perceptions of on-line purchasers in Hong Kong. *Journal of Hospitality and Tourism Research*, *27*(1), 118–124.

Lepp, A., & Gibson, H. (2003). Tourist roles, perceived risk and international tourism. *Annals of Tourism Research*, *30*(3), 606–624.

Litvin, S.W., & Goh, H.K. (2002). Self-image congruity: A valid tourism theory? *Tourism Management*, *23*(1), 81–83.

Lo, A., Cheung, C., & Law, R. (2002). Information search behavior of Hong Kong's inbound travelers — A comparison of business and leisure travelers. *Journal of Travel and Tourism Marketing*, *12*(3), 61–81.

Lucas, A.F., & Bowen, J.T. (2002). Measuring the effectiveness of casino promotions. *International Journal of Hospitality Management*, *21*(2), 189–202.

Lynn, M. (2003). Restaurant tips and service quality: A weak relationship or just weak measurement. *International Journal of Hospitality Management*, *22*(3), 321–325.

Lynn, M., & Sturman, M.C. (2003). It's simpler than it seems: An alternative explanation for the magnitude effect in tipping. *International Journal of Hospitality Management*, *22*(1), 103–110.

Macintosh, G. (2002). Building trust and satisfaction in travel counselor/client relationships. *Journal of Travel and Tourism Marketing*, *12*(4), 59–74.

Matovic, D., & McCleary, K.W. (2003). Marketing in the next decade: A qualitative study of the U.S. hotel industry. *Journal of Travel and Tourism Marketing*, *14*(2), 47–65.

Mattila, A.S. (1999). An examination of factors affecting service recovery in a restaurant setting. *Journal of Hospitality and Tourism Research*, 23(3), 284–298.

Mattila, A.S., & Mount, D.J. (2003). The role of call centers in mollifying disgruntled guests. *Cornell Hotel and Restaurant Administration Quarterly*, 43(4), 75–80.

Mazanec, J.A. (2002). Tourists' acceptance of Euro pricing: Conjoint measurement with random coefficients. *Tourism Management*, 23(3), 245–253.

Middelkoop, M.V., Borgers, A., & Timmermans, H. (2003). Inducing heuristic principles of tourist choice of travel mode: A rule-based approach. *Journal of Travel Research*, 42(1), 75–83.

Miller, A.R., & Grazer, W.F. (2003). Complaint behavior as a factor in cruise line losses: An analysis of brand loyalty. *Journal of Travel and Tourism Marketing*, 15(1), 77–91.

Money, R.B., & Crotts, J.C. (2003). The effect of uncertainty avoidance on information search, planning, and purchases of international travel vacations. *Tourism Management*, 24(2), 191–202.

Monty, B., & Skidmore, M. (2003). Hedonic pricing and willingness to pay for bed and breakfast amenities in Southeast Wisconsin. *Journal of Travel Research*, 42(2), 195–199.

Morais, D.B., & Zillifro, T. (2003). An examination of the relationships established between a whitewater rafting provider and its male and female customers. *Journal of Hospitality and Leisure Marketing*, 10(1/2), 137–150.

Moschis, G., Curasi, C.F., & Bellenger, D. (2003). Restaurant-selection preferences of mature consumers. *Cornell Hotel and Restaurant Administration Quarterly*, 43(4), 51–60.

Mount, D.J., & Mattila, A. (2002). Last chance to listen: Listening behaviors and their effect on call center satisfaction. *Journal of Hospitality and Tourism Research*, 26(2), 124–137.

MSI. (2004). Marketing Science Institute. http://www.msi.org

Mueller, R.D., Palmer, A., Mack, R., & McMullan, R. (2003). Service in the restaurant industry: An American and Irish comparison of service failures and recovery strategies. *International Journal of Hospitality Management*, 22(4), 395–418.

Murphy, J., & Tan, I. (2003). Journey to nowhere? E-mail customer service by travel agents in Singapore. *Tourism Management*, 24(5), 543–550.

Namasivayam, K., & Hinkin, T.R. (2003). The customer's role in the service encounter: The effects of control and fairness. *Cornell Hotel and Restaurant Administration Quarterly*, 44(3), 26–36.

NFSMI. (2004). National Food Service Management Institute. http://www.nfsmi.org

NRAEF. (2004). National Restaurant Association Educational Foundation. http://www.nraef.org

Oh, H. (2002). Transaction evaluations and relationship intentions. *Journal of Hospitality and Tourism Research*, 26(3), 278–305.

Oh, H. (2003). Reexaming recovery paradox effects and impact ranges of service failure and recovery. *Journal of Hospitality and Tourism Research*, 27(4), 402–418.

Oh, H., & Parks, S.C. (1997). Customer satisfaction and service quality: A critical review of the literature and research implications for the hospitality industry. *Hospitality Research Journal*, 20(3), 35–64.

Oliver, R.L. (1997). *Satisfaction: A behavioral perspective on the consumer*. Irwin/McGraw-Hill, New York.

Pan, G.W. (2003). A theoretical framework of business network relationships associated with the Chinese outbound tourism market to Australia. *Journal of Travel and Tourism Marketing*, 14(2), 87–104.

Parasuraman, A., Zeithaml, V.A., & Berry, L.L. (1988). SERVQUAL: A multiple-item scale for measuring consumer perceptions of service quality. *Journal of Retailing*, 64(1), 12–40.

Pearce, D.G. (2002). New Zealand holiday travel to Samoa: A distribution channels approach. *Journal of Travel Research*, 41(2), 197–205.

Pearce, P.L., Morrison, A.M., & Moscardo, G.M. (2003). Individuals as tourist icons: A developmental and marketing analysis. *Journal of Hospitality and Leisure Marketing*, 10(1/2), 63–85.

Pellinen, J. (2003). Making price decisions in tourism enterprises. *International Journal of Hospitality Management*, 22(2), 217–235.

Petrick, J.F. (2002). An examination of golf vacationers' novelty. *Annals of Tourism Research*, 29(2), 384–400.

Petrick, J.F., & Backman, S.J. (2002). An examination of the determinants of golf travelers' satisfaction. *Journal of Travel Research*, 40(3), 252–258.

Pike, S. (2003). The use of repertory grid analysis to elicit salient short-break holiday destination attributes in New Zealand. *Journal of Travel Research*, 41(3), 315–319.

Pizam, A., Reichel, A., & Uriely, N. (2002). Sensation seeking and tourist behavior. *Journal of Hospitality and Leisure Marketing*, 9(3/4), 17–33.

Pullman, M.E., & Thompson, G.M. (2002). Evaluating capacity- and demand-management decisions at a ski resort. *Cornell Hotel and Restaurant Administration Quarterly*, 43(6), 25–36.

Randal travel marketing, Inc. (2003). Top ten travel and tourism trends 2003. Retrieved June 20, from http://www.rtmnet.com

Rittichainuwat, B.N., Qu, H., & Mongknonvanit, C. (2002). A study of the impact of travel satisfaction on the likelihood of travelers to revisit Thailand. *Journal of Travel and Tourism Marketing*, 12(2/3), 19–43.

Schall, M. (2003). Best practices in the assessment of hotel-guest attitudes. *Cornell Hotel and Restaurant Administration Quarterly*, 44(2), 51–65.

Seddighi, H.R., & Theocharous, A.L. (2002). A model of tourism destination choice: A theoretical and empirical analysis. *Tourism Management*, 23(5), 475–487.

Shoemaker, S., & Bowen, J.T. (2003). Commentary on "Loyalty: A strategic commitment." *Cornell Hotel and Restaurant Administration Quarterly*, 44(5/6), 47–52.

Sigala, M. (2003). Developing and benchmarking Internet marketing strategies in the hotel sector in Greece. *Journal of Hospitality & Tourism Research*, 27(4), 375–401.

Sirakaya, E., Uysal, M., & Yoshioka, C.F. (2003). Segmenting the Japanese tour market to Turkey. *Journal of Travel Research*, 41(3), 293–304.

Song, H., & Wong, K.K.F. (2003). Tourism demand modeling: A time-varying parameter approach. *Journal of Travel Research*, 42(1), 57–64.

Stafford, G., Yu, L., & Armoo, A.K. (2002). Crisis management and recovery how Washington, D.C., hotels responded to terrorism. *Cornell Hotel and Restaurant Administration Quarterly*, 43(5), 27–40.

Sui, J.J., & Baloglu, S. (2003). The role of emotional commitment in relationship marketing: An empirical investigation of a loyalty model for casino. *Journal of Hospitality and Tourism Research*, 27(4), 470–489.

Sundaram, D.S., Jurowski, C., & Webster, C. (1997). Service failure recovery efforts in restaurant dining: The role of criticality of service consumption. *Hospitality Research Journal*, 20(3), 137–149.

Tan, A.Y.F., McCahon, C., & Miller, J. (2002). Modeling tourist flows to Indonesia and Malaysia. *Journal of Travel and Tourism Marketing*, 12(1/2), 63–84.

Taylor, G.A., & Long-Tolbert, S. (2002). Coupon promotions in quick-service restaurants: Preaching to the converted? *Cornell Hotel and Restaurant Administration Quarterly*, 43(4), 41–47.

TIA. (2004). Travel Industry Association of America. http://www.tia.org

Tsaur, S., Chang, T., & Yen, C. (2002a). The evaluation of airline service quality by fuzzy MCDM. *Tourism Management*, 23(2), 107–115.

Tsaur, S., Chiu, Y., & Huang, C. (2002b). Determinants of guest loyalty to international tourist hotels — A neural network approach. *Tourism Management*, 23(4), 397–405.

Tse, A.C. (2003). Tipping behaviour: A disconfirmation of expectation perspective. *International Journal of Hospitality Management*, 22(4), 461–467.

TTRA. (2004). Travel and Tourism Research Association. http://www.ttra.com

Tyrrell, T.J., & Johnston, R.J. (2003). Assessing expenditure changes related to welcome center visits. *Journal of Travel Research, 42*(1), 100–106.

USDA. (2004). U.S. Department of Agriculture. http://www.usda.gov

Verma, R., & Plaschka, G. (2003). The art and science of customer-choice modeling: Reflections, advances, and managerial implications. *Cornell Hotel and Restaurant Administration Quarterly, 44*(5/6), 156–165.

Verma, R., Plaschka, G., & Louviere, J.J. (2002). Understanding customer choices: A key to successful management of hospitality services. *Cornell Hotel and Restaurant Administration Quarterly, 43*(6), 15–24.

Vogt, C.A., & Andereck, K.L. (2003). Destination perceptions across a vacation. *Journal of Travel Research, 41*(4), 348–354.

Walsh, K. (2002). Service-delivery strategies: Three approaches to consulting for hospitality. *Cornell Hotel and Restaurant Administration Quarterly, 43*(6), 37–48.

Wang, Y., Yu, Q., & Fesenmaier, D.R. (2002). Defining the virtual tourist community: Implications for tourism marketing. *Tourism Management, 23*(4), 407–417.

Wei, S., & Milman, A. (2002). The impact of participation in activities while on vacation on seniors' psychological well-being: A path model application. *Journal of Hospitality & Tourism Research, 26*(2), 175–185.

Weilbaker, D.C., & Crocker, K. (2002). The importance of selling abilities in corporate hospitality sales to corporate customers. *Journal of Hospitality & Leisure Marketing, 9*(3/4), 51–66.

Wilkie, W.L., & Moore, E.S. (1999). Marketing's contributions to society. *Journal of Marketing, 63*(special issue), 198–218.

Wong, J., & Law, R. (2003). Difference in shopping satisfaction levels: A study of tourists in Hong Kong. *Tourism Management, 24*(4), 401–410.

Yoon, T., & Ekinci, Y. (2003). An examination of the SERVQUAL dimensions: Using the Guttman scaling procedure. *Journal of Hospitality and Tourism Research, 27*(1), 3–23.

Zins, A.H. (2002). Consumption emotions, experience quality and satisfaction: A structural analysis for complainers versus non-complainers. *Journal of Travel and Tourism Marketing, 12*(2/3), 3–18.

PART I:

"IT" MARKETING

Introduction

Metin Kozak and Luisa Andreu

The definition of "the tourism market" concept needs to be reconsidered as the information technology (IT) possibly has an opportunity to bring demand and supply on the virtual market together. While the main element of tourism demand as being the consumer who needs to satisfy their leisure requirements remains the same, computers could serve as suppliers or have the responsibility of suppliers. In addition to the specific feature of the accommodation industry being open for 24 h a day, computers may improve the non-stop services offered by the tourism and travel industry generally. A great number of hotel and airlines companies have launched their web sites on the Internet and are about to activate them as a two-way communication channels. An IT user can now search for the hotel and the flight company or the destination where they want to spend their holiday and complete reservations simply by giving details such as name, address and credit card number or other payment options. Once the reservation is accepted, the ticket is delivered to the user in a couple of days or e-ticket is provided promptly and the booking fare is transferred from the users' account into the company's account.

Taking into consideration the revolutionary effects of IT on the industry by reshaping the operation of activities in tourism, the first chapter presents the historical development of IT and its applications in tourism in a framework which will enable tourism companies and/or authorities to evaluate growth process of IT and to create a vision for their future. Even though users need to find suppliers or intermediaries rather than vice versa, it is also true that suppliers or intermediaries need to reach potential users via computers or other advertising tools to make them more aware of their products or services provided on the screen. Therefore, in light of a massive use of several IT applications not only by end-users but also service providers and a growing intention to develop new ones in the near future, it should be necessary to redefine the role of intermediaries as "cyber-mediaries" (or artificial agents) and the concept of marketing as "cyber-marketing" (Schuster, 1998). On the condition that the growth of IT applications keeps its current momentum at the same level, cyber-mediaries seem to be the only competitors of traditional intermediaries in tourism and travel marketing in the near future.

The second chapter is about the investigation of whether the industry people use electronic brochures and documents as a means of sustainable tourism marketing. Until recently, it was a commonly held belief among people that information technologies (ITs) and the Internet would create a paperless world. Nevertheless, present statistics reveal the opposite. According to claims put forward by "Paper Com Alliance" consisting of number of associations and a group of companies from the paper industry, new economy results in more paper consumption. According to one approach supporting the "paperless office" concept, the paper will be less needed because every kind of communication and information storage will be able to be achieved in a digital environment. However, improvements against this expectation have taken place and particularly with more widespread use of the Internet, printer, photocopy and due to the rich content provided by the Internet the paper consumption has increased to a level higher than ever. Considering the fact that 93% of the consumed paper is still obtained from the wood, it can be seen that both environment and sustainable tourism activities are under the threat of this new situation. Departing from this point, this chapter highlights the present situation by carrying out a survey among accommodation facilities and travel agencies operating in Mugla, Turkey. The findings reveal that tourism practitioners believe in the realization of "paperless environment"; however, there seem to be some pitfalls in practice and due to the conventional and habitual use of paper, electronic documents and brochures cannot be exploited adequately.

Revisiting the above-debate on whether traditional purchasing process will be replaced with an alternative option to purchase using ITs, the purpose of the next chapter of this part is to investigate consumers' intentions to buy travel products from online travel agencies. This study also investigates the demographics of Internet users, their online purchasing satisfaction experiences, their attitudes and perceptions toward purchasing electronically, the average time spent each day with electronic communications, online consumer incentives and online consumer benefits. An analysis of the actual means suggested that consumers find "price" to be the most important variable when purchasing a travel product online. This finding may suggest that online travel products are commoditized. Quality is ranked as the second most important variable followed by security, variety and brand. This difference might suggest that consumers are becoming more willing to reveal personal credit card information over the Web. However, there is a negative relationship between the likelihood of purchasing travel products over the Web using an online travel agency and the personal significance factors "important" and "significant". The differences within personal significance may suggest that consumers find it less likely to purchase from online travel agencies when it is very important to purchase.

Reference

Schuster, A. G. (1998). A Delphi Survey on business process re-engineering from the tourism and hospitality industries: The case of Alpha Flight Services. In: D. Buhalis, A. M. Tjoa, & J. Jafari (Eds), *Information and communication technologies in tourism* (pp. 224–234). Wien: Springer.

Chapter 2

A Historical Development of "IT" in Tourism Marketing

Yasar Sari, Metin Kozak and Teoman Duman

Introduction

"Intelligence and access to information have become the new basis for power in the world" (Godbey, 1997, p. 55). The advances in information technologies (ITs) show that destinations and tourism enterprises will lose their competitive advantages unless they adopt themselves to current electronic distribution channels and apply this electronic transformation to their businesses (Buhalis, 1998). Mostly as services, tourism products cannot be evaluated comprehensively before the actual experience because these products are generally purchased away from residence (Morrison, 1989). Information about tourism products is composed of descriptions of services that are produced by travel agencies, which have important effects on tourist-decision processes. Therefore, information that is current and that matches the needs and wants of the tourist is key to meet the tourism demand. In other words, for consumers, the satisfaction of needs and wants and for marketers, the successful promotion of tourism products depends on successful deliverance of current information through distribution channels (Sari & Kozak, 2004). Accordingly, tourism is one of the areas where IT is heavily and widely used (Sheldon, 1993).

As a definition, information technology (IT) implies the latest developments in electronics and communication through which information is compiled, decomposed, saved, analyzed, processed and distributed (Senn, 1998; Bensghir, 1996). To this end, the tourism industry has heavily used IT for last 20 years under the names of virtual realities, electronic commerce, digital currencies, teleconference, CD-ROM and Internet. Nowadays, the use of technology plays a crucial role in tourism marketing. The development of IT along with the rapid changes in network technologies has created a number of opportunities for tourism enterprises. As the creation, compilation, processing, saving and transmitting of information ease the daily business activities, IT is becoming a more important element of business applications in tourism. Moreover, the mutual growth of demand for and supply of tourism resulted in the heavier use of IT in the industry. It is generally accepted in tourism academia that developments in IT has revolutionary effects on the industry and result in significant reshaping of operation of activities in tourism (Stamboulis & Skayannis, 2003). Hence, it is necessary to overview the gradual development of IT in tourism. The purpose of this paper is to analyze the development of IT in tourism with a historical perspective. The historical development of IT and its applications in tourism is presented in a framework, which will enable tourism companies to evaluate growth process of IT and to create a vision for their future.

Literature Review

Mentioning about the turning points in the past, well-known futurologist Alvin Toffler argued that two important transformations had been experienced long ago and the third one is being experienced in today's time. According to Toffler, the first societal turning point was the appearance of agriculture and the second one was industrial revaluation. These two transformations were experienced in long time periods in the past. About 10,000 years ago, the humans scattered around all over the world and they adapted to a new way of life with the agriculture revolution. Through the end of 17th century, in Europe, the second big transformation in human past, the industrial revolution, came about before agriculture revolution had lost its effects on human life. This process, which is frequently called as "industrialization", had its effects on nations and continents much faster than the first one. During the last two centuries, the effects of agricultural revolution have slowed whereas the effects of industrial revolution have spread around the world especially in Europe, North America and in some other parts of the world quickly. Today, in many parts of the world, the effects of industrial revolution are still continuing and many of the countries whose economies depend heavily on agriculture have still been building steel production facilities, automotive and textile factories and railways.

As the effects of industrial revolution had been continuing through the beginning of 20th century, the third wave of changes started to show its effects on human history. At the roots of this change were information and technology. Especially, during the years after the World War II, this third wave of changes started to influence every aspect of human life and showed its effects in the US during the mid-1950s. Later, its effects have spread to other industrialized countries up till now. Still, many developed countries have been struggling to transform their heavy industrial structures that carry the effects of second wave of development to today's information-based technological structure. Beyond the hardware technology, IT is also making travel and tourism markets more competitive, as in other markets.

Large-scale transformations in human history also brought about new societies with them. Peter Drucker calls the society that appeared after the World War II with new wave of changes as "society beyond capitalism". In this respect, main economic sources for the new generation are not or will not be capital, labor or natural resources but information. In an economical analysis presented in 1941, it was argued that a typical economy had three components, the primary of which was agriculture, the secondary was production and industry, and the tertiary of which was services. In other words, an economy is composed of these three components at varying proportions. If an economy is becoming industrialized, much of the labor is employed in production related units. As a national income is to increase due to differences between sectoral productivity levels, the need for services and information will also increase. From this point of view, a number of European theorists pointed out the importance of information and technology in the transformation of industrial nature of many economies.

Therefore, the unification occurs between qualified labor, science and technology. D. Bell and A. Touraine who are known for their work on post-industrial societies argue that there are no industrial societies in developed countries. According to Bell, in post-industrial societies theoretical information is centralized and the share of services in the economy is getting larger with the influences of professionals, engineers, technicians and scientists on the economy. Touraine has also talked about societies that are defined with new bureaucratic and expert classes and information-based occupation trends. Despite the differences in the details, these types of definitions imply a drastic socio-economic transformation processes. These processes have brought about information societies, which are quite different from agricultural and industrial societies. Information society is defined with labor most of which is employed in information-related occupations. Also, information societies are characterized by the use and application of information in most parts of the economy.

The number of people employed in agriculture, industrial and information sectors differ between nations. Differences in the number of people in different sectors are more apparant in developed nations. For example, in 1980 only three percent of the total labor was employed in the agriculture sector in the US while 76 percent was employed in the services and information related sectors. Furthermore, more than eighty percent of new business ventures in the US are reported as related to service and information sectors. Similarly, a number of western European nations are becoming information societies just as the US, Canada and Japan (Akin, 2001). A number of socio–economic changes appear with effect of information societies. Some of these changes are as follows:

1. A deviation from goods production to services production. A rise in the professional, technical, educational, health and fast-food sectors.
2. The change in the nature of tasks.
3. The increase in the number of professional and technical jobs.
4. The technological change toward more advanced technologies. Widespread use of small and capable devices used for compilation and managing of information through microelectronics and semi-conductors.
5. The spread of informatics and the use of telecommunication parallel to the advancements in computer technology for coordination with far points.

It is generally accepted that the information era starts with the years that follow the World War II. Some writers propose that the year of 1957 during which the number of white collars overrode the number of blue collars is a strong indication of the start of information era. With the start of information era, a number of sectors in the economy including tourism started to be heavily influenced by the changes this new time period brought about. As a part of worldwide services sector, tourism industry can also be considered as an information industry. The retrieval and use of information in production and consumption of services and in daily activities are more important for tourism industry than for many other industries (Yarcan, 1998). Because of the nature of tourism product, the consumer or the tourist purchases or acquires the information before the actual product. For the tourist, the acquisition of information becomes more important as the distance between buyer and seller increases. On the same time, tourism enterprises want to collect information about their prospective customers for planning purposes. The mutual need for information between tourism product buyer and seller entails that the information exchange be correct, fast and low cost. In tourism industry, information flows through many channels that comprise consumers, producers, research units, destination organizations and governmental units (Yolal, 2003).

As very well known, most tourism products are consumed where they are produced. Therefore, most of the time, potential tourists have no chance to sample or physically investigate the components of the product they plan to purchase. Therefore, initially tourists purchase an image of what they expect. This image is a result of information they collect through different channels. The nature and the quality of information presented before the actual experience becomes crucial because this information is the source of expectations which are used for evaluation of service quality following the experience (Zeithaml, Parasuraman, & Berry, 1990). Similarly, the supply of up-to-date information that includes details of the tourism product becomes important for creating reasonable expectations. The widespread use IT has also triggered a number of changes in tourism consumer behavior. The easy reach of information about tourism products and services has created more demanding tourists who are less loyal, more selective about product and service quality, and are more apt for frequent and short-term holidays. A natural result of such behaviors is shorter decision-making periods that may create inclination for last minute deals. These changes in holiday buying behavior are also reshaping tourism-marketing efforts in many destination countries (Sarı, 2003).

According to Poon (1993), information acts as a cement for tourism-product producers (i.e. airlines, tour operators, travel agencies, hotels, car-rental agencies). The connection between the producers focuses on the information in all aspects of business not on the product *per se*. This information flows through different channels and connects the producer to the end consumer. For this reason, the interconnection between producers and consumers in tourism necessitates a well-organized information network (Wertner & Klein, 1999). Furthermore, most of the time, the information flow in tourism is not only between producers and consumers but also between other markets, competition and related governmental entities. In general, the information within and outside sources is necessary for cost-control, sustainable competitive advantage and more efficient marketing functions. As a result, today information is ultimate source for retaining and maintaining quality in service production.

In general, IT is defined as means and applications that are used for retrieval, storage and distribution of information (Senn, 1998). It encompasses computers, computer networks, printers, national or international cable or cordless communication devices (telephone, satellite communication systems etc.), printed, auditory or visual media devices (radio, TV etc.) and the like (Maddison & Darnton, 1996). IT has become a means of reaching development, prosperity and competitive advantage at the macroeconomic level. Similarly, at the microeconomic level, it serves as a means of efficient operational management that is also necessary for keeping up with competition in business (Buhalis, 1998). The use of IT provides the management with synchronic decision-making and control opportunities, which are necessary for instant problem solving. In other words, the use of IT makes quick, dependable and cost-effective interchange of data possible within businesses, customers and public agencies. As a result, it seems unlikely for businesses to reach sustainable competitive advantage, producing quality goods and services, increasing productivity in business practices and developing long-term customer relations without benefiting IT opportunities.

Historical Development of ITs

An overview of historical development of IT and its use in tourism is presented in Figure 2.1. As shown in the figure, initial developments in IT start with the invention and use of telegraphy during the second quarter of 1800s. From late 1800s through the mid-1900s, telephone, radio, fax and TV technologies appeared and later followed by computer technology. Computer use kept pace with the developments in network technology during 1970s. Computers were used for a number of purposes from conception and reservation to production and communication. Until 1980s, companies heavily used IT for operational purposes. Computers were used for payroll productions, business correspondence, inventory and accounting records, stocking and customer database development by the businesses. With the enhancements in data stocking and processing capacities with smaller and cost effective devices through 1980s, computer use has become widespread in every aspect of business practices.

After 1980s, increasing competition in the world forced companies to use IT more heavily for marketing purposes. Managerial and operational use of IT continued with an increasing pace but companies started to put more emphasis on collecting information about markets and reaching customers through 1990s. During the last decade, primary functions of IT has been to produce better quality services and promote products more effectively by research and product differentiation. Today, a number of innovations (i.e. virtual reality, multimedia kiosks, hard storage devices, intranet and extranet, home shopping and interactive TV, intelligent agents, intelligent cards, space technologies) promise more future developments in IT. Use of IT in production, presentation and promotion of services will bring about competitive edge to future businesses.

Use of IT within Organizations

Initially, most companies used computers for organizational purposes. Some of the intra-organizational uses of computers included payroll productions, business correspondence, inventory and accounting records keeping, stocking and customer database development. In other words, computers were initially used for computation, storage, search, listing and printing purposes. As for the use of IT in travel and tourism, airline companies were the first to adapt IT to their business practices. During late 1950s, high communication costs due to heavy data processing forced airlines to use computers in all aspects of their business. In time, these companies have developed specific airline reservation system softwares that have been used for flight reservation, seat arrangements, ticket confirmation, ticket sale and related services (O'Connor, 1999; Yarcan, 1998).

Systematic use of information technologies in tourism	System labels	Airline Reservation Systems	Computer Reservation Systems (CRSs)	Global Distribution Systems (GDSs)	Global Travel and Tourism Information and Reservation Systems
	Governance forms	Intra organizational systems	Inter-organizational systems	Electronic markets Systems for specific travel and tourism components.	Electronic markets Systems for a large variety of travel and tourism products
	Access	Inventory systems -Payroll preparation, -Business correspondance, -Inventory and accounting records, -Stocking ve keeping customer database	- Single Access systems	- Co-hosted systems - Multiple Access systems	De-hosted multiple access systems
Developments in IT		Telegraphy	Telephone, Radio, Fax and TV	Computer Technology	Developments in Microelectronics -PC Usage -Network technology	Internet and World Wide Web (www) - e-mail, chat e-markets -Travel portals	-Virtual reality -Multimedia kiosks -Hard storage devices -Intranet and Extranet -Home shopping and interactive TV - Intelligent agents -Intelligent cards -Space and mobile technologies -Data mining -Geographical information systems
YEARS		1825-1870	1870-1955	1955-1965	1965-1980	1980-2000	2000 and after

Figure 2.1: Developments in IT and its use in tourism.
Source: Adapted from O'Connor (1999, p. 14) Buhalis (1998), and Berce (1997, p. 337).

Nowadays, despite being highly costly, most tourism companies have adopted IT in their operational systems. Most business functions are completed with electronic devices and systems that bring out important operational efficiency. A number of hospitality companies set examples with their high-tech operational systems where the effects of such systems on customer loyalty and profitability have been shown (Siguaw & Enz, 1999). Examples of these systems include HOTELEXPERT of Barbizon Hotel and Empire Hotel New York, SOURCE of Marriott Courtyard and POWER-UP of Cendant Corporation. These organizational computer systems eliminated most paperwork, improved communication through the organization and eased managerial decision-making. The returns of such systems are known to be reduced costs, increased productivity, occupancy and ultimately profits.

Computer Reservation Systems (CRSs)

The computer reservation systems (CRSs) imply a centralized reservation network between interconnected companies such as airlines, travels agencies and hotels. In tourism, this network enables the firms to make and confirm reservations and to get information about customers and other firms recorded in the system. It is generally accepted that the electronic era for tourism businesses starts with these systems. Through 1990s, the scope of CRSs widened and these systems turned into global distribution systems (GDSs) (Buhalis, 1998). The range of products and services reserved through CRSs increased rapidly and large GDSs such as Amadeus and Galileo came about during last decade. Not only have these companies served as reservation agents but also they have operated airlines and accommodation companies (Buhalis, 1998).

Global Distribution Systems (GDSs)

In 1978 in the US, air carrying capacity increased about 94% following the deregulation of air transportation system. Increasing capacity and deregulation brought about fiercer competition, declines in prices and profitability (Werthner & Klein, 1999). This resulted in managerial and marketing partnerships between airlines in the world. Airlines initially developed their own reservation systems and after that they created global distribution systems by merging their systems with accommodation, travel agency, car rental and tour operator systems. In time, these computer networks progressed both vertically and horizontally. Horizontally, a number of airlines combined their networks to provide better air travel services while vertically they created partnerships with other travel and tourism companies to increase the quality and variety of services (i.e. hotel reservations, entertainment organizations, car rental, ferry tickets). Because GDSs combine a number of travels, tourism and intermediary organizations with computer networks, they lead to standardizations of many services and easier control of market shares in the industry (Buhalis, 1998). The centralized GDSs in the tourism industry are also called travel distribution supermarkets. As the computerized reservation systems develop and are interconnected, the number of monopolistic electronic formations increases. In other words, monopolistic sale of tourism products becomes more common with increasing electronic partnerships.

Internet and World Wide Web (www)

The first Internet use was launched by American Defence Ministry in 1970 with a project called ARPAnet. The purpose of the project was to develop a communication network for recovery after a possible nuclear war. During the years of peace, this project served a common purpose of fast communication. Until 1980s, Internet was mostly used by large academic institutions, but later it became popular among larger audiences with the development of www applications. Fast developments in Internet technology in 1990s (i.e. new communication protocols that ease the traffic in the networks, appearance of www applications, computer technology innovations) changed the way to do business to a greater extent and the term "electronic commerce" (e-commerce) entered into the world business terminology. Electronic commerce can be defined as reliable exchange of knowledge, goods and services through computer networks and supplemental digital infrastructure (Buhalis, 2003). During 1990s, commercial use of Internet was commonwide and tourism marketers started to use this new technology for promotion and sale of tourism products. Today, tourism is the second larger industry to use Internet applications for business purposes after the computer industry (Sheldon, 1997).

The rise of the importance of electronic commerce and the growth of business potential through it forced tourism industry to move an important share of its business practices into Internet and to benefit more from opportunities electronic commerce has brought to business world. One of the consequences of global development of Internet was the change in the traditional intermediaries of travel and tourism products. Previously, travel intermediaries were composed of tour operators, international travel agencies and domestic travel agencies, which commonly used computerized reservation systems, global distribution systems, travel networks and teletexes. However, as electronic commerce has become commonwide, tourism and travel services providers (i.e. airlines, car rental companies, hotel chains) developed e-commerce applications in their business practices and tried to have their potential customers to directly reach their systems. Currently, a number of destinations, along with single or multiple tourism service providers are structuring electronic-marketing systems through which they try to inform current or potential customers about their products. Traditional service providers in tourism are continuously adapting their businesses to IT and attempting to reach their markets through vertical and Internet portals (Buhalis, 2002). A summary of electronic marketing applications in tourism is provided in Table 2.1.

Travel portals are one of the fastest growing business types on Internet. There are a number of online travel agencies that make accommodation and ancillary service reservations electronically and that can respond to traveler needs as they arise during travel. Such leading travel agencies are "expedia.com" in the US and "orbitz.com" in Europe. Through these portals, travelers have a chance to reserve their plane tickets, hotel rooms and rental cars electronically in a few minutes. According to Jupiter Research Company, online travel sales that reached 24 billion dollars in 2001 is expected to reach 64 billion dollars in 2007. "In 2000, 42 percent of online travel planners made online reservations" (Morrison, 2002). While travel and accommodation companies are benefiting from Internet opportunities to solve capacity problems (e.g. last minute pricing), travelers enjoy value pricing by using electronic systems. The ease of reservation and price opportunities increases the business potential of travel intermediaries on the Internet (Greenspan, 2003).

Table 2.1: E-marketing applications in tourism.

E-business	Company	Consumer	Government
Company	B2B Communication networks between hotels and tour operators (extranet)	B2C E-business applications where airline tickets are purchased	B2G Business relations with government offices (i.e. approval of plans for hotel construction)
Consumer	C2B Specific requests of consumers from hotels or airlines	C2C Sharing of positive or negative experiences between consumers	C2G Consumer applications for entrance visa or information requests about destinations
Government	G2B Informing of businesses about food safety and taxes by government	G2C Informing of consumers about judicial arrangements, safety, visa or vaccine requirements	G2G Governments' receival of technical assistance about tourism policy from international organizations such as World Tourism Organization

Source: Buhalis (2003, p. 42).

Conclusions and Implications

In today's business world, as the scope of Internet technology widens day by day, the way of presenting information becomes as important as reaching it. Presenting information on Internet by virtual reality technology that utilizes pictures and animation gives users a chance to have a taste of products and services planned for purchase. "Virtual reality technology enables participants to enjoy computer-generated environments that offer three-dimensional perspectives through the use of sound, sight and touch technology (Rimmington & Kozak, 1997, p. 71). These programs offer users artificial experiences that can be viewed from home or business environments. Accordingly, it seems that virtual reality has a great potential for future tourism marketing efforts. Presentation and sale of tourism products are getting much easier due to persuasive power of such technology.

Another recent technological advancement promising wide application in tourism marketing is multimedia kiosks. This technology is becoming an important part of e-marketing in tourism. Through this technology, such procedures as information gathering and reservation making are made possible by the use of touch-screens in public places such as airports and markets (Kircova, 2002). Through these touchable computer terminals tourists can gather information about programs or places and make reservations for accommodation or activities. Two of the current web-based applications include intranet and extranet.

Intranets are generally operated within a single organization while extranets operated between organizations (O'Connor, 1999). Both systems limit entering the system by usernames and passwords for speed and security. In the future, both systems are expected to find wide application in travel and tourism because of safe, fast and efficient operation of transactions. The scope of extranet systems is widening day by day to include communication with governmental and non-governmental organizations (Buhalis, 2004).

Advancements in IT suggest prevalent use of computers in tourism companies. More specifically, the effect of technology on marketing of tourism products seems to be unescapable due to widespread and easy use of computers. State of the art computers, which can be operated by touching, viewing or even speaking, not only ease organizational operations but also facilitate public's interactions with business procedures. Latest developments in IT have widened the scope of electronic data transfer, distribution and communication systems in the world. It is generally accepted today that winners in business will be those that adopt current technologies into their business activities. Databanks, intelligent cards, automation in production and communication networks have important effects on competition. These changes affect any type of business as well as travel and tourism companies. Especially, www applications and Internet's role on distribution systems have become more apparent these days. It is argued that the effects of technological advancements on tourism (i.e. sound-recognition systems, data mining, artificial intelligence applications, virtual reality and geographical information systems) will be much more in the future (Rimmington & Kozak, 1997).

Humanity is experiencing a transformation process of information and technology. Throughout the history, the passage from agriculture economy to industrial economy increased the need for information and technology and this need laid the foundations of information era. The passage from production economy to information economy is being experienced in today's world and this changed the economic structure of the world dramatically. Information is one of the most important elements of today's economic structures. Developments in transportation and information technologies have increased the demand for travel and tourism. For today's traveler it is much easier to get information about destinations, book accommodation and reach the farthest places in the world. The changes in IT, importance of local and international cooperations between companies, increasing competition between companies and changes in consumer needs and expectations have all pushed tourism industry to a transformation and restructuring period. This trend is expected to continue even a faster pace parallel to the developments in IT.

Keeping abreast of technological advancements should be the priority for travel and tourism companies today because tourist needs, wants and expectations are becoming more complicated with new technology. A direct outcome of these changes is fiercer competition and hence difficulty of profit making. Those companies that keep a balance between modern tourist expectations and fast and effective technological response will be the winners of tomorrow. IT is becoming increasingly vital for the efficient and effective management of operations and managing the distribution of products and services with the tourism and travel industry. Everything from information centers to check out processes can potentially be integrated. Businesses seem highly ambitious to set up new IT applications which will enable customers to manage their own information-gathering and booking arrangements. The evidence seems to be that many users find such facilities valuable and the volume of business transacted through them is growing substantially. Changes in service distribution as a result of such developments will potentially impact the structure of the tourism and travel industry.

Finally, even though users need to find suppliers or intermediaries rather than vice versa, it is also true that suppliers or intermediaries need to reach potential users via computers or other advertising tools to make them more aware of their products or services provided on the screen (Berthon, Pitt, & Watson, 1996). Therefore, it should be necessary to redefine the role of intermediaries as "cybermediaries" (or artificial agents) and the concept of marketing as "cybermarketing" (Schuster, 1998). Cybermediaries or artificial agents have been introduced into cyber tourism and travel marketing as a bridge that interacts information between the end-user and the producer. Cybermediaries seem to be the competitors of traditional intermediaries in tourism and travel. A traditional intermediary is defined as "any third party or organisation between producer and consumer that facilitates purchases, the transfer of title to the buyer, and sales revenue to the producer" (Middleton, 1994, p. 203). There appear to be no reasons why cybermediaries are not accepted as intermediaries since both concepts' tasks fit into each other.

References

Akın, B. (2001). *Yeni Ekonomi: Strateji, Rekabet, Teknoloji Yönetimi.* Konya: Çizgi Kitabevi Yayınları.
Bensghir, T. K. (1996). *Bilgi Teknolojileri ve Örgütsel Değişim.* Ankara: Türkiye Ortadoğu Amme İdaresi Enstitüsü Yayını.
Berce, J. (1997). Information age and tourism. In: A min Tjoa (Ed.), *Information and communication technologies in tourism* (pp. 336–341). Austria. Springer Verlag.
Berthon, P. L. Pitt., & Watson, R. T. (1996). Marketing Communication and the World Wide Web, Business Horizons, September-October: 24–32.
Buhalis, D. (1998). Strategic use of information technologies in the tourism industry. *Tourism Management, 19*(5), 409–421.
Buhalis, D. (2003). *eTourism/information technology for strategic tourism management.* Gosport: Prentice-Hall.
Buhalis, D. (2004). eAirlines: Strategic and tactical use of ICTs in the airline industry. *Information and Management, 41*(7), 805–825.
Buhalis, D., & Licata, M. C. (2002). The future of etourism intermediaries. *Tourism Management, 23*(3), 207–220.
Godbey, G. (1997). *Leisure and leisure services in the 21st century.* Pennsylvania: Venture Publishing.
Greenspan, R. (2003). Hotel Industry Makes Room for Online Bookings, http://www.clickz.com/-stats/sectors/travel/article.php/6071_1567141 (30.11.2004)
Kırcova, İ. (2002). *Internette Pazarlama*, 2.b. İstanbul: Beta Yayınları.
Maddison, R., & Darnton, G. (1996). *Information systems in organizations.* London: Chapman & Hall.
Middleton, V. T. C. (1994). *Marketing in travel and tourism.* Oxford: Butterworth Heinemann.
Morrison, A. M. (1989). *Hospitality and travel marketing.* Delmar: NY, Albany.
Morrison, A. M. (2002). *Hospitality and travel marketing* (3rd ed.). Delmar: NY: Albany.
O'Connor, P. (1999). *Electronic Information Distribution in Tourism and Hospitality, Institut de Management Hôtelier International Groupe ESSEC.* Cergy-Pontoise France: CABI Publishing.

Poon, A. (1993). *Tourism, technology and competitive strategies*. Oxford: CAB International.
Rimmington, M., & Kozak, M. (1997). Developments in information technology: Implications for the tourism industry and tourism marketing. *Anatolia: An International Journal of Tourism Hospitality Research*, 8(3), 59–80.
Sari, Y. (2003). Bölgesel Web Sitelerinin Turizm Talebine Etkisinin Araştırılması: Muğla Bölgesinde Bir Uygulama (Basılmamış Doktora Tezi), Muğla Üniversitesi Sosyal Bilimler Enstitüsü.
Sari, Y., & Kozak, M. (2004). Yabancı Turistlerin Internet'i Kullanma Eğilimleri: Uluslar Bazında Bir Karşışılaştırma. *Anatolia: Turizm Araştirmalari Dergisi*, 15(2), 169–183.
Schuster, A. G. (1998). A Delphi survey on business process re-engineering from the tourism and hospitality industries: The case of alpha flight services. In: D. Buhalis, A. M. Tjoa, & J. Jafari (Eds), *Information and communication technologies in tourism* (ss. 224–234). Wien: Springer.
Senn, J. A. (1998). *Information technology in business*. Englewood Cliffs, NJ: Prentice-Hall Inc.
Sheldon, P. J. (1993). Destination information systems. *Annals of Tourism Research*, 20(4), 633–649.
Sheldon, P. J. (1997). *Tourism information technology*. Wallingford: CAB International.
Siguaw, J. D., & Enz, C. A. (1999). Best practices in information technology. *Cornell Hotel and Restaurant Administration Quarterly*, 40(5), 58–71.
Stamboulis, Y., & Skayannis, P. (2003). Innovation strategies and technology for experience-based tourism. *Tourism Management*, 24(1), 35–43.
Werthner, H., & Klein, S. (1999). *Information technology and tourism – a challenging relationship*. Wien: Springer.
Yarcan, S. (1998). *Türkiye'de Turizm ve Uluslararasilaşma*. Boğaziçi Üniversitesi Yayınları, İstanbul.
Yolal, M. (2003). *Türkiyedeki Küçük ve Orta Büyüklükteki Konaklama İşletmelerinde Bilgi Teknolojileri Kullanımı (No.144)*. Anadolu Üniversitesi Yayınları, Eskişehir.
Zeithaml, V. A., Parasuraman, A., & Berry, L. L. (1990). *Delivering quality service: Balancing customer perceptions and expectations*. NewYork: Free Press.

Chapter 3

Use of Electronic Documents and Brochures for Sustainable Tourism Marketing

Yasar Sari, Ismail Cinar and Dogan Kutukiz

Introduction

Information transfer process starting with clay tablets and continuing on to optical recording devices started to be performed in different dimensions, particularly in some service industries. With the combination of optical devices with microelectronics, the concept of paperless office was introduced, and paperless offices, considered to be a dream even recently, have nowadays come to be established in a convincing manner (Odabas, 1999; Baillie, 1997; Hilgen, 2000; Heresniak, 1997). With the use of different technology in the same fields through integration, one may see that the formerly separate fields integrate with each other, and some concepts and principles undergo structural changes. As a result of the adaptation of communication technologies via computer technologies, public needs are catered to by means of distant interaction; the consumer cannot see the sales person nor can they touch the product.

Information technologies (ITs) entering public life particularly through the banking sector, have been claimed to have almost completely eradicated the use of paper; nevertheless, studies conducted in recent years show that most of the work carried out in the computer environment has also been printed on paper (Odabas, 1999; Phelan, 2003; Sellen & Harper, 2003). Contrary to what has been claimed, this stimulates paper consumption. In the same way, according to the claims of Paper Com Alliance established by a number of associations and groups of companies from the paper industry, the "new economy" promises increased paper consumption (BT Vizyon, 2001). Considering the fact that 93% of consumed paper is still obtained from wood, it can be seen that both environment and sustainable tourism activities are under the threat of this new situation. From this perspective, this chapter aims to highlight the present situation by carrying out a survey among accommodation facilities and travel agencies.

Literature Review

In the past, when the word "office" was uttered, what came to mind were furniture, desk, chair, typewriter, and telephone. People who had this equipment could open an office and conduct transactions. Later, with the invention of the photocopy machine by the Xerox company, multiplication of documents became possible. Initially, because it was too expensive, not everybody could own a photocopy machine and photocopying emerged as a new branch of business. Those who are in business now can clearly remember the hours spent in photocopy shops getting their documents photocopied. Printers and fax machines followed the photocopy machine. Following this, with the introduction of personal computers (PC) into offices and computers' communicating with each other via network, shared use of office equipment became possible. Office equipment of varying sizes used commonly by everyone in the office has improved with the addition of new functions every year. Starting as separate machines, not capable of interaction with the computer, and working as analog, photocopy, printer, scanner, and fax machines have improved together with technology and became machines that can operate in a network. Then, they became components of a compact machine serving the functions of photocopy, fax, printer, and scanner (Isaacs, 2002). Finally, speed and printing quality have greatly been improved, and they reached speeds of over 180 page-printing capacities per minute.

The final stage of these developments is the use of the Internet. With the opportunities provided by the Internet and network technologies, computers started to communicate with each other independent of space. Due to the Internet, grouping and classification of increased information and digital document management issues have emerged, because management of documents has become impossible through conventional approaches. This problem has been alleviated via software programs developed by different companies. Digital document management software programs have prevented chaos by making it possible to classify and store the information produced especially by big companies. With the encouragement provided by the introduction of the digital document management concept, the term "paperless office" was proposed (Hemphill, 2001). According to this, paper would no longer be needed and every kind of communication and information storage would be done in digital medium (Cross, 1986).

Nevertheless, contradictory developments have taken place, particularly with more widespread use of the Internet, printer, photocopy and due to the rich content of the Internet, paper consumption has increased to a level higher than ever (Liu & Stork, 2000). Xerox previously had a research conducted throughout the world in order to determine paper use and consumption inclinations. They announced these findings in 2001, which indicated that the spread of computer and Internet use had increased paper consumption. A short time ago, certain findings were obtained with respect to this issue in England through a study carried out by Richard H.R. Harper of the University of Surrey and Abigail Sellen of the Hawlett Packard (2003). This study revealed that computer users print and file the document they create, and if they need the document again they prefer referring to the paper document instead of locating the digital file. Moreover, another concrete finding from this study is that office workers print out of even small notes and unimportant documents (Kaplanseren, 2004).

The ease in which IT is used can be accepted as the main reason for the increased printing of documents. This also makes users produce more document and brochures unnecessarily. In addition to that, lack of confidence and knowledge in virtual reality causes users to print out more documents. Researchers claiming that wastefulness brought about by technology having increased paper consumption by at least 40% say that images existing in the computer somehow meet with the paper. The primary cause underlying this increase in wastefulness is the easiness and comfort provided by the use of technology. By pushing one button any number of pages on the screen can be printed on paper. Every year, for the production of millions of tons of paper, millions of trees are destroyed. In 1994, world paper production in 153 countries reached 265.5 million tons (Kaplanseren, 2004). In the past 20 years, while paper consumption has increased by 74%, a significant increase, 110%, has taken place in the production of printing and writing paper. Average paper consumption per capita is nearly 51 kg. every year. Realization of 60% of whole paper consumption by 12% of world population managing the world economy is another interesting statistic. This same circle consumes 45% of printed paper in the world (Kaplanseren, 2004). With 93%, the majority of world paper consumption is derived from trees. This ratio equals the one-fifth of the material obtained from the forests in our planet. This high rate of paper consumption is threatening both our environment and accordingly sustainable tourism activities. If prevented through some measures of thrift and recycling, a reduction of atmospheric pollution and water pollution by 74% and 35%, respectively, could be realized (Karahasan, 2004).

Electronic Documents and Brochures

Electronic documents and brochures can be defined as a file consisting of every kind of text, voice, image, and graphic that can be transferred to the computer environment by means of devices such as keyboard, scanner, camera, video, stereo, electronic mail, telex, and fax. In the dictionary of Archiving Science Terms, electronic documents and brochures are defined "documents/archives generally recorded on a medium like encoded magnetic disc, magnetic tape, perforated card and whose content can only be read through machines and which are organized in line with provenance principle different from data archives" (Ataman, 1999). As one can understand from these definitions, information in electronic document and brochure is formed and protected by various technological devices and is converted into electrical signals when transferred from one place to another. Electronic documents and brochures are used in almost every sector, primarily in banking and tourism.

Though what electronic medium offers us does not match exactly with the principles of the science of archiving, people encounter more services based on computers with every passing day. When viewed generally, the goal of automation is the realization of the present paper-based transaction scheme in a computer environment; and thus, tries to decrease document and brochure production and correspondingly, paper consumption. Documents and brochures existing in an electronic environment both decreases vital costs such as posting, transferring, document security, and archiving, as well as enabling rapid access to documents when necessary. Electronic data which are in a state of continuous transition in intra- and inter-firm networks, force the users to familiarize with ITs and concepts of electronic documents and brochures (Odabas, 1999).

Promotion and advertisement in the tourism industry are both imperative to success. Promotion broadly aims to reach the consumer, to explain the potential benefits of the product and service, to inform them about the product and to persuade them to buy the product. When it comes to advertisements; they are composed of sales, sales development, individual sales, and P.R. Instruments used in the promotion and advertisement fields are printed materials, i.e. brochures, pamphlets, and posters. Newspaper advertisements are composed of radio and TV commercials, outdoor advertisements (Icoz, 2001). Those instruments may increase the existing or actual tourism demand as well as the potential demand. For that reason, tourism markets in developed countries prefer to use electronic documents and brochures. This enables them to spend a greater amount on advertisements and brochures used in the industry. It has been realized that promotion and ad activities are major instruments in demand of tourism activities.

Methodology

As can be understood from the above arguments, studies throughout the world show that making use of electronic documents and brochures has steadily become more commonplace, and there is a significant amount of increase in paper consumption. This is contrary to what was expected. Up to this point there has been no research concerning the use of electronic document and brochure in the tourism industry in our country. With this as a reference, a field study investigating the use of paper, electronic document and brochure by both accommodation facilities and travel agencies in Mugla, Turkey was conducted by employing the questionnaire survey. Those organizations which have Internet websites were included in the study. In reference to sample selection, in order to ensure representation of the main mass as objectively as possible, a method of simple random sampling based on equal chance was preferred. Separate questionnaires were developed for accommodation and travel agencies from which data was gathered. A total of 110 questionnaires for accommodation facilities and 110 for travel agencies were distributed by hand between August and September 2005 over a period of two months. At the end, 109 questionnaires were returned (68 from accommodation facilities and 41 from travel agencies). Special attention was paid to ensure that the person completing the questionnaire held the office of manager of information processing center of the organization, an individual in the managerial position responsible for information technologies familiar with the field. Data were initially transferred into a file established in Statistical Packages for Social Sciences (SPSS) and then recoded to facilitate its use by various statistical analysis.

Beginning from April 2004, a comprehensive research was initiated to prepare the questionnaires which will be used to collect data. Primarily we started a comprehensive study using the Internet to download related sample questionnaires. Moreover, some university libraries were scanned for material, and pertinent books, articles, journals, and theses were used in the preparations of questionnaires. In addition, researchers interested in this field have been consulted via e-mails. Although some of the questions appear similar, the questionnaires for accommodation and travel agencies were prepared separately as some questions differ.

Discussion of Findings

Accommodation businesses in the research area of Mugla which have websites and answered the questionnaire are composed of 2, 3, 4, and 5 star hotels, apart hotels and holiday villages. Travel agencies which responded to the questionnaires are mainly "A" type agencies with their own websites. Services provided in the websites of the organizations responding to the questionnaires are given in Table 3.1. As this table demonstrates, services provided consist mainly of e-mail addresses, product and service promotion and providing helpful information services. The low rates of online reservation and customer feedback show that these sites are not dynamic at desired levels but still have static structures. Moreover, the low level of intra-firm information sharing shows that intra-firm communication is still carried out mainly via conventional methods (i.e. paper, telephone, and face-to-face).

Table 3.2 displays the items used in electronic documents and brochures that were chosen for product and service promotion in the websites of the organizations. Values given in

Table 3.1: Services offered in the websites of the organizations.

Offered services	Yes		No		No response	
	N	Ratio %	N	Ratio %	n	Ratio %
Product and service promotion	103	94.5	6	5.5	-	-
Providing helpful information (weather, exchange rates, etc.)	102	93.6	6	5.5	1	0.9
e-mail services	96	88.1	12	11.0	1	0.9
Online reservation	70	64.2	35	32.1	4	3.7
Customer feedback	65	59.6	38	34.9	6	5.5
Intra-firm information sharing	62	56.9	43	39.4	4	3.7

Table 3.2: Advertisement and promotion items used in electronic documents and brochures in the websites of the organizations.

Electronic document and brochure items	Yes		No		No response	
	n	Ratio %	N	Ratio %	n	Ratio %
Items consisting of pictures, photographs, drawings, animations, and texts	88	80.7	12	11.0	9	8.3
Items consisting of voiced video images	55	50.5	49	45.0	5	4.6
Items consisting of three dimensional virtual reality images that can be seen with the help of the mouse	34	31.2	70	64.2	5	4.6

Table 3.3: Opinions of the organizations about their own paper consumption in the years following a website possession.

Sort of paper	N	Mean[a]
Expenses for promotion and advertisement brochures such as leaflets and booklets	102	2.19
Expenses for paper used for intra-organization transactions	109	2.14
Expenses for paper used to get in contact with customers	101	1.52

[a] 3 = increased, 2 = unchanged, 1 = decreased.

the table show that most of the items used in electronic documents and brochures are almost the same as those used in classic paper printing. This result reiterates the idea that these organizations websites are static. Moreover, this result also shows that the organizations are not exactly aware of the Internet environment and opportunities offered by this environment in terms of advertisement and promotion. Thus, it seems that for the organizations there is not much difference between the advertisement and promotion through normal paper printing than that of the Internet.

Table 3.3 refers to the weighted mean values indicating the opinions of the organizations about their annual average paper consumption throughout the years following the development of their own website. When the values given in the table are analyzed, an increase in paper use in advertisement and promotion and inner office paper is shown. Some decrease is observed with regards to mailing activities. Based on these values, it can be speculated that the Internet is primarily used by the organizations for the purpose of communicating with customers; however, conventional ways are drawn upon more than the Internet for promotion activities and intra-organization transactions. In this case, it can be argued that the Internet is perceived as an alternative, but not adequately efficient promotion medium by the organizations.

When looking at the results of the questionnaire that asked the accommodation business to rating of the given ideas and judgments according to penta 5 scale, a value of 3.68 indicates that websites of accommodation businesses were heavily visited by foreign tourists. However, more than half of the businesses had a clear idea about their number of their web site visitors (52.3%). The other group (43.1%) declared that they had no idea how many website visitors they had. When the above-mentioned business accommodations asked about the "use of the Internet reduces paper consumption" their agreement rate of 2.90 weighed mean out of 5 indicates that they either generally agree or would like to believe that. But owing to the structure of the Internet medium technologies which leads to some problems and unreliability, it can be said that they were not able to reflect this in their applications.

Conclusions and Implications

In the globalizing- and technology-based developing world economy, the tourism industry also has been developing new methods to provide information exchange between service providers, middlemen, and consumers. The development of ITs, emergence of E-trade practices, and wide use of the Internet lead to important changes in the structure, marketing, booking, and sales within tourism. The most important of these are online ticket reservations and sales. This type of IT usage results in excessive use of paper rather than the intended paperless environment. This research has been designed to cover accommodation and travel businesses which have websites on the Internet and are operating within the district of Mugla, a popular tourist destination located in the south-west part of Turkey.

The first suggestion would be to turn the websites into active environments rather than static, so that they can be used by both visitors to these sites and staff of the organizations conveniently and comfortably. This way people will be able to use the Internet and consequently the businesses' websites to communicate. Many items which are impossible to present on paper can be used in the websites. Awareness of this issue within the organizations should be raised and they need to be educated in the use of three dimensional virtual reality items equipped with video and voice which can offer more than that provided through paper. Moreover, every organization should find some way of having precise information about the number of visitors to their sites. Thus, over time, they will be aware of the fact that documents and brochures printed on paper have become obsolete. From the information obtained from open-ended questionnaire items and face-to-face interviews, it seems clear that tourism service providers believe or at least are willing to believe that improvements in ITs and the Internet would decrease paper consumption.

On the other hand, whether in public or private sector or educational institutions, in working environments, the most commonly used material is, as we all know, paper. People feel more secure with paper because it is conventional. Most of the time, an electronic document in a computer is read from its print out. People feel as if it would not be understood when read from the screen. However, in reality, there is nothing that gets changed, lost or misunderstood; it is just a matter of perception. Regardless of how closely people are engaged with ITs, they find them less secure than traditional methods. All of us, from time to time, experience computer crashes and loss of invaluable data. It is highly reasonable for a person who has had such an experience not to rely on electronic documents. In this respect, information-processing managers and authorities have considerable responsibilities to provide data security and to find the ways of backing up data. Raising the consciousness of users with regards to having their personal backups, providing incentives and control and performing periodic and flawless institutional backing up activities as well are of great importance in terms of data security and encouraging electronic document use.

Secondly, in transition to electronic documents and brochures, it is important not only to raise institutional awareness of the environment, but also to get personnel to realize the necessity of the use of recycled paper. This consciousness raising will provide a good motivation for people to look for alternatives to paper. Finally, the use of electronic documents makes meeting bureaucratic requirements easier for the individual. Besides preventing some documents from being kept under desk pads, it will make enable better use of control mechanisms. In this way, the reduction of efficiency's through document traffic would be prevented and the individual would aim to fulfill his responsibilities as best he can without being bogged down among documents. After that, the concepts of paperless office, digital office or paperless environment will be evaluated from different perspectives, and perhaps one day, paper will really be redundant. However, present trend indicates that at least for a while both paper and electronic documents and brochures will be in use simultaneously, but who knows what will happen in 10 years.

Conscientious use of ITs not only reduces paper consumption but also supports tourism activities and reduces the cost of communication and coordination. Changing cost structures also lead to new market structure and emerging new middlemen. The Internet especially offers strong marketing opportunities. Marketing in the Internet is much more flexible compared with the traditional marketing instruments. Marketing units can update according to customer feedbacks and add new products accordingly. Cost of updating in the Internet is cheaper than traditional pamphlets and catalogues. Another advantage of the Internet is availability; consumers can reach any information about the product and buy it at any time without a middleman. Furthermore, multi-dimensional medium and virtual reality applications provide the product a realistic visibility, process can take less time and data entry is faster and more flexible which are some of the advantages of using information technologies.

This chapter can be accepted as the first study in this subject. For that reason, the study may be used as a guidepost to lead comprehensive researches in this field. In Mugla, commercial institution activities make up an important share of the businesses. In coastal areas generally the main public income is based on tourism activities, i.e. accommodation and travel agencies. According to this study, the personnel working in these industries are not aware of the environmental destruction because of the increase in the consumption of paper products. Attention should be paid to develop a project to raise awareness of increased paper consumption within the area and promote and develop programs for efficient use of ITs.

References

Ataman, B. K. (1999). *Science of archiving terms dictionary*. İstanbul: Librairie de Pera.
Baillie, J. (1997). Moving one step closer to the paperless office? *People Management*, *3*(April 3), 44.
BT Vizyon (2001). *Developing environment system unit and paperless office concept*. http://www.btvizyon.com.tr/viz_dergi_dosya.phtml?kulakcik_nox=26&konu_dosya_no x=45 (01.12.2004)
Cross, J. A. (1986). *A paperless environment for group effort in document development*. Computer Science Department, Indiana University of Pennsylvania, ACM, pp. 97–101.
Hemphill, B. (2001). Paperless or less paper. *Financial Planners' Guide to Technology*, *14*(7), 22–25.
Heresniak, E. J. (1997). The paperless office. *Across the Board*, *34*(February), 15.
Hilgen, D. (2000). Going paperless. *Best's Review*, *101*(3), 124.
Isaacs, L. (2002). Following the paperless trail. *American City and County*, *117*(6), 51–60.
Icoz, O. (2001). *Turizm İşletmelerinde Pazarlama*, 2.b. Ankara: Turhan Kitabevi.
Kaplanseren, E. (2004). Technology is increasing paper consumption. *Mesaj*, http://www.nethaber.com/haber/haberler/0,1082,48537_3,00.html (01.12.2004)
Karahasan, F. (2004). Marks – Trends. *Milliyet*, 25.04.2004, pp. 3–4.

Liu, Z., & Stork, D.G. (2000). Is paperless really more? Rethinking the role of paper in the digital age. *Communications of the ACM, 43*(11), 94–97.

Odabas, H. (1999). Electronic documents and archives. *Adventure of information: Past, present and future ... society of Turkish libraries foundation 50 years international symposium's announcements* November, Ankara, pp. 17–21.

Phelan, S. E. (2003). A paperless success story. http://www.aicpa.org/pubs/jofa/ oct2003/phelan.htm (20.06.2005)

Sellen, A. J., & Harper, R. H. R. (2003). *The myth of the paperless office*. USA: The MIT Press.

Chapter 4

Online Travel Purchases from Third-Party Travel Web Sites

Cihan Cobanoglu, Jonathan H. Powley, Ali Şukru Cetinkaya and Pamela R. Cummings

Introduction

Internet resources and Web sites have become a form of advertising for products and services in the past decade (Best Practice B2C, 2001). They have had an impact on the business world, affecting consumers, producers and physical companies, such as travel agencies. The use of the Internet has also sparked globalization and today it allows companies to compete globally (Globalization puts power, 2002). Many organizations are discovering the benefits of the Internet. Utilizing the Internet for marketing purposes has become a new priority. Marketing through the Internet may allow consumers to skip the middleman, ultimately reducing costs. In the last year, the estimated number of worldwide Internet users has increased by 18% and the Internet is now estimated to have 580.78 million users (Nua Internet Surveys, 2002).

The cyber market, however, is somewhat different than the physical market. It demands that people have a larger set of skills to understand technology (Keaveney & Parthasarathy, 2001). Cyber marketing has the potential to become a significant opportunity if the industry learns how to successfully communicate to the online consumers (Jarvenpaa & Todd, 1996). Once cyber positioning has been established, a strategy for each segment needs to be developed to enhance success and opportunities (Wan, 2000). The purpose of this chapter is to investigate customers' intentions to buy travel products from online travel agencies. This chapter also investigates the demographics of Internet users, their online purchasing satisfaction experiences, their attitudes and perceptions toward purchasing electronically, the average time spent each day with electronic communications, online consumer incentives, and online consumer benefits.

Literature Review

In 1999, organizations exchanged US$20 billion worth of products and services through business to consumer Web sites and this number is predicted to be as high as US$184 billion in 2004 (E-commerce Shopping Around, 2000). Researchers in the hospitality industry found that the Internet revolutionized the way business was done in the 1990s and early 2000s, causing a huge growth in e-commerce (Ranganathan & Ganapathy, 2002). These researchers also suggest that for tourism and hospitality marketers to successfully communicate with their customers and to implement effective online marketing activities, they need to study the behavior of consumers. If managers are aware of how consumers make online purchasing decisions, they can adapt their marketing plans and strategies to fit this new mode of business.

Online marketing tools are important to marketers to establish communication between the consumer and the company (Tools for Success, 2002). These marketing tools include promoting consumer awareness and interest, providing information and consultation, facilitating two-way communication with customers through e-mails and chat rooms, and enabling customers to place orders online. By creating a Web site, companies can increase their conventional communication with the clients 24 h a day with a relatively low cost. Marketing and communication through the Internet are essential in the hospitality industry (McMillian & Hwang, 2002). To understand online activities and consumers, such as ways of informing customers with what a business has to offer, one must study the behavior of customers (Gurau, Ashok, Ranchhod, & Hackney, 2003). The Internet has made it possible for organizations to disseminate a wide variety of material, from operations information to offering discounts on products and services around the world (Lovelock, 2001).

To understand the transition from mass marketing of physical retailing to personalized click and order e-tailing, one needs to profile who is now shopping online and who will use online shopping in the future (Sin & Tse, 2002). Companies working on e-business strategies need to start thinking about the psychology of online behavior and tracing the attitudes and motivations of online customers (Digital Psychology, 2000). The Internet represents the new wave of technological communication that has become the next best communication median, second only to telecommunications (Rhee & Riggins, 1999). According to consumer behavior experts, the Internet changed consumer shopping habits as consumers become active participators, rather than passive receptors (Lagacherie & Matthews, 1998). A 2001 survey suggested that tourists consider the Internet almost four times better than travel agents and tour operators as a way of getting information (Travelmole, 2001). Cobanoglu's study (2001) indicated that 70% of business travelers search hotels on the Internet regardless of whether they book online or offline.

Roehl's Study (2001) suggested that education, income and attitudes toward the use of credit cards for online purchases are statistically significant in predicting customers' behavior. Webber and Roehl (1999) reported that World Wide Web (WWW) users who purchase travel products online are most likely to be 26–55 years of age, have a higher income, be employed in management, professional or computer related occupations and have more years of online experience. Cobanoglu's study (2001) illustrated that most business travelers have access to the Internet at home or at work, and also have e-mail addresses. This study showed that more than a third of them spend up to an hour on the

Internet per day, and a significant proportion of them (43.8%) purchase a product on the Internet up to four times a year.

Lang (2000) argues that initial access to the Internet tended to be linked to affluent, young, educated and "upscale" individuals. However, this trend has been changing rapidly. The Boston Consulting Group (Graham, 2002) has produced numerous consumer behavior reports in relation to the online environment. They found that consumers are more passionate about the Internet than ever before, because it is convenient, it provides access to vast selection, and it saves time. The study also showed that online purchases in North America totaled $51.3 billion in 2000, which is up 21% from the last year (Graham, 2002).

The Internet is changing buying habits (Beirne, 2001). Travelocity.com, Expedia.com and Priceline.com all posted profits for the first time in the second quarter of 2001. On the basis of their projections, consumers will spend $63 billion on online travel by the year 2006. A survey of 10,000 consumers showed that 70% of the respondents who were not bound by corporate policies requiring them to use their company travel agent, said they were more likely to purchase online. Researchers have generated revenue results that found e-commerce increased 200% in 1999 from $15 billion in 1999 to $45 billion in 2001 (E-commerce Times, 2001). It is projected that if consumer behavior continues in this U.S., e-commerce will increase to $269 billion in the year 2005 (Growing Internet Usage, 2001). On the basis of all these facts, the hypothesis being tested is that there is a significant relationship between the Web site quality, travel information source, product motivation, personal significance, attitudes and the likelihood of purchase and the likelihood of purchase travel products over the Web using an online travel agency.

Methodology

The target population consisted of managers who were current paid members of the American Management Association (AMA). A two stage random sampling method was used. In the first stage, a proportionate stratified sampling procedure was employed to draw representative sample of 1000 from a target population of 74,000. The proportionate stratified sample is "a stratified sample in which the number of observations in the total sample is allocated among the strata in proportion to the relative elements in each stratum in the population" (Churchill, 1996, p. 517). The number of sample for each state was calculated by the following formula:

$$\text{Sample size of a state} = \frac{\text{Number of member managers in a state}}{\text{Number of member managers in target population}} \times 1000$$

After determining the state sample size, the second stage was implemented. A simple random sample of elements was chosen randomly from each state. All member managers in each state were printed in alphabetical order of last name. Then a number was given to each. The random sample table in Pedhazur (1997) was used to select a pre-calculated number of samples from each state. The researchers selected a number randomly in the table. The member that corresponded to that number was selected. The researchers continued to select the remainder of the sample randomly in this fashion until it was completed. A self- administered questionnaire was created from the information obtained from the literature research using the research questions generated. A pilot study of this questionnaire was conducted among 400 Hotel Restaurant and Institutional Management Undergraduate students to test the efficacy and clarity of the questionnaire. Revisions were made based on the recommendations of the pilot participants. The survey included eight sections. The first section asked questions related to Internet use such as how often they accessed the WWW, how many hours on average they spent on the Web, and how long have they been using the Web. The second section consisted of questions about the respondents' primary use of the web, how often they purchase online, and their favorite online travel agents.

The third section listed statements that assessed their personal and motivational involvement when purchasing travel online. In this section, the respondents were asked to rate how much they agreed with the statement that was provided. A 7-point Likert scale was provided (1 = Strongly Disagree; 7 = Strongly Agree) to assess motivational involvement. A 5-point scale was provided to (1 = Strongly Disagree; 5 = Strongly Agree) measure personal involvement. In section four, a 5-point Likert scale was provided (1 = Never; 5 = Always) to examine how frequent consumers used different travel information sources to locate the best financial deal. In section five, a 5-point Likert scale (1 = Not important at all; 5 = Very Important) was used in assessing the importance of various when purchasing from online travel agents. The attitude questions made up section six and another 7-point Likert scale response format (1 = Strongly Disagree; 7 = Strongly Agree) was used. It was determined on prior research that the 7-point scale format would increase the quality of the responses (Shifflet, 1992). The seventh section asked respondents about their future online behavior if they were to travel in the next 6 months. The final section of the survey consisted of demographic questions that dealt with gender, marital status, age, educational background, annual income, job title, industry, area of expertise, and how many trips the respondents' took last year.

This study employed online survey methodology where the survey instruments were disseminated by e-mail/Web-based forms. With the development of the Web, the biggest concern for using e-mail or Web-based surveys is that not all members of the population have access to e-mail and to the WWW. However, this study only researched the consumers who were online, so the entire population had access to the WWW and this was not a concern.

Discussion of Findings

One thousand surveys were distributed to manager members of the AMA. The response rate yielded a usable sample of 184 members with an 18.4% response rate. Table 4.1 shows the demographic information about the respondents. There were 114 (62.0%) male respondents and 70 (38.0%) female respondents. Over 90% (92.4%) of the respondents were over the age of 35 years old. In terms of educational background of respondents, 71 (38.6%) have earned a Bachelors Degree, 60 respondents (32.6%) earned their Master's Degree, while 24 respondents (13.0%) received a Doctoral Degree in their fields. There were only six (3.3%) of the respondents who had only a high school diploma. The most frequent level of income reported was between "$75,001 and $100,000" by 40 respondents (21.7%). The second most frequent level of income was between "$100,001 and $150,000" reported by 34 respondents (18.5%). The third highest income reported by 28 respondents (15.2%) was "$150,001 or more." However, 38 respondents (20.7%), did not report the amount of income earned per year.

Table 4.1: Demographic information of sample.

Gender	n	%	Education	n	%
Female	70	38.0	High school	6	3.3
Male	114	62.0	Associate degree	23	12.5
			Bachelor degree	71	38.6
Age			Masters degree	60	32.6
			Doctorate degree	24	13.0
Under 35 years	14	7.6			
36–45	54	29.3	**Expertise area**		
46–55	80	43.5	Accounting	33	17.93
56 or older	36	19.6	Sales	17	9.24
			Engineer	17	9.24
Income			Education	14	7.61
$25,001–$50,000	4	2.2	Computer related	20	10.87
$50,001–$75,000	22	12.0	Human resources	11	5.98
$75,001–$100,000	40	21.7	Law	5	2.72
$100,001–$125,000	34	18.5	Finance	11	5.98
$125,001–$150,000	8	4.3	Business management	26	14.13
$150,001 or more	28	15.2	Administration	4	2.17
Prefer not to answer	38	20.7	Medical	6	3.26
			Other	14	7.61
Marital status			Missing	6	3.2
Single/widowed/separated	28	15.2			
Married with children	118	64.1	**Working or not**		
Married with no children	18	9.7	Yes I work	180	97.8
Prefer not to answer	16	8.7	No I do not work	4	2.2
Missing	4	2.1			
Single/widowed/separated	28	15.2	**Region**		
			New England	12	6.5
			The Mid-Atlantic	80	43.5
			The South	22	12.0
			The Mid-west	4	2.2
			The Southwest	36	19.6
			The West	26	14.1

Table 4.2 reported the Internet behavior of respondents. The majority of the respondents reported their Internet access as "Primarily work/school but also at home." There were 54 respondents (29.3%) that use their Internet access "primarily at home, but also at work." Finally, there were only six respondents (3.3%) who access the Web only from work. The average consumer took 7.53 business trips, 2.97 personal trips, and 1.88 leisure trips per year that involved at least one night's stay at a hotel. The most frequent average use of the WWW browser is "1 to 4 times/day," reported by 56 respondents (30.4%), 50 respondents (27.2%) access the WWW browser "more than 9 times per day, 26 respondents (14.1%) access it between "5 to 8 times per day," 46 of the respondents (25.0%) use the WWW browser a few times a week, while only two respondents (1.1%) use the WWW browser only "once per week."

Table 4.2: Internet behavior.

Primary place of Internet access	n	%
Primarily work/school but also at home	108	58.7
Primarily at home but also at work/school	54	29.3
Work only	16	8.7
Home only	6	3.3
Average use of WWW browser		
More than 9 times a day	50	27.2
5-8 times/day	26	14.1
1-4 times/day	56	30.4
A few times a week	46	25.0
Once a week	2	1.1
Once a month	2	1.1
Missing	2	1.1
Length of time using Internet resources		
1-3 years	4	2.2
4-6 years	85	46.2
7 or more years	94	51.1
Missing	1	0.5
Primary use of Web		[a]
Work/business	176	95.7
Shopping/gathering product information	140	76.1
Gathering information for personal needs	114	62.0
Education	97	52.7
Entertainment	54	29.3
Communication with others	40	21.7
Wasting time	28	15.2
Other	6	3.3

[a]The total may not add up to 100%, because multiple selections were allowed.

Table 4.3 shows the frequency of online purchasing behavior of respondents. Ten respondents (5.4%) had never purchased anything on the Web, 14 respondents (7.6%) purchase once a year, 68 respondents (37.0%) purchase between "2 to 5 times a year," 34 respondents (18.5%) purchase between "6 to 12 times a year," while 44 respondents (29.3%) purchase online "more than 12 times a year". The majority of the respondents (70.1%) reported purchased "airline tickets" online through online agencies. Other purchases through online travel agents include 110 respondents (59.8%) who purchase "hotel, motel or bed and breakfast reservations," 88 respondents (47.8%) purchase "car rentals," 30 respondents (16.3%) purchase "train tickets," 17 respondents (9.2%) reported purchasing "vacation packages," 6 respondents (3.3%) purchase "cruise trips," while 18 respondents (9.8%) purchase other travel products through online travel agents.

Table 4.4 illustrates the average amount spent for both business and personal online travel purchases per year. The most frequent average amount spent for business travel purchases was "more than $500" by 70 respondents (38.0%), 58 respondents (31.5%) spent "less than 100," and 40 respondents (21.7%) spent "between $101 and $500" on business travel purchases. The most frequent average amount spent for personal travel purchases is "more than $500" by 67 respondents (36.4%), 73 respondents (39.7%) spent between "$101.00 and $500.00" for personal travel purchases, while only 34 respondents (18.5%) reported spending "less than $100.00."

The most popular online travel Web site was Expedia.com chosen by 53 respondents (29.4%), followed by Travelocity.com by 38 respondents (21.1%), Orbitz.com by 34 respondents (18.8%), Cheaptickets.com by 13 respondents (7.2%) Priceline.com by 12 respondents (6.6%), and the following online travel agencies were selected by less than 5% of the respondents: rosenbluth.com, sidestep.com, qixo.com, carlsontravel.com,

Table 4.3: Purchasing behavior online.

Frequency of purchases online	n	%
Never purchased anything on the Web	10	5.4
Once a year	14	7.6
2-5 times a year	68	37.0
6-12 times a year	34	18.5
More than 12 times a year	54	29.3
Missing	4	2.1
Travel products purchased online through online agencies		[a]
Airline tickets	129	70.1
Hotel or motel or bed and breakfast reservations	110	59.8
Car rentals	88	47.8
Train tickets	30	16.3
Other	18	9.8
Vacation packages	17	9.2
Cruise ships	6	3.3

[a]The total may not add up to 100%, because multiple selections were allowed.

Table 4.4: Online travel expenditures per year.

Avg. amount spent online	n (Business)	Percent (Business)	n (Personal)	Percent (Personal)	χ^2
Less than $100	58	31.5	34	18.5	9.613*
Between $101-$500	40	21.7	73	39.7	12.140*
More than $500	70	38.0	67	36.4	2.458
Missing	16	8.8	10	5.4	5.245

*Significant at 0.05 level.

sadmral.com, travelzoo.com. cheaphotels.com, yahootravel.com, aaa.com, cruise.com, travelsavers.com, hotwire.com, hotel.com, and lodging.com.

Three different factor analyses were conducted. The first factor was done for Web site quality. There were 26 variables about Web site quality used in this study. Factor analysis was used to condense the information contained in these attributes and to confirm the notion that distinct dimensions existed. Utilizing Statistical Package for Social Sciences (SPSS), a factor analysis was performed on all 26 variables to determine possible underlying factors. Initially, a Spearman rank-order, inter-item correlation matrix was calculated for these items. It was observed that the majority of the variables were correlated highly with each other, indicating that this was suitable data for factor analysis.

Two statistics were used to test if the factor analysis was appropriate for this study (Hair et al., 1998). First, the Kaiser–Meyer–Olkin (KMO) statistic was calculated as 0.782 for online purchasing factors which is meritorious (Kaiser, 1974). Since KMO was very close to 0.80, the variables were interrelated and they shared common factors (Hair et al., 1998). Second, Bartlett's Test of Sphericity was conducted, yielding a significant χ^2 value in order to test the significance of the correlation matrix ($\chi = 2511.809$, df = 378, Sig. = 0.000). Both tests indicated that factor analysis was appropriate for this study. After the viability of the factor analysis was determined, a principal axis factor analysis with a varimax rotation was completed. The varimax, rather than quartimax rotation, was adopted, because the investigators expected to find several dimensions of equal importance in the data. Items with factor loadings of 0.30 or higher were clustered together to form constructs, as recommended by Hair et al. (1998).

In addition, the communalities ranged from 0.50 to 0.79 with an average value of 0.64, suggesting that the variance of the original values were fairly explained by the common factors. The reliability coefficient for items in this study ranged from 0.38 to 0.98, above the minimum value of 0.50 that is considered acceptable as an indication of reliability for basic research (Cronbach, 1951). Therefore, the *convenience* factor ($r = 0.38$) reliability coefficient is somewhat low to be considered reliable. The factor analysis explained 56.73% of the total variance. The contents of the five factor dimensions were analyzed and named as follows: *efficiency, Web extras, speed and quality of design, convenience and attractiveness* (see Table 4.5).

The second factor analysis was done for online purchasing motivators. A KMO statistic was calculated as 0.65 for the online purchasing motivators. Then Bartlett's Test of Sphericity

Table 4.5: Summary of factor analysis: Web site quality.

Factor name	EV[1]	PV[2]	CV[3]	Component variables	Factor loading
Efficiency	6.257	23.347	22.347	Convenient to use	0.847
				Usefulness	0.797
				Online reservation via Web site	0.769
				Clarity	0.744
				Finding companies general information	0.589
				Guaranteed accurate information	0.532
				Multimedia effects	0.469
Web extras	3.531	12.610	34.957	VIP membership	0.794
				Auction	0.773
				Personalization	0.735
Speed and quality of design	2.365	8.447	43.405	Quick downloads	0.866
				2-3 clicks for needed information	0.847
				Speed of page loading	0.650
				Finding customer support	0.356
Web site convenience	1.991	7.110	50.514	Product organization	0.913
				Easy to sign up	0.855
				Chat rooms	0.568
Web site attractiveness	1.741	6.219	56.733	Colorful Web site attractiveness	0.871
					0.745

[1]Eigen value.
[2]Percent of variance.
[3]Cumulative variance.

was conducted yielding a significant Chi-Square value in order to test the significance of the correlation matrix of information sources ($\chi = 695.91$, df = 66, Sig. = 0.000). This has suggested that the data were suitable for factor analysis. In addition, the communalities ranged from 0.54 to 0.79 with an average value above 0.66, suggesting that the variance of the original values were fairly explained by the common factors. After the viability of the factor analysis was determined, a principal axis factor analysis with a varimax rotation was completed. The varimax, rather than quartimax rotation, was adopted, because the investigators expected to find several dimensions of equal importance in the data. Items with factor loadings of 0.30 or higher were clustered together to form constructs, as recommended by Hair et al. (1998). The reliability coefficient for items in this study ranged from 0.44 to 0.83, above the minimum value of 0.50 that is considered acceptable as an indication of reliability for basic research. Therefore, the *personal image* factor ($r = 0.44$) coefficient is somewhat low to be considered reliable. The contents of four factor dimensions were analyzed and named as follows:

personal interest, risk of mispurchase, complexity of choice, and personal image. Table 4.6 shows the factors that emerged from the purchasing motivator statements factor analysis.

The third factor analysis was done for travel information source variables. A third KMO statistic was calculated as 0.84 for travel information sources, which is meritorious (Kaiser, 1974). Since KMO was more than 0.80, the variables were interrelated and they shared common factors. Bartlett's Test of Sphericity was conducted yielding a significant χ^2 value in order to test the significance of the correlation matrix (χ = 522.397, df = 28, Sig. < 0.000). Both tests indicated that factor analysis was appropriate for this study (Hair et al., 1998). After the viability of the factor analysis was determined, a principal axis factor analysis with a varimax rotation was completed. The varimax, rather than quartimax rotation, was adopted, because the investigators expected to find several dimensions of equal importance in the data. Items with factor loadings of 0.30 or higher were clustered together to form constructs, as recommended by Hair et al. (1998). In addition the communalities ranged from 0.39 to 0.76 with an average value of 0.57, suggesting that the variance of the original values were fairly explained by the common factors. The reliability coefficient for

Table 4.6: Summary of factor analysis: purchasing motivators.

Factor name	EV[a]	PV[b]	CV[c]	Component Variables	Factor loading
Personal interest	3.276	27.299	27.299	I find it pleasurable	0.839
				Buying it feels like giving myself a gift	0.775
				I am interested in it	0.759
				I attach importance to it	0.753
				I enjoy buying it for myself	0.727
Risk of mispurchase	2.363	19.695	46.994	It is annoying to make and unsuitable purchase	0.874
				A poor choice would be upsetting	0.852
				It is a big deal if I make a mistake in choosing it	0.821
Complexity of choice	1.183	15.105	62.099	I feel a bit at a loss in choosing it	0.881
				Choosing it is complicated	0.877
				It is a big deal if I make a mistake in choosing it	0.821
Personal image	1.075	8.954	71.053	In purchasing it, I am certain of my choices	0.808
				What I buy reflects the kind a person I am	0.740

[a]Eigen value.
[b]Percent of variance.
[c]Cumulative variance.

Table 4.7: Summary of factor analysis: Travel information source.

Factor name	EV[a]	PV[b]	CV[c]	Component variables	Factor loading
Offline	3.565	44.562	44.562	Brochure from travel agent	0.824
				Free tourist information leaflets	0.824
				Travel guide	0.834
				Other written information (e.g. magazines, newspapers)	0.802
				Television and radio programs	0.760
Online	1.499	18.737	63.299	Direct e-mail from company	0.723
				Surfing/browsing	0.555

[a]Eigen value.
[b]Percent of variance.
[c]Cumulative variance.

items in this study ranged from 0.39 to 0.88, above the minimum value of 0.50 that is considered acceptable as an indication of reliability for basic research. Therefore, the *online* factor (0.3967) is somewhat reliable for basic research. The contents of two factor dimensions were analyzed and named as follows: *offline* and *online* (see Table 4.7).

An ordinary least-square regression analysis was employed to explore the impact of the individual factors on the likelihood of purchasing travel products online. The hypothesis proposes that a bundle of the Web site quality purchasing motivators, personal significance, travel source information and attitudes affect the likelihood of consumers who purchase travel products over the Web using an online travel agency. To test the hypothesis, linear regression is used to determine the impact of the bundle of the five determinants on the likelihood of purchasing travel products online. The dependent variable was "the likelihood of purchasing a travel product over the Web using an online travel agency." The independent variables are five summated factor scales of the total that were obtained from factor analysis and variables in attitudes and personal significance scales. The regression model for the impact of the total on the likelihood of purchasing travel products over the Web using an online travel agency is proposed as follows:

$$Y_s = \beta_0 + \beta_1 (X_1) + \beta_2 (X_2) + \cdots + \beta_{24} X_{(24)}$$

where
Y_s = the likelihood of purchasing travel products over the Web using an online travel agency.
β_0 = constant (coefficient of the intercept)
$\quad X_1$ = Web Site Quality "Efficiency"
$\quad X_2$ = Web Site Quality "Web Extras"
$\quad X_3$ = Web Site Quality "Speed and Quality of Design"
$\quad X_4$ = Web Site Quality "Convenience of Web Site"
$\quad X_5$ = Web Site Quality "Attractiveness of Web Site"
$\quad X_6$ = Purchasing Motivators "Personal Interest"
$\quad X_7$ = Purchasing Motivators "Risk of Mispurchase"
$\quad X_8$ = Purchasing Motivators "Complexity of Choice"

X_9 = Purchasing Motivators "Personal Image"
X_{10} = Personal Significance "Important"
X_{11} = Personal Significance "Means a lot to me"
X_{12} = Personal Significance "Does not matter to me"
X_{13} = Personal Significance "Significant"
X_{14} = Personal Significance "Of concern to me"
X_{15} = Travel Information Source "Online"
X_{16} = Travel Information Source "Offline"
X_{17} = Attitudes "Inexpensive"
X_{18} = Attitudes "Enjoyable"
X_{19} = Attitudes "Easy"
X_{20} = Attitudes "Confident"
X_{21} = Attitudes "Personal"
X_{22} = Attitudes "Safe"
X_{23} = Attitudes "Fast"
X_{24} = Attitudes "Helpful"

Hair et al. (1998) suggests that variance inflation factors (VIF) and tolerance value play an important role in determining the correlation between independent variables. VIF and tolerance value reports the degree to which each independent variable becomes a dependent variable and is regressed against the remaining independent variables. Small tolerance values and high VIF denote high collinearity. According to Hair et al. (1998), a common cutoff threshold is a tolerance value of 0.10, which corresponds to a VIF value above 10. Therefore, all variables ("Important," "means a lot to me," "significant") that had a VIF value above 10 were excluded from the regression analysis and a regression analysis was conducted with the remaining variables. Table 4.8 shows the results of final regression analysis.
The final prediction equation is

$Y = 2.751 + 0.512$ Enjoyable $+ 0.586$ Confident $+ 0.407$ Safe $- 0.364$ Complexity of choosing. The hypothesis was supported.

The first significant variable is enjoyable ($p = 0.030$), indicating that there is a positive relationship between *enjoyable* and the likelihood of purchasing travel products over the Web using an online travel agency. In other words, one unit of increase in the *enjoyable* factor would lead to a 0.512 unit increase in the likelihood of purchasing travel products over the Web using an online travel agency. The second variable of significance is *confident* ($p = 0.001$), indicating that there is a positive relationship between *confident* and the likelihood of purchasing travel products over the Web using an online travel agency. In other words, one unit of increase in the *confident* factor would lead to a 0.586 unit increase in the likelihood of purchasing travel products over the Web using an online travel agency. The third variable of significance is *safe* ($p = 0.046$), indicating that there is a positive relationship between *safe* and the likelihood of purchasing travel products over the Web using an online travel agency. In other words, one unit of increase in the *safe* factor would lead to a 0.407 unit increase in the likelihood of purchasing travel products over the Web using an online travel agency. The fourth variable of significance is *complexity of choice* ($p = 0.032$), indicating that there is a negative relationship between *complexity of choice* and the likelihood of purchasing travel products over the Web using an online travel agency. In other

Table 4.8: The results of regression analysis.

Dependent variable: The likelihood of purchasing travel products over the Web using an online travel agency.

Independent variables: enjoyable, confident, safe, complexity of choice

Goodness of fit
Multiple $R = 0.701$
$R^2 = 0.491$
Adjusted $R^2 = 0.332$
Standard error of the estimate $= 1.26$

Analysis of variance	Sum of squares	Df	Means square	F	Sig.
Regression	103.414	21	4.924	3.079	0.000
Residual	107.148	67	1.599		

Variable	B	SE β	St. β	T	Sig.
Constant	2.751	2.355		1.168	0.247
Enjoyable	0.521	0.230	0.408	2.224	0.030
Confident	0.586	0.167	0.462	3.506	0.001
Safe	0.407	0.200	0.338	2.033	0.046
Complexity of choice	−0.364	0.166	−0.308	−2.194	0.032

words, one unit of increase in *complexity of choice* factor would lead to a 0.364 unit decrease in the likelihood of purchasing travel products over the Web using an online travel agency.

Conclusions and Implications

The study showed that consumers used both online and offline sources to locate the best online travel products or deals. Consumers indicated that direct e-mail from companies and surfing the Web are the most significant ways of locating travel information. This might suggest that online consumers prefer purchasing online through travel agents, because they are not pressured to buy while online. This finding shows the importance of customer relationship management (CRM) strategy for on online travel agency. CRM is a business strategy aimed at maximizing the relationship with customers (internal and external) via better service and sales with appropriate use of people, process and technology (Cobanoglu, 2002). Through CRM tools, the online travel agency may communicate with its customers and hence increase the sales. It can be concluded that since consumers rely heavily on surfing and browsing the Web for the best travel deal, an offline travel agency might design and utilize an online Web site for their business as well.

This study indicates that there was a positive relationship between the likelihood of purchasing travel products over the Web using an online travel agency and the personal involvement factor "means a lot to me." This positive personal significance is consistent with a study in 2001 of Internet Users' intention to purchase holidays online that suggests that one of the strategies of the online marketing communication should be to increase the level of involvement in order to stimulate purchasing behavior (Ekinci, Park, & Cobanoglu, 2002). However, there was a negative relationship between the likelihood of purchasing travel products over the Web using an online travel agency and the personal significance factors "important" and "significant." The differences within personal significance may suggest that consumers find it less likely to purchase from online travel agencies when it is very important to purchase. Another possible speculation for this negative correlation, might indicate consumers' rather call a travel agency and let them do the work booking their trip rather than searching online and increasing their odds of mispurchasing when the personal significance factor "important" is high.

The travel agents might overcome this problem by attempting the level of involvement in order to stimulate purchasing behavior. For instance, if a travel product is perceived to be very important or very significant, such as taking a family holiday in a foreign country for the first time, an advertising message should contain detailed information about this holiday such as grading of accommodations, room types, arrival and departure times, expected weather conditions, prices, etc. Also, customers should be informed about their online purchase and its consequences. If the product is considered to be in a low involvement category, such as buying an ordinary plane ticket to a domestic city, much detail may not be required. The research found that purchase motivators such as "complexity of choice" had a negative correlation with the likelihood of purchasing travel products over the Web using an online travel agency. Consumers who "feel a bit at loss choosing it," "find it complicated in choosing" and think "it is a big deal if they make a mistake in choosing it" are less likely to purchase travel products over the Web using an online travel agency. This may suggest that online travel agency marketers need to decrease the difficulty of choosing what to purchase online by increasing the clarity of Web sites.

Purchasing over the Web through an online travel agent can be promoted as "safe" and "enjoyable" and "confident." As indicated by the attitude research, consumers describe feeling safe and enjoyable while purchasing over the Web through an online travel agent. The research may suggest that consumers are feeling safe to do considerable progress in secure electronic transaction (SET), popularizing online credit card purchasing. Likewise, a study conducted by Butler and Peppard (1998) found similar findings commending progress made in encryption, to the point where sellers will even guarantee to make good fraudulent losses arising from Internet transactions.

This study also provides various recommendations for practitioners. First, online travel agency marketers should concentrate on keeping experiences "enjoyable." A few recommendations to accomplish this task may be to keep the online travel agency Web site fun and simple. Another important way of accomplishing this task is to keep it easy to search and find information. Second, online travel agency marketers should concentrate on keeping consumers "confident" about purchasing. A few recommendations to accomplish this task are to guarantee to the consumer the lowest rates, increase Web site security and guarantee safe transactions. Third, online travel agency marketers should concentrate on keeping consumers feeling "safe" about purchasing. A few recommendations to accomplish this task would be to invest in purchasing a privacy seal for your Web site so that consumers feel safe about sharing their personal information with the online travel agency. Another recommendation would be to publish clear privacy information clearly stating that you will protect the consumers' personal information. Finally, online travel agency marketers should concentrate on keeping consumers feeling "less confused" about purchasing. Recommendations to accomplish this task would include keeping the Web sites navigation easy, implementing a simple and clean Web design and making choices simple not complex.

References

Beirne, M. (2001). Upping the Ante, *Brandweek*, *42*(33), 30–36.

Best Practice B2C eCommerce in Food and Drink: Online Strategies to meet the demand of your consumers.(2001, December1) American Marketing Association [online] Available http://www.ama.org/index.php?&Session_ID=49fbf5513032d497b883498a53656ad

Butler, P., & Peppard, J. (1998). Consumer purchasing on the Internet: Processes and prospects, *European Management Journal*, *16*(5), 600–610.

Churchill, A. G. (1996). *Basic marketing research*. Orlando, FL: Dryden Press.

Cobanoglu, C. (2001). *An analysis of hotel selection and satisfaction*. Unpublished Ph.D. thesis, Oklahoma State University, Stillwater.

Cronbach, L. J. (1951). Coefficient alpha and the internal structure of tests, *Psychometrika*, *16*, 297–334.

Digital Psychology. (2000). *Business Europe*, *40*(15), 1–2.

E-commerce shopping around the Web. (2000). *The Economist*, 5–6.

E-commerce Times (2001). Growing Internet usage is generating revenue and changing Consumer Behavior: Usage is generating revenue results. [online] Available: http://www.ecommercetimes.com/

Ekinci, Y., Park, J., & Cobanoglu, C. (2002). An examination of the factors affecting internet users' intention to purchase holidays online. *33rd Annual TTRA Conference Proceedings*, Virginia, USA.

Globalization puts power out of reach. (2002, May 5) American Marketing Association (online] Available: http://www.ama.org/index.php?&Session_ID=49fbf5513032d497b883498a53656ad

Graham, L. (2002). Online sales in 2001 generated profits for more than half of all U.S. retailers selling online. Boston Consulting Group Publications. [online] Available http://www.bcg.com/publications/publication_view.jsp?pubID=926&language=English

Gurau, C., Ranchhod A., & Hackney, R. (2003). Customer-centric strategic planning: Integrating CRM in online business systems. *Information Technology and Management*, *4*(2–3), 199–214.

Hair, J. F., Anderson, R. E., Tatham, R. L., & Black, W. C. (1998). *Multivariate data analysis* (5th ed.). Upper Saddle River, NJ: Prentice-Hall.

Jarvenpaa, S. L., & Todd, P. A. (1996). Consumer reactions to electronic shopping on the World Wide Web. *International Journal of Electronic Commerce*, Winter 96–97, *1*(2), 59–88.

Kaiser, H. F. (1974). An index of factorial simplicity. *Psychometrika*, *39*, 31–36.

Keaveney, S. M., & Parthasarathy, M. (2001). Customer Switching Behavior in Online Services: An Exploratory Study of the Role of Selected Attitudinal, Behavioral, and Demographic Factors. *Journal of the Academy of Marketing Science*, *29*(4), 374–390.

Lagacherie, F., & Matthews, A. (1998). Pushing opportunities on the Internet. *British Telecommunications Engineering*, *17*(1), 164–169.

Lang, T. (2000). The effect of the internet on travel consumer purchasing behavior and implications for travel agencies. *Journal of Vacation Marketing*, *6*(4), 368–385.

Lovelock, C. (2001). *Service marketing: People technology and strategy*. Upper Saddle River, NJ: Prentice-Hall.

McMillian, S. J., & Hwang, J. (2002). Measures of perceived interactivity: An exploration of the role of direction of communication, user control and time in shaping perceptions of interactivity, *Journal of Advertising*, *31*(3), 29–42.

Nua Internet Surveys. (2002, February). The Worlds Leading Resource for internet trends and statistics [online] Available: http://www.nua.ie/surveys/how_many_online/world.html

Pedhazur, E. J. (1997). *Multiple regression in behavioral research* (3rd ed.). Forth Worth, TX: Harcourt Brace College Publishers.

Ranganathan, G., & Ganapathy, S. (2002). Key dimensions of business-to-consumer web sites, *Information & Management*, *39*(1), 457–465.

Rhee, S., & Riggins, F. (1999). *Internet users' perception of world wide web vendors and their support of consumer mercantile activities*. Centre for Electronic Commerce at the Dupont College of Management at Georgia Tech.

Roehl, W. S. (2001). Survey of U.S state and territory tourism office web site practices. [online] Available: http://www.ttra.com/pub/uploads/012.pdf

Sin, L., & Tse, A. (2002). Profiling internet shoppers in Hong Kong: Demographics, psychographic, attitudinal, and experiential factors. *Journal of International Consumer Marketing*, *15*(1), 7–29.

Shifflet, D. K. (1992). Bringing in the business travelers. *Hotel & Resort Industry*, *15*(11), 66–72.

Tools for Success. (2002). Marketing Solutions [online] Available: http://au.solutions.yahoo.com/campaign/marketing.html

Travelmole. (2001). The online community for travel and tourism. [online] Available: http://www.travelmole.com/

Wan, H. A. (2000). Opportunities to enhance a commercial website. *Information & Management*, *38*(1), 15–21.

Webber, K., & Roehl W. (1999). Profiling people searching for and publishing travel products on the world wide web, *Journal of Travel Research*, *37*, (February), 291–298.

PART II:

DESTINATION MARKETING AND COMPETITIVENESS

Introduction

Metin Kozak and Luisa Andreu

As Porter (1985) highlights, regardless of the type of industry, competitiveness can become much fiercer when new competitors enter the market. A number of examples can be given for the tourism and travel industry. Eastern Mediterranean or North African destinations now compete directly with western Mediterranean destinations in the European market. Despite the fact that there are thousands of destinations around the world, tourist destinations are subject to intense competition because of potential tourists' ability to choose any destination from their awareness set (Woodside & Sherrell, 1977; Woodside & Lysonski, 1989). Choice of a particular destination depends on tourists' awareness and familiarity with the destination and the marketing of the destination, recommendation by friends or other things causing it to be in the consideration set (refers to destinations that a tourist is likely to visit). When tourists select a destination for a given holiday, competing destinations lose their opportunity to be the destination for that visit.

The existence of several determinants affecting consumer behavior is important to bear in mind (Oliver, 1999). Overall, perceptions of tourists may depend on external factors that are difficult for destination management or local tourism businesses to influence. Factors disrupting flows to a destination may be economic, political or temporal features appearing in tourist-generating countries as well as in tourist-attracting countries (tourist destinations), i.e. motivation, distance, risk and existence of alternative destinations. There are also such uncontrollable factors as image directed from outside of a country, which may have lasting affect when they happen. The view that image is a critical factor in choosing destinations is widely supported (e.g. Pike, 2002). However, the industry-specific nature of these studies limits the generalization of the findings and leads to adopt a destination-specific perspective because a significant gap still exists in the tourism literature in explaining factors influencing the marketing of tourist destinations to enhance the competitive edge.

This part begins with a chapter on developing a framework for future research on destination marketing. Although pivotal to the travel and tourism system, the destination is widely acknowledged to be one of the most difficult products to manage and market. Over the coming decade, the challenges facing destination marketers are likely to be even greater with a whole host of issues likely to impact on the future marketing of destinations. This chapter proposes an exploratory framework that brings together those issues deemed to be of significance to the future marketing of the destination product. The chapter concludes that *via* collaboration and a desire to work together in solving problems deemed too demanding to solve in isolation, destinations can counter many of the challenges to be confronted over the coming decade.

With relevance to tourism services marketing, the second chapter outlines why it is necessary to know who is involved in the direct provision of tourism services when studying tourism destinations as clusters or networks. The classification of tourism product-supplying industries according to the Tourism Satellite Account is discussed and a new market oriented classification of tourism industries is introduced. The new classification includes only those industries that have direct contact with tourists and therefore represent the link between tourists and the network or system that supplies tourism products. The authors suggest that such classification will help to assess each region or destination on the basis of their competitive positions. The chapter also presents recommendations for the application of this classification and future research.

During the last decade, there has been a growing interest in the tourism literature about the notion of 'competitive destination'. In the preceding decades competition in tourism was very often identified with the price component and quite often restricted to the micro level. But since the beginning of the 1990s, the tourism practitioners and tourism scientists have been aware that besides comparative advantages and prices, many other variables determine the competitiveness of a tourism enterprise or a destination. The notion 'competitive destination' contains two elements: destination and competitiveness. The next chapter presents a detailed analysis of competitive approaches for tourism destinations. The models included in this assessment are those postulated by Porter, Poon, Bordas, Dwyer, WES and Crouch and Ritchie. The chapter concludes that the developed conceptual models to enhance competitiveness are very different while there is some agreement about the content of the notions 'destination' and 'competitiveness'.

In recent years, a growing number of countries have faced tourism crises as a direct result of terror attacks, natural disasters, epidemics, etc. Countries including the US, Spain, Thailand and UK now have to fight for a favorable image in the global tourism market. At the same time, leaders of many countries around the world believe that the unfavorable images and stereotypes associated with their names are an obstacle preventing them from becoming more attractive, and in fact forestall a brighter future. Thus, the succeeding final chapter suggests media strategies that decision-makers can employ to deal with their countries' image crises and to reverse negative images. The chapter first deals with place promotion, country image management, place branding and the nature of tourism crises. It then presents 10 strategies to improve a country's negative image, in order to overcome the crisis and restore a positive, favorable image. The chapter also presents current examples from various countries on how such strategies have been incorporated into the practice.

References

Oliver, R. L. (1999). Whence consumer loyalty. *Journal of Marketing, 63*, 33–44.

Pike, S. (2002). Destination image analysis: A review of 142 Papers from 1973 to 2000. *Tourism Management, 23*(5), 541–549.

Porter, M. E. (1985). *Competitive advantage: Creating and sustaining superior performance*. New York: Free Press.

Woodside, A. G., & Lysonski, S. (1989). A general model of traveler destination choice. *Journal of Travel Research, 27*(4), 8–14.

Woodside, A. G., & Sherrell, D. (1977). Traveler evoked, inept and inert sets of vacation destinations. *Journal of Travel Research, 16*(1), 14–18.

Chapter 5

Destination Marketing: A Framework for Future Research

Alan Fyall, Brian Garrod and Cevat Tosun

Introduction

The destination lies at the very heart of the travel and tourism system, representing as it does an amalgam of products that collectively provide a tourism experience to consumers. Indeed, the array of components that make up the destination product, the complexity of the relationships that exist between them and the strengthening of this complexity due to the tendency for a large number of different stakeholders to be involved is such that the destination is widely acknowledged to be one of the most difficult products to manage and market. Over the coming decade, the challenge facing destination marketers is likely to be even greater with a whole host of issues likely to impact on the future marketing of destinations.

In view of the above context, a destination-marketing framework is proposed that serves as a 'route-map' for professionals and researchers in the field. The framework proposed is not derived from any one particular research study, but is the outcome of the combined experience of the authors — both in a professional and academic capacity. It is therefore experience based and a reflection of the thoughts, ideas and frustrations of the authors and their students in addition to the views of a select few authors in the field who have passed a variety of similar judgements — albeit less comprehensive — in the past.

Literature Review

Two studies that set the context for the future marketing of destinations particularly well are those by Bennett (1999) and King (2002). Although a little outdated now, Bennett introduces a range of potential future pressures for those marketing destinations. These include the need to take due consideration of the needs, wants and expectations of more mature and knowledgeable customers, and the need for more up-to-date and reliable information upon which to base such decision-making. Bennett highlights also the considerable pressures caused by the sustained presence and influence of intermediaries, as well as the parallel imbalance of channel power for destinations in the tourism system. With regard to transportation and technological pressures, developments in useful destination management systems have taken place, which now afford them necessity status, while the systematic growth of discount airlines and the surplus of new destinations continues to ensure severe competition among destinations for tourist spend. Of all these forces however, it is, according to Bennett, the longstanding 'dividing line' between the public and private sectors that remains the prime catalyst for change; a dividing line that Bennett considers to have been holding back the potential of destination marketing for far too long.

More recent work by King (2002) acknowledges the existence of a number of similar pressures. However, he raises also the scenario of traditional distribution channels being increasingly bypassed in the future with more direct contact between the consumer and the supplier likely to take place. King also suggests that a reduction in booking lead times is likely, as is a steady downturn in the demand for mass tourism products leading to a greater pressure for the destination to deliver satisfactions and meet expectations of an increasingly independent tourist. King is very critical of many existing destination management organisations (DMOs), in that the majority remain focused on 'what the destination has to offer' and continue to use 'mass marketing techniques more suited to the passive customer' (King, 2002,p. 106). He develops this theme by alluding to the fact that the customer is now very much an active partner in the marketing process. For destinations to be a success, marketers will therefore need to engage the customers as never before, as well as to be able to provide them with the types of information and experience they are increasingly able to demand. It is now 'the customer who can decide how and when they access their travel and tourism information, and how and through what process they access and purchase their travel and tourism arrangements' (King, 2002,p. 106).

In the same study, King advances a number of so-called 'new realities' for destination marketers. These include the need for: even greater emphasis on a strong brand image, with clearly identified and projected brand values that resonate with key target segments; more direct engagement with the customer to identify their holiday motivations, anticipate their needs and fulfil their aspirations; the establishment of ongoing, direct, two-way and networking consumer communication channels, and for key customer relationship strategies to take place with the eventual development of mass customisation marketing and delivery capabilities; greater emphasis to be given to the creation and promotion of holiday experiences that link key-brand values and assets with the holiday aspirations and needs of key customers; and a move away from a relatively passive promotional role to include greater intervention, facilitation and direction in the conversion process. The authors are in agreement with many of the sentiments and issues raised by King and Bennett and in an attempt to provide some structure for future research in the domain of destination marketing propose a framework to bring together the key themes and research priorities. The remainder of this chapter will outline the framework and offer a prioritisation of research for the academic and practitioner communities.

The 15 Cs Framework

Although at a developmental phase, and in no way intended to represent a definitive list, the authors believe that the framework proposed — the 15 Cs Framework — provides a suitable synthesis of the key challenges facing the domain of destination marketing for the next decade. Clearly their degree of importance will vary according to the destination in question. However, the omission of even one of the challenges in the design and implementation of destination marketing strategies is likely to hinder the effectiveness of the final plan or strategy in that an inadequate understanding of the wider destination environment is evident. Each component of the framework is now to be discussed in greater depth.

Complexity

The complexity of the destination product is not in dispute. What remains an issue for the future is that the destination is likely to become even more complex due to the myriad of forces and stakeholders both internal and external to it. For example, the complexity of the destination as a product to be marketed is further increased when the consumer and community dimensions are taken into consideration. For the former, individual consumers of the destination product will frequently differ in their perceptions, expectations and desired satisfactions of the 'tourism-place'. Few, if any, are likely to regard the destination as a neatly encapsulated bundle of suppliers, as might be the case from the supply perspective (Buhalis, 2000). For the short, medium and longer-term, the destination is likely not only to have multiple stakeholders, multiple components and multiple suppliers but also to convey multiple meanings to multiple markets and market segments.

Internally, pressures within DMOs exist to raise revenue from members and stakeholders while at the same time presenting marketing strategies that appeal to the needs and wants of an expectant market. These pressures are particularly evident within the UK at present *vis-à-vis* the devolution and regionalisation of tourism organisation and funding, and the migration from member-led 'bottom-up' strategies to centrally funded 'top down' strategies determined by the regional development agencies (RDAs) — who have a strategic remit for the development of tourism — and the regional tourism organisations (RTOs) who retain responsibility only for the marketing of the destination.

Control

Closely related to the above is the issue of control in that one of the principal frustrations for many destination marketers is their inability to control elements of the destination product as well as its destiny in the marketplace. This viewpoint is shared by Scott, Parfitt, and Laws (2000, p. 202) who argue that 'the difficulties of co-ordination and control have the potential to undermine a strategic approach to marketing based on destination branding because campaigns can be undertaken by a variety of tourist businesses with no consultation or co-ordination on the prevailing message or the destination values being promoted'. Hopper (2002), meanwhile, identifies many of the above issues as contributing to why London has struggled historically to make a sustained impact in terms of brand positioning. Although the emphasis here is on branding, these comments are pertinent to the entire domain of managing destinations. It is true that developments are being made in the need to bring tourism's information base up-to-date (see Ritchie & Ritchie, 2002) as there is considerable evidence to suggest that the design and implementation of destination management systems (DMSs) are taking place to the extent that for most destinations, rather than being an aspirational element of their marketing armoury, they are now afforded necessity status and represent a very real opportunity for destination marketers to gain greater control of their product.

Change

Change is evident in any line of business and is thus not unique to the marketing and management of destinations. One particular aspect of change that is particularly needed in the domain of destinations, however, is the migration from the traditional division that has always existed between the public and private sectors. As discussed earlier, Bennett considers this division as the principal catalyst for change in that it has held back the potential of destination marketing for far too long. To date, most countries around the world — the USA apart — retain a strong public bias in their organisational and funding structures. Not only does this result in the retention of a predominantly public 'organisational' mindset but also it serves as a barrier to the raising of additional funding and the speed with which DMOs can react to forces in the external environment.

Crisis

Although crises have always been a feature of tourism, the terrorist atrocities in New York in September 2001 served as a reminder to all destination marketers that crises impact significantly on the demand for tourism, especially international tourism. Foot and Mouth Disease in the UK, the outbreak of SARS across South East Asia, hurricanes in the Caribbean and terrorism — or the perceived threat of terrorism — in many outposts around the world, have all, to varying degrees impacted negatively on tourism demand. Work by Baral, Baral, and Morgan (2004), Beirman (2002) and Money and Crotts (2003) has begun to explore the dynamics of such crises. One anticipates, however, that this is merely the beginning of what is likely to become a burgeoning domain of research activity. For example, recent events in India, Sri Lanka, the Maldives, Indonesia, Thailand and Malaysia as a consequence of the Tsunami that hit each of their shores in December 2004 — although, clearly tragic for the domestic populations at large — has decimated much of the tourism infrastructure, most notably in Sri Lanka and the Maldives, as has it engendered in the minds of tourists a fear of nature's elements to an extent hitherto unheard of. The outcomes for all destinations affected are at present clearly uncertain.

Any destination-marketing organisation that does not now incorporate some form of crisis management planning into its strategic marketing planning cycle can now be accused of grossly ignoring the realities of modern tourism. Acknowledging the crisis is one thing. Understanding its impact is, however, a little more difficult in that many destinations are still coming to terms with the changing tourist flows that accompany crises and their related spend and accommodation requirements. In London, for example, the loss of one visitor from the United States in economic terms requires two European visitors and three and a half domestic visitors to compensate. This statistic alone highlights the need for continued market diversification with less reliance on traditional markets and continual new product development, promotion and public relations.

One crisis that is often overlooked is that of economic crises. Economic crisis in the major generating countries such as Germany or Japan are economically far more damaging for tourist receiving countries than more high-profile — media-hungry — events such as 911, the outbreak of Chicken Flu in Thailand and the recent Tsunami in Asia.

Complacency

Continual change and fear of crises should be sufficient in themselves to prevent complacency among those marketing destinations. One of the problems for many destinations, however, is that for so long now specific markets have been such reliable sources of custom. Although destinations can perhaps be excused in the past for being slow to react to forces in the external environment, recent crises alone ought to be sufficient in themselves to demonstrate that that the *status quo* of visitors to destinations can no longer be taken for granted. 9/11 was significant in one way in that although many destinations clearly suffered from very rapid drops in demand, tourists continued to travel albeit intra-regionally or domestically. Tourism has thus yet again been proved to be a highly robust phenomenon in that although travel patterns may change, the act of travelling remains steadfast in that to many markets it is now a necessity rather than a luxury; especially in the developed world.

Customers

The complexity of the destination as a product to be marketed is further increased when the consumer dimension is taken into consideration. For example, individual customers of the destination product will frequently differ in their perceptions, expectations and desired satisfactions of the 'tourism-place'. Few, if any, are likely to regard the destination as a neatly encapsulated bundle of suppliers, as might be the case from the supply perspective (Buhalis, 2000). The task of managing the tourist destination is therefore never going to be an easy one for the destination is likely not only to have multiple stakeholders, multiple components and multiple suppliers but also to convey multiple meanings to multiple markets and market segments.

In many instances, destination marketers need to be more innovative in their adoption of marketing techniques and strategies in meeting the needs of more demanding customers. For example, the highly competitive global market for tourists serves as a catalyst for tourism destinations to seek more innovative 'relationship' marketing strategies so as to engender a degree of loyalty and stimulate lucrative repeat business among their visitor base.

Studies conducted by a variety of authors (see for example, Bowen & Shoemaker, 1998; Fyall, Callod, & Edwards, 2003; Kozak, 2001; Oppermann, 2000; Riley, Niininen, Szivas, & Willis, 2001; Wang, 2004; Yuksel, 2001) have begun to explore many of the issues but far greater insights are required to move the debate and application of such strategies on. For example, in a context of many destinations competing in price-driven, low-margin markets, the costs and benefits to be derived from relationship marketing require significant research before tourism destinations are able to accept the concept as a new paradigm or potential solution to maintain/expand their share of the market for visitors. In view of the inherent imbalance of power, resources and experience between tourism destination 'actors', generating cohesion, mutual trust and respect within the tourism system stand as significant challenges for those marketing tourism destinations in the future.

Culture

The issue of culture is relevant to both demand and supply-side perspectives of destination marketing. For example, as identified in the component of change, the cultural division between the public and private sectors within tourism continues to represent a barrier for progress across many countries. Although there is evidence to suggest that change is beginning to happen, albeit slowly, the particular characteristics of the destination and its fundamental reliance on 'public goods' as part of its wider appeal is likely to ensure that the two cultures will have to continue working alongside each other for the foreseeable future. On the demand side, however, one means by which destinations — and especially those that have acquired 'commodity' status in recent years, can differentiate themselves in the future is via the development of niche tourism strategies; often driven by the development of cultural products, more often than not of a heritage genre — for the more discerning visitor. Further work is clearly needed in determining the true worth of such strategies to domestic and international markets.

Competition

The aforementioned need to differentiate the destination product is testament to the sheer number of destinations now available for sale in the 'tourism supermarket'. In the European context the dearth of destination competition has been driven ostensibly by the continual growth of discount airlines making hitherto inaccessible destinations real alternatives for many tourists from the key generating markets of the UK, Scandinavia, and Germany. The surge in ownership of second homes — most notably in France and Spain — also serves as an indirect competitive threat in that an increasingly significant percentage of the market now no longer needs variety in their choice of destinations as via their purchase of a second home they have expressed their loyalty, albeit to varying degrees, to a particular destination. Competition is at its most cutthroat post-crisis with evidence from recent disasters suggesting that although the overall volume of trips taking place remains relatively static, the shift in travel patterns is significant in that domestic and intra-regional travel to more familiar and perceived 'safe' destinations have become the norm.

Commodification

The increase in competition across all regions of the world is such that over periods of time more and more destinations are likely to share similar if not identical 'selling points'. The 'commodified' destination is already a reality — particularly in parts of the Mediterranean, South East Asia and the Caribbean — where the pressure is now to differentiate as much as possible between one destination and another. One of the outcomes of commodification of the destination product is the continual downward pressure on prices. Although highly beneficial to the tourist the reduction in yield poses a significant headache for destination markers in that increasingly more marketing — and marketing spend — has to be conducted in return for a decreasing yield from tourists. Niche tourism developments are the means to counter such a trend — as best demonstrated by marketing strategies adopted by the Tourism Authority of Thailand and their development of the brand Amazing Thailand brand and its annual niche-oriented marketing 'straplines'.

Creativity

The aforementioned need for greater branding of destinations is just part of the need for a wider appreciation of greater creativity across the whole spectrum of marketing activity. Branding is the most obvious development, especially with regard to attempts made to position destinations outside of the mass of commodity destinations around the world. One of the biggest hurdles for destination marketers in this regard, however, is their limited ability to build destination-wide brands. The lack of product control and tight budgets as well as the potential for political interference, all inhibit the ease with which brands can be developed. This in turn helps to explain why there is such a paucity of brand innovation in the destination sector as compared to other sectors within the tourism industry. In part, studies conducted by Caldwell and Freire (2004), Konecnik (2004), Morgan, Pritchard, and Piggott (2002, 2003), Prideaux, Agrusa, Donlon, J. and Curran (2004) and White (2004) have begun to address some of the issues related to branding. That said, far greater work needs to be commissioned with regard to the need for more clarity and consistency with the brand proposition and an even greater emphasis on a strong brand image with clearly identified and projected brand values that resonate with key target segments; more direct engagement with the customer to identify their holiday motivations, anticipate their needs and fulfil their aspirations

Communication

The need for greater creativity is particularly apparent in the context of communication. Traditionally, a disproportionately high percentage of marketing budgets has been spent on brochures and leaflets and although in many parts of the world this remains the case more varied communication efforts are now needed for a more educated and increasingly sophisticated clientele (Dore & Crouch, 2003; Foley & Fahy, 2004). Clearly, this statement varies according to the generating market in question in that what maybe true for developed markets such as Germany and the UK may not be so for emerging markets such as Korea and Russia. According to King (2002) much greater emphasis needs to be given to the creation and communication of holiday experiences that link key brand values and assets with the holiday aspirations and needs of key customers. In parallel he advocates a move away from a relatively passive promotional role to include greater intervention, facilitation and direction in the conversion process. The migration to an economy based on 'experience' opens the door to the establishment of ongoing, direct, two-way and networking consumer communication channels, and for key customer relationship strategies to take place with the eventual development of mass customisation marketing and delivery capabilities.

Channels

This and the issue that immediately follows — cyberspace — are closely related in that they both are concerned with the aspect of distribution of the destination product. With disintermediation of much of the tourism marketing system now taking place — in part driven by the increase in independent travel in many origin markets — as at the same time reintermediation beginning to take place due to the uncertain travel patterns of some key markets, it is clear that the issue of channels is very much in a state of flux at the current moment in time. Although there have been significant developments *vis-à-vis* computer reservation systems and global distribution systems, for the destination it is the growth of destination management and marketing systems that are the principal competitive tool for destinations in their quest for gaining greater control over the distribution of the destination product. Irrespective of the location, scale and type of destination in question, the development of a suitable destination management system — whether unilaterally or with other like-minded destination(s) is a priority that can no longer be ignored.

Cyberspace

As alluded to above, the emerging role and influence of the Internet is a significant force in the future distribution and management of tourism across generally and the destination in particular. The emergence over the past decade of virtual intermediaries such as Expedia, Travelocity and Opodo continue to represent a significant threat to destinations in that their expertise and scope of operation brings considerable economies of scale that further enhance their position in the marketplace. The emergence of the Internet and its application in the domains of tourism, travel and hospitality is significant in that it has underpinned significant changing patterns of consumption — as has it impacted the entire buying processes — and the entire means by which tourism, travel and hospitality products are packaged and sold. A large number of studies have been conducted in this area — see for example Buhalis (1998) — as academia and the wider industry continue to learn from the e-revolution. The complexity of the destination product and the co-ordinating role practised by destination marketers clearly makes the development, implementation and management of destination-wide web sites particularly challenging. However, as with the rest of the wider tourism industry, it is a challenge that destinations cannot afford to ignore.

Consolidation

The example of Thomas Cook AG represents a typical illustration of a common trend across most industries — the significant growth in recent years in the number of mergers and acquisitions taking place. This trend has impacted significantly on the global tourism industry, most notably in the domains of travel in the form of airlines, hospitality in the form of large international hotel groups and tourism in the form of intermediaries; such as Thomas Cook AG (WTO, 2002). Indeed, according to Wahab and Cooper (2001) it is the development of new integrated corporate structures as a result of alliances, mergers and acquisitions that is likely to cause the greatest structural impact on the tourism industry.

For destinations this issue throws open a number of challenges in their attempt to counter the power imbalance that often results from such developments.

Collaboration

For destination marketing to be effective and succeed both now and in the future — and to counter the threat of increasing consolidation across the industry — it is clear that destinations need to bring all of the individual partners together to co-operate rather than compete, and to pool resources towards developing an integrated marketing mix and delivery system (Buhalis & Cooper, 1998; Prideaux & Cooper, 2002; Telfer, 2001). Whether one is referring to intra-destination networks (von Friedrichs Grängsjö, 2003), relational brands (Hankinson, 2004) or forms of collaboration governance (Palmer, 1998; Palmer & Bejou, 1995), this move towards the need for greater collaboration is referred to by King (2002) as the 'network economy', in that DMOs will probably enter into strategic relationships with industry partners who can together provide a seamless experience for the customer. This is because it will be the 'relevance of the experience they offer the customer, rather than the destination they promote, which will be the key ingredient for success in the future' (King, 2002, p. 108). Bennett (1999) shares this viewpoint with Fyall and Garrod (2005), who call for much more collaboration between all those involved in the destination product in order to take destinations forward. Collaboration is not considered a luxury in this instance, but as a necessity for destinations to survive in the face of considerable competition and environmental challenges.

Conclusions and Implications

If one single issue is to be identified as that which most comprehensively encapsulates those fifteen challenges identified in the 15 Cs Framework, it is the latter issue of collaboration and the need for destinations to work together in solving problems deemed too demanding to solve in isolation. This was identified initially in the mid-1990s when Palmer and Bejou stated that 'a *free market* solution to tourism destination marketing in which there is no collaboration among stakeholders gives rise to a number of potential problems for them' (1995, p. 617). Three main reasons were given for this. (1.) The stakeholders are able to create less promotional impact on potential visitors by working independently than by joining together to put in place a promotional campaign in which resources are pooled. (2.) The market mechanisms typically fail to support and share the benefits of the collective promotion of an area. (3.) In the marketing planning process that stakeholders can achieve their objectives more effectively by recognising their interdependencies. For collaboration to succeed in the context of destinations, the DMO needs to act as a strong unifying force that is able to discourage the conception of splinter groups, which at a later stage can frustrate or otherwise oppose destination-wide strategies. If a strong counter-body does emerge, this may well generate significant confusion in the marketplace and engender dysfunctional behaviour within the destination.

Collaboration is, therefore, likely to represent the *sine qua non* for successful destination marketing in the future. With regard to its centrality to the 15 Cs Framework, tourism destinations are clearly *complex* domains, which almost always involve a wide range of stakeholders, the constraints and aspirations of whom are typically highly divergent. It is only via the adoption of collaboration strategies that destinations will be in a position to unify their component parts and present a single message to the market. Likewise the destination's ability to gain — and maintain — *control* over its destiny in the market is more often than not dependent on inter-destination solutions while the need for a *change* in organisational culture, in the UK at least, is beginning to emerge in the form of cross-border (be it local or regional) destination marketing partnerships. It is most likely that for the foreseeable future the destinations impacted by the devastation caused by the Tsunami will work together in promoting the collective appeal of the region post-*crisis*, for many working with destinations previously considered to be *competition*. This in itself provides evidence of destinations confronting previously *complacent* attitudes and that they are more in tune with the needs and wants of *customers*. Clearly such a move requires a shift in the *cultural* mindset of destination marketers, the historical orientation of *competition* being replaced by a more relational collaborative orientation where more often than not, destinations of a *commodified* nature are being forced to work with other destinations in attempts to distinguish themselves in an increasingly cluttered marketplace. Via *creative* branding and more traditional *communication* techniques, often via *channels* of distribution — and increasingly in *cyberspace* — destinations can work in isolation or together with other destinations in developing destination management systems to counter the competitive threat of multinational organisations that have come together as a consequence of merger and acquisition activity and are testament to the trend of concentration and *consolidation*.

If the 15 Cs Framework is to have any impact on the so-called 'real world' of destination marketing, the onus is on the research community to scrutinise each issue and its consequent impacts in depth through a mix of contemporary case material and the rigorous application of academic thought. Too often in the past, have researchers of tourism generally — and destinations more specifically — applied a somewhat superficial gloss over much of the rigour applied in the mainstream Marketing literature in their attempts to help understand and explain the dynamics of marketing and market orientation within the domain of destinations. And, consistent with the message coming out of this chapter, the dynamics of collaboration marketing and relational market orientation within the domain of destinations.

References

Baral, A., Baral, S., & Morgan, N. (2004). Marketing Nepal in an uncertain climate: Confronting perceptions of risk and insecurity. *Journal of Vacation Marketing*, *10*(2), 186–192.

Beirman, D. (2002). Marketing of tourism destinations during a period of prolonged crisis: Israel and the Middle East. *Journal of Vacation Marketing*, *8*(2), 167–176.

Bennett, O. (1999). Destination marketing into the next century. *Journal of Vacation Marketing*, 6(1), 48–54.

Bowen, J., & Shoemaker, S. (1998). Loyalty: A strategic commitment. *Cornell Hotel and Restaurant Administration Quarterly*, *39*(February), 12–25.

Buhalis, D. (1998). Strategic use of information technologies in the tourism industry. *Tourism Management, 19* (5), 409–421.

Buhalis, D. (2000). Marketing the competitive destination of the future. *Tourism Management. 21*(1), 97–116.

Buhalis, D., & Cooper, C. (1998). Competition or co-operation: The needs of small and medium sized tourism enterprises at a destination level. In: E. Laws, B. Faulkner & G. Moscardo (Eds), *Embracing and managing change in tourism* (pp. 324–346). London: Routledge.

Caldwell, N., & Freire, J. R. (2004). The difference between branding a country, a region and a city: Applying the Brand Box Model. *Journal of Brand Management, 12*(1), 50–61.

Dore, L., & Crouch, G. I. (2003). Promoting destinations: An exploratory study of publicity programmes used by national tourism organisations. *Journal of Vacation Marketing, 9*(2), 137–151.

Foley, A., & Fahy, J. (2004). Incongruity between expression and experience: The role of imagery in supporting the positioning of a tourism destination brand. *Journal of Brand Management, 11*(3), 209–217.

Fyall, A., Callod, C., & Edwards, B. (2003). Relationship marketing: The challenge for destinations. *Annals of Tourism Research, 30*(3), 644–659.

Fyall, A., & Garrod, B. (2005). *Tourism marketing: A collaborative approach*. Clevedon: Channel View Publications.

Hankinson, G. (2004). Relational network brands: Towards a conceptual model of place brands. *Journal of Vacation Marketing, 10*(2), 109–121.

Hopper, P. (2002). Marketing London in a difficult climate. *Journal of Vacation Marketing, 9* (1), 81–88.

King, J. (2002). Destination marketing organisations: Connecting the experience rather than promoting the place. *Journal of Vacation Marketing, 8*(2), 105–108.

Konecnik, M. (2004). Evaluating Slovenia's image as a tourism destination. A self-analysis process towards building a destination tool. *Journal of Brand Management, 11*(4), 307–316.

Kozak, M. (2001). Repeaters' behavior at two distinct destinations. *Annals of Tourism Research, 28*(3), 784–807.

Money, R. B., & Crotts, J. C. (2003). The effect of uncertainty avoidance on information search, planning and purchases of international travel vacations. *Tourism Management, 24*(2), 191–202.

Morgan, N., Pritchard, A., & Piggott, R. (2002). New Zealand, 100% pure: The creation of a powerful niche destination brand. *Journal of Brand Management, 9*(4/5), 335–354.

Morgan, N. J., Pritchard, A., & Piggott, R. (2003). Destination branding and the role of stakeholders: The case of New Zealand. *Journal of Vacation Marketing, 9*(3), 285–299.

Oppermann, M. (2000). Tourism destination loyalty. *Journal of Travel Research, 39* (1), 78–84.

Palmer, A. (1998). Evaluating the governance style of marketing groups. *Annals of Tourism Research, 25*(1), 185–201.

Palmer, A., & Bejou, D. (1995). Tourism destination marketing alliances. *Annals of Tourism Research, 22*(3), 616–629.

Prideaux, B., Agrusa, J., Donlon, J., & Curran, C. (2004). Exotic or erotic – contrasting images for defining destinations. *Asia Pacific Journal of Tourism Research, 9*(1), 5–17.

Prideaux, B., & Cooper, C. (2002). Marketing and destination growth: A symbiotic relationship or simple coincidence? *Journal of Vacation Marketing, 9*(1), 35–51.

Riley, M., Niininen, O., Szivas, E., & Willis, T. (2001). The case for process approaches in loyalty research in tourism. *International Journal of Tourism Research, 3* (1), 23–32.

Ritchie, R. J. B., & Ritchie, J. R. B. (2002). A framework for an industry supported destination marketing information system. *Tourism Management, 23*(5), 439–454.

Scott, N., Parfitt, N., & Laws, E. (2000). Destination management: Co-operative marketing, a case study of Port Douglas Brand. In: B. Faulkner, G. Moscardo, & E. Laws (Eds), *Tourism in the 21st century* (pp. 198–221). London: Continuum.

Telfer, D. (2001). Strategic alliances along the Niagara wine route. *Tourism Management*, *22*(1), 21–30.

von Friedrichs Grängsjö, Y. (2003). Destination networking: Co-opetition in peripheral surroundings. *International Journal of Physical Distribution & Logistics Management*, *33*(5), 427–448.

Wahab, S., & Cooper, C. (2001). *Tourism in the age of globalisation*. London: Routledge.

Wang, D. (2004). Tourist behaviour and repeat visitation to Hong Kong. *Tourism Geographies*, *6*(1), 99–118.

White, C. J. (2004). Destination image: To see or not to see. *International Journal of Contemporary Hospitality Management*, *16*(5), 309–314.

WTO (2002). *Tourism in the age of alliances, mergers and acquisitions*. Madrid: World Tourism Organization.

Yuksel, A. (2001). Managing customer satisfaction and retention: A case of tourist destinations, Turkey. *Journal of Vacation Marketing*, *7*(2), 153–168.

Chapter 6

A Reclassification of Tourism Industries to Identify the Focal Actors

David Ermen and Juergen Gnoth

Introduction

Researching and developing the competitive advantage of destinations is taking a prominent position in strategic destination management because of a rapid, global growth of destinations. However, in order to base comparative analyses for marketing purposes on a sound footing, we lack an argued basis for a stratification of industry members. The heterogeneity of providers (Tremblay, 1998), different life cycle stages (Butler, 1980), and structures of destinations (Flagestad & Hope, 2001), as well as different levels of involvement and commitment by individual companies are factors that contribute to the difficulty in comparative research. For the purpose of analyzing, understanding and developing the competitive advantage and marketing strategies of tourism destinations, the question is, which or what types of companies should, in principle, be involved? In other words, what sorts of businesses would need to be contacted and studied in order to identify a country's tourism clusters or the dynamics of destination networks?

The purpose of the present chapter is to establish an argued basis for the selection and actual listing of types of businesses that need to be studied when analyzing and managing the dynamics of destinations from the business or supply perspective. The primary methodologies that aid in such an inquiry are cluster, network, and systems theory. Deriving from economic geography, clusters are " ... a functionally defined group of firms and supporting institutions that produce and market goods and services from a group of related industries that are concentrated in a specific geographical locale" (Wolfe & Gertler, 2004). Recently, clusters have received renewed attention especially since Porter (1998) linked this to his concept of competitive advantage of regions and nations. A parallel construct is network theory (Granovetter, 1973, 1985, 1992), which is based in sociology focusing on the social interaction among network members and has been used extensively to analyze the interaction between firms in industrial markets (Achrol & Kotler, 1999;

Anderson, Hakansson, & Johanson, 1994; Hakansson & Ford, 2002; Hakansson & Snehota, 1989).

Literature Review

In tourism, both cluster and network approaches have been used in order to enrich our understanding of the dynamics of destinations (Jackson & Murphy, 2002). In addition, Bieger (2004) adopted and developed the concept of self-referential systems, which stems from previous conceptualizations of systems theory, as a third approach to tourism (Sessa, 1984). These are systems, which are cyclically interconnected, i.e. which are in contact with and influencing each other. Rather than focusing on environmental factors exerting influences on the system, self-referential system theory concentrates on the systemic elements themselves and their internal relationships. Conceptually, the latter is thus closely related to and overlaps with network theory.

While all of these approaches are being developed, little thought has gone into the definition of what is a destination from the supply point of view. How do we identify tourism clusters or tourism systems in national economies? Which types of businesses do we need to concentrate on while attempting comparative studies of different destinations, e.g. urban versus resort destinations, especially when they are at different stages of development? In other words, while individual analyses (Pavlovich, 2003; Von Friedrichs Grangsjo, 2003) and comparisons (for example, Jackson & Murphy, 2002) of destinations have been conducted, most of these have been snapshots of destinations in time and only a few have involved longitudinal studies of the change in destination over time (Pavlovich, 2001, 2003; Selin & Chavez, 1995; Von Friedrichs Grangsjo, 2003). In both types of studies, researchers have discussed fundamental issues such as businesses involved, structures, sizes, age, and intensity of interactions or the presence of institutions either in a vacuum, as it were, or they have abstracted from specific situations so that comparisons or generally applicable lessons could be offered.

Notwithstanding the legitimacy of these approaches and the benefits snapshots may render, there is a general methodological concern with both cluster (Jackson & Murphy, 2002; Wolfe & Gertler, 2004) and network theories (Anderson et al., 1994; Gummesson, 1996) as neither of these have clear criteria for defining their boundaries. The members of each cluster, network, and system are thus often defined according to the individual purpose of any given research but would make standardized comparisons between research results difficult. Similarly, while trying to compare the stages of destination life cycles (Butler, 1980) what are the indicators and which units, especially which types of businesses, should be included needs to be decided. As destinations develop, we see both the generation of new businesses and also other businesses folding. Are these new openings just a consequence of a successful destination or do these and the decline of other businesses indicate a more fundamental change at the destination? With particular reference to services marketing and management of market-oriented firms and destinations, and to answer the above and similar questions, we require a methodology for the identification of tourism clusters and destination networks as well as a measure of the dependency of the region on that industry.

Destination networks need to orientate themselves toward the market much like individual firms, where market orientation requires a firm to focus on their customers, suppliers and the environment (Kohli & Jaworski, 1990). As such, market orientation generates a self-referential system that includes various groups and companies the firm monitors and interacts with. The firm itself determines the system's boundaries as well as the intensity and efficiency with which this orientation is pursued. However, because of the particular nature of the tourism product, it is not always transparent, for example, which other companies constitute suppliers to a tourism firm. Especially in the case of Free and Independent Tourists, where one firm in the destination often does not know which other firm supplies other elements of the synergistic tourism product. This circumstance has a number of consequences related to transaction costs (Williamson, 1975) and also to issues relating to generating an effective and efficient destination brand (Gnoth, 2002). In order to overcome the bound rationality of small firms immersed in day-to-day issues that often prevent more strategic approaches, the present study seeks an argued development to what companies should be involved in the strategic market orientation of the destination. Given the individual company's limited resources, the development needs to focus on the necessary rather than all companies involved but one that goes beyond opportunistic or haphazard parameters of self-referential systems.

Notwithstanding the benefits of a market-oriented approach, it has been argued that the company's marketing function constitutes the link to the market (Moorman & Rust, 1999) and therefore to successful market orientation. Due to its particular skills, the marketing function co-ordinates the operation and its processes with a view on maximum effectiveness and efficiency in serving customers. In this light, it is argued here that the tourist-oriented focus creates a hierarchy according to which a market orientation could be organized. This means that the hierarchy of firms in the tourism-supply net should start with those firms that directly serve tourists as the first tier. The focus of this study therefore turns to the discussion of Tourism Satellite Accounts (TSAs) and their common methodology. On the face of it, TSAs give us a lead to the questions stated above, as their input–output tables include all types of businesses that contribute to the provision of goods and services in tourism. However, TSAs have been configured to measure the economic impact of tourism to a destination. Hence, being driven by macro-economic concerns, they can serve as a start but not as an unconditional reference for marketing-oriented network and cluster research. They are thus not an easily adaptable catalog of businesses from which a destination-network analysis could be designed in terms of the businesses, which should be included. On the other hand, the TSA, as it is being adopted by more and more countries, can function as a common base for cross-destination network and cluster research.

Classification of Tourism Industries through Tourism Satellite Account

Tourism Satellite Accounts are used to estimate the monetary value of the tourism industry in New Zealand and elsewhere, for example Canada, France, UK, Poland, Morocco, USA, Singapore, and many others. It is based on an argued methodological framework arranged and adopted by the World Tourism Organization (WTO, 1999) and an ever-increasing number of countries across the world. They measure tourism's direct and indirect contribution of value to GDP, which allows the comparison to normal commodity producing industries (Statistics New Zealand, 2002). The measure of the contribution is based on the national input–output framework, which provides 'product level' detail of both the structure of industry output and the demand for these products by final consumers. To achieve this, a multitude of tourism products are described, which are then categorized as either 'tourism characteristic', 'tourism related' or 'non-tourism related' products, based on what percentage of the product is thought to be consumed by tourists (Statistics New Zealand, 2002).

On the supply side, which is of particular interest to the current study, the industries that are thought to provide these products are then, for the purpose of the TSA, also divided into two groups. These are 'Tourism Characteristic Industries' (TCIs) and 'Tourism Related Industries' (TRIs). TCIs are those in which at least 25% of the industry's total output is purchased by tourists directly. Their products would essentially not be offered if it were not for tourists. This means that the product or service needs to pass directly from companies in the industry to the tourist. This criterion excludes both manufacturing and wholesaling industries (Statistics New Zealand, 2002). TRIs are those where 5–25% of the total output is sold to tourists and which have direct physical contact with tourists. This once again excludes manufacturing and wholesaling, leaving retailing as the only real tourism related industry (Statistics New Zealand, 2002). As such, the TSA identifies and measures the tourism value chain. All industries that do not fall into these two categories are considered to be 'non-tourism specific' (Statistics New Zealand, 2002). Overall, this classification provides a good starting point for the investigation of which industries should be included in studies of tourism businesses, because they are thought to play a part in supplying tourism products.

Which Industries are Included in the Tourism Satellite Accounts Classification

For the purpose of the TSA, Statistics New Zealand works at the industry group level of industry classification. Any lower industry subgroup levels are not evaluated individually, but are aggregated into the group's description. Table 6.1 shows which industries have been included in the TSA on both the ANZSIC (Australian New Zealand Standard Industry Classification) Industry Group level and the industry subgroup level. Table 6.1 shows that some of the industries included in the TSA seem to be of little direct relevance to tourism-destination marketing management. For example, the industry group 'Services to Transport' includes both the subgroup 'Travel Agency Services' and the subgroup 'Road Freight Forwarding'. The former is very much a tourism characteristic industry, but the latter is unlikely to have any contact with tourists or make any direct sales to tourists since it is involved in freight transport. In addition, while, ultimately, freight forwarding supports tourism and is therefore of importance (e.g. in cases of lost luggage or the supply of sport gear to shops), this industry exists with or without tourism, albeit benefiting from tourism. It is the airline or the sports shop, which utilizes the service in order to better produce its own service to the tourist. There is the caveat that a freight forwarder at a destination may totally depend on tourism enterprises for its business in which case the TSA would classify it as a tourism-characteristic business as its total turnover comes from tourism. However, it can be argued that the freight forwarder has no direct contact with tourists and is therefore not part of the 'consumer-activated network' (Gnoth, 2002) that supplies the tourist with the tourism product.

Table 6.1: All industry groups and subgroups included in the TSA analysis (Statistics New Zealand, 2002).

Tourism characteristic industries		Tourism related industries	
ANZIC industry description Group description	Industry subgroups (if applicable)	ANZIC industry description Group description	Industry subgroups (if applicable)
Accommodation	Accommodation Hotels (accommodation) Motels and motor inns Hosted accommodation Backpacker and youth hostels Caravan parks and camping grounds Accommodation (nec)[a]	Supermarket and grocery stores	Supermarkets Groceries & dairies
		Specialised food retailing	Fresh meat, fish and poultry retailing Fruit and vegetable retailing Liquor retailing Bread and cake retailing Takeaway food retailing Fish chips and ethnic food takeaway stores Chicken takeaway stores Ice-cream parlors and mobile vendors Pizza takeaway stores Other takeaway food stores nec Milk vending Specialized food retailing nec
Pubs, taverns & bars			
Cafes & restaurants			
Clubs (hospitality)			
Long distance bus transport			
Short distance bus transport including tramway			
Taxi and other road passenger transport			
Rail transport			

(*Continued*)

Table 6.1: (Continued)

	Tourism characteristic industries		Tourism related industries
Water transport	International sea transport Coastal water transport Inland water transport	Department stores Clothing and soft good retailing	Clothing retailing Footwear retailing Fabric and other soft good retailing
Air and space transport	Scheduled international air transport Scheduled domestic air transport Non-scheduled air and space transport	Furniture, houseware and appliance retailing	Furniture retailing Floor covering retailing Domestic hardware and houseware retailing Domestic appliance retailing Recorded music retailing
Other transport	*Pipeline transport* Transport nec		
Services to transport	*Parking services* Services to road Transport nec *Stevedoring* *Port operators* *Services to water transport nec* Services to air transport Travel agency services *Road freight forwarding* *Freight forwarding*	Recreational good retailing	Sport and camping equipment retailing Toy and game retailing Newspaper, book and stationery retailing Photographic equipment retailing Marine equipment retailing

A Reclassification of Tourism Industries   93

	(except road) *Customs agency services* *Services to transport nec*	Other personal and household good retailing	Pharmaceutical/cosmetic/toiletry retail Antique and used good retailing Garden supplies retailing Flower retailing Watch and jewellery retailing Retailing nec
Storage	*Grain storage* *Storage nec*	Household equipment repair services	Household equipment repair service (electrical) Household equipment repair services nec
Machinery and equipment (hiring and leasing)	Motor vehicle hiring *Other transport equipment leasing* *Plant hiring or leasing*	Motor vehicle retailing and service	Car retailing Motor cycle dealing Trailer and caravan dealing Automotive fuel retailing Automotive electrical services Smash repairing Tyre retailing Automotive repair and services nec
Libraries, museums and the Arts	Libraries Museums Zoological and botanical gardens Recreational parks and gardens Music and theater productions Creative arts		

(Continued)

Table 6.1: (Continued)

Tourism characteristic industries		Tourism related industries
		[a]Not elsewhere classified.
	Sound recording studios	
	Performing arts venues	
	Services to the Arts nec	
Sport and recreation	Horse and dog racing	
	Racing clubs and track operation	
	Horse and dog training	
	Sports grounds and facilities nec	
	Sports and services to sports nec	
	Gambling services	
	Lotteries	
	Casinos	
	Gambling services nec	
	Other recreation services	

The essential criterion for a tourism product to exist is that the critical services of transport, accommodation, attraction, and hospitality are provided for tourists. Together or apart, whether providers are known to each other or not, the tourism product is perceived only by the tourist and may be arranged independently by himself/herself. Essentially, the services facilitating the experience are often activated by the tourist (Gnoth, 2002). The impetus for economic activity thus begins with the interaction between the tourist and these types of service providers. A further argument for these types of businesses as the basis for any identification and comparison of clusters and networks is the demand for a market-oriented approach that begins with the customer. The organization of the production-process, then, including all additional products and services is a matter of service process design and organization as, for example, discussed in service blueprints (Shostack, 1982). So it would be hard to understand, for example, if a tour operator who bundles part or all of the above critical services was not included in the tourism industry. On the other hand, while electricity is often necessary to provide a tourism service, it constitutes a necessary commodity but one that could be provided by any supplier. The latter would neither have to be a specialist in tourism nor would such skills make any difference to the tourists' experiences.

Indeed, the marketing efforts of tour operators are part of tourism's success. The tour operator is therefore included in the 'tourist activated network' because a tour operator has direct contact with tourists, and is reliant on tourists for business. While being potentially part of the value-chain, freight-forwarders therefore are not included in our considerations for two reasons: (a) because they are not in direct contact with the tourist and (b) because they could exist without tourism as a generic industry as could hairdressers as another example. Overall, the central attribute of service providers to be included in our re-classification of Tourism Characteristic Operations is that they (a) require the presence of the tourist and (b) would not exist without tourists. Tourism Related Operations includes those that have (a) direct contact with the tourist and (b) 5–25% of sales going to tourists but could exist without them. The combination of these criteria is the fundamental difference to the TSA classification as it is based on a market-oriented approach to the destination phenomenon. Benefiting from the existing data as gathered in TSAs yet relevant to market-oriented destination research and management, the three criteria that are suggested to be used to determine the true tourism characteristic and related industries are:

1. Is the tourist directly participating in the service delivery or (service) production process of the business?
2. Is it a tourism related industry? In other words are between 5 and 25% of its sales going to tourists (but could exist without it)?
3. Is the industry a tourism characteristic industry? In other words, is it likely to have more than 25% of its sales going to tourists (and is unlikely to exist without it)?

These criteria will exclude all peripheral and support industries, including wholesale suppliers, to critical tourism services. They provide a 'clean' picture of those industries that are directly involved in servicing the tourist and therefore form the direct link between the tourism network and the market. It is suggested that these firms are the focal companies that generate and manage the success of a destination. They are proposed to be central in their rise and fall and the formation of the competitive advantage and brand of a destination.

The reason for this is that they are essentially the frontline staff of the destination and are, in the tourists' eyes, directly responsible for the satisfaction of the tourists' needs, although the support industries are also vital in making the whole network function. The new classification of tourism businesses that are thought to be directly related to tourism and fulfill the criteria listed above is outlined in the next section.

A New Classification of Tourism Businesses

This section presents the new classification of both TCIs and TRIs based on the previously introduced criteria. The industries classified as tourism characteristic are all thought to receive more than 25% of their sales from tourists and those classified as tourism related are thought to receive between 5 and 25% of their sales from tourists. Industries in both categories have direct contact with the tourists, during the provision of their service, and are therefore part of the 'consumer activated network'. The reclassification of the industries was based on the industry descriptions in the ANZSIC manual (Statistics New Zealand, 1996), which outlines the primary activities of the industry attached to each code. The application of the criteria to the original list of industries from Table 6.1 has excluded some industries completely and has reclassified others. These changes have been introduced in the boldened categories in Table 6.1 and italicized. They are further listed and are explained below.

Tourism Characteristic Industries

Thirteen subgroups from the original classification have been excluded from the new classification and although these industries may support tourism firms and play a secondary part in the provision of tourism services, they do not fulfill the criteria for inclusion in this reclassified industry list. To give an example of why this was necessary, 'Pipeline Transport' is included in the original classification under the broader classification of transport, which means that if the more detailed levels of classification are ignored, this obviously not tourism-related industry would be included. However, when the three criteria are applied to this subgroup it becomes clear that it is not a tourism characteristic industry and should therefore be reclassified. The 13 industries are listed in Table 6.2 and are all

Table 6.2: Industries excluded from the new classification.

Subgroup name	
Pipeline transport	Plant hiring or leasing
Services to water transport	Grain storage
Road freight forwarding	Storage nec
Freight forwarding (except road)	Services to the arts nec
Services to transport nec	Horse and dog training
Stevedoring	Lotteries
Port operators	

excluded, because they do not have any direct contact with tourists and are unlikely to make more than 5% of their sales to tourists.

Related Tourism Industries

All the original retailing industries are still classified as TRIs and five of the originally tourism characteristic ones have been moved here, because although they have direct contact with tourists, it is unlikely that they would have sales of more than 25% to tourists (Table 6.3). Hence, they only qualify as TRIs, not TCIs. An example of this is 'Gambling Services nec', which is classified as a TCI in the original classification under the broader heading of 'Sport and Recreation', an industry that has direct contact with tourists, but is unlikely to have sales of more than 25% to tourists, since its definition includes bookmakers, betting shops and totalizator agencies, which will largely target local and resident customers.

This section introduced a new classification of tourism industries that eliminates a number of the subgroups originally included in the TSA classification. The new classification delimits industries participating in the hybrid tourism industry based on (a) whether they have significant sales to tourists and (b) whether they have direct contact with tourists. These criteria provide a market-oriented industry classification, which allows the identification of those industries that are likely to be involved in the 'consumer activated networks' (Gnoth, 2002) that the tourist creates around himself/herself to provide the tourism experience. This type of classification should provide a good picture of who services tourists directly and is therefore an immediate target for measures of destination development and management as they are directly contributing value to the destination network (Jarillo, 1995).

Hence, these industries are most likely to initiate tourism-focused marketing activities and be the leaders in networks, at a destination level, that are aiming to service tourists. Supporting industries are vital to the successful delivery of the tourism product by these focal industries. Leaving the supporting industries out of this classification by no means indicates that they are not important to the provision of tourism but are less likely to dominate the tourism experience and, in the first instance, of destination development and management. While the theory of self-referential systems mentioned earlier cautions us that there are events that may bring other systems (industries) into play, the proposed reclassification constitutes any destination's focal companies that need to network in order to create a competitive advantage. Since they have direct contact with the tourist, they provide the link or point of interaction between tourists and the network or system that is responsible for the provision of tourism at the destination level.

Table 6.3: Industries reclassified as TRIs in the new classification.

Subgroup name	
Parking services	Sound recording studios
Customs agency services	Gambling services
Other transport equipment leasing	

Conclusions and Implications

The chapter has presented a new classification of tourism characteristic and tourism related industries based on the definitions and framework of the TSA. The objective was to identify those industries that are necessary to provide tourism and that have direct contact with tourists. These should be the foundation for any study using network or cluster theory to identify the economic and competitive dynamics that occur at a destination, because they act as the link or point of interaction between tourists and the network or system that provides the tourism product. The next step is to test this classification on a dataset to determine whether key tourism regions in New Zealand can be identified as clusters. If this is the case, this new classification of tourism industries will allow the comparison of different regions within New Zealand based on what percentage of businesses are part of the tourism characteristic and tourism-related industries. It will lead to a quantification of how many businesses operate in these industries and how many people they employ in each region.

Another dynamic that is thought to make the group decision-making in destinations particularly difficult is that there is constant change in the 'make up' of the destination. In other words, there is an expectation that companies will be entering and exiting the destination constantly, which continuously changes the group of Small to Medium Tourism Enterprises (SMTEs) that are the destination. This would make it very difficult to develop consistent decision-making procedures with regard to marketing decisions, like mission statements and branding, as well as the management of communal assets, like the destination's reputation. Now that we know what industries to focus on, it is possible to analyze the birth and death dynamics in these industries and compare these with the overall growth at the destination over time.

The main theoretical contribution of this study is that it lays the foundation for the more consistent study of tourism destinations from the supply side, because it provides a list of those firms that provide the direct link between the tourism-destination network and the market. This will enable researchers to more clearly identify the focal actors in their studies and make it possible for others to repeat the study in a different context, using the same focal actors. In doing so they can build on the insight gained by previous authors and develop their research further. The implications for future research are that if this can be repeated in other countries then similar classifications can be developed internationally to allow the comparison of the supply side of destinations at a global level. Since similar industries will form the link between the destination network and the market in most international settings, this ought to be just a matter of applying the same criteria to whatever industry classifications are available in a given country. In addition to this, managers of or in destinations will be able to use this classification to analyze the supply side of their destination and develop management programs that take into account those actors that form the core of tourism destinations. They will then be able to work backward from there and understand the support or supply system that underlies these focal actors in order to gain a more holistic perspective of the business environment in which they are operating.

References

Achrol, R. S., & Kotler, P. (1999). Marketing in the network economy. *Journal of Marketing*, *63*(Special Issues), 146–163.

Anderson, J. C., Hakansson, H., & Johanson, J. (1994). Dyadic business relationships within a business network context. *Journal of Marketing*, *58*(4), 1–15.

Bieger, T. a. L., C. (2004). *Tourismuslehre- Ein Grundriss*. Bern: Haupt Verlag.

Butler, R. W. (1980). The concept of a tourist area cycle of evolution: Implications for management of resources. *Canadian Geographer*, *XXIV*(1), 5–12.

Flagestad, A., & Hope, C. A. (2001). Strategic sucess in winter sports destinations: a sustainable value creation perspective. *Tourism Management*, *22*(5), 445–461.

Gnoth, J. (2002). Consumer activated networks: Towards a dynamic model for tourism destinations. Paper presented at the marketing networks in a global economy, Monash University, Kuala Lumpur.

Granovetter, M. (1973). The strength of weak ties. *American Journal of Sociology*, *78*(May), 1360–1380.

Granovetter, M. (1985). Economic action and social structure: The problem of embeddedness. *American Journal of Sociology*, *91*(November), 481–510.

Granovetter, M. (1992). Problems of explanation in economic sociology. In: N. Nohria & R.G.Eccles (Eds), *Networks and organizations: Structure, form and action* (pp. 25–56). Boston: Harvard Business School Press.

Gummesson, E. (1996). Relationship marketing and imaginary organizations: A synthesis. *European Journal of Marketing*, *30*(2), 31–44.

Hakansson, H., & Ford, D. (2002). How should companies interact in business networks? *Journal of Business Research*, *55*(2), 133–139.

Hakansson, H., & Snehota, I. (1989). No business is an island: The network concept of business strategy. *Scandianvian Journal of Management*, *5*(3), 187–200.

Jackson, J., & Murphy, P. (2002). Tourism destinations as clusters: Analytical experiences from the new world. *Tourism and Hospitality Research*, *4*(1), 36–52.

Jarillo, J. C. (1995). *Strategic networks: Creating the borderless organization*. Oxford: Butterworth-Heinemann.

Kohli, A. J., & Jaworski, B. J. (1990). Market orientation: The construct, research propositions, and managerial implications. *Journal of Marketing*, *54*(2), 1–18.

Moorman, C., & Rust, R. T. (1999). The role of marketing. *Journal of Marketing*, *63*(Special Issue), 180–197.

Pavlovich, K. (2001). The twin landscapes of Waitomo: Tourism networks and sustainability through the landcare group. *Journal of Sustainable Tourism*, *9*(6), 491–504.

Pavlovich, K. (2003). The evolution and transformation of a tourism destination network: The Waitomo Caves, New Zealand. *Tourism Management*, *24*(2), 203–216.

Porter, M. E. (1998). Clusters and the economics of competition. *Harvard Business Review*, *76*(6), 77–90.

Selin, S., & Chavez, D. (1995). Developing an evolutionary tourism partnership model. *Annals of Tourism Research*, *22*(4), 844–856.

Sessa, A. (1984). The contributions of economics to tourism. *Annals of Tourism Research*, *11*(2), 283–302.

Shostack, G. L. (1982). How to design a service. *European Journal of Marketing*, *16*(1), 49–61.

Statistics New Zealand. (1996). *Australian and New Zealand standard industrial classification (New Zealand use version)*. Wellington: Statistics New Zealand.

Statistics New Zealand. (2002). *Tourism satellite account 1997–1999*. Wellington: Statistics New Zealand.

Tremblay, P. (1998). The economic organization of tourism. *Annals of Tourism Research, 25*(4), 837–859.

Von Friedrichs Grangsjo, Y. (2003). Destination networking: Co-opetition in peripheral surroundings. *International Journal of Distribution and Logistics Management, 33*(5), 427–448.

Williamson, O. E. (1975). Markets and hierarchies, analysis and antitrust implications: a study in the economics of internal organization. New York: Free Press.

Wolfe, D. A., & Gertler, M. S. (2004). Clusters from the inside and out: Local dynamics and global linkages. *Urban Studies, 41*(5–6), 1071–1093.

WTO. (1999). *Tourism Satellite Account (TSA) The conceptual Framework (English Version)*: World Tourism Organisation.

Chapter 7

A Comparative Analysis of Competition Models for Tourism Destinations

Norbert Vanhove

Introduction

'Competitiveness in tourism' can be described with the elements that make a destination competitive as defined by Ritchie and Crouch (2003), '... its ability to increase tourism expenditure, to increasingly attract visitors while providing them with satisfying memorable experiences and to do so in a profitable way, while enhancing the well-being of destination residents and preserving the natural capital of the destination for future generations'. We find the same elements with WES (1994) and Poon (1993). From this content, we can derive that competitiveness in tourism has several dimensions: economic, socio-cultural and environmental. Competitiveness has become a central point of tourism policy. As competition increases and tourism activity intensifies, tourism policy focuses on improving competitiveness by creating a statutory framework to monitor, control and enhance quality and efficiency in the industry and to protect resources (Goeldner, Ritchie, & McIntosh, 2000). Although there is some agreement about the content, the developed conceptual models to enhance competitiveness are very different.

These models are neither predictive nor causal. Ritchie and Crouch (2002) are right when they state '... models should not be used to make a decision; they assist in decision making but should be no substitute for the role of the decision maker'. Five of the below mentioned models focus exclusively on destination competitiveness. However, Porter's oldest competitive concept based on the competitive forces can be applied to destinations. This chapter gives an overview of the most well-known models with respect to competitiveness and emphasise the great differences in approach analysing the competitiveness of a tourism destination. At the same time we make a link to tourism policy. What should be understood by tourism policy? 'A set of regulations, rules, guidelines, directives and development/promotion objectives and strategies that provide a framework within which the collective and individual decisions directly affecting tourism development and the daily activities within a destination are taken' (Goeldner et al., 2000). Contemporary tourism policy focuses on competitiveness and sustainability; they are also the major parameters of tourism destination management (TDM). Successful TDM involves economic/business management skills balanced with environmental management capabilities.

Literature Review

It cannot be denied that for a destination as well as for an enterprise, price is a vital element of competitiveness (Dwyer, Forsyth, & Rao, 2000). But since the beginning of the 1990s (see AIEST, 1993; Poon, 1993; Goeldner et al., 2000) the tourism industry and tourism scientists are aware that besides comparative advantages and prices, many other variables determine the competitiveness of a tourism enterprise or a destination. More and more authors and practitioners are focusing on 'Competitive destination'. The notion 'competitive destination' contains two elements: destination and competitiveness. A tourism destination is a well-defined geographical area within which the tourist enjoys various types of tourism experiences. Ritchie and Crouch (2003) distinguish several types and levels of tourism destinations:

- country;
- a macro-region, consisting of several countries (e.g. Africa);
- a province or another administrative entity;
- a localised region (e.g. Flanders, Normandy);
- a city or town (e.g. Istanbul); and
- a unique locale with great drawing power (e.g. a national park, Iguaçu Falls).

In relative terms, very few tourists visit a macro-region or country, such as Spain, USA, etc. Tourists are interested in regions and towns, such as Andalucia in Spain, the Algarve in Portugal, New York in the US, the Flemish art cities. They are 'tourism clusters'. Porter (1998) defines clusters as 'geographic concentrations of interconnected companies and institutions in a particular field. Clusters encompasses an array of linked industries and other entities important to tourism'. Applied to tourism, we can define a cluster as a group of tourism attractions, enterprises, and institutions directly or indirectly related to tourism concentrated in a specific geographical area. Competition in tourism is mainly between clusters and not so much between countries (Bordas, 1994). 'The fundamental product in tourism is the destination experience. Competition, therefore, centres on the destination' (Ritchie & Crouch, 2000). For most tourists this experience takes place in a rather small geographical area, such as a town or a region. That is an entity, which from the tourism management point of view is managerial. The following models are dealt with the competitive forces and generic strategies of M. Porter; the 'Porter diamond' or the determinants of competitive advantage; the Poon concept; the WES approach; the Bordas demand model; the conceptual model of destination competitiveness of Ritchie and Crouch; and the price competitiveness approach of Dwyer et al. The most well-known model is the Porter diamond. However, the other models have their origin in the tourism industry. We start with the oldest model of Porter, which can and has been applied to tourism.

The Competitive Forces of M. Porter

In contrast to the other mentioned concepts, Porter's theory about competitive forces and his theory about determinants of competitive advantages do not find their origin in the tourism industry. It is only later on that tourism scientist have applied the theory to the tourism industry. According to Porter (1980), the essence of formulating competitive strategy is relating a company to its environment. In his book 'Competitive strategy', Porter proposes the model of the 'five forces' for investigating the competitive environment:

- the threat of entrants;
- the power of suppliers;
- the power of buyers;
- the threat of substitutes; and
- competitive rivalry.

Is this theory of competitive forces applicable to tourism destinations? There can be no doubt if one considers a destination as a cluster at regional or local level. The cluster is in reality a big firm composed of hundreds of molecules. For a practical example, we refer the Caribbean area (Vanhove, 2005). The combined strength of these five forces determines the profit potential (in the case of tourism destinations potential value added of the industry) and its marketing strategy. For each firm and also for each destination, one can develop a specific competitive strategy reflecting the particular circumstances of a firm, industry or destination. For Porter, an effective competitive strategy takes offensive or defensive action in order to create a defendable position against the five competitive forces and thereby yield a superior return on investment for a firm, or in our case value added for a destination. He formulates three potentially successful generic strategic approaches to outperforming other firms or other destinations: cost leadership, differentiation and focussed or niche strategy.

The Determinants of Competitive Advantage in Tourism

In his book 'The Competitive advantage of nations', Porter developed a model, which attracted much attention in the tourism industry. Taking into account the examples in his book and paraphrasing on the title of his book, one can speak of 'The competitive advantage of regions'. In the context of this contribution and referring to the introduction of this paper, a title' The competitive advantage of tourism destination' makes sense, especially as Porter together with Bordas (THR), applied his model to Barcelona, a city, which is very successful in the short holiday and MICE market. Porter claims that the success of a firm does not only depend on its strategy and positioning (see the five competitive forces of Porter) but also on it's embedding in their environment. Regions, destinations/clusters succeed in a particular industry or activity because their home environment is the most dynamic and the most challenging, and is stimulates firms to upgrade their advantage. This is his central thesis. The starting point for the development of strategies to improve the competitive position of a destination is identical to the determinants of competitiveness (Smeral, 1996). Based on the Porter model, competitive advantages of a destination emerge in a dynamic system consisting of four interdependent determinants, which together form

Table 7.1: The determinants of competitive advantage in tourism.

Factor conditions	or the destination's position in factors of production necessary to compete in the tourism industry (e.g. factor endowments)
Demand conditions	or the nature of (home) demand for tourism products and services (e.g. position in fast-growing markets)
Related and supporting industries	or the presence or absence in the region of supplier industries and related industries (e.g. a souvenir industry)
Firm strategy, structure, organisation and rivalry	or the conditions in the nation (destination) governing how companies are created, organised and managed, and the nature of (domestic) rivalry (e.g. a strategic tourism plan)
Two additional variables — government and chance	or they can influence the system in important ways and are necessary to complete the theory

a diamond, a term Porter uses to refer to these determinants (Porter, 1990). These determinants are shown in Table 7.1.

The 'diamond' is a mutually reinforcing system. The effect of one determinant depends on the state of the others. Favourable demand conditions for example, will not lead to competitive advantage unless the state of rivalry is sufficient to cause firms (e.g. hotels) to respond to them. Advantages in one determinant can also create or upgrade advantages in another. In tourism there are many clusters, such as groups of companies directly and indirectly related to tourism and concentrated in a specific geographical area. A tourism product as a composite product — attractions, accommodation, transport and other facilities — stimulates the clustering process (see Michael, 2003). Typical examples of tourism clusters are Bruges, Ibiza, Iguaçu, Istanbul, Venice and many others. The Porter model can be very helpful to detect the strengths and the weaknesses of a destination. Let us illustrate this with an application for Bruges (Vanhove, 2002). The growth of tourism activity in Bruges in the last two decades has been spectacular. The performance would not be possible without a number of strong points. They are presented in Table 7.2.

Although one would estimate that the strong points of tourism policy dominate, following the Porter model, there are indeed a number of weaknesses. They are summarised in Table 7.3. The major weaknesses are: absence of a strategic plan (meanwhile a strategic plan is prepared and accepted); insufficient communication budget; absence of a quality plan; inadequate MICE infrastructure; and lack of a destination management (DM) information system.

The Poon Concept

Poon (1993) emphasises the changes in tourism where she opposes new tourism (flexible, segmented, diagonally integrated, environmentally-conscious) to old tourism (mass, standardised and rigidly packaged) with respect to consumers, management, technology, production and

Table 7.2: Strengths with respect to competitiveness — the case of Bruges (2002).

Determinant	Strengths
Factor conditions	• Product policy • Cultural patrimony • Historic town centre recognised as UNESCO world heritage site • Interesting museums • Good hotel accommodation • Price policy and price level • Geographical location in Europe • Language knowledge • Small-scale atmosphere • Professional reception infrastructure for tourists (new projects in implementation) • Security
Demand conditions	• Market size and growth potential • Many international visitors • No dominance of organised group travel
Related and supporting activities	• Accessibility • Parking facilities • Shopping facilities • Typical souvenirs • Gastronomy and good food in general • Hotel schools
Market structure, rivalry, organisation and strategy	• Well-organised hotel sector: 'vzw Hotels Brugge' • Alliance between art cities in Flanders
Local government	• Bruges: cultural capital of Europe in 2002

frame conditions. For her, new tourism changes the rules of the game and calls for new strategies to ensure competitive success. 'The more rapid the changes in the firm's environment, the more important becomes strategy formulation and implementation. The travel and tourism industry is undergoing rapid and radical transformation. Therefore, competitive strategies are more important than ever for the survival and competitiveness of industry players' (Poon, 1993). Poon's central thesis is 'Innovation — introduction of new products — is far more important than low cost, differentiation or focus'. The Poon concept of competitive strategy has two dimensions: a micro and a macro level. She deals with 'competitive strategies for industry players' and 'strategies for tourism destinations'.

Competitive strategies for industry players New tourism changes the rules of the game in the industry and calls for new strategies to ensure competitive success. The author has identified four key principles of competitive success and for each there are a number of strategies associated: put consumer first; be a leader in quality; develop radical innovations; and strengthen your strategic position. Some of these principles and associated

Table 7.3: Weaknesses or points for improvement with respect to competitiveness — the case of Bruges (2002).

Determinant	Weaknesses or points for improvement
Factor conditions	• Inadequate MICE infrastructure • International hotel chains (brands) • More active cultural experience required • Evening activities and the hinterland as a support
Demand conditions	• Attitude (a minority of local population) towards tourism • Headquarter zone
Related and supporting activities	• TGV connection to Lille • Lack of a national air carrier as coordinator • Risk degrading quality level (prices) of services (e.g. some taxi drivers and restaurant keepers)
Market structure, rivalry, organisation and strategy	• No strategic planning • Low communication budget • Lack of a quality plan • No DM information system • Public–private partnership • Insufficient joining with international hotel networks
Local government	• Hotel stop

strategies need further explanation. We emphasise five topics. The first one relates to the holistic approach. A holiday experience is much more than the bed-nights at a hotel or apartment. It begins on arrival. The actions of immigration officers or customs, the attitude of taxi drivers are a part of the holiday experience. At the destination other critical factors for holiday experience are the food, the behaviour of the police, the beggars on city streets, dirty streets, harassment of tourists on the beach or in restaurants and so many other factors. Poon states that the success of certain holidaymakers — Disneyland, SuperClubs, Sandals, Center Parks — is because they have taken a holistic approach to the holiday experience. Secondly, Poon claims that 'quality' will be the most significant factor for competitive success among industry players. Tourists want quality, flexibility and value for money.

Therefore, creative recruitment of personal, the empowering of the front line, investment in education and motivation are very important. Thirdly, radical innovation is a little bit misleading. It is not possible to develop a new holiday concept each year, but one can, at regular intervals, consider exploring new markets, providing new services, developing new processes, developing a culture for innovation and encouraging new ideas. Fourthly, what does it mean to seek an advantageous position in the value chain? A value chain is an analytical tool developed for tracing the process of value creation in an industry (Porter, 1987). The value chain can be thought of as all the interconnecting operations that make up the whole consumer experience of a product. Poon applied it to the tourism industry to provide insights into how the industry creates value. According to the author, two basic principles are necessary in order to gain an advantageous position in the value chain. There is the need (a) to influence the process of wealth creation and (b) to build strategic alliances.

Strategies for tourism destination The second dimension of Poon's concept of competitive strategy is at the macro or destination level. The issue is not whether to develop tourism but rather how to develop the industry in such a way that the destination benefits. Questions related to this thesis are: how to use tourism to generate other sectors; how to limit tourism's negative social and cultural impacts; and how to build a dynamic private sector? Similarly to the competitive strategies for tourism players, Poon identifies four strategies that tourism destination needs to enhance the development of a new and sustainable tourism. The basic strategies with respect to destinations are:

- Putting the environment first
- Making tourism a lead industry
- Strengthening distribution channels in the market place
- Building a dynamic private sector.

Let us focus on some of these strategies. Firstly, so far not all countries and destinations have respected the principle of responsible tourism. Capacity control is still an exception (e.g. Bermuda, The Seychelles) and comprehensive planning is not yet the rule in tourism destinations (WTO 1992; Bosselman, Peterson, & McCarthy , 1999). Fortunately there are many more examples of visitor's management. Secondly, making tourism a leading industry deserves special attention. Indeed tourism can activate a lot of services and activities, such as car rental, food, crafts, souvenirs, construction, incoming tour operating, etc. Special attention should be paid to avoid leakages. Thirdly, the plea for a transformation of the role of National (Regional) Tourist Offices from promotion to product development deserves attention. Fourthly, public/private partnership at destination level is a necessity if one is to reach an effective tourism policy, to bring all noses in the same direction and gather together the necessary financial means to implement a strategic marketing plan. Last but not least, also at destination level, quality management is considered as a basic strategy. Governments must take steps to establish and enforce standards and to stimulate quality plans at destination level.

The WES Approach

The WES approach finds its origin in a demand of the Inter American Development Bank to analyse the competitive position of a number of countries in the Caribbean area. Special attention was given to the explanation of the differences in the competitive position of these Caribbean destinations and to formulate how to improve these competitive positions. Long-term competitiveness was the focus. Competitiveness was defined as its capacity to reach its objectives in the long run in a more efficient way than the international or regional average. This means that a competitive destination is able to realise a higher profitability than the average, with the lowest social costs and without damaging the environment and available resources. From the beginning a clear distinction was made between (a) indicators

Table 7.4: Factors conditioning the competitive position.

Factors	Variables

Macro-economic factors	• Income-generating countries
	• Real exchange rate
	• Availability and cost of capital
	• Fiscal policy
	  ◦ Import taxes
	  ◦ Cost price increasing taxes
	  ◦ Taxes on profit
	  ◦ Tourism tax
	  ◦ Cruise tax

Supply factors	• Tourist product
	  ◦ Attractions
	  ◦ Accommodation
	  ◦ Price level
	• Labour
	  ◦ Availability
	  ◦ Cost
	  ◦ Quality and training
	• Infrastructure
	  ◦ Transport
	  ◦ Public utilities

Transport factors	• Availability of regular services • Availability of charter services • Availability of cruise services
Demand factors	• Market dependence • Penetration in distribution channels • Marketing efforts • Presence in future growth product markets
Tourism policy	• Institutional framework • Policy formulation • Planning capacity • Commercialisation • Government budgetary support

Source: WES (1993).

of competitive performance and (b) factors which contribute to competitiveness. The former are historical measures, which describe how a destination performed in the past (e.g. international arrivals, tourist nights, etc.). The factors are capabilities or conditions, which it is believed, will contribute to or detract from the ability of a destination to be competitive in the future. They are summarised in Table 7.4. The WES approach reveals a number of decisive factors of competitiveness. Typical for the WES approach is the attention paid to macro-economic factors. Application of multiple regression analysis shows the impact of the income factor in the generating markets and the real exchange rate.

The Price Competitiveness Approach

The preceding sections may give the impression that price is an irrelevant factor with respect to competitiveness. Most models neglect or minimise factor price. Price elasticity cannot be overlooked. This is also the idea of Dwyer et al. (2000) where they state, 'changing costs in particular destinations relative to others, adjusted for exchange rate variations, are regarded as the most important economic influence on destination shares of total travel abroad'. Also Edwards (1995) underlines the role of factor price when he maintains that a fall in relative cost is linked to a rise in market share. Dwyer et al. define destination competitiveness as: 'a general concept that encompasses price differentials coupled with exchange rate movements, productivity levels of various components of the tourist industry and qualitative factors affecting the attractiveness or other wise of destination'. Consequently, these authors consider besides price two other groups of factors: (a) socio-economic and demographic factors and (b) qualitative factors. The latter category comprises variables, such as tourist appeal, image, quality of tourist services, destination marketing and promotion, cultural ties, etc. Price factors or the cost of tourism to the visitor includes the cost of transport services to and from the destination and the cost of ground content.

The Bordas Model

The Bordas model was for the first time presented at the AIEST (1993) congress in Argentina and further developed at the TRC meeting in Swansea (1994). It is a typical demand (marketing) model and does not fit into the general concept of competitiveness. Furthermore, this model has been conceived for long haul destinations. In this marketing model for the long haul destinations there are two key elements. The first one is the 'perceived value' of the destination where the image is the central point. The authentic benefits should be well known. Potential tourists have an image of the destination. Very often the image has been created independently of any tourism activity. In the case of a bad image, it is difficult to change it. Tourism promotion will in most cases not be successful in changing an existing image. Only an improvement of the supply side and the creation of new and/or upgraded products can be helpful. The second element is the 'perceived cost'. The latter has several facets: the economic costs, the physical efforts, the psychological costs and the difficulties to have access to information and what Bordas calls the sales system. The farther away from home the more the uncertainty about travel and living costs, the higher the physical cost of travel (waiting time in airports, stress, jet-lag, immobility in the aircraft, etc.) and the growing importance of psychological cost (hygiene, health care and risks of all kinds). A lot can be done to reduce those costs and to enhance the competitiveness of the destination. There are three important drawbacks to this model. Firstly, it is a one-sided model or only demand oriented. Secondly, the model is still a gross concept without any test. Thirdly, some variables are difficult to measure. Nevertheless, the model underlines a number of factors neglected or underestimated in other approaches.

Ritchie and Crouch's Conceptual Model of Destination Competitiveness

The most comprehensive model is without any discussion the Ritchie–Crouch model. During the past 10 years, the concept has been improved and elaborated and has led to the publication of an interesting handbook 'The Competitive Destination' by Ritchie and Crouch (2003). The cornerstone of the publication is the conceptual model of destination competitiveness. It is a device that provides a useful way of thinking about a complex issue. Their starting point of the model is the thesis that destination success is determined by two different kinds of advantages: *comparative advantages* and *competitive advantages*. The first kind reflects the resource endowments of the destination, provided either by nature or by the overall society within which the destination resides. Competitive advantages are those that have been established as a result of effective resource deployment (maintenance, growth and development, efficiency, effectiveness and audit). In other words, how well does the destination utilise the available resources or what is the destination's ability to add value to the available resources. But for the authors comparative advantage and competitive advantage are generic concepts. Greater depth is necessary. What do these concepts mean in the context of a tourist destination? To be managerially useful, they further examined the categories or components that constitute resource endowments and resource deployments in order to understand how these constructs are best made operational to determine destination competitiveness. The components of the model are:

- the global (macro) environment;
- the competitive (micro) environment;
- core resources and attractors;
- supporting factors and resources;
- destination policy, planning and development (DPPD);
- Destination Management (DM); and
- qualifying and amplifying determinants.

We consider DPPD and DM as the two core components. The authors also draw particular attention to these two categories. *The global (macro) environment* recognises that tourism is an open system. It is subject to many influences and pressures that arise outside the system itself. All these forces create threats and opportunities. A destination manager should be aware of these challenges and opportunities and possibly, together with the industry, formulate the right policy.

The competitive (micro) environment is part of the tourism system; it concerns the actions and activities of entities in the tourism system that affects the goals of each member of the system (companies and organisations). The '*core resources and attractors*' component of the model describes the essence of destination appeal or the pulling force. It is these factors that are the key motivators to visit a destination. Ritchie and Crouch distinguish seven categories: physiography and climate (e.g. scenery, wildlife, beach); culture and history; a broad range of activities; special events; types of entertainment; superstructure (e.g. cathedral of La Sagrada Familia in Barcelona); and market ties (e.g. religion, ethnic roots).

Most of these attractors speak for themselves. Nevertheless, the local DM organisation can do a lot to enhance the attractiveness of each of these categories and so increase the competitiveness of the destination. Indeed competitive advantage relates to a destination's ability to use the attractions effectively over the long term. A further component in the model is *the supporting factors and resources*. They support or provide a foundation upon which a successful tourism industry can be established. This category contains elements (e.g. infrastructure, accessibility, hospitality) that enhance the destination appeal. Their absence or insufficiency will be a constraint for the destination to pull tourists. The *qualifying and amplifying determinants* are described as factors of competitiveness that either moderate, modify, mitigate and filter or strengthen, enhance and augment the impact of all other factors, DPPD and DM included. They are situational conditioners on which a destination has no or little influence (e.g. location, destination safety, destination cost level and destination image). But destinations with an eye on these conditioners will be more likely to act proactively; they can foresee opportunities and threats. The DPPD and DM are the other two categories of the model. In the framework of resource deployment and modern management of a region or destination they might be considered as the key categories.

What do the authors have in mind when they talk about DPPD and DM? 'DPPD is essentially an intellectual process that uses information, judgement and monitoring to make macro-level decisions regarding the kind of destination that is desirable, the degree to which ongoing performance and related changes in the nature of visitation and the physical character of the destination are contributing to the achievement of the kind of destination that stakeholders want .... DM is more a micro-level activity in which all the stakeholders carry out their individual and organisational responsibilities on a daily basis in efforts to realise the macro-level vision contained in policy, planning and development'. Indeed a highly competitive destination does not exist by chance. It requires a well-planned environment within which the appropriate forms of tourism development are encouraged and facilitated. Tourism policy is the key to providing this environment. Strategic planning is the cornerstone of DPPD (see also Morrison, 1989). The DPPD component creates the framework for a competitive destination. The DM component of the Ritchie–Crouch model focuses on those activities that implement the tasks prescribed by the DPPD. As such, it seeks to enhance the appeal of the core resources, strengthens the quality and effectiveness of the supplying factors and resources and adapts best to the constraints or opportunities imposed or presented by the qualifying and amplifying determinants.

Meanwhile Dwyer and Kim (2004) have developed a new model — 'Integrated model of destination competitiveness', which contains many of the variables identified by Crouch and Ritchie. At the moment of ending this chapter, the publication was not yet available. We can find the basic ideas in a contribution of Dwyer, Kim, Livaic, and Mellor (2004) with an application of the model to Australia and Korea. The key elements of their model are:

- core resources and supporting factors; the core resources are subdivided into two categories: endowed and created; supporting factors relate to general infrastructure, quality of service, accessibility, etc.;
- DM factors (public sector and private sector activities);
- demand conditions; the three main elements are awareness, perception and preferences;
- situational conditions (economic, social, cultural, political, legal, etc.; cfr qualifying and amplifying determinants of Ritchie and Crouch).

Table 7.5: The major competition variables by model

Variable/characteristic	Porters 1 and 2 1980	Porters 1 and 2 1990	Poon	WES	Dwyer	Bordas	Ritchie/Crouch
Comparative advantage	−	+	+	+	−	−	++
Macro-economic factors	−	−	−	++	+	−	+
Exchange rate	−	−	−	++	++	−	−
Axis of development	+	−	++	−	−	−	+
Tourism policy	−	+	+	++	−	−	++
Strategic planning	++	++	+	+	−	−	++
Strategic alliance	−	+	++	−	−	−	+
Demand factors	−	++	−	++	−	++	+
Marketing	−	+	+	+	−	++	+
Image	−	−	−	−		++	++
Promotion	−	−	−	+	−	+	+
Supply factors	−	++	−	++	−	−	++
Attractions	−	+	−	+	−	−	++
Innovation	−	++	++	−	−	−	+
Human resources	−	+	++	+	−	−	++
Price	++	+	−	++	++	++	+
Accessibility	−	+	++	++	−	−	++
Quality	−	++	++	+	+	−	+
Supplying and supporting factors	−	++	+	−	−	−	++
Supplying and supporting factors	−	++	+	−	−	−	++
Environment	−	−	++	−	−	−	++
Destination management	−	+	−	+	−	−	++
Qualifying and amplifying fact	−	−	−	−	−	−	++
Audit	−	−	−	−	−	−	+
Entrepreneur-oriented	++	−	++	−	−	−	−
Destination-oriented	−	++	++	++	−	++	++

+, important; ++, very important.

In order to cope with this oversimplification, we summarise the major competition variables and characteristics in a comparative table (Table 7.5). Very important variables are shown with a double ++; important factors have one + sign. The valuation is based on a personal interpretation of the different models.

Conclusions and Implications

Needless to say the analysed competition models are of a different nature. The starting point and/or the line of approach is not the same. But each of them has the merit of emphasising one or more particular aspects: Porter (1980) is focussing on the competitive forces of enterprises, to a lesser extent of destinations, and the related generic competitive strategies. Tourism enterprises and destinations are faced with a strong competition. The second Porter model emphasises the home environment and related determinants. It is very useful to detect strengths and weaknesses of tourism destinations. The Bruges case is a good illustration. Poon pays a lot of attention to innovation, quality and making tourism a lead industry. The WES model is influenced by the application area (Caribbean region); this model shows how important macro-economic factors and tourism policy are to make a destination competitive. The Dwyer approach is the only one, which gives a great attention to the price component. The Bordas model is marketing oriented and is focussing on perceived value and perceived costs. Ritchie and Crouch bring the most comprehensive model; central points are destination policy, planning and development and DM.

From this general overview three important final conclusions can be derived. Firstly, competitiveness of a destination is not a matter of one or two factors. Tourism is a complex issue and many factors are involved. This conclusion should not be considered as a criticism of the Dwyer et al. approach. These authors have tried to show the great price discrepancy between destinations and how to measure the differences in tourism purchasing power. They also recognise the role of productivity levels of various components of the tourism industry and qualitative factors affecting the attractiveness of a destination. Secondly, the Ritchie–Crouch concept is by far the most comprehensive model. But also the Porter diamond and WES model contain a great variety of components. Poon's concept is also based on a large number of factors but focuses more on typical factors, such as innovation, quality and the role of tourism in the development of a destination, region or country. Thirdly, The Ritchie–Crouch, the Porter and WES models have one common denominator. All three emphasise strategic planning (tourism policy), attractions, supply and demand factors and accessibility. To a certain extent there is a great complementary between the different models. The choice between them is to large extent influenced by the kind of research topics and tourism policy applications.

References

AIEST. (1993). *Competitiveness of long haul tourist destinations*, 43rd AIEST Congress, Bariloche.

Bordas, E. (1994). Competitiveness of tourist destinations in long distance markets. Paper presented at TRC meeting, Swansea.

Bosselman, F., Peterson, C., & McCarthy, Cl. (1999). *Managing tourism growth*. Washington: Island Press.

Dwyer, L., Forsyth, P., & Rao, P. (2000). The price competitiveness of travel and tourism: A comparison of 19 destinations. *Tourism Management*, 21, 9–22.

Dwyer, L. and Kim, C. (2004). Destination Competitiveness: Determinants and Indicators; Current Issues in Tourism.

Dwyer, L., Kim, C., Livaic, Z., & Mellor, R. (2004). Application of a model of destination competitiveness to Australia and Korea. In: S Weber, & R Tomljenovic (Eds), *Reinventing a tourism destination*. Zagreb, Scientific Edition Institute for Tourism.

Edwards, A. (1995). *Asia-pacific travel forecasts to 2005*, Research report, EIU, London.

Goeldner, R., Ritchie, J., & McIntosh, R. (2000). *Tourism. Principles, practices, philosophies* (8th ed.). New York: Wiley.

Michael, E. (2003). Tourism micro-clusters. *Tourism Economics*, 2(9), 133–145.

Morrison, A.M. (1989). *Hospitality and travel marketing*. New York: Delmar Publishers Inc.

Poon, A. (1993). *Tourism, technology and competitive strategies*. Wallingford: C.A.B International.

Porter, M. (1980). *The competitive strategy: Techniques for analysing industries and competitors*. New York: The Free Press.

Porter, M. (1987). From competitive advantage to corporate strategy. *Harvard Business Review*, (1), 43–60.

Porter, M. (1990). *The competitive advantage of nations*. London: The Macmillan Press.

Porter, M. (1998). Clusters and the new economics of competition. *Harvard Business Review*, (Nov–Dec), 77–90.

Ritchie, J.R.B., & Crouch, G. (2000). The competitive destination: A sustainability perspective. *Tourism Management*, 21, 1–8.

Ritchie, J.R.B., & Crouch, G. (2002). Country and city state destinations. *Tedqual*, (1), 13–15.

Ritchie, J.R.B., & Crouch, G. (2003). *The competitive destination. A sustainable tourism perspective*. Wallingford: CABI Publishing.

Smeral, E. (1996). *Globalisation and changes in the competitiveness of tourism destinations, in globalisation and tourism*, 46th AIEST Congress, Rotorua.

Vanhove, N. (2002). Tourism policy between competitiveness and sustainability: The case of Bruges. *The Tourism Review*, 3, 34–40.

Vanhove, N. (2005). *The economics of tourism destinations*. Oxford: Elsevier-Butterworth-Heinemann (see chapter 5: Competition and the tourism destination).

WES. (1994). *The competitive situation of tourism in the Caribbean area and its importance for the region's development*. Washington/Brugge, unpublished report.

WTO, An Integrated Approach to Resort Development, Madrid, 1992.

Chapter 8

Media Strategies for Improving National Images during Tourism Crises

Eli Avraham and Eran Ketter

Introduction

In recent years, a growing number of tourist destinations has been facing image crises. Living in the ever-changing world of the 21st century, facing crises has become an everyday problem for many countries. Popular tourist destinations such as New York, London and Madrid have suffered from terrorist attacks, the tsunami tidal wave swept the beaches of Thailand, India and Sri Lanka and the epidemics of SARS and foot-and-mouth disease had a severe effect on tourism in the UK, China and Canada. According to Kash and Darling (1998, cited in Ritchie, 2004), facing a crisis is no longer a question of "if" a country will face a crisis, but a question of "when", "what type", and "how prepared" it will be. In the age of the World Wide Web, satellites, global TV networks and global economy, crises such as those mentioned above are widely covered in the international media and overnight can empty out hotels, cancel flights and leave tourist attractions deserted. In addition, due to the globalization process, a crisis in tourism in one country affects other countries, such as the effect of the 9/11 terrorist attack on worldwide tourism. On the other hand, in contrast to sudden unexpected crises, countries such as those of Africa, the former communist countries of Eastern Europe, Middle Eastern countries and many more, can gradually develop a negative image as the cumulative result of a problematic past.

In both these cases, the gradual negative image and the sudden downturn in image resulting from a particular crisis, an unfavorable image is projected in the media and has a correspondingly negative effect on the international tourism industry and on a country's economics, investments and commerce. Whatever the cause of the negative image, many destinations suffer from being identified as frightening, dangerous, boring or gloomy; places a tourist would have no interest in visiting. Many decision makers in the international tourism industry stand by helplessly, frustrated by their knowledge that in most cases, the negative image is not based on well-grounded facts. Given that stereotypes are not easily changed or dismissed, the challenge facing these decision makers is great. Analyses of many tourist crises, however, show that numerous countries throughout the world have managed to change a negative image into a positive one, thus bringing tourists back to visit. To achieve this worthwhile goal, a number of communications strategies were used. This article proposes to analyze public relations, advertising and promotion strategies in order to present those most successful in altering an unflattering public image.

Literature Review

"Place promotion" has many different definitions in literature; a summary of most of them can be found in Short, Breitbach, Buckman, and Essex (2000), who declare that "Place promotion involves the re-evaluation and re-presentation of place to create and market a new image for localities to enhance their competitive position in attracting or retaining resources" (p. 318). This definition emphasizes the re-presentation of a place in order to create and market a new image geared to compete over the retaining and attracting of various resources. Nielsen's (2001) definition of place promotion is similar, but he stresses the difficulty of achieving the task, especially when dealing with an image-related crisis: "Promoting a destination in normal circumstances is a difficult task, but promoting a destination that faces tourism challenges — whether from negative press, or from infrastructure damage caused by natural disasters or man-made disasters — is an altogether more arduous task" (pp. 207, 208). Place marketing attempts to improve the images and public perceptions of places. Kotler, Haider, and Rein (1993) define the image of a place as "the sum of beliefs, ideals, and impressions people have toward a certain place". They argue that an image represents a simplification of a large number of associations and pieces of information related to a certain place, and is a cognitive product of the attempt to process large amounts of information.

Country Image

A country's image is composed of many components including its location, leadership, kind of regime, economic situation, government stability and more. Although the design of an image seems very dynamic, it is actually based on a stereotype. We think of a country in a stereotypical manner, and that is why these images are so hard to change (Elizur, 1986). Many countries internalize the importance of their image, and invest much time and effort in order to improve it. Four major techniques are commonly used in this effort: advertising, public relations, direct mailing/marketing and sales promotion. Public relations are used in order to influence the way the destination is represented in the various media. Destination spokespeople or public relations advisors try to create a favorable image through the promotion of special events and positive stories, and at the same time attempt to prevent the publication of any unfavorable stories, especially during crises. The use of the advertising technique is the most popular tool for marketing destinations, and is based on purchasing advertisements in the international media and delivering messages to target populations (Avraham, 2003, 2005).

In recent years, there has been a rise in the use of the phrase "branding", along with an increase in the use of PR and advertising. There are many definitions for branding; a concluding one might be: "Compared to products and services branding, country branding is the [continuous and strategic] process whereby a country actively seeks to create a unique and competitive identity for itself, with the aim of positioning the country internally and internationally as a good destination for trade, tourism and investments" (Nworah, 2005). In the academic literature, one can find an analysis of many case studies of countries and tourist destinations that tried to re-brand themselves (e.g., see Morgan, Pritchard, & Pride, 2002; Pink, 1999).

Dealing with Tourism Crises

When dealing with an image crisis, Parsons (1996, cited in Ritchie, 2004) suggests a method to distinguish among three types of crises: (1) immediate crises, where little or no warning exists, as in the case of the tsunami tidal wave in South East Asia; (2) emerging crises, which develop slowly, and may be stopped or limited, as in the outbreak of the foot-and-mouth disease epidemic; (3) sustained crises that may last for weeks, months or even years, such as the ongoing conflict in the Middle East. In any of the three types of crisis listed, the media takes a significant role in handling the situation.

Recovering from any kind of crisis takes much more than just crisis communications: the country has to take positive actions in order to change reality, or the new image will be labeled as a fake or fraud. It is important to distinguish between attempts to change a destination's image while changing its actual reality (Beriatos & Gospodini, 2004), and attempting to alter an image without making any concrete changes. In the case of Jamaica, for example, the country tried to recover from its negative image by launching a campaign stressing safety and friendliness. The expensive campaign instead actually caused damage, when many unsatisfied tourists went back home and told their friends about the unpleasant experiences they had on their Jamaican visit (Kotler et al., 1993). Another important aspect of changing reality has to do with the ongoing improvement in the infrastructure, services and tourist attractions. Although making a deep and meaningful change in the reality is vital, this article will focus on communication strategies that can be used in order to improve a country's image and not with strategies to improve the actual reality. An effective way to deal with an actual tourism crisis can be found in the professional literature (see e.g., Faulkner, 2001; Ritchie, 2004; Blake & Sinclair, 2003).

Ten Strategies for Improving the Image of a Country Facing a Tourism Crisis

1. The "We Have No Crisis" Approach. When a country is facing an image crisis, one of the easiest things it can do is to actually do nothing, and pretend as if nothing has happened (Avraham, 2005). In other words, some destinations choose to ignore the damage to their image after negative events and act as though there never was a crisis, in the hopes that new events, and the passing of time, will cause tourists to forget about the crisis. Spain, for example, chose to employ a "business as usual" approach following a period of terrorist attacks in several cities (Efrati, 2002). In the tourism advertisements for these cities no mention was made of these events in any way. In Turkey, a similar policy was adopted after the several terrorist attacks in 2003–2005.

In any event, it is not always possible to ignore a crisis when the media demands explanations or reaction. In that case, there is a tendency to diminish the magnitude of the negative events, that caused the crisis. For example, after a terrorist attack in Djerbe, a Tunisian official said: "There is no terrorism in Tunisia! Why do you always focus on that?" He added that only one synagogue was attacked and that "it is not the end of the world" (The Media Line, 2004, p. 2). This was also the case after the suicide bomber attack in Cairo, Egypt. Officials tried to convince the media that the terrorist acted alone and was not part of a new terror network (*Ha'aretz*, 10.4.2005). In these last two cases, officials were trying to promote the idea that the events were rare occurrences and that the chance that similar negative events would occur was very small.

2. Employing a Counter-Message. Another strategy for handling an image crisis is to produce a counter-message, which focuses on information that is contrary to that which led to the crisis. Launching a counter-message in order to fight a negative image and preserve a positive one is also known as a "counter-messages offensive" (Kotler et al., 1993). Two main methods are used to accomplish this strategy. The first includes specific references in public relations and advertising campaigns to the source of the negative components of the image; the second attempts to reposition the destination.

When the first possibility is employed, counter-messages are sent which are geared toward changing the negative components of the image so that the destination is no longer perceived as unsafe, unstable or dangerous. If a destination is perceived as unsafe, advertisements can be used in which visitors say how much they enjoyed their visit and how safe they felt. Similarly, a country, which has suffered from terrorist attacks that were covered in the international media in the context of number of victims, blood and chaos, etc., can create a campaign, that is totally different from these images.

For example, after a terrorist attack in 2002 in which 20 people were killed, Tunisia's tourism office adopted an ad campaign aiming to inspire "peace and tranquility" in visitors (The Media Line, 2004). Tunisia did not use this strategy very long, but many other countries such as Syria, Israel, Northern Ireland, among others tried to promote the fact that they are safe for tourists. The "counter-message offensive" strategy has also been used for other issues beyond security. When a highly publicized health problem among British tourists to the Dominican Republic created a crisis in 1997, part of the recovery strategy was to show through statistics that less than 1% of the 2 million British tourists in the past year had fallen ill. This fact emphasized the hundreds of thousands of people who had traveled safely to this country (World Tourism Organization, 2005).

Although India is perceived as a major tourist destination, only a small number of American tourists arrive each year. For most Americans, India is associated with epidemics, floods and poverty. In the spring of 2001, the Indian Tourist Bureau launched a campaign aimed at creating a counter-message image. In the campaign, India is presented as a peaceful, beautiful and spiritual place. Repositioning India as counter to the common stereotype is an efficient way to change the negative image of the country (*Ha'aretz*, 29.6.2001).

In the summer of 2003, the German Culture Bureau composed a campaign aimed at the European market, delivering a counter-message image. Trying to recover from the image of the German people as humorless workaholics, as well as from the Nazi stigma of World War II, the new campaign emphasized contemporary life in Germany. The advertising campaign showed a refreshing image of the country, complete with love parades, short workdays and long vacations, featuring the supermodel Claudia Schiffer, the soccer player Yorn Kleinsman and the world famous tennis player Boris Baker (*Ha'aretz*, 11.7.2003).

3. Acknowledging the Negative Image. At times, acknowledging the negative image directly is the most effective — even if not the most convenient — course of action. This strategy may come in use during a crisis, or immediately after it has passed, in order to maintain or regain a trustworthy image. After the crisis is over, an advertisement may be placed presenting the message that the place, although it may have previously been unsafe, boring or lacking in tourism services, has been improved and is now a great place to visit (Burgess, 1982). Such a slogan acknowledges the difficult past and thus creates a feeling of trust between the advertisers and the external audience.

This strategy also includes the initiative employed by some countries to acknowledge that a problem exists in a specific region, and to frankly advise tourists not to go there. A prime example is the approach taken by the London Tourist Board during England's much-publicized outbreak of foot-and-mouth disease, which emphasized that the problem was only in rural areas (Hopper, 2003; Frisby, 2002). Similar approaches have been used by Israel, Nepal and the Philippines (Beirman, 2002; Baral, Baral, & Morgan, 2004). In the case of Nepal, the Nepal Tourism Board proclaimed that much of the violence took place in remote, rural areas, while top tourist destinations were secure and free of violent incidents. In addition, it emphasized that tourists had never been targeted by the rebels and that the media created a misconception (Highlander, 2005). In addition, there are countries that admit they are not familiar to tourists or that they have a distorted image. Lichtenstein, for example, hired a London-based advertising firm in order to promote its image and to show that the country was not only a place for questionable business deals but also for tourism as well (*Ha'aretz*, 18.8.2004).

4. Geographic Isolation Strategy. When a destination is identified within a country or a geographical region that is suffering from a negative image, a good strategy to use might be that of geographical isolation. Distancing itself from the problematic region with which it is identified can help a country to reverse its negative image and produce a positive image. In his analysis of safety and security issues, Santana (2003) notes that "as far as tourism is concerned, security issues (real or perceptive) always have a spillover effect. That is, tourists tend to associate a security incident with an entire region" (p. 305).

This strategy, which has been called "destination-specific" (Pizam & Mansfeld, 1996) or "isolation strategy" (Beirman, 2002), is recommended when promoting destinations located in countries suffering from ongoing image crises. Beirman (2002) added another example when he mentioned that Jordan aimed "to differentiate destination Jordan from destination Israel" (p. 174), after the start of the latest outbreak of conflict between Israel and the Palestinians at the end of 2000. Another example for the use of the geographic isolation strategy is in the case of Nova Scotia, Canada. A survey of the U.S. travel market in

1985 found that most of the Americans who had been surveyed had no intention of visiting Canada. In response, the province of Nova Scotia launched a creative campaign, presenting it as a freestanding entity. The result of this surprising campaign was a 90% increase in U.S. visitors to Nova Scotia (Kotler et al., 1993).

5. Spinning Liabilities into Assets. This strategy takes the key point of a previous strategy — acknowledging the negative image — a step further, by acknowledging a negative factor responsible for the image and spinning it into a positive trait. For example, Lapland, a geographical region in Scandinavia, was known for many years as being extremely cold, a fact that damaged the destination's image and kept people away. Today, however, these cold winters are marketed as unique and have become a tourist attraction, with various winter cultural events and festivals catering to many, under the slogan: "Vitality from Nature".

Haiti has a prolonged negative image, associated with poverty, violence and voodoo. In an effort to transform these liabilities into assets, Haiti launched a tourism campaign using the slogan: "Haiti, it's Spellbinding". With this slogan, Haiti was trying to take the negative image of voodoo witchcraft and turn it into a positive, mysterious and mystical image (Kotler et al., 1993). Similar to Haiti, Romania was also struggling with a negative image. Known as the homeland of the mythical vampire, Count Dracula, Romania has been associated with horror stories, blood and darkness. In 1995, the Romanian Tourism Office launched the first international Dracula congress, trying to turn the mythical vampire into a glamorous top-selling attraction (Kotler, Asplund, Rein, & Haider, 1999).

Another use for the spinning liabilities into assets strategy is in the case where a country has a weak or poor image. Images like these can be transformed into assets. For example, the U.S. state of Georgia used to have a weak image as an undeveloped region which attracted only a very few tourists. In a campaign launched in the 1970s, Georgia tried to turn this weak image into a wild and exotic one, using the slogan "Georgia, the Unspoiled" (Canfield & Moore, 1973). Another example of this strategy is the case of South Korea, which had little tourism and a weak image for many years. In a new campaign, the marketers of South Korea tried to spin this liability into assets, by referring to itself as "South Korea — Asia's Best Kept Secret". For many years, Indonesia had suffered from a negative image, being an area of many violent interracial conflicts. Having such a well-defined image, the marketers of Indonesia decided to turn the multi-cultural diversity of the country into an asset, with the slogan, "Indonesia — Endless Beauty of Diversity". In all these examples, those characteristics seen as responsible for the negative image are presented with a new twist, so as to turn them from liabilities into assets.

6. Changing a Destination's Name, Logo or Slogan. When one thinks of a country, the first elements that usually come to mind are its name, logo or slogan. Being aware of the primary effect that these elements have, some place marketers believe that in order to change a destination's image, one should first change its name, logo or slogan. Some destinations have names that are beneficial to marketing, whereas others have names associated with negative stereotypes and perceptions that harm their attractiveness. There are cases in which a destination's image is so unfavorable that the local authorities have given up any hope of rectifying the situation. Some of these places simply change their names in the hope that the negative image associated with the old name will disappear along with it (Avraham, 2005). An interesting example is that of the U.S. state of North Dakota, which has begun taking measures to rid itself of the prefix "North" and be known simply as "Dakota", since the term "North" leads to perceptions of the state as cold, isolated and unattractive (Singer, 2002).

Along with names, the destinations' symbols and logos, components of marketing campaigns, are also important. Thus, a destination in transition may also need to change its symbols. For example, a Polish marketing agency recently suggested making a kite the new national logo, in order to promote tourism and to improve the nation's general image. According to the agency, kites symbolize a plethora of positive attributes, including freedom, youth, love of life and hope. The idea is that associating Poland with these concepts via the logo will help to undo the stereotype of Poland as gray, boring, cold, conservative and poor (Boxer, 2002). Spain has rebranded itself — in part by using Joan Miro's bright and lively "Espana" painting as a national logo and as a symbol of the nation's post-Franco optimism (Pink, 1999).

Like logos, slogans are effective methods of delivering messages. One of the classic slogans used to foster fondness for a place is the well-known "I ❤ New York". A good slogan may be used for many years and through several different campaigns; it can lay out a destination's vision, reflect its spirit and create enthusiasm and momentum. Formulating a slogan depends on the target population and on the goals of the campaign, but the slogan must also be at least somewhat congruent with reality (Kotler et al., 1993). A destination undergoing a change could replace its slogan, emphasizing this together with its new look, as in the case of Malaysia, whose new slogan includes "Malaysia, Truly Asia", or Thailand with "Amazing Thailand".

7. Hosting Public Opinion Leaders. Common knowledge among place marketers is that once a place image is made, it is very difficult to change. For countries that have suffered from a problematic past, this common knowledge soon becomes a common problem. Some of those destinations have probably discovered that even if a positive change in reality occurs, unfavorable opinion persists (Strauss, 1961). In the public's mind, unfavorable stereotypes are firmly established, and it is very difficult to overcome them. No matter how much effort is made to change reality, if the negative stereotypes keep the crowds away, no one will see the changes. In such cases, the best course of action is to stage events designed to bring in visitors who otherwise would not come. This can be accomplished by holding conferences, exhibitions, tours and press conferences, among other special events. The main advantage of visiting a destination is that the image holder has a chance to personally experience the objective reality within the destination, without being dependent on mediators or secondary agents. When this happens in destinations associated with negative stereotypes, it may become clear to visitors that these stereotypes are false.

In addition to bringing visitors, destinations need to convince decision makers and public opinion leaders to come to the destination and "see it with their own eyes". Germany, after World War II, hosted many public opinion leaders from all over the world in order to show them the "new Germany". For many years, Israel annually hosted at least 2000 public opinion leaders such as academics, clergies, journalists, politicians and community leaders in order to show them that the country — its sights and people — are very different from those seen through the media coverage. The same tactics were used by India, which hosted many journalists from all over the world after the outbreak of epidemics and showed them that the crises were over, and also by Nepal after the political unrest, that threatened to put a halt to the tourists' flow (Baral et al., 2004). All of these countries believe that their public opinion leaders will spread the fact that a crisis is over — to students, the religious community, the media audience — and that it is safe to visit.

8. Hosting Spotlight Events. During 2005, some of the most popular tourist destinations competed to host the 2012 Olympic Games: New York, Paris, London, Moscow and Madrid. Although these cities did not suffer from severe image crises, all of them believed that hosting the games would contribute a great deal to the city's future and image. At least two of these cities hoped to gain some benefits related to the crises they had undergone. New York hoped that hosting the games would help the city to recover from the events of the September 11th, and Paris hoped to reshape the city with the new infrastructures needed for the games.

One of the most famous examples of using spotlight events (often referred to as "hallmark" or "mega" events) to improve a place image was the Nazis' use of the 1936 Olympic Games to project a positive image of their regime (Nielsen, 2001). Since then, many places have used the Summer and Winter Olympics, the World Expo, the Cultural Capital of Europe title, the Eurovision song competition and, in the U.S., the Republican and Democratic national conventions, as major platforms for massive public relations-led image campaigns (Beriatos & Gospodini, 2004). These events focus attention on a particular location for a short, concentrated period, allowing the destination to promote certain chosen images to the international media, which could be used to improve a negative image.

This was the case when Beijing hosted the 1990 Asian Games and used media attention to improve China's image after the Tiananmen Square massacre (Hall & O'Sullivan, 1996). The aim of hosting these events was to create positive news to shift the international media attention from negative news about the country. In another example, Egypt tried to shift international attention from a series of terrorist attacks by hosting some special international events and promoting visits to its ancient archeological sites (Wahab, 1996). Similarly, Northern Ireland is trying to overcome its negative image created by IRA terror by promoting local music, dance, literature and theater festivals, (*Ha'aretz*, 30.6.1998; Witt & Moore, 1992, cited in Sonmez, Apostolopoulos, & Tarlow, 1999).

9. Ridicule the Stereotype. This strategy is aimed at presenting a negative stereotype of a country, taking it to an extreme and then breaking it down by showing how ridiculous it actually is. The joining of the countries of Eastern Europe to the European common market has evoked the fear of an inexpensive labor force coming into Western Europe. In France, a few local politicians who oppose the EU constitution expressed their fears by declaring that the "Polish plumber" will come to work in France and will take the place of local labor. In response, the tourist bureau of Poland launched a campaign aimed at attracting French tourists. In the campaign advertisement, there is a picture of a young, sexy and handsome Polish plumber, wearing simple overalls and holding plumbing tools, with views of Poland in the background. The slogan on the ad in French read: "I'm staying in Poland — come". On the next ad in the campaign, a beautiful young nurse is featured with the slogan: "Poland: I'm waiting for you". In the campaign, the stereotype being attributed to the Polish people is taken to an extreme, in an attempt to dispel it. This is part of Poland's long ongoing campaign to shed its communist, gloomy, dark, poor and cold image (Ha'aretz, 18.7.2005, 1.7.2005).

Another use for this strategy can be found in different circumstances as well, as in the case of Israel. Dealing with its negative image as an unsafe place, Israel's tourist representatives handed out condoms to American students who were considering coming to Israel for a visit. The condom wrappers were in the colors of the Israeli flag and carried the slogan: "Israel — It's still safe to come".

10. Changing the Campaign's Target Audience. A final strategy for handling an image crisis can be to address a specific target audience that would be less affected from the crisis. In some cases, the crisis is so severe that within the existing target audience there is virtually no chance of overcoming it, and the destination decision makers should find an alternative target audience. When these decision makers change their target audience or type of tourism, they begin to concentrate on a different market segment that is less affected by the issues raised in the negative coverage.

In the beginning of the new century, several countries in the Middle East employed this strategy (Avraham, 2005). In Israel, for example, as a result of the damage caused to general tourism by political issues, advertising campaigns began to concentrate on drawing religious tourists from the U.S. and Europe, with the assumption that tourists of this type would be less sensitive to security issues. Jews and Evangelical Christians became a prime target audience, while internal tourism was also encouraged at new levels. The new campaign attempted to use the potential tourists' religious identity to convince them to visit the Holy Land, using the slogan "Don't let your soul wait any longer. Come visit Israel" (Ha'aretz, 5.6.2003; The Media Line, 2004).

Another example of this strategy can be found in Syria, another country that suffered a tourism crisis after the terrorist events of September 11th. As a result of the crisis, Syria began a campaign based on the slogan "Syria, Land of Civilizations" in order to attract tourists from throughout the Arab world who no longer felt comfortable traveling in the West (Ha'aretz, 30.7.2002). Jordan and Lebanon took a similar approach, and began concentrating on regional tourism, attracting visitors from Gulf nations and neighboring countries (The Media Line, 2004).

Conclusions and Implications

This chapter analyzes ten communication strategies that are used by countries in order to improve their negative image and re-attract tourists, after having experienced an immediate or an ongoing crisis. It is now only natural for one to ask which strategy a country should choose when facing a crisis. The choice, obviously, is a matter of the circumstances. Countries that receive constant coverage in the international media concerning terrorism cannot ignore that fact and choose the "We have no crisis" strategy. Choosing the "Hosting public opinion leaders" strategy might be a disaster if the new image projected by the country is totally different from the reality encountered during their visit.

Handling an image crisis is a multi-dimensional mission, which involves much more than delivering a counter-message. When facing this kind of a mission, changing slogans and logos is insufficient; one needs to come up with a long-term process, which would deal with all the different aspects concerning crises, including cooperation with the Ministries of Foreign Affairs, Tourism and International Commerce. Despite the importance of a country's image, one should remember that making a meaningful change in reality itself is much more important than launching a campaign. If a country is being perceived as unsafe for tourists due to a high rate of crime, the best way to handle this image crisis is to significantly reduce the crime rate.

There is no doubt that the best way to handle an image crisis is to be ready for it. Decision makers in the tourism industry of every country should try to predict which kinds of crises they might have to face, and what preparations should be made to handle them. The international media has a major effect on a country's image during a time of crisis, and being familiar with crisis communications techniques would be advantageous. Being prepared to face a crisis can significantly reduce its negative and long-term effects on the country's image, and even help to create and maintain a positive image.

References

Avraham, E. (2003). Behind media marginality: *Coverage of social groups and places in the Israeli press.* Lanham, MD: Lexington Books.

Avraham, E. (2005). Public relations and advertising strategies for managing tourist destination image crises. In: Y. Mansfeld, & A. Pizam (Eds), *Tourism and security: A case approach* (pp. 233–249). London: Butterworth-Heinemann.

Baral, A., Baral, S., & Morgan, N. (2004). Marketing Nepal in an uncertain climate: Confronting perceptions of risk and insecurity. *Journal of Vacation Marketing*, 10, 186–192.

Beirman, D. (2002). Marketing of tourism destinations during a prolonged crisis: Israel and Middle East. *Journal of Vacation Marketing*, 8, 167–176.

Beriatos E., & Gospodini, A. (2004). "Glocalising" urban landscapes: Athens and the 2004 Olympics. *Cities*, 21, 187–202.

Blake, A., & Sinclair, M. T. (2003). Tourism crisis management: US responses to September 11. *Annals of Tourism Research*, 30(4), 812–832.

Boxer, S. (2002). New Poland, no joke. *New York Times*, 12th December.

Burgess, J. (1982). Selling places: Environmental images for the executive. *Regional Studies*, 16, 1–17.

Canfield, B. R., & Moore, H. F. (1973). *Public relations: Principles, cases and problems.* Homewood, IL: Richard D. Irwin, Inc.

Efrati, B. (2002). Not welcoming. *Kol Ha'ir,* (September 6) (in Hebrew).

Elizur, J. (1986). *National images.* Jerusalem: Hebrew University.

Faulkner, B. (2001). Towards a framework for tourism disaster management. *Tourism Management*, 22, 135–147.

Frisby, E. (2002). Communication in a crisis: The British tourist authority's responses to the foot-and-mouth outbreak and 11th September, 2001. *Journal of Vacation Marketing*, 9, 89–100.

Ha'aretz. (10.4.2005, 29.6.2001, 11.7.2003, 18.8.2004, 30.6.1998, 18.7.2005, 1.7.2005, 5.6.2003, 30.7.2002).

Hall, C. M., & O'Sullivan V. (1996). Tourism, political stability and violence. In: A. Pizam, & Y. Mansfeld (Eds), *Tourism, crime and international security issues*. Chichester, UK: Wiley.

Hopper, P. (2002). Marketing London in a difficult climate. *Journal of Vacation Marketing*, 9, 81–88.

Highlander. (2005). *Go to Nepal and enjoy its beauty* (June 22). Retrieved June 26, 2005, from http://www.highlandernepal.com/currentNews/common/view_news_details.php?id=342

Kotler, P., Asplund, C., Rein, I., & Haider, D.H. (1999). *Marketing places, Europe*. Edinburgh, UK: Financial Times, Prentice-Hall.

Kotler, P., Haider, D.H., & Rein, I. (1993). *Marketing places*. New York: Free Press.

Media Line, The. (2004). *Tourism in the face of terror* (June 14). Retrieved June 30, 2004, from http://themedialine.org/news/news_detail.asp?NewsID=5768

Morgan, N., Pritchard, A., & Pride, R. (Eds). (2002). *Destination branding: Creating the unique destination proposition*. Woburn, MA: Butterworth-Heinemann.

Nielsen, C. (2001). *Tourism and the media*. Melbourne: Hospitality Press.

Nworah, U. (2005). *Nigeria as a brand* (April 5). Retrieved April 25, 2005 from http://www.nigeriavillagesquare1.com/Articles/Nworah/2005/04/nigeria-as-brand.html

Pink, D. (1999). The brand called UK. *Fast Company*, 22, 172–175.

Pizam A., & Mansfeld Y. (Eds). (1996). *Tourism, crime and international security issues* (pp. 105–121). Chichester, UK: Wiley.

Ritchie, B. W. (2004). Chaos crisis and disasters: A strategic approach to crisis management in the tourism industry. *Tourism Management*, 25, 669–683.

Santana, G. (2003). Crisis management and tourism: Beyond the rhetoric. *Journal of Travel and Tourism*, 15, 299–321.

Short, J. R., Breitbach, S., Buckman, S., & Essex, J. (2000). From world cities to gateway cities. *City*, 4, 317–340.

Singer, M. (2002). True north. *The New Yorker*, February 18, 25, pp. 118–123.

Sonmez, S. F., Apostolopoulos, Y., & Tarlow, P. (1999). Tourism in crisis: Managing the effects of terrorism. *Journal of Travel Research*, 38, 13–18.

Strauss, A. L. (1961). *Image of the American city*. New York: The Free Press.

Wahab, S. (1996). Tourism and terrorism: Synthesis of the problem with emphasis on Egypt. In: A. Pizam, & Y. Mansfeld (Eds), *Tourism, crime and international security issues* (pp. 175–186). Chichester, UK: Wiley.

World Tourism Organization. (2005). *Crisis guidelines for tourism industry*. Retrieved July 20, 2005, from http://www.world-tourism.org

PART III:

MARKET SEGMENTATION

Introduction

Metin Kozak and Luisa Andreu

The strategy of market segmentation seeks to achieve competitive advantage by focusing on a specific type of customer segment and designing the existing products and services according to their values or socio-economic and socio-demographic characteristics. Those who expect the same benefits or are in the same category of consumption patterns are classified as one segment of the market. Having reviewed earlier studies in the literature, it is possible to suggest several categories of market segmentation strategies relating to the marketing of tourism products or destinations, e.g. by socio-economic and demographic characteristics such as nationality, age, income and occupation, by product-related characteristics such as types of activity, number of repeat visits and length of stay, by psychographic characteristics such as attitudes, interests and motivation, and by geographical characteristics such as day trippers, domestic and foreign tourists (Goodall, 1990; Heath & Wall, 1992). A facility or a destination might offer cheaper services to those with lower income levels in the off-season or attract only explorers for adventure tourism.

The socio-economic and socio-demographic profiles of tourism demand in the potential markets are a determinant for affecting the choice to vacation and its direction towards particular tourism products or destinations. The level of age, income, occupation, time, whom to travel with and personality play a significant role in determining the destination choice process (Um & Crompton, 1990). Visitors will be likely to choose destinations where any or all of these variables are better matched with what the destination offers. Heath and Wall (1992, p. 91) states that "market segmentation is based on the assumption that different market segments have different needs [and different sets of personality, expectations and wants], different levels of present and potential consumption, different levels of awareness of the product and are exposed to different communication channels". Thus, different marketing mix concepts should be devised for different market segments. As every facility or destination has a different product to attract customers from different markets, it is unlikely that all facilities or destinations are able to compete for all market segments. In this sense, the most important and competitive products should be developed in each segment.

The first chapter of this part on market segmentation explores Timothy's classification of visitors to historical settings according to their perception of the heritage presented (as World, National, Local or Personal), in segmenting visitors' expectations of on-site interpretation. The study, conducted at the Anne Frank House in Amsterdam, included 208 participants. The results indicate that visitors to heritage settings are not interested in an educational or cognitive experience alone, but also in its emotional dimension. Overall, three main expectations were identified: the visitors' wish for the interpretation to provide an emotional experience, provide information about WWII and allow an active learning process. As such, visitors' perceptions of the site as personal are linked to their expectation that the interpretation will generate emotional involvement. Additionally, perception of the site by all other dimensions is relevant to the expectation for an educational experience. These findings are of helpful to implement different marketing strategies according to how heritage is perceived by each segment.

As a result of the waning ability of traditional socio-demographic variables to explain the motivations of individuals in the area of tourism, a need has arisen to go into more detail and show their dependence upon another variable, lifestyle, hitherto neglected in this industry. The second chapter first demonstrates the relevance of segmenting the tourist market and then justifies the need to do it on the lifestyle basis. It then reviews current methodological trends. An application of analytic techniques indicates that motivations and tourist behaviour depend on the variables identified by one of the approaches: AIO (Activities, Interests and Opinions). An evidence of a very significant increase in the dependence of lifestyle tourist variables has been confirmed when homogeneous segments of the population are determined. This signals a need to segment the market using this criterion as well as to apply differentiated marketing strategies for each segment established on the basis of such variables.

As already mentioned earlier, choosing a tourist destination often involves dealing with various types of perceived risks. While investigating the perceived risk of travelers, several questions should be taken into consideration to come up with solid conclusions and implications at the end. For example, do tourists differ in their perceptions of risk associated with a particular destination? Can tourist characteristics be identified to distinguish between various risk perceptions as well as between various risk reduction strategies? Is the choice of a particular type of tour associated with specific types of risk? Does the country of origin matter in terms of perceived risk? In order to attempt to answer these questions, the next chapter attempts to examine the relationships between destination risk perceptions, risk reduction strategies, tourist characteristics and type of tour. First, the chapter clarifies the concept of tourist destination risk perception and elaborates through the notion of tourist as a consumer faced with a decision about intangible services. It then analyses the various dimensions of destination risk perceptions in relation to risk reduction strategies as well as tourist characteristics and the type of preferred tour. The findings may serve as a basis for establishing a thorough segmentation strategy that could be useful for dealing with effective destination marketing solutions.

Finally, segmented, either differential or discriminatory, pricing is a widely applied pricing strategy in the hospitality and tourism industry; however, in Turkey as elsewhere, there is an application of price differentiation that is contradictory to the requirements of sustainable tourism development. It is the purpose of the final chapter of this part to discuss the potential reasons of such a contradictory price differentiation and generate solutions to avoid the negative consequences. To this end, a few hotel managers experienced in the Turkish tourism industry were surveyed on this issue using an online research mode. The chapter presents potential outcomes of such a controversial pricing strategy as well as better coping strategies for different market segments, e.g. domestic tourists, foreign tourists, travel agencies. Generally speaking, the study findings confirm that there is price differentiation between domestic and foreign tourists in Turkey, which is in disadvantage to the former market segment.

References

Goodall, B. (1990). Opportunity sets as analytical marketing instruments: A destination area view. In: G. Ashworth, & B. Goodall (Eds), *Marketing tourism* (pp. 63–84). London: Routledge.

Heath, E., & Wall, G. (1992). *Marketing tourism destinations: A strategic planning approach*. Canada: Wiley.

Um, S., & Crompton, J.L. (1990). Attitude determinants in tourism destination choice. *Annals of Tourism Research*, *17*, 432–448.

Chapter 9

Using the Experientially based Approach to Segment Heritage Site Visitors

Avital Biran, Yaniv Poria and Arie Reichel

Introduction

Researchers and practitioners in the field of heritage tourism management widely rely on a supply-side perspective, emphasizing the tourist's presence at a site defined, by a governmental or some form of preservation organization, as a "heritage site" (Apostolakis, 2003). Using this approach overlooks the heterogeneous nature of visitors' perceptions of the heritage presented, and their expectations of the experience provided by on-site interpretation. While understanding visitors' preferences is a key element in designing the tourist experience, the current studies in the field of heritage management commonly ignore the consumer, i.e the visitor (Goulding, 1999). In contrast to the supply side perspective, and in line with the "experientially based" (Apostolakis, 2003, p. 799) approach to the understandings of visitors' behavior, it is argued that historic spaces are multifunctional goods serving diverse users, who behave in different ways (Ashworth, 2001). Based on this notion it is suggested that segmentation of visitors according to the experiential approach could be beneficial to the management of heritage tourism attractions, since it may be relevant to the understanding of tourists' behavior at historical settings.

In line with the experientially based approach, the current chapter attempts to provide an assessment of Timothy's model as a practical tool for differentiating between heritage site visitors. To do so two main research objectives were defined. First, to identify visitors' expectations of the interpretation provided at a heritage site and second, to search for possible links between visitors' perception of the site (according to Timothy's classification as World, National, Local or Personal heritage) and their expectations of the interpretation. It should be noted that Timothy's (1997) classification is theoretical in nature, and thus far has not yet been subject to empirical investigation. Understanding the nature of the relations between visitors' perceptions and their expectations of on-site interpretation may provide practical implications to the management of heritage settings, in addition to theoretical aspects for the research of heritage tourism.

Literature Review

The existing literature recognizes that visitors vary in their behavior at heritage settings (e.g. Dierking, 1998; Silberberg, 1995). Researchers and practitioners have attempted to provide a rationale that distinguishes between varying types of visitors at heritage sites. Swarbrooke (2002), for example, suggests that demographic and socio-demographic characteristics (e.g. age, gender, income) are among the most commonly used indicators by heritage site managers to differentiate between visitor types. However, socio-demographic characteristics do not provide insight into the needs, expectations and desired experiences of visitors (Prentice, 1995). Additional studies attempted to distinguish between visitor types based on the motivation for the visit. McCain and Ray (2003), for example, use motivation to differentiate legacy tourism from other special interest tourism, such as ecotourism. Moscardo (1996), differentiated between visitor types based on their need to be educated or entertained. Important to this study is Moscardo's suggestion that segmentation, by motivation for the visit, is helpful in understanding visitors' on-site behavior.

Other attempts at segmentation are in line with the experientially based approach, which highlights tourists' experience derived from the relationships between the visitor and the heritage presented. In this context, Poria, Butler, and Airey (2003, 2004) argued that the understanding of tourists' behavior should be based on their perception of the site in relation to their own personal heritage. In a series of studies, they indicate that different individuals display diverse behaviors according to their perception of the site as part of their own personal heritage (or not part of their own heritage). Similarly, Timothy (1997, also in Timothy & Boyd, 2003) suggests a classification of heritage tourists by their perception of the heritage presented as World, National, Local or Personal. Furthermore, Timothy indicates that visitors' experiences at a site, and the feelings it may evoke in them, differ according to their subjective perception of the site. Timothy (1997) considers four types of heritage sites, as indicated in Table 9.1. Timothy also argues for the existence of an 'overlapping', when the same site is perceived differently by different people.

The interpretation provided at a heritage site is a key element in a tourist's experience, linked to his/her satisfaction with the visit (Goulding, 1999; Moscardo, 1996). The literature assigns to the interpretation at heritage settings three main objectives (Timothy & Boyd, 2003). First, to educate and provide visitors with knowledge of the site. Second, to entertain. In the past entertainment was perceived as the opposite of education but is now recognized as facilitating learning (Light, 1995). Third, to increase awareness. Ultimately, the interpretation is designed to increase the visitor's awareness of the need to preserve the heritage presented. The definitions of the interpretation's goals provided by the literature raise two critical issues relevant to the current study.

First, as reflected in the literature, a great deal of attention, both by researches and practitioners, is devoted to the interpretation in heritage settings as an educational experience. Nevertheless, since a visit to a heritage site is not merely a cognitive experience, interpretation aimed only to educate provides visitors with only a partial understanding of the site (Uzzell & Ballantyne, 1998). Relevant to this research is Uzzell and Ballantyne's suggestion that sites hold personal values, beliefs and memories for the visitor (e.g. battlefields, memorials). These elements affect visitors' emotional reactions to the heritage presented and should be included in the interpretation provided.

Table 9.1: Timothy's classification of heritage sites.

World heritage sites	"may invoke feelings of awe", but "probably do not invoke a feeling of personal attachment" (p. 752)
National heritage sites	"may rouse strong feelings of patriotism ... and national pride" (p. 752)
Local heritage sites	"stir emotions and contribute to a local heritage experience" (p.753). This type of site is often a matter of local pride and prestige (Richards, 2001a, p. 11 in Timothy & Boyd, 2003)
Personal heritage sites	Where individuals "possess emotional connections to a particular place" (p. 753). Note: Timothy indicates that the emotional connection can be associated with specific interest groups to which the individual belongs (e.g. ethnic groups)

Source: Timothy (1997).

Second, by emphasizing the educational experience (e.g. Moscardo, 1996; Light, 1995) researchers and site managers perceive visitors as homogeneous in their preferences and expectations. There is very limited research that examines the link between the visitor and the heritage presented. Specifically lacking are studies that explore visitors' expectations of the interpretation at heritage sites (Prentice, 1993). Nevertheless, few studies provide evidence that different people are interested in different kinds of interpretation. Stewart, Hayward, Devlin, and Kirby (1998) distinguish four types of visitors based on the interpretive media they chose to use, and the type of information that interests them ('seekers, stumblers, shadowers and shunners'). Bruner (1996), who investigated visitors to Elmina Castle in Ghana, noticed that different visitors are interested in different aspects of the interpretation, according to the subjective meaning the site holds for them. For example, Dutch visitors prefer to hear about the period under Dutch rule and visit the Dutch cemetery, while British visitors are more interested in the colonial rule of the Gold Cost.

Currently heritage attractions provide visitors with the same interpretation, under the assumption that visitors are homogeneous in their needs. The use of segmentation in the context of interpretation design would allow heritage sites to provide visitors with an experience better suited to their expectations. The current research set out to clarify the possibility of using Timothy's (1997) model as a basis for segmenting heritage site visitors and as an indictor of their expectations of the interpretation provided. To summarize, this study has two main objectives. First, to explore visitors' expectations of the interpretation provided at a heritage site, and second, to search for a possible links between the individuals' perception of the site (as world, national, local or personal heritage) and their expectations of the interpretation.

Methodology

The site chosen for the focus of the current research was the Anne Frank House in Amsterdam. At this site Anne Frank, a German-Jewish teenager, hid from the Nazis during the Holocaust and wrote her diary about events surrounding her. Since its publication in 1947, Anne Frank's Diary has been translated into at least 67 languages, with over 31 million copies sold worldwide. On 1960, the 'Anne Frank House' opened its doors as a museum. The museum is now considered one of the most famous heritage sites in Amsterdam (In 2003, the site had more than 900,000 visitors from all over the world, Anne Frank Museum Official Web Site, 2003).

A quantitative research approach was adopted. The questionnaire designed for the study opened with a series of queries about visitors' perception of the site. Since Timothy's (1997) definitions of National, Local and Personal heritage are rather general, it was decided to adopt the following approach: First, tourists' perception of the heritage as personal was assessed through the use of a set of questions suggested by Poria et al. (2003, 2004). Second, to establish a clearer understating of the notions of 'Local' and 'National' in the context of the Anne Frank House, an exploratory study was conducted on site. The pilot study revealed that the term 'Local' is interpreted in different ways (e.g. Dutch heritage, the heritage of Amsterdam, Dutch-Jewish heritage). The term 'National' was also perceived differently as the heritage of the State of Israel, or European heritage or Jewish heritage. Based on these observations, eight types of heritage classifications were included in the final version of the questionnaire: (1) World heritage, (2) European, heritage, (3) Dutch heritage, (4) Jewish heritage, (5) Amsterdam heritage, (6) State of Israel heritage, (7) Dutch-Jewish heritage and (8) Personal heritage. Participants were given a six-interval scale, (0 — disagree, 5 — agree), to indicate their perception of the site (Schwarz & Hippler, 1995).

Questions about respondents' expectations concerning the interpretation provided were also included. Participants were asked to state their answers using the above 0–5 scale. This section was largely based on an exploratory study that included 40 short interviews with potential visitors conducted in Holland and Israel. In these interviews, participants were asked to give possible preferences and expectations of the interpretation, should they visit the Anne Frank House. Data were collected through face-to-face interviews by one of the authors. The questionnaire was completed using 'systematic sampling' (every Nth visitor was approached) while participants waited in line to enter the museum. The objective of this sampling strategy, (a theoretical sample), was to ensure diversity — which in turn enables generalization of the findings. The sample included only visitors above the age of 15 who were able to speak and understand English (Apter, Hatab, Tyano, & Weiziman, 1998). The feasibility study took place in December 2002. The main study took place between December 2002 and January 2003. In total, 208 interviews were conducted. Approximately 10% of the visitors approached chose not to participate, claiming to be unfamiliar with the English language.

Discussion of Findings

The entire sample was composed of 208 participants (57.8% female and 42.2% male). Of the sample, 153 were Christian (74.6%), 33 identified themselves as 'no affiliation' (16.1%), 7 were Jewish (3.4%) and 12 were from other religions (5.9%). The three most common places where participants spent most of their lives were the USA (24.5%), Britain

(19.2%) and the Netherlands (15.9%). Among those who gave their age group, the mode response was 20–29 (51.9%). Of the sample, 82.6% (n = 172) had not visited Anne Frank House before and 56.3% (n = 117) had read the Diary of Anne Frank.

Visitors' Perception of the Heritage

Visitors were asked to reply to six questions aimed at capturing their perception of the site in relation to their own personal heritage. The questions and the distribution of answers are presented in Table 9.2. As indicated in Table 9.2, most participants' answers were distributed between 0 and 3, categories 4 and 5 were relatively less chosen, except for the third statement. The disparate nature of responses indicates that participants differ in their perception of the site in relation to their own heritage. In addition, the value of the Cronbach's alpha statistic was relatively high (0.85), suggesting that the six questions used measure the same latent variable.

Table 9.2: Perception of the site in relation to visitors' personal heritage (N=208).

	Disagree (0)	**1**	**2**	**3**	**4**	**Agree (5)**
The site represents something which relates to your identity	27.5% (n=57)	16.4% (n=35)	23.2% (n=48)	20.3% (n=42)	7.2% (n=15)	5.3% (n=11)
The site represents something which is relevant to your present existence	20.7% (n=43)	15.4% (n=32)	17.3% (n=36)	20.7% (n=43)	18.8% (n=39)	7.2% (n=15)
The site has symbolic meaning for you	10.6% (n=22)	6.3% (n=13)	14.0% (n=29)	21.3% (n=44)	27.5% (n=57)	20.3% (n=42)
The site generates a sense of belonging for you	23.8% (n=50)	15.5% (n=32)	21.8% (n=45)	22.3% (n=46)	10.7% (n=22)	5.8% (n=12)
Anne Frank House represents part of your own personal heritage	23.7% (n=49)	16.4% (n=35)	17.9% (n=37)	17.9% (n=37)	14.0% (n=29)	10.1% (n=21)
You consider the site to be part of your own personal heritage	34.3% (n=72)	18.8% (n=38)	15.0% (n=31)	13.0% (n=27)	13.5% (n=29)	5.3% (n=11)

Cronbach's alpha=0.85

Based on the mean score of the six questions presented in Table 9.2, an index was created representing tourists' perception of the heritage displayed as their personal heritage. The respondents were classified into three groups: (1) those who perceive the site as part of their personal heritage (average answer above 3.4), (2) those who do not perceive the site as part of their personal heritage (average answer below 1.7) and (3) those who are 'in between' (average answer between 1.7 and 3.4). Based on Timothy's model (1997) and the results of the exploratory study, participants were asked to indicate their perception of the site as a World/State of Israel/Amsterdam/European/Dutch/Jewish/Dutch-Jewish heritage. The findings are presented in Table 9.3. From Table 9.3 it can be seen that most participants' answers were distributed between 4 and 5 in all types of classification presented. This pattern suggests that visitors do not vary much in their classification of the site.

To gain a clearer understanding of the results, visitors were classified into 3 (or 2) groups according to their perception of the heritage presented. Since in the case of 'World', 'Amsterdam' and 'The State of Israel' their perception of the heritage was diverse, visitors were classified into 3 groups: (1) those who perceive the site as 'World/Amsterdam/State of Israel' heritage (answers 4 and 5), (2) those who do not perceive the site as being part of the 'World/Amsterdam/State of Israel' heritage (answers 0 and 1) and (3) those who are 'in between' (answers between 2 and 3).

Regarding the other classifications (European, Dutch, Jewish and Dutch-Jewish heritage), since the number of visitors who selected answers 0 or 1 was smaller, it was decided in those cases to include only those visitors who gave an answer between 2 and 5. Therefore in these dimensions, visitors where divided into two groups only: (1) those who perceive the site as 'European/Dutch/Jewish/Dutch Jewish' heritage (answers 4 and 5) (2) and those who do not perceive the site as being part of the 'European/Dutch/Jewish/Dutch

Table 9.3: Perception of the site as world, national and local heritage ($N=208$).

Anne Frank House represents part of the:	Disagree (0)	1	2	3	4	Agree (5)
World's heritage	0.5% ($n=1$)	5.3% ($n=11$)	7.2% ($n=15$)	20.7% ($n=43$)	30.8% ($n=64$)	35.6% ($n=74$)
European heritage	1.0% ($n=2$)	1.0% ($n=2$)	6.3% ($n=13$)	15.4% ($n=32$)	27.4% ($n=57$)	49.0% ($n=102$)
Dutch heritage	1.0% ($n=2$)	2.4% ($n=5$)	5.8% ($n=12$)	11.6% ($n=24$)	26.6% ($n=55$)	52.7% ($n=109$)
Jewish heritage	0% ($n=0$)	0% ($n=0$)	1.0% ($n=2$)	5.8% ($n=12$)	24.0% ($n=50$)	69.2% ($n=144$)
Amsterdam's heritage	1.4% ($n=3$)	4.3% ($n=9$)	3.8% ($n=8$)	14.4% ($n=30$)	27.4% ($n=57$)	48.6% ($n=202$)
State of Israel's heritage	6.7% ($n=14$)	5.8% ($n=12$)	15.9% ($n=33$)	23.1% ($n=48$)	21.6% ($n=45$)	26.9% ($n=56$)
Dutch-Jewish	1.9% ($n=4$)	1.9% ($n=4$)	5.8% ($n=12$)	15.5% ($n=32$)	29.0% ($n=60$)	45.9% ($n=95$)

Jewish' heritage (answers 2 and 3). The distinction into groups would later be explored as a basis for segmentation.

Expectations of On-Site Interpretation

Following the questions dealing with tourists' perception, participants were asked to state their expectations concerning the interpretation provided on site. The mean scores of visitors' expectations are presented in Table 9.4. Table 9.4 shows that overall, visitors stated a high willingness that the interpretation provided would allow them to learn something new, and provide them with information about Dutch-Jewry during the WW II period. Moreover, it is noticeable that the statement referring to the visitors' expectation that the interpretation will make them emotionally involved is ranked relatively high (mean score of over 3). This suggests that visitors to Anne Frank House seek more than just an educational experience.

To explore whether underlying common dimensions for expectations of the interpretation can be found, a Factor Analysis technique was utilized. Owing to the exploratory nature of this study, and as commonly implemented in social research studies (Malhotra & Birks, 2003), Principal Component Analysis was carried out using oblique rotation. This is based on the assumption that the factors may be correlated. The determination about the number of factors was made according to Eigen value greater than 1 and the Scree plot (Tabachnick & Fidell, 1996). In order to determine which variables are included in each factor, it was decided to include those loaded above 0.4 (Hatcher, 1994). Table 9.5 presents the loading values of the various expectations. As can be seen, three factors were identified, explaining 62.2% of the variance.

Table 9.4: Tourists' expectations of on-site interpretation.

You would like the interpretation at this site:	Mean	S.D.
To allow you to learn something new	3.86	1.24
To provide you with information about Jewish people in Holland during WW II	3.72	1.16
To deal with racism today	3.24	1.45
To emphasize the role of the Dutch during WW II	3.20	1.36
To provide you with information about WW II in general	3.17	1.34
To make you feel emotionally involved	3.11	1.39
To be interactive	3.04	1.42
To provide you with information about other groups who have suffered racism	2.83	1.48
To emphasize the link between you and those who lived in Anne Frank House	2.82	1.40
To involve multimedia	2.82	1.52
To make you feel connected to your own heritage	1.97	1.56

Based on Table 9.5, there is a clear distinction among the three factors. The first relates to visitors' willingness that the interpretation will generate an emotional involvement with the heritage presented. This factor was named 'emotional experience'. The second factor highlights participants' interest in information about the period surrounding WW II. This factor was named 'information about WW II'. The third factor involves independent and active processes that allow the visitor to engage in an educational activity. This factor was named 'independent learning'.

Expectations of the Interpretation and Visitors' Perception of the Site

To explore differences between visitor's expectations of the interpretation based on their perception of the site, one-way Anova and T tests were employed. It should be noted that only differences significant at the 0.05 level are reported. Statistical means of the questions based on the results of the Principal Component Analysis were produced. Table 9.6 presents differences between the three/two categories of tourists based on their perception of the site as

Table 9.5: Factor analysis of visitor's expectations of on-site interpretation.

	Emotional experience 1	Information about WW II 2	Independent learning 3
To provide you with information about Jewish people in Holland during WW II		0.904	
To provide you with information about WW II in general		0.897	
To emphasize the role of the Dutch during WW II		0.578	
To provide you with information about other groups who have suffered racism	0.824		
To emphasize the link between you and those who lived in Anne Frank House	0.751		
To deal with racism today	0.741		
To make you feel emotionally involved	0.664		
To make you feel connected to your own heritage	0.661		
To be interactive			0.818
To involve multimedia			0.807
To allow you to learn something new			0.783
Eigen value	4.024	1.610	1.208
% of variance	36.578	14.638	10.983
Cronbach's alpha	0.785	0.762	0.737

Notes: Extraction method: principal component analysis; rotation method: promax with Kaiser normalization; and rotation converged in five iterations.

'World/European/Dutch/Jewish/Amsterdam/State of Israel/Dutch Jewish/Personal heritage, and the three factors identified in Table 9.5.

Two issues arise from the results presented in Table 9.6. First, clear differences can be found between visitors based on the extent to which they perceive the site as part of their own personal heritage. The more participants perceive the site to be part of their own personal heritage, the more they want on-site interpretation to provide them with an emotional experience. However, visitors' appear not to differ in their expectations for information about WW II, or for an independent learning experience based on their perception of the site as part of their personal heritage. Second, it is noticeable that when segmenting visitors' expectations according to their classification of the site by all other dimensions, (besides that of the heritage of the State of Israel), a different pattern is revealed. Those who classify the heritage presented as 'World/Amsterdam/European/Dutch/Dutch Jewish/Jewish' expect the interpretation first and foremost to provide them with an educational experience. Moreover, the more participants saw the site as 'World/Amsterdam/European/Dutch/Dutch Jewish/Jewish' heritage, the more they wanted it to provide them with knowledge about WW II, or independent learning possibilities. Exception to this is the 'State of Israel' heritage in which differences were found both in relation to 'emotional experience' and 'information about WW II'.

Conclusions and Implications

Currently the main focus in the research of interpretation is given to its role as an educational experience and facilitator of a learning process (e.g. Prentice, Guerin, & McCugan, 1998). The results indicate that visitors to heritage settings are not interested in an educational or cognitive experience alone, but also in its emotional dimension. Overall, three main expectations were identified: (1) the visitors' wish for the interpretation to provide an emotional experience, (2) provide information about WW II and (3) allow an active learning process. These findings are congruent with those reported in previous studies, although examining motivations for heritage tourism, Poria's et al. (2003, 2004) identified tourists' willingness to feel connected and emotionally involved with the heritage presented. Moreover, this finding is in accord with visitors' experiences at heritage settings as identified by Beeho and Prentice (1997): educational, recreational (which was not referred to in the current study) and emotional experiences.

Another aim of this study is to explore whether visitors' perception of the site according to Timothy's (1997) classifications could serve as a basis for segmentation. The findings indicate that the more respondents perceive the site as part of their own personal heritage, the more they expect the interpretation to generate emotional involvement. In contrast, those who perceive the site by all other dimensions (as 'World/European/Dutch/Jewish/Amsterdam/State of Israel/Dutch Jewish') showed greater interest in the interpretation as a tool to enrich their knowledge of the WW II and as meaningful for their educational experience at the site. This supports Beeho and Prentice (1997) observation that one interpretation is not suitable for all visitors.

Another topic arising from the findings is that tourists' expectations of the interpretation differ, based on their perception of the site. This may be explained by literature,

Table 9.6: Expectations of the interpretation in relation to perceptions of the site.

	Group 1	Group 2	Group 3	Difference found (one-way Anova)	Differences found between the groups	Scheffe test
Personal heritage						
Emotional experience	2.23 ($n=78$)	2.98 ($n=98$)	3.62 ($n=30$)	$F=25.412$ Sig. $=0.44$	1 and 2 1 and 3 2 and 3	0.000 0.000 0.009
Information about WW II	3.14 ($n=78$)	3.47 ($n=98$)	3.62 ($n=30$)	$F=3.174$ Sig. $=0.44$	NS	
Independent learning	3.12 ($n=78$)	3.32 ($n=97$)	3.36 ($n=30$)	$F=0.842$ Sig. $=0.432$	Sig. $=0.000$	
World heritage						
Emotional experience	2.21 ($n=12$)	2.65 ($n=58$)	2.90 ($n=136$)	$F=2.985$ Sig. $=0.053$	NS	
Information about WW II	2.41 ($n=12$)	3.18 ($n=58$)	3.52 ($n=136$)	$F=7.645$ Sig. $=0.001$	1 and 3	0.002
Independent learning	2.44 ($n=12$)	3.21 ($n=58$)	3.34 ($n=136$)	$F=3.641$ Sig. $=0.028$	1 and 3	0.026
State of Israel heritage						
Emotional experience	2.13 ($n=26$)	2.59 ($n=81$)	3.13 ($n=99$)	$F=12.134$ Sig. $=0.000$	1 and 3 2 and 3	0.000 0.003
Information about WW II	2.85 ($n=26$)	3.23 ($n=81$)	3.61 ($n=99$)	$F=6.701$ Sig. $=0.002$	1 and 3 2 and 3	0.005 0.048
Independent learning	2.94 ($n=26$)	3.13 ($n=81$)	3.43 ($n=99$)	$F=2.618$ Sig. $=0.075$	NS	
Amsterdam heritage						
Emotional experience	2.46 ($n=12$)	2.46 ($n=38$)	2.90 ($n=156$)	$F=3.104$ Sig. $=0.47$	NS	
Information about WW II	3.30 ($n=12$)	2.82 ($n=38$)	3.50 ($n=156$)	$F=6.647$ Sig. $=0.002$	2 and 3	0.002
Independent learning	2.41 ($n=12$)	2.93 ($n=38$)	3.40 ($n=156$)	$F=6.380$ Sig. $=0.002$	1 and 3	0.013

	Group A	Group B	Difference found (T test)		
European heritage					
Emotional experience	2.63 ($n=45$)	2.86 ($n=157$)	$t=-1.279$ Sig. $=0.202$		

(Continued)

Table 9.6: (*Continued*)

	Group A	Group B	Difference found (*T* test)
Information about WW II	3.00 (*n*=45)	3.49 (*n*=157)	*t*=−2.785 Sig. =0.006
Independent learning	2.94 (*n*=45)	3.37 (*n*=157)	*t*= −2.266 Sig. =0.025
Dutch heritage			
Emotional experience	2.57 (*n*=36)	2.85 (*n*=162)	*t*=−1.39 Sig. =0.165
Information about WW II	2.93 (*n*=36)	3.50 (*n*=162)	*t*=−2.985 Sig. =0.003
Independent learning	3.12 (*n*=36)	3.34 (*n*=162)	*t*=−1.057 Sig. =0.292
Dutch-Jewish heritage			
Emotional experience	2.75 (*n*=44)	2.86 (*n*=153)	*t*=−0.617 Sig. =0.538
Information about WW II	3.06 (*n*=44)	3.51 (*n*=153)	*t*=−2.631 Sig. =0.009
Independent learning	3.01 (*n*=44)	3.40 (*n*=153)	*t*=−2.075 Sig. =0.039
Jewish heritage			
Emotional experience	2.47 (*n*=14)	2.81 (*n*=192)	*t*=−1.202 Sig. =0.231
Information about WW II	2.47 (*n*=14)	3.43 (*n*=192)	*t*=−3.332 Sig. =0.001
Independent learning	2.61 (*n*=14)	3.30 (*n*=192)	*t*=−2.206 Sig. =0.028

Notes: Group 1: Those who 'Do not perceive the site as being part of their personal/world/state of Israel/Amsterdam heritage'; Group 2: Those who 'Somewhat perceive the site as being part of their personal/world/state of Israel/Amsterdam heritage'; Group 3: Those who 'Perceive the site as being part of their personal/world/state of Israel/Amsterdam heritage'; Group A: Those who 'Do not perceive the site as being part of the European/Dutch/Dutch Jewish/Jewish heritage'; Group B: Those who 'Perceive the site as being part of the European/Dutch/Dutch Jewish/Jewish heritage'.

arguing that visitors arrive at the site with their own personal agenda, which influences their experience, their reaction to the exhibits and the effectiveness of the interpretation provided (Beeho & Prentice, 1997; Uzzell & Ballantyne, 1998). Finally, the findings reflect that the possibility of using Timothy's model as a segmentation tool is not of a trivial nature. While visitors' perception of the heritage as a part of their own personal heritage is highly relevant in revealing their expectations for the interpretation to generate emotional involvement, it is unhelpful when required to indicate their expectations for an educational experience. This finding is in line with previous studies indicating the link between the site's personal meaning to visitors and their desire for an emotional experience (e.g. McCain & Ray, 2003; Uzzell & Ballantyne, 1998). The pattern characterizing segmentation by all other dimensions of visitors' perception is quite the opposite. While examining visitors' perception of the site by other dimensions (other than personal heritage) makes it possible to differentiate between visitors in the context of expectations for an educational experience, it does not provide insight on their expectations for an emotional experience.

The revealing of two dissimilar patterns of behavior when segmenting by personal heritage or by 'other' heritages implies that perhaps examining both dimensions is not sufficient, and that the interaction between them should also be considered. Though this approach for segmenting is more complex in comparison to other commonly used bases of segmentation, it provides greater understanding of visitors' expectations of the interpretation and the experience consumed, in the context of heritage settings.

The study findings contribute both to the academic literature and to the management of heritage settings. First, the findings indicate the need for a more holistic view in the exploration of tourist's behavior at heritage sites. Namely, taking into consideration of the site's attributes, tourist's characteristics and the relationships between the two. This approach is in contrast to the customary approach, which highlights either the supply or the demand side perspective (Timothy & Boyd. 2003; Apostolakis, 2003). Second, the current study provides a better understanding of tourists' expectations of on-site interpretation, an important element that has received little academic attention so far.

The results presented have significant managerial implications. Managers of heritage sites are advised to identify visitors based on their perceptions of the site and provide them with different interpretations. For those who perceive the site as part of their own personal heritage, it is recommended to structure an emotional visiting experience. For visitors who perceive the site as part of the world's heritage, national or local heritage, it is recommended that managers provide them with information of a more general context and to make use of interactive guiding techniques. In the broader sense of heritage sites management, it is possible to implement different marketing strategies according to the different segments. For example, market the site as an emotional experience for those who perceive it as personal heritage, or as enriching visitors' knowledge of historical events, for those who perceive it as world, national or local heritage.

However, when discussing the need to segment visitors to heritage sites according to their perception of the site, one should bear in mind that perceptions are not easily recognized by site managers. Therefore, to implement this mode of visitors' segmentation, it is necessary to connect visitors' perceptions to a more recognizable tourist's characteristic such as demographic, socio-demographic or geographic. Namely, make use of these characteristics as a proxy for tourist's perception of the site.

Unavoidably, this research has a number of limitations. First, the suggested approach for segmenting was explored in relation to one site only. Second, the site chosen for the research is a 'must see' tourist attraction and might have unique characteristics that influenced the results. Finally, it is suggested that the results of the current study reflect that Anne Frank House is associated with human atrocities. Clearly, future research should investigate the approach presented here in other sites with attributes different to those of the Anne Frank House, as to allow for the generalization of the findings. Further research could also explore the relationships between the individual and the site in relation to other behavioral patterns of importance to heritage site management (e.g. satisfaction, visitors' experiences).

References

Anne Frank Museum Official Web Site. (2003). Over 3 million visitors to 3 major Amsterdam Museums. Retrieved 8 June 2004, from http://www.annefrank.org

Apostolakis, A. (2003). The convergence process in heritage tourism. *Annals of Tourism Research*, 30(4), 795–812.

Apter, A., Hatab, J., Tyano, S., & Weiziman, A. (1998). *Child and adolescent psychology*. Tel Aviv: Dyonon Publishing (in Hebrew).

Ashworth, G. J. (2001). Heritage, tourism and cities: A review of where we are. In: G. Wall (Ed.), *Contemporary perspective on tourism* (pp. 143–180). Waterloo: Department of Geography Publication Series, University of Waterloo.

Beeho, A. J., & Prentice, R. C. (1997). Conceptualizing the experiences of heritage tourists. *Tourism Management*, 18(2), 75–87.

Bruner, E. M. (1996). Tourism in Ghana: The representation of slavery and the return of the black diaspora. *American Anthropologist*, 98(2), 290–304.

Dierking, L. D. (1998). Interpretation as a social experience. In: D.L. Uzzell, & R. Balantyne (Eds), *Contemporary issues in heritage and environmental interpretation* (pp. 37–55). London: The Stationary Office.

Goulding, C. (1999). Interpretation and presentation. In: A. Leask, & I. Yeoman (Eds), *Heritage visitor attractions: An operation management perspective* (pp. 54–67). London: Cassell.

Hatcher, L. (1994). *A step-by-step approach to using the SAS system for factor analysis and structural equation modeling*. Cary, NC: SAS Institute Inc.

Light, D. (1995). Heritage as informal education. In: D. T. Herbert (Ed.), *Heritage, tourism and society* (pp. 116–145). London: Mansell.

Malhotra, N. K., & Birks, F. D. (2003). *Marketing research: An applied approach* (2nd European ed). Harlow: Prentice-Hall.

McCain, G., & Ray, N. M. (2003). Legacy tourism: The search for personal meaning in heritage travel. *Tourism Management*, 24(6), 713–717.

Moscardo, G. (1996). Mindful visitors: Heritage and tourism. *Annals of Tourism Research*, 23(2), 376–397.

Poria, Y., Butler, R., & Airey, D. (2003). The core of heritage tourism: Distinguishing heritage tourists from tourists in heritage places. *Annals of Tourism Research*, 30(1), 238–254.

Poria, Y., Butler, R., & Airey, D. (2004). Links between tourists, heritage, and reasons for visiting heritage sites. *Journal of Travel Research*, 43(1), 19–28.

Prentice, R. (1993). *Tourism and heritage attractions*. London: Routledge.

Prentice, R. (1995). What the consumer wants: The customer base for the interpretation of Scotland's built heritage. *Interpretation Journal*, 57(winter), 4–9.

Prentice, R., Guerin, S., & McGugan, S. (1998). Visitor learning at a heritage attraction: A case study of discovery as a media product. *Tourism Management, 19*(1), 5–23.

Schwarz, N., & Hippler, H. J. (1995). The numeric values of rating scales: A comparison of their impact in mail surveys and telephone interviews. *International Journal of Public Opinion Research, 7*(1), 72–74.

Silberberg, T. (1995). Cultural tourism and business opportunities for museums and heritage sites. *Tourism Management, 16*(5), 361–365.

Stewart, E. J., Hayward, B. M., Devlin, P. J., & Kirby, V. G. (1998). The "Place" of interpretation: A new approach to the evaluation of interpretation. *Tourism Management, 19*(3), 257–266.

Swarbrooke, J. (2002). *The development and management of visitor attractions*. Oxford: Butterworth Heinemann.

Tabachnick, B. G., & Fidell, L. S. (1996). *Using multivariate statistics*. NY: Harper Collins College.

Timothy, D. J. (1997). Tourism and the personal heritage experience. *Annals of Tourism Research, 24*(3), 751–754.

Timothy, J. D., & Boyd, S. W. (2003). *Heritage tourism*. Harlow: Prentice-Hall.

Uzzell, D., & Ballantyne, R. (1998). Heritage that hurts: Interpretation in a postmodern world. In: D. L. Uzzell, & R. Balantyne (Eds), *Contemporary issues in heritage & environmental interpretation* (pp. 152–171). London: The Stationary Office.

Chapter 10

Motivations and Lifestyle: Segmentation Using the Construct A.I.O

Ana M. González Fernández, Miguel Cervantes Blanco and Carmen Rodríguez Santos

Introduction

The study of tourist demand can be undertaken from different perspectives, according to the factors influencing tourist travel. There are various classifications of these factors; broadly speaking, those of an economic nature on the one hand, promoting or restricting demand and, on the other, personal and social factors which strengthen the idea of tourist activity as something fundamentally human. The human factor brings with it certain peculiarities, which show up in personal requirements on the demand side, bringing about the existence of multiple forms of tourism and encouraging diversity in the present and possible future supply. It is thus essential to include this human factor when selecting suitable business strategies to meet the needs and wants of consumers. Having identified these influencing factors and being heterogeneity one of the principal characteristics, this analysis focuses on the fact that tourist demand comes from many types of tourists with different behaviours deriving from a wide range of motivations and the variety of factors influencing them, such as lifestyle. If the dependence between both groups of variables was demonstrated, that would bring about the need of undertaking market segmentation.

In this context, the first aim of this chapter is the search for any direct relationship between the variables, which are the subject of the chapter: lifestyle and tourist motivations. If this was borne out, the need to use these variables and their efficacy in gaining deeper knowledge of consumers would be confirmed. This would be because the definition of strategies based on this type of variable and adapted to the groupings emerging from the study would become possible. Owing to it, once proved the existence of such relations, a second objective is to group individuals according to the construct lifestyle. After testing these relationships for the sample as a whole and having segmented the tourism market, the next objective is to test this hypothesis for each segment separately, analysing whether these proposed relationships become stronger or weaker in the light of segment identification. Finally, the groups identified are characterised as a function of lifestyle variables, analysing motivations and tourist behaviour of each segment.

Literature Review

The tourism market is characterised by being composed of heterogeneous clients with differentiated needs and wishes. This feature of demand, as explained above, makes segmentation of holiday travel a line of investigation and practice especially relevant in marketing, in both academic and business approaches to this field. The segmentation process allows division of the market into homogeneous sub-groupings with a view to implementing differentiated commercial strategies for each of them. This allows the needs of each to be met in the most effective way and companies' business targets to be attained.

The segmentation criteria, which can be used in splitting up the market concerned, can be classified in broad terms, distinguishing between *general* and *specific, objective* and *subjective* (Frank, Massy, & Wind, 1972). Nevertheless, the explanatory value of the criteria traditionally used in breaking down tourists into groupings (economic and socio-demographic variables, included among the objective general criteria) is steadily decreasing (Ritchie & Goeldner, 1987; Fisher, 1990; Mitchman, 1991; Witt & Moutinho, 1994; González Fernández & Bello Acebrón, 2002). The reality seen among the individuals who compose the market is that every day, very similar behaviour can be noted on the part of people who are quite different in socio-economic and demographic terms, and *vice versa*. A growing personalisation of consumer behaviour can be observed, and this is the reason for the variables mentioned above being used solely as descriptive of the market as a whole. Furthermore, if the profound and rapid changes that society is undergoing are taken into account, the conclusion must be reached that the evolution of society is the principal cause for a need to use other criteria, such as lifestyle, to round out knowledge of consumers.

This justifies an approach investigating the possibilities offered by these subjective general criteria for dividing up the tourist market, obtaining homogeneous groups, which can be selected as objective segments. To each of these a different marketing mix can be applied, specifically oriented towards the needs, interests and preferences of the consumers making up each segment, since they present distinct motivations that induce different behaviours. The concept of lifestyle was introduced by Lazer (1963) who considered it to be related to the notion of system, referring to the various ways of life (in the broadest sense) adopted by society as a whole or by sections of it. It relates to the different elements or peculiarities, which describe the way of life of a cultural or economic group, allowing it to be distinguished from other groups. It includes the structures, which develop and emerge from the dynamics of life in society.

Since this first approach a number of different methodologies have been developed. However, two clearly distinct tendencies can be distinguished: lifestyle on the one hand and values on the other, with appropriate sub-divisions being made within each. Lifestyles focus on specific situations or objects, and prove especially useful in the analysis of consumer motivations and the understanding of behaviour. Values are more abstract beliefs concerning states of affairs not linked to specific situations. They are a supposedly universal model of collective thought patterns and conduct, involving the introduction of an ideal norm.

In connection with tourism, one of the most widely proven methods of approach is AIO (activities, interests, opinions). Its first applications were made in about the middle of the 1970s, very often combined with social, economic and demographic variables, advancing towards the identification of the features of the segments so as to complete their description and compare such criteria. However, many researchers referring to tourism use such variables instead of general variables, which means that, in fact, they are measuring the style of tourism. Table 10.1 shows some surveys that apply this methodology with regards to tourism considered interesting in connection with this research effort.

Methodology

This research proposes the development of a methodology based on AIO. Selection of AIO variables as components of the construct "lifestyle" is principally due to the high degree of specificity shown by beliefs, opinions and preferences. These allow behaviour to be predicted to the extent that they reveal a predisposition (Hustad & Pessemier, 1974; Triandis, 1979), forming part of the modern concept of attitude as an affective state of individuals linked to their tendency to act in a given way when faced with some stimulus (Vázquez Casielles, Trespalacios Gutiérrez J. A. and Rodríguez del Bosque, I. A. (2005) or the capacity to react on the basis of experience. This exerts a direct and dynamic influence on the responses of individuals to situations they confront, predisposing them to a given type of action when confronted with a specific situation.

When it comes to activities, these are a concept related to how individuals spend the time available to them. This may refer to work at a trade or profession, necessary day-to-day actions such as sleeping and so forth, housework or leisure activities (Feldman & Hornik, 1981). However, since the first three of these relate to statements including interests and opinions, this part of the concept will deal exclusively with those activities having to do with spare time. In a preliminary research, a direct relation between travellers' lifestyles and their behaviours in trips has been proved (González Fernández & Bello Acebrón, 2002). On this basis, the main objective of this chapter is to demonstrate that distinct lifestyles influence on the existence of different tourist motivations.

In order to attain this objective, an empirical study was carried out using a personal survey completed in the homes of the interviewees. Those interviewed constituted a representative sample of the population under investigation. The technical details are shown in Table 10.2. The tool used for collecting information was a structured questionnaire designed to fit the aims of the research. The order of subjects and questions to be followed was not random. It was on a basis of ascending order of difficulty, allowing interviewers to familiarise themselves with and understand its objectives. This ruled out any type of susceptibility on those questions which could be considered more personal. The final distribution was as follows:

The first block of questions taken as a whole relates to various aspects of travel such as the social motivation for travel and the real total undertaken over the year (both short trips and long journeys). The second block is divided into two sections. The first includes various questions made up of batteries of items intended to elucidate the interests and opinions of the interviewees with regard to various topics such as family, work, politics, religion and so forth. The second incorporates leisure activities, including, among others, sports, open-air

Table 10.1: Applications of AIO in tourism (in alphabetical order).

Author(s)	Year	Variables	Research
Abbey	1979	Demographic Specific AIO	Lifestyles let salesmen make tours package in accordance with travellers' motivation and attitudes
Crask	1981	General AIO	Segmentation in the tourist market
Davis, Allen, and Cosenza	1988	Specific AIO	They measure and segment residents from Florida so as to make a welcoming atmosphere to tourists
González Fernández, and Bello Acebrón	2002	General AIO	Segmentation in the tourist market. Study of the relationships of dependency between an individual's lifestyle and tourist behaviour
Hay Associates	1978	Specific AIO	Study of the travel market in Great Britain
Hawes	1988	Demographic Specific AIO	Segmentation of elderly women in the tourist market
	2000		Mass media preferences
Lawson	1991	General AIO Specific AIO	Contrastive study of segmentation between general and given lifestyles on tourism
Mayo	1975	Specific AIO Demographic Trip characteristics National parks' evaluation	Determines the motivations for which a group feels attracted to National parks offer
Pearch and Caltabiano	1983	Specific AIO	Deduce motivations from travellers' experiences
Perreault, Darden, and Darden	1977	Socio-economic Specific AIO Predisposition Tourist and common behaviour	Segmentation of tourist market related to different holiday predispositions

Raaij	1986	Attitudes Specific and general AIO Socio-demographic	Description of segments so as to improve the behaviour understanding Defining promotion and advertising campaigns
Schewe and Calantone	1978	Specific and general AIO Demographic Socio-economic Aim of the trip Main destination	Segmentation of the tourist market from Massachusetts. Development of communication programme adapted to lifestyles profiles
Schul and Crompton	1983	Specific AIO Socio-demographic	Lifestyle variables are more effective than socio-demographic ones as for the forecast of outward search behaviour
Silverberg, Backman, and Backman	1996	Specific AIO	Differ segments of traveller market according to nature
Vyncke	2002	General AIO	Meaningful lifestyle typologies, comparable with traditional demographic segmentation criteria. They used the technique of cluster analysis
Wahlers and Etzel	1985	Individual stimulus (lifestyle) Ideal stimulus	The relationship between preferences of holiday activities and necessities of individual stimulus
Woodside and Pitts	1976	Specific AIO Demographic	Suggest using lifestyle variables in this market segmentation to forecast the behaviour of an abroad and domestic trip

Table 10.2: Technical specifications.

Sample group	People aged over 15[a] who had gone on one or more trips during a one-year period and resident in capitals of more than 100,000 inhabitants within an inner Spanish region
Sample size	400 valid interviews carried out at the interviewees' homes
Sample error	$\pm 5\%$ ($p = q = 50$)
Standard of confidence	95.5% ($K = 2\sigma$)
Sample design	Random, stratified, multiphase sample, with proportional assignment by sex, age and city of residence
Selection of individuals	System of random routes

[a]People aged over 15 were used in the study, since the WTO's standards consider all those under that age to be children.

activities, reading, television and radio. This section overall relates to the lifestyle variable. The third block is aimed at gathering socio-demographic data for each interviewee.

To ensure the quality of the information collected, a process of selection and training of interviewers who would be involved in implementation of the field work was carried out. The questionnaires were subjected to strict quality control with the aim of detecting possible omissions or contradictory answers in which case the questionnaire was automatically discarded. Valid questionnaires were processed by computer, creating the database from which the results given here are drawn.

Discussion of Findings

The aim of the analysis was to verify if individuals' lifestyles have a real influence on their social motivations leading them to given mindsets and consequent intentions to purchase tourist services. If these were borne out, the need to use these variables and their efficacy in gaining deeper knowledge of consumers would be confirmed. This would be because the definition of strategies based on this type of variable and adapted to the groupings emerging from the study would become possible. Hence, those products or services meeting consumer needs, motivations and desires could be offered. The stated aim can be achieved through testing the following hypothesis: *There is a direct relationship between individuals' lifestyles, as measured through Activities, Interests and Opinions, and social motivations leading to travel.*

As a method of gaining knowledge of consumers through the variables affecting their decision-making processes, when once the latter had been defined, several *multivariate statistical techniques* were applied in this research. In order to get around one of the most serious problems faced by lifestyle methodologies used hitherto — the excessive length of questionnaires caused both by the variables included and by the measurement system aiding determination of individual lifestyles — this study adopted a two-phase data collection procedure. Exhaustive screening was performed on the items included in the questionnaire, in an attempt to avoid collecting superfluous data, which would unnecessarily lengthen the survey. In addition, qualitative variables were measured using two types of scale: Likert and nominal multiple choice. One of the main aims of this study was to obtain the same amount of information in much less time than other approaches to lifestyle, hence avoiding bias deriving from excessive survey length. In this way, it is possible to reduce the cost of field work and thus of a whole research project, allowing resource substitution and conforming better to company budgets for such tasks.

The best choice for handling the variables proved to be a combination of two statistical techniques, *factorial analysis of principal components* for application first to motivations (a variable gathered through 14 items), and second to interests and opinions (43 items), variables which have to be measured using Likert scales. This is because it was of interest to take into account the information obtained by measuring goodness of fit using the statistical package SPSS (Statistical package for social science). The other technique was *factorial analysis of multiple correspondences*, used on activities, nominal qualitative multiple-choice variable (110 items), through the statistical package SPAD (Système Portable pour l'Analyse des Donnés). The main purpose behind application of these two techniques was *to homogenize the information*, allowing replacement of answers by factorial scores. For this reason, there is little value in interpreting the factors obtained, as interpretation is not used to reduce the number of variables. The results of analyses using these techniques are new variables encapsulating exactly the same information as the originals. They constitute the inputs for analysis carried out subsequently without any statistical information being lost.

Next, testing of the first hypothesis: *that there is a direct relationship between individuals' lifestyles and the social motivations which lead them to travel*, was performed using the multivariate technique of *canonical correlation analysis* (performed using Bartlett's χ^2 statistical test). The statistical package used for this was BMDP (Biomedical Package). This was initially used for the sample as a whole. It covered the set of factorial results on lifestyles as independent variables, these being obtained from the factorial analyses of principal components and of multiple correspondences mentioned above. As dependent variables, the factors resulting from principal component analysis of variables relating to social motivation of travel were used. This was done instead of direct application to the original variables so as to eliminate the potential risk of multicolinearity, as the factors are linearly independent. Thus, possible instability in the canonical weights obtained and potential problems owing to the structure of the matrix are avoided, since in the case of orthogonal variables the two matrices are identical (Levine, 1986; Richard, LeMay, Taylor, & Turner, 1994) (Figure 10.1).

The result was positive, showing a direct relationship between individuals' lifestyles and social motivations leading them to travel for the sample as a whole. However, this did not reach high levels, since the maximum score from the canonical correlations was 0.66. As the hypothesis suggested was borne out, the question arose whether this relationship would be stronger or weaker in the light of the identification of market segments defined by lifestyle criteria, that is, with different lifestyles. If any strengthening were observed, it would underpin the need to segment, since a higher value for canonical correlation on a segmental basis would confirm the hypothesis put forward in this research, "comparison of a homogeneous lifestyles segmentally differentiated with similarly differentiated tourist motivation." This would demonstrate a need to segment the market on grounds of lifestyle

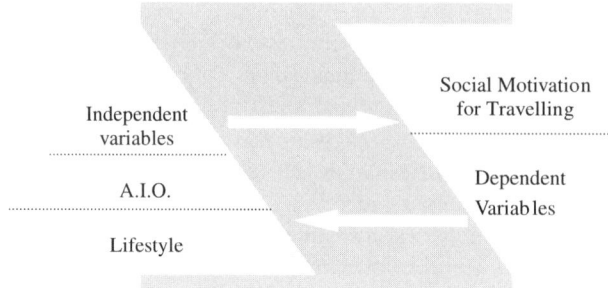

Figure 10.1: Hypothesis.

so as to identify consumer sub-groups evincing different requirements. Those which could be offered a tailor-made commercial package could then be selected, increasing the efficiency and profitability of companies' commercial activities.

As this would be the positive outcome for the hypothesis proposed and the easiest to test, the methodology applied to segmentation of the market under study was *cluster analysis*. The variable used to differentiate tourist consumers is the construct lifestyle. Use of this information sharpened segment identification, hence the factors previously obtained were introduced as information inputs in the classification of subjects. The method employed in classification was the algorithm *K-means* and the measure of proximity selected was *Euclidean distance*. Assignment of individuals to clusters was carried out following the criterion of the nearest centroid. As optimum number of groupings was not known beforehand, in an attempt to choose the most suitable on objective grounds, several successive iterations were performed.

With a view to choosing the optimum number of groups, the definition of each of them was first observed. This means that the degree of association between the elements within any group should be high, while that between elements belonging to different groupings should be the lowest possible, analysis of variance of the clusters formed being used as a measure of this. When this process was carried out, the most appropriate number of groups proved to divide the market into five segments: home-loving, idealistic, autonomous, hedonistic and conservative (Table 10.3). After analysis, interpretation of the results, group sizes, proximity between clusters and application of a further technique, discriminant analysis, allowed confirmation that this was the correct division. This is

Table 10.3: Breakdown of population by segments.

Segment	% of population
Home-loving	6.25
Idealistic	13.00
Autonomous	12.25
Hedonistic	35.75
Conservative	32.75

because the overall percentage of correct classification through cluster analysis in this research was shown to be 94% and it also permitted reclassification in accordance with the discriminatory functions of those items which should be in another group. The system for selecting the most discriminant variables was stepwise using the Mahalanobis distance.

Finally, after the hypothesis proposed had proved acceptable for the sample as a whole and after segmentation of the tourism market, the question arose of what direction would be taken by this proposed relationship, in other words, whether it would become stronger or weaker in the light of segment identification. For this reason, the following stage involved testing the hypothesis of this research for each segment separately, so as to detect any relationships between lifestyle dimensions and tourist motivation. The aim was to demonstrate a need to segment the market and gain in-depth knowledge of individual lifestyles.

The methodology applied in testing the hypotheses for separate market segments was identical to that used for the sample as a whole, analysis of canonical correlations. This was used independently on each grouping, in search of the dependency relationships among the groups of variables established. In the event, the segments on which this method was used so as to test the hypotheses were only segments four and five, which were of greater size. In the rest, the number of variables exceeded the number of individuals. However, the methodological process would have been the same if this restriction had not applied, the results being equally comparable. The hypothesis intended to measuring the relationship between individuals' lifestyles and the social motivations which led them to travel, was tested by introducing the same inputs as for the whole sample, but in this case for each of the previously defined segments.

The results recorded segment by segment allow the hypothesis to be accepted. This is because a very striking increase was noted in the values for relationships between lifestyles and social motivations for travel relative to what had previously been obtained on an overall basis (Table 10.4). Quantification of the canonical correlations calculated shows evidence of a *very significant increase in the dependence of lifestyle tourist variables* when determined for homogeneous segments of the population. This points to a need to segment the market using this criterion as well as to apply differentiated marketing strategies for each segment established on the basis of these variables. Analysed the relationship between lifestyles and motivations, the most outstanding characteristics are described in Table 10.5.

Conclusions and Implications

This chapter conclusively demonstrates the dependence upon the construct lifestyle of the social motivation that leads individuals to undertake leisure travel. This construct has been measured by the generic individuals' AIO methodology. An implication of the high-explanatory power of the lifestyle variable in the segmentation of tourism market, that has been proved in the research, is the convenience of using this criterion to divide consumers into homogeneous groups. In this way, objective segments are obtained, to which different marketing strategies can be applied. Use of stepwise discriminant analysis renders it possible to put new individuals after the event into one of the five groups established, giving an important predictive capacity. Furthermore, the result of 22

Table 10.4: Lifestyles and tourist motivations.

Home-loving	Idealistic	Autonomous	Hedonistic	Conservative
Interests and opinions				
Focus on family life	Commitment to a better world and to fight against injustice	Personal success linked with freedom and independence	Work life	Home-loving people
Enjoy a quiet and happy private life	Not appropriate to work only at home	Enjoy life	To have an enthusiastic job, with success, which allows to fulfil their aims in life	Focus on the well being of their family
Have children and to up bring them	Set special store by matters relating to the workplace	Not interested in working at home	Human relationships	They do not fulfil their expectations
Work at home	Achieve collaborative part in the enterprises	Work as a duty and for social projection	Not attracted to managerial posts	Work as a duty
Get satisfaction from carrying out the tasks involved	Want to have an enthusiastic job	Consider their salaries not high		Their jobs are not stimulating
Not materialistic	Not interested in taking on managerial responsibilities			Identify success with working efficiently
Value friendship	Importance to relations with friends			Set store by managerial positions that would allow upward social mobility
Conservative	Flexible and responsible	Flexible in politics, religion and social views	Tolerant regarding discipline and politics	Responsible
Inflexible	Tolerant in matters of politics, religious and public order	Considerable liberal	Ecological	Strict with regard to social order
Religious				
Cautious towards the future	Strict regarding product quality	Accept social reality	Consumers of new products	Practising tolerant religious
Optimistic about society and future	Consumers of new products	Optimistic about future		Practical people.
Strict regarding product quality				Thrifty
				Pessimistic about future and society

Activities				
Cultural activities	Vist family and friends	Cinema	Listening to music	Visiting beautiful outstanding
Visits to beautiful places	Relax and disconnect from every life	Enjoy nightlife	Reading: magazines (professional, business), newspapers (local and national)	Sports: walking, bicycle, skiing
Sports: swimming and footing	Know and meet new people	Not interested in cultural activities		Not interested in nightlife, music or cinema
Attend to sporting events, concerts, theatre, dancing…	Sports	Sports: tennis and team sports		Participating in social or religious associations
Music in general (specially classical)		Music: pop, rock, disco and ballads		
Reading: magazines (on politics), newspapers (local and national)		Television: films	Television: news, films	
Television: sports, debates				Television: regional news, reality shows, game shows, gossip programmes
Newspapers (local and regional)				
Television: news, documentaries, current affairs, debates and travel programmes				
Tourist motivations				
Well-deserved rest		Something to tell your acquaintances	Knowing countries and their cultures	Joining families
Joining families		Well-deserved rest	Disconnecting from working	Making new friends
Enjoying the weather		Have a good time		Developing personality
Developing personally		Meeting new people		Enjoying the weather
Shopping		Educative activite		

Table 10.5: Comparison of the relationship between lifestyle and social motivation of the travel. Whole sample/segments.

	Maximun canonical correlation
Whole sample	0,66152
Segment 4	0,82814
Segment 5	0,87665

discriminant variables, among which can be found: personal realisation, quality–price relation, innovation, hedonism, will allow to predict the tourist motivations of new individuals using a much smaller and easier questionnaire, in which these more discriminant variables are included.

The methodology utilised in establishing the construct lifestyle shows, among others, two immediate areas of usefulness for the planning of companies' operational marketing decisions: product and communication policies. Thus, when deciding these policies a firm should take into account the characteristics of the segment to which they are directed. In this sense, for example, a firm which wanted to focus on the hedonistic segment, it should take into account that this is a group with a lifestyle mainly related to the satisfaction and the search for the personal realisation in the labour field as well as to the interest for trying new products that preserve the environment.

In spite of the positive results achieved by the application of the above-mentioned method of approach to general lifestyles described above, it presents certain limitations. The strongest criticism it deserves might be that population segmentation according to general lifestyles fails with regards to practical aspects from the operational point of view, because it requires the use of excessively long questionnaires, the cost of which is too high for certain businesses and, in addition, it is not meticulous enough and may lead to biased results as a consequence of its duration. Furthermore, the interpretation of results may be difficult for firms in the industry.

On the other hand, research projects that use the methodology of specific lifestyles are often based on the habits of tourists rather than on lifestyles properly, or travel styles. Quite frequently, when building up the AIO they practically refrain from introducing two significant sets of variables such as interests and opinions, not justified by earlier research, as a result of which it would seem that they measure tourism activities carried out in travel, which shows that they are mainly measuring consumer activities. For this reason, an interesting research project that is being carrying out at present on the basis of the results obtained from this actual work, is to conceive an easier system for measuring general lifestyles of tourists, which should benefit from the justified properties of already used general lifestyles, but applying it directly to tourism. The new lifestyle method of approach is going to be applied to a very defined group of tourists, those that travel because of cultural motivations and consequently present *a priori* similar general characteristics, in order to be able to detect the existence of significant differences according to their lifestyle when traveling, so as to subsequently be able to verify whether, as occurred in the preceding research effort, the motivations of their travel do depend on their lifestyles.

References

Abbey, J. R. (1979). Does life-style profiling work? *Journal of Travel Research, 18*(1), 8–14.

Crask, M. R. (1981). Segmenting the vacationer market: Identifying the vacation preferences, demographics and magazine readership of each group. *Journal of Travel Research, 20*(2), 29–34.

Davis, D., Allen, J., & Cosenza, R. M. (1988). Segmenting local residents by their attitudes, interests, and opinions toward tourism. *Journal of Travel Research, 27*(2), 2–8.

Feldman, L., & Hornik, J. (1981). The use of time: An integrated conceptual model. *Journal of Consumer Research, 7*(4), 407–419.

Fisher, A. B. (1990). What consumers want in the 1990's. *Fortune, 29*(January), 108–112.

Fodness, D. D. (1994). Measuring tourist motivation. *Annals of Tourism Research, 21*(3), 555–581.

Frank, R. E., Massy, W. F., & Wind, Y. (1972). *Market segmentation*. NY: Prentice-Hall.

González Fernández, A. M. (1998). *El estilo de vida como criterio de segmentación en el mercado turístico: propuesta metodológica y contrastación empírica*. Thesis Doctoral, Universidad de León, Spain.

González Fernández, A. M., & Bello Acebrón, L. (2002). The construct lifestyle in market segmentation. The behaviour of tourist consumers. *European Journal of Marketing, 36*(1–2), 51–85.

Hawes, D. K. (1988). Travel-related lifestyle profiles of older women. *Journal of Travel Research, 27*(2), 22–32.

Hawes, D. K. (2000). Travel-related lifestyle profiles of older women. *Consumer behavior in travel and tourism, Haworth hospitality press* (pp. 481–511). NY.

Hay Associates. (1978). *United Kingdom: A study of the international travel market*. Washington, DC: United States Travel Service, Department of Commerce.

Hustad, P., & Pessemier, E. (1974). The development and application of psychographic life-style and associated activity life-style and associated activity and attitude measures. In: W. Wells (Eds), *Life-style and psychographics* (pp. 32–70). Chicago: American Marketing Association.

Lawson, R. (1991). What is psychographic segmentation?: A comparison between general consumer analysis and product specific analysis. *Conference: New horizons in tourism and hospitality education, training and research*. The University of Calgary, 2–5 July, pp. 445–455.

Lazer, W. (1963). Life-style concepts and marketing. In: Greyser et al. (Eds), *Toward scientific marketing* (pp. 130–139). Chicago, IL: American Marketing Association.

Levine, M. S. (1986). *Canonical analysis and factor comparison*. Beverly Hills, CA: Sage.

Mayo, E. (1975). Tourism and the national parks: A psychographic and attitudinal study. *Journal of Travel Research, 14*(14), 14–18.

Michman, R. (1991). *Lifestyle market segmentation*. NY: Praeger.

Pearch, P. L., & Caltabiano, M. L. (1983). Infering travel motivation from traveler's experiences. *Journal of Travel Research, 20*(2), 16–20.

Perreault, W. D., Darden, D. K., & Darden, W. R. (1977). A psychographic classification of vacation life styles. *Journal of Leisure Research, 9*(3), 208–224.

Raaij, F. van. (1986). Consumer research on tourism. Mental and behaviour constructs. *Annals of Tourism Research, 13*(1), 1–9.

Richard, M. D., LeMay, S. A., Taylor, G. S., & Turner, G. B. (1994). A canonical analysis of extrinsic satisfaction in a transportation setting. *Logistics and Transportation Review, 30*(4), 327–338.

Ritchie, J. R. B., & Goeldner, C. R. (1987). *Travel, tourism and hospitality research: A handbook for managers and researchers*. NY: Wiley.

Schewe, C., & Calantone, R. (1978). Psychographic segmentation of tourists. *Journal of Travel Research, 16*(3), 14–20.

Schul, P., & Crompton, J. L. (1983). Search behavior of international vacationers: Travel specific lifestyles and sociodemographic variables. *Journal of Travel Research, 22*(2), 25–31.

Silverberg, K. E., Backman, S. J., & Backman, K. F. (1996). A preliminary investigation into the psychographics of nature-based travelers to the southeastern United States. *Journal of Travel research*, *35*(2), 19–28.

Triandis, H. (1979). *Attitude and attitude change*. NY: Wiley.

Vazquez Casielles, R., Trespalacios Gutiérrez J. A., & Rodríguez del Bosque, I. A., (2005). *Marketing: Estrategias y Aplicaciones Sectoriales*. Navarra: Thomson-Cívitas (4ª Ed).

Vyncke, P. (2002). Lifestyle segmentation. *European Journal of Communication*, *17*(4), 445–464.

Wahlers, R. G., & Etzel, M. J. (1985). Vacation preference as a manifestation of optimal stimulation and lifestyle experience. *Journal of Leisure Research*, *17*(4), 283–295.

Witt, S. F., & Moutinho, L. (1994). *Tourism marketing and management handbook*, 2nd ed. London: Prentice-Hall.

Woodside, A. G., & Pitts, R. E. (1976). Effects of consumer life styles, demographics and travel activities on foreign and domestic travel behavior. *Journal of Travel Research*, *14*(winter), 13–15.

Chapter 11

Correlates of Destination Risk Perception and Risk Reduction Strategies

Galia Fuchs and Arie Reichel

Introduction

Choosing a tourist destination often involves dealing with various types of perceived risks ranging from disappointment with the expected experience through the waste of precious vacation time, to the fear of physical harm due to disease, crime or terror. When faced with risk associated with purchasing a new product or service, consumers often utilize risk reduction strategies that tend to adjust the level of the perceived risk. Do tourists differ in their perceptions of risk associated with a particular destination? Can we identify tourist characteristics that distinguish between various risk perceptions as well as between various risk reduction strategies? Is the choice of a particular type of tour associated with specific types of risk? Does the country of origin matter in terms of perceived risk? In order to attempt to answer these questions, this exploratory study attempts to examine the relationships between destination risk perceptions, risk reduction strategies, tourist characteristics and type of tour. First, the concept of tourist destination risk perception is clarified and elaborated on through the concept of tourist as a consumer faced with a decision about intangible service. The various dimensions of destination risk perceptions are analyzed in relation to risk reduction strategies as well as tourist characteristics and the type preferred tour.

Consumer behavior literature has been discussing the theory of perceived risk for over four decades (Assael, 1995; Engel, Blackwell, & Miniard, 1995). The theory assumes that consumers perceive risk in their purchasing behavior and generally act to reduce it. Perceived risk is defined as "a consumer's perception of the overall negativity of a course of action based upon an assessment of the possible negative outcomes and the likelihood that those outcomes will occur" (Mowen & Minor, 1998, p. 176). According to "classical" consumer behavior literature (Jacoby & Kaplan, 1972; Peter & Ryan, 1976), consumer perceived risk is composed of a number of types of risk: physical — the risk of physical harm to the consumer as a result of the functioning of the product; financial — the risk that the money invested in the product will be lost; performance — the risk identified with the possibility that the product will not function as expected; social — the fear that the purchase will not conform to the standards of the reference group; psychological — the fear that the product will not be compatible with the self-image of the consumer; time — the possibility that the consumption of the product will be overly time consuming; and opportunity loss — the risk that by taking a course of one action, the consumer will miss out on doing something else he or she would prefer to do. As soon as consumers have experienced a certain level of risk, their behavior changes, from delaying the purchase to using strategies designed to reduce the risk level to a "tolerable" one (Mowen & Minor, 1998; Roselius, 1971).

Literature Review

Despite the importance of consumer risk perception, tourism literature has only recently turned its attention to this subject. Roehl and Fesenmaier (1992) were among the first to study risk perception in tourism. Utilizing factor analysis, they identified three basic dimensions of perceived risk: physical-equipment risk, vacation risk and destination risk. Tsaur, Tzeng, and Wang (1997) focused on two main types of risk: physical risk, which refers to the possibility that an individual's health is likely to be exposed to injury and sickness because of conditions such as law and order, weather and hygiene, as well as equipment risk, which refers to the dangers arising from the malfunctioning of equipment, such as insufficient telecommunication facilities, unsafe transportation and breakdown of vehicles. One of their main findings is that law and order was the most important aspect of tourist perceived risk.

Mitchell and Vassos (1997) found that the risk factor deemed most risky to holiday tourists was "Your hotel may not be as nice as it appears in the brochures", and the least risky was "Your representative guide will not participate in activities such as windsurfing or scuba diving". Mäser and Weiermair (1998) found that perceived risk could be used in part as a variable in explaining decision-making processes of tourists: The higher the perceived risk, the more information tourists seem to seek and the more rational the decision process becomes. Sönmez and Graefe (1998b) examined types of risk associated with international travel and the overall degree of safety felt by the tourists. They identify several types of risk such as equipment/functional risk ("possibility of mechanical, equipment, organizational problems occurring during travel or at destination (transportation, accommodations, attractions), financial risk, health risk, physical risk, political instability risk, psychological risk, satisfaction risk, social risk, terrorism and time risk. The results revealed that perceived risks were found to be strong predictors of the likelihood of avoiding destinations. The higher the perceived risk of the foreign destination, the higher the likelihood that consumers will decide to avoid visiting it (Sönmez & Graefe, 1998a, b).

The present study explores the concept of destination risk perception and attempts to reveal the possible relationships between tourist destination risk perception, tourist characteristics, type of travel and usage of risk reduction strategies. It is assumed that tourist characteristics such as country of origin, age, religious persuasion, motivation to visit the destination and past experience have an effect on the level of destination risk perception. Moreover, the type of travel is related to risk perception in the sense that, for example, group-based package tours require fewer decisions and presumably involve less risk.

Furthermore, risk reduction strategies are clearly related to destination risk perception. These exploratory interrelationships have to date not been studied simultaneously with respect to a specific tourist destination.

Methodology

A structured tourist destination risk perception questionnaire (see Fuchs & Reichel, 2004; 2006) was developed. Questions asked about the respondents include: (a) overall destination risk perception; (b) types and dimensions of destination risk; (c) risk reduction strategies; (d) socio-demographic characteristics, including type of tour. The target population of the main field study was international tourists to Israel, a country known for a long history of tourist crises (Mansfeld, 1999). The choice of a highly risky destination enables to focus on tourists who are in the midst of consuming a risky "tourist products" and to examine variations in attitudes and perception toward risk and risk reduction strategies.

During July 2000, letters were sent to managers of hotels around the country, with the exception of the resort city of Eilat. They were asked for permission to interview tourists staying at the hotels they run. Eilat was excluded from the sample because according to the statistics and expert opinions during the months the research took place (August and September) most of the tourists in Eilat are Israelis. Of the hotels whose managers answered positively to the request and which hosted international tourists in the relevant period, interviews were conducted in 18 hotels and 3 youth hostels in Jerusalem, Tel Aviv, Tiberias, the Dead Sea, Arad, Netanya and in the Solarium at the Dead Sea. Within each site the respondents were randomly approached. The hotels and youth hostels represent a wide range of accommodation, from budget to the luxurious.

The questionnaire was translated from English into French, German and Russian by professional translators and then retranslated into English and Hebrew to assure accuracy of meaning. Fourteen English, German and Russian speaking students trained for interviews were able to conduct 776 face-to-face interviews from August 17, 2000 through the onset of the Palestinian Al-Aksa Intifada at the end of September 2000. Emphasis was placed on the fact that the research should be conducted in as short a timeframe as possible to avoid interference resulting from various unexpected events such as political, economic or terrorist acts.

The study's response rate was extremely high: 98%. The remaining 2% were tourists from the former Soviet Union. It is assumed that this is due to cultural biases associated with the long tradition of avoiding expressing opinion to strangers. The high consent rate may have been due to the interviewing techniques of qualified interviewers and by their approaching the tourists at the right and convenient time for the tourists while in their hotels and not on sites visited. Also, the interviewers reported a very high desire to express feedback on the visit, both negative and positive, as part of the interview process. A total of 760 questionnaires were completed, 415 female respondents (54.6%) and 345 male respondents (45.5%). The ages ranged from 18 to 70+, as presented in Table 11.1. The tourists were asked to state their country of residence: the largest category was United States and Canada ($n=207$, 27.2%), while the smallest category was Jordan ($n=8$, 1.1%). Table 11.2 presents the distribution of perceived average income.

Table 11.1: Age distribution of interviewees.

Age group	Frequency	Percentage
18–29	190	25.0
30–39	94	12.4
40–49	136	17.9
50–59	132	17.4
60–69	150	19.7
70+	58	7.6
Total	760	100.0

Table 11.2: Perceived average income.

Income perception	Frequency	Percentage
Much below average income	34	4.5
Below average income	72	9.5
Same as average income	286	37.6
Above average income	262	34.5
Much above average income	61	8.0
Refused to answer	45	5.9
Total	760	100.0

Discussion of Findings

To test the construct validity of the questionnaire, a factor analysis was utilized, employing the method of principal component with Varimax rotation. The summary of the results of the factor analysis is presented in Table 11.3. The cutting point of variable inclusion in a particular factor was above 0.5. Accordingly, 18 variables were grouped into six factors accounting for 53.5% of the variance. The following questions were not included in any factor due to low loading (< 0.5): Q27 — "Tourist behavior"; Q32 — "Possible strikes"; Q12 — "Value for money"; Q38 — "Status in life"; Q19 — "Epidemics"; Q21 — "Personal satisfaction"; and Q28 — "Food would not be good".

Factor 1, "human-induced risk" includes the questions that measured crime, terror, political instability and crowded sightseeing. This factor reflects the risk perception of possible physical harm stemming from human activities. Factor 2, "financial risk", includes the questions that measure expenses in Israel, the assumed costs of touring Israel as compared to touring other destinations, extra expenses at home and the influence of the trip to Israel on the financial situation of the tourist. This factor reflects the financial risk perception in selecting a particular destination. Factor 3, "service quality risk", includes the questions that measure the friendliness of the hosts, quality of facilities

Table 11.3: Validation results: Factor analysis results (Varimax rotation).

Factor	Loading	Eigenvalues	% of Variance	Cronbach's alpha	Pearson
Factor 1 "human-induced risks"		2.90	11.10		
Q35 Political unrest	0.81			0.75	—
Q31 Terrorism	0.79				
Q29 Crime	0.61				
Q23 Crowded	0.51				
Factor 2 "financial"		2.58	9.90		
Q14 Extra expenses at the destination	0.73			0.71	—
Q20 More expensive than …	0.71				
Q26 Incidental expenses at home	0.61				
Q30 Impact on financial situation	0.61				
Factor 3 "service quality"		2.50	9.67		
Q37 Israelis would not be friendly	0.72			0.75	—
Q34 Facilities would not be acceptable	0.52				
Q18 Hotels unsatisfactory	0.50				
Factor 4 "socio-psychological"		2.40	9.34		
Q17 What friends think	0.74			0.68	—
Q33 What family thinks	0.72				
Q15 Self-image	0.65				
Factor 5 "natural disasters and car accidents"		1.81	6.96		
Q22 Natural disasters	0.67			0.35	0.25
Q25 Car accidents	0.64				
Factor 6 "food safety problem and weather"		1.70	6.54		
Q11 Food safety	0.73			0.37	0.23
Q13 Weather	0.58				

in the country visited and level of satisfaction with the hotels. This factor reflects the risk that the service quality, whether human or physical, at the destination will not be satisfactory. Factor 4, "socio-psychological risk", includes questions that measure the opinions of families and friends of the tourist and the compatibility of the trip with self-image. This factor reflects the socio-psychological risk stemming from the decision to travel to Israel. Factor 5, "natural disasters and car accidents", includes questions that measure the possibility of these occurrences while staying in Israel. Factor 6, "food safety and weather", reflects the risk perception stemming from food safety and bad weather conditions.

In addition, overall destination risk perception was measured by an index consisting of the following statements: (1) Israel is a safe country for tourists; (2) I expected my friends would worry about my safety while I was in Israel; (3) Prior to your trip did you consider Israel more dangerous than other places around the world? (4) Considering your experience in Israel so far, how would you rate Israel in terms of risk? (5) To what extent do your friends and relatives see Israel as a risky place to visit?

In the following sections, variables associated with the above destination risk perception factors will be presented in terms of statistically significant T-test results as well as ANOVA along with Post-Hoc Scheffe results. Specifically, numerous possible relations among risk factors and tourist characteristics were examined in exploratory fashion. Yet, only significant results will be presented below, as related to country of origin, age, religious persuasion, motivation for visiting the destination and past experience in international travel. The relationship between risk perception factors and risk reduction strategies were examined by Pearson correlations. In order to explore risk perceptions and risk reduction strategy variations between tourists who chose different types of tour (FIT vs. group travel) a two-group discriminant analyses were utilized.

Tourist Characteristics

Country of origin (residence) The overall destination risk perception of tourists from Germany was higher than that of tourists from the USA and Canada, France and other Western European countries (mean of 3.63 vs. 3.04, 2.80 and 2.90, respectively). The human-induced risk perception of tourists from Germany was higher ($m=3.18$) than that of tourists from France ($m=2.53$). With regard to financial risk, tourists from Germany and France perceived higher levels of risk than those from the USA and Canada (means of 2.58, 2.59 vs. 2.01, respectively). Furthermore, it was found that tourists from Africa perceived higher levels of socio-psychological and food safety and weather problems than tourists from Germany, USA and Canada (socio-psychological: mean=1.97 vs. 1.30, 1.22, respectively; food safety: mean=3.21 vs. 1.97 and 2.39, respectively).

Age The sample was divided into six age groups: 18–29, 30–39, 40–49, 50–59, 60–69 and 70+. The risk perception of the youngest group was higher than that of all other age groups in terms of the overall destination risk perception, human-induced risk, financial risk as well as service quality risk. For example, with respect to overall risk perception, the group of 18–29, mean=3.46 vs. $m=2.50$ in the age group of 60–69. Also, human-induced risk: the 18–29 group's mean=3.26 vs. mean=2.5 in the 60–69 group.

Religious persuasion The overall and the human-induced risk perceptions of Jewish tourists were lower than those of Catholic and Protestant tourists, and of those who claimed "no religious affiliation" (the overall risk: 2.6 vs. 3.28, 3.37, 3.35, respectively; human-induced risk: 2.37 vs. 2.95, 3.17, 3.10, respectively). Service quality risk and natural disasters and car accidents risk perceptions of Catholic tourists were lower than that of Jewish tourists and those with "no religious affiliation" (service risk: 1.65 vs. 2.09, 2.52 respectively; natural disasters and car accidents: 1.35 vs. 1.79, 1.82, respectively).

Motivation for visiting the destination The overall destination risk perception and the human-induced risk perception of tourists, whose principal motive for visiting the destination was visiting friends and relatives, were lower than those of tourists whose motives for visiting were sightseeing, religious or cultural. For example, the overall risk perception mean of the visiting friends and family segment was 2.54 vs. sightseeing = 3.47; religious segment = 3.21 and cultural tourism = 3.11.

Past experience in international tourism Financial, service quality, socio-psychological, natural disaster and car accidents, food safety and weather risk perceptions of tourists with no past experience in international tourism were somewhat higher than those of experienced tourists. For example, in terms of financial risk, the formers mean was 2.88 vs. 2.36 of the latter. However, past experience was not found to be a factor that influenced the overall destination and human-induced risk perceptions. Furthermore, it was found that the greater the past experience in visiting the particular destination (Israel), the lower the overall risk perception ($r = -0.21$).

Risk Reduction Strategies

The analyses of the study's results imply that tourists use various strategies to reduce the level of destination risk perceptions to levels that enable them to actually visit the destination. The strategies of risk reduction include purchasing inexpensive tourist products, developing loyalty (to hotels in which they have stayed before, to the travel agent or to a particular destination), searching for information (from brochures, tourist organizations, the Internet, friends and relatives), cooperative decision making, consulting people who have visited the destination in the past, watching television programs on the destination and reading articles about the destination.

The results indicate that the higher the overall risk perception of the destination and its components, the higher the utilization of risk reduction strategies. The strategies most used were the following (in decreasing order): (1) consulting with past visitors to the destination (Israel); (2) reading articles on the destination; (3) loyalty to hotels they had stayed at in the past; and (4) gathering information from friends and relatives. A link was also found between several risk reduction strategies and various risk dimensions. For example, a positive moderate association was found between the perceived human-induced risk and the search for information from friends and relatives ($R^2 = 0.23$) and between the planning of an inexpensive trip and the financial and service quality perceived risk ($R^2 = 0.27$).

The above analyses focused on destination risk perceptions and socio-demographic characteristics of the tourists as well as the motivation for visiting the destination, past experience in international tourism and risk reduction strategies. It is also interesting to see if the choice of travel mode reflects particular destination risk perceptions. Specifically, would tourists on a group tour exhibit different destination risk perception patterns than those who chose to travel on their own (FIT)? The differences between the two groups were examined by means of discriminant analysis.

Type of Travel and Destination Risk Perceptions

Table 11.4 depicts the results of the discriminant analysis comparing FIT and group travel in terms of destination risk dimensions. As demonstrated in Table 11.4, FIT travelers are associated with natural disaster and car accident, service quality and financial destination risk dimensions. Group travelers, on the other hand, are associated with general risk, human-induced risk, food safety and weather and socio-psychological risk dimensions. The classification results indicated 67.6% correctly classified cases.

Type of Travel and Risk Reduction Strategies

The choice of a type of travel is assumed to correlate with preferences for the usage of risk reduction strategies. As noted earlier, risk reduction strategies include collecting information from travel agents, friends and relatives, the Internet, TV programs, articles and consulting with people who have previously visited the destination. Moreover, making the vacation short and relatively inexpensive. The results of the discriminant analysis of FIT vs. group travel in terms of risk reduction strategies are presented in Table 11.5. As can be seen in Table 11.5, the FIT segment is associated mainly with choosing inexpensive trips, searching information on the Internet, preference for short trips. On the other hand, the group travelers are associated mainly with acquiring information through travel agents, reading articles about the destination, watching TV programs and gathering information from friends. The discriminant function correctly classified 62.2% of the cases.

Table 11.4: Discriminate analysis results FIT vs. groups travelers risk dimensions.

Risk dimensions	**Standardized coefficients**
Natural disaster and car accident	0.53
Service quality	0.49
Financial	0.34
General risk	−0.30
Human-induced risk	−0.19
Food safety and weather	−0.17
Socio-psychological	−0.05

1. FIT centroid 0.47
2. Group centroid -0.39

Table 11.5: Discriminate analysis FIT vs. groups, travelers, risk reduction strategies.

Risk reduction strategies	Standardized coefficients
Inexpensive tourist products	0.60
Gather information from travel agent	−0.49
Search for information on the Internet	0.41
Read articles about Israel	−0.33
Make a short trip	0.15
Watch TV programs about Israel	−0.12
Search for information from friends and relatives	−0.07
1. FIT centroid 0.26	
2. Group centroid -0.22	

Conclusions and Implications

Within the limits of an exploratory study conducted during a specific period and destination (Israel), it is possible to attempt to draw conclusions. First, given the finding that the risk perception of a tourist destination is reflected in various dimensions, it is possible to adopt a market segmentation method based on risk perceptions. Specifically, it is possible to appeal first to segments whose overall risk perception is relatively low. In addition, it is possible to identify segments with high perceived-risk components that can be reduced relatively easily. For example, appealing to market segments with a high financial risk perception, which is easier to deal with (e.g., by offering discounts or low-price packages) compared, for example, to market segments characterized with a high human-induced risk perceptions. In such cases, it is possible to take advantage of risk-reduction strategies that can be applied by the marketers and supply potential customers with appropriate information about the nature of the destination via means such as Web sites, advertisements and possibly offering tour options that shield the tourist from potential risk factors. Note, however, that most risk reduction strategies are not at the disposal of the marketers.

The results of the study have also segmentation implications in terms of differences found between the group tours vs. FIT. Specifically, the FIT travelers are concerned with service quality in sites they choose to visit, dine and stay. Also, they are concerned with the financial implications of their decisions during their visit. It is less clear why they are worried about natural disasters and car accidents more than the group segment. It is possible to speculate that those independent tourists, who, for example, rent cars, tend to fear accidents. Moreover, they are on their own to deal with possible natural disaster. On the other hand, the group segment is characterized with a sense of overall destination risk perception that might be related to the idea not to travel independently. Yet, they may feel some uneasiness concerning problems of human induced risk and food safety and weather risk that group travel may not guarantee. Clearly, the choice of the travel type (group tour) does not give them choice in terms of deciding how to deal with human induced and food safety and weather risk. The study's results also indicate that the FIT segment adopts risk reduction strategies that entail product control. Specifically, purchasing inexpensive and short trips. They also search for the appropriate items via the Internet. On the other hand, the group tour segment adopts risk reduction strategies that focus on information search. They derive information from travel agents, articles dealing with the destination, watching TV programs and consulting friends and family. Clearly, the need for information, weather printed, human or electronic, cannot be overstated.

In conclusion, this exploratory study suggests an integrative framework for understanding and applying the concept of risk perception of a tourism destination and its dimensions. It clearly demonstrates the multi-faceted nature of destination risk perception. As an exploratory study, it also presents a set of variables associated with risk, namely tourist characteristics, type of tour and risk reduction strategies. These findings can serve as a basis for a thorough segmentation scheme that could be useful for dealing with destination promotional efforts. Further studies are needed to examine the utilization of risk reduction methods in various market segments. Additionally, the vulnerability of tourist destinations to issues such as the actual occurrences of terrorist acts, natural disasters, economic crises and the impact of the mass media needs to be examined in relation to tourist risk perception. Furthermore, it is important to examine tourist destination risk perceptions in terms of the weight or contribution of each of its dimensions to the decision regarding the selection of a specific destination.

References

Assael, H. (1995). *Consumer behavior and marketing action* (5th ed.). Cincinnati: South-Western College Publishing.

Engel, J., Blackwell, R., & Miniard, P. (1995). *Consumer behavior* (7th ed.). NY: Dryden Press.

Fuchs, G., & Reichel, A. (2004). Cultural differences in tourist destination risk perception: An exploratory study. *Tourism, 52*(1), 21–37.

Fuchs, G., & Reichel, A. (2006). Tourist destination risk perception: The case of Israel. *Journal of Hospitality and Leisure Marketing, 14*(2), 18–106.

Jacoby, J., & Kaplan, L. (1972). The components of perceived risk. *Advances in Consumer Research, 3*(3), 382–383.

Mansfeld, Y. (1999). Cycles of war, terror and peace: Determinates and management of crisis and recovery of the Israeli tourism industry. *Journal of Travel Research, 38*(1), 30–36.

Mäser, B., & Weiermair, K. (1998). Travel decision-making from the vantage point of perceived risk and information preferences. *Journal of Travel and Tourism Marketing, 7*(4), 107–121.

Mitchell V.-W., & Vassos, V. (1997). Perceived risk and risk reduction in holiday purchases: A cross-cultural and gender analysis. *Journal of Euromarketing, 6*(3), 47–97.

Mowen, J., & Minor, M. (1998). *Consumer behavior* (5th ed.). Englewood Cliffs, NJ: Prentice-Hall.

Peter, P., & Ryan, M. (1976). An investigation of perceived risk at the brand level. *Journal of Marketing Research, 13*(May), 184–188.

Roehl, W. S., & Fesenmaier, D. R. (1992). Risk perception and pleasure travel: An exploratory analysis. *Journal of Travel Research, 30*(4), 17–26.

Roselius, T. (1971). Consumer rankings of risk reduction methods. *Journal of Marketing, 35*(January), 56–61.

Sönmez, S., & Graefe, A. (1998a). Influence of terrorism risk on foreign tourism decisions. *Annals of Tourism Research, 25*(1), *1*, 112–144.

Sönmez, S., & Graefe, A. (1998b). Determining future travel behavior from past travel experience and perceptions of risk and safety. *Journal of Travel Research, 37*(November), 171–177.

Tsaur, S. H., Tzeng, G. H., & Wang, K. C. (1997). Evaluating tourist risks from fuzzy perspectives. *Annals of Tourism Research, 24*(4), 796–812.

Chapter 12

Segmented (Differential or Discriminatory) Pricing and Its Consequences

Asli D. A. Tasci, Ali Kemal Gurbuz and William C. Gartner

Introduction

Segmented (differential or discriminatory) pricing means selling a product or service at different prices without proportional differences in costs (Kotler, 1997; Kotler & Armstrong, 1996; Kotler, Bowen, & Makens, 2003). Loomis and Walsh (1997), define three degrees of price differentiation, perfect, imperfect and segment-based. In perfect degree, the entire potential consumer surplus is extracted with a price equal to the maximum willingness to pay per unit. In imperfect degree, some of the consumer surplus is extracted with discounts for groups of units rather than per unit, and the third degree "involves separating buyers into groups with different elasticities of demand and setting prices so that marginal revenue equals marginal cost in each" (1997, p. 356). There are several ways of applying segmented pricing. The same product or service could be sold at different prices at different places. A differential park entrance fee at different places is a good example of this practice. Another way of segmented pricing has to do with the timing of production and consumption; the same product could be sold at different prices at different times. Hospitality and tourism products are highly seasonal; therefore, segmented pricing at different times is very pertinent to the hospitality and tourism industry. In another way, the same product or service could be sold at different prices to different segments of customers (Kotler, 1997, p. 513). In the context of a destination as an international tourism product, it would be logical to assume that residents, the real owners of the place, would have cheaper access to tourism sites and facilities. The reasons could be residing in avoidance of conflicts in social rights as well as the lower income levels of resident populations.

However, in Turkey as elsewhere, there is an application of price differentiation that is contradictory to the above-mentioned assumption, as well as the requirements of sustainable tourism development. In addition to a few studies (Association of Turkish Travel Agencies, 1999), ample personal accounts with domestic tourists and hospitality business establishments reveal that it is a commonly observed fact that some hotels and resorts in Turkey apply segmented pricing for their domestic and foreign customers, toward the advantage of foreigners. Despite the fact that many demand-side and supply-side groups are aware of and complaining about this seemingly unfair price differentiation between foreign and domestic tourists, there is a lack of focus on this subject matter in the literature. This study was designed to fill this gap in the literature by surveying managers with ample experiences in the Turkish tourism industry. Acquiring more insight into the reasons for price differentiation applications in the Turkish tourism industry would help reveal better coping strategies. It is the purpose of this study to discuss the potential reasons of such a contradictory price differentiation and generate solutions to avoid the negative consequences. To this end, a few hotel managers experienced in the Turkish tourism industry were surveyed on this issue using an online research mode. The online mode was considered appropriate for this study due to the high rate of computer and Internet use by this segment of the Turkish population (State Institute of Statistics, 2004). The next section provides the theoretical background of the study followed by the description of the methods used, the results of the study, discussion and implications.

Literature Review

It is the first inclination to think that Turkish hotels and resorts charging different prices for domestic and foreign tourists, might be offering different products to the customers of different nationalities. This idea comes from the consumer behavior theory that consumers of different nationalities would have different needs, wants, motivations, and expectations (Litvin, Crotts, & Hefner, 2004; Pizam & Reichel, 1996; Reisinger & Turner, 2002; Suh & Gartner, 2004). Nationality defines even where tourists choose to go for vacation purposes. For example, in Turkey, Bodrum is a tourist destination crowded by English tourists, while Antalya, is frequented by German tourists, in general. However, offering different products at different prices for different nationalities is not the case here.

Charging different prices for different products has to do with efficient and effective use of resources as well as increasing sales in today's heterogeneous consumer markets (Liebermann, 1995). However, charging different prices for the same product, namely segmented pricing, has a wider range of explanations. Segmented pricing could be discussed by using references to economics, marketing, and consumer behavior literature due to its intimate relationship with several paradigms in this field. First of all, price differentiation is found in discussions regarding monopolistic power (Dinler, 1993). According to the model of monopolistic price differentiation, even at the level of a price set for profit maximization, there are some customers, who are willing to pay even a higher price for the product; thus, these customers still receive benefits beyond what would normally be purchase price. To achieve higher revenues, a monopolistic firm charges these customers higher prices than the others. For example, a doctor can charge his/her patients different fees depending on their income levels. There has to be some conditions to achieve such price differentiation: segments must be differentiated clearly, it should not be possible to buy a product or service at cheaper prices and sell at higher prices, and different segments need to have different price elasticity. The assumption that this kind of price differentiation would work for monopolies resides in the fact that there is lack of competition in the market thereby allowing this strategy to be easily adopted.

It should also be mentioned that most government agencies, which control public attractions, essentially have a monopoly over them. But instead of acting as monopolistic powers and maximizing revenue, they act to provide social welfare in the form of lower admission fees for country residents. Examples of this can be found in most developing countries where international tourists are present. Attraction entrance fees, when segmented pricing is practiced, will almost always be lower for domestic tourists than for foreign tourists. For example in Vietnam, local authorities and private organizations set different prices for visitors and residents. One reason is that the Vietnamese government has reduced prices at some attractions and services to encourage domestic travel (Tran, 2004).

Price differentiation is also related to the concept of 'asymmetric information', in which one party in an exchange relationship (seller or buyer) has more knowledge about the product or service (Akerlof, 1970; Spence, 1974; Rotschild & Stiglitz, 1976). Assuming the clearinghouse model, a model of price dispersion and consumer behavior, Morgan, Orzen, and Sefton (2003), conceive two types of consumers, those who are 'informed' about the entire distribution of prices and buy the product with the lowest price, and those 'captive' consumers whose purchasing behavior is based on factors other than price. They postulated that when the proportion of 'informed' consumers increased, prices paid by both consumers decreased; similarly, they postulate, when the number of competing sellers are increased, 'informed' consumers pay lower prices, while 'captive' consumers pay higher prices. In this case, we can consider foreign tourists as 'informed' of other competing destinations and domestic tourists as 'captive' for several reasons including inability to travel abroad due to financial constraints. An increasing number of foreign tourists do not seem to be lowering the prices paid by the domestic tourists so the second part of their postulation seems to hold true in this case: increased number of other similar destinations (i.e. competition) decrease prices paid by foreign tourists, while the prices paid by domestic tourists increase or stay the same.

As is stressed by Kotler (1997), for this type of pricing to work, several conditions are necessary, one of which is that it should not cause customer ill will or resentment. A good example of consequences of overlooking this condition is provided by Cox (2001) who discussed loyal customers' perception of the unfair price differentiation conduct of "Amazon.com Company" between its loyal and new customers to the advantage of the new customers. Assuming that their loyal customers would buy from the company anyway, Amazon.com charged its loyal customers higher prices for the same product than for new customers. When they received negative reactions from their loyal customers, they asserted it to be an experiment investigating the price sensitivity of their customers and paid the price difference back to their loyal customers.

The presumably unfair pricing practice of some hospitality business establishments in Turkey might be defended by looking for the source of the problem in the different steps of pricing defined by Kotler (1997). Firstly, there could be a hidden or articulated objective of this price differentiation between domestic and foreign tourists. Kotler (1997) defines common pricing objectives as 'survival', 'maximum current profit', 'maximum current revenue', 'maximum sales growth', 'maximum market skimming', 'product quality leadership' and other objectives pursued by public or nonprofit organizations (pp. 496–497).

'Survival' and 'maximum sales growth' sound logical for this pricing strategy of Turkish hospitality establishments. They might be motivated to survive in the fierce competition of home and abroad by attracting as many foreign tourists as possible, namely mass-producing and covering variable costs and some of the fixed costs, to stay in business. They also might be aiming to gain a bigger market share by offering lower prices in the short run to retain a bigger consumer base in the long run, when they can set more profitable prices. If this is the case, then the method of pricing must be 'value pricing', where a fairly low price is charged for a relatively good quality product (Kotler, 1997, p. 506). This is the case in Malaysia where the government often supports new resorts by utilizing the services of its national airline to offer no cost stopovers and by advertising new resort properties in an attempt to create repeat visitation and positive "word of mouth".

Turkish hospitality establishments might also have other objectives similar to those of nonprofit and public organizations. One such objective that comes to mind immediately is that of image betterment of Turkey as a travel destination by offering first-hand experience at lower costs. The image of Turkey is reported to be relatively more negative compared to other similar Mediterranean destinations with similar tourist products (Baloglu & McCleary, 1999; Ozsoy, 1999; Sonmez & Sirakaya, 2002). First-hand experience with a destination is commonly believed to improve the image of a destination (Dann, 1996; Fakeye & Crompton, 1991; Gartner, 1993). The idea that Turkish hospitality establishments practice such price differentiation between domestic and foreign tourists for the image betterment of Turkey sounds a little far fetched, though it is not impossible. Public tourism organizations might be the supporting player behind these practices by offering incentives, such as tax discounts, to these establishments, in some ways similar to the example of Malaysia. Considering that no written policy exists that discusses or mentions this strategy regarding Turkish tourism development this sounds even more far-fetched.

The source of the problem could reside in the second step, 'determining demand'. The domestic and foreign segments' price elasticity might be different. Morgan, Orzen and Sefton's (2003) study results suggest that increased competition, where consumers are able to easily substitute lower-priced products, results in increasing competition and lower prices. Having other Mediterranean destinations as substitutes in their choice set, foreign tourists might be more price sensitive, less elastic, and choose other destinations easily. On the other hand, for most domestic tourists, about 97% (Seckelmann, 2002), other Mediterranean countries cannot be in their choice set due to high costs of transportation involved in traveling abroad. Comparing choices of vacations in Turkish destinations versus another country, reveals that Turkey is a lower cost choice among most of its competitors. If this is the case, then the pricing method must be 'perceived-value pricing' (Kotler, 1997, p. 505); in which a vacation in Turkey is perceived to provide higher value compared to other choices.

The idea that domestic tourists have higher price elasticity than foreign tourists is potentially true. According to the economic theory, items with high cost in proportion to one's income level would usually lead to higher price elasticity (Dinler, 1993). There are exceptions and these relate to products that are essential to life such as prescription medicine. Having a relatively lower income level than most other European countries, and thus, lower propensity to travel, Turkish people's portion of tourism expenditures in their consumption basket is relatively lower than those of its neighbors (Seckelmann, 2002).

Therefore, their price elasticity for tourism products should be higher than that exhibited by foreign tourists of other European nationalities.

The problem could also source from the third step, 'estimating costs'. As a determinant of pricing, costs of offering the same product to domestic and foreign tourists might be different in terms of not only monetary expenses, but also time and energy spent by the staff while serving these two different segments. The differentiation might be related to variable costs rather than fixed costs. The domestic tourists, who may be less tolerant and more demanding, might increase variable costs, with higher consumption of items such as food and drinks, as well as require more serving time from the frontline personnel. Thus, management might be applying a more math-based pricing method such as 'target return pricing' or 'markup pricing' (Kotler, 1997) in setting differentiated prices for different segments to cover their differing costs incurred.

The fourth step of pricing could also be the source of the problem, 'analyzing competitors' costs, prices, and offers'. Turkish hospitality establishments might be conducting price benchmarking compared to other establishments in domestic and foreign markets. They might be benchmarking their prices against those of their competitors and apply a pricing method of 'going-rate pricing' (Kotler, 1997) or even lower prices than those of the going-rate. Though effective in expanding the market share in the short run, establishing lower prices than competitors' might backfire as a negative perception on product quality since "many consumers use price as an indicator of quality" (Kotler, 1997, p. 508). It might also increase usage without a balanced return to the economy of an area, which can cause environmental degradation in a shorter period of time.

Turkish hospitality establishments might be applying 'price discounts and allowances' for the foreign markets' acts of 'volume purchases' 'early payment', and 'off-season buying' which are all common through use of bulk purchasers such as tour operators and travel agencies when dealing with foreign markets. Vacation planning is one of the most distinguishing factors between domestic and foreign tourists. Domestic tourists not only use travel wholesalers and subsidiaries such as travel agencies and tour operators less than foreign tourists, but also make their vacation reservations, and thus, make their down-payments considerably, later than foreign tourists (Association of Turkish Travel Agencies, 1999). Therefore, domestic tourists cannot acquire the low prices that travel wholesalers and subsidiaries can offer to those early-planning, bulk buying foreign tourists (Association of Turkish Travel Agencies, 1999). In addition, as outlined in the marketing exchange model by Peter and Olson (1999), consumer costs include more than monetary values (see Figure 12.1). The nonmonetary costs incurred by foreigners could be surpassing those incurred by domestic tourists due to time and cognitive activity and behavior effort involved in planning activities with travel wholesalers and subsidiaries and traveling to and from another country. That is why, the total sum of all costs incurred by foreign tourists may approach or exceed those incurred by domestic tourists.

Methodology

Online modes are reported to be effective and efficient data collection techniques for studying organizational populations, such as managers, who have higher education levels

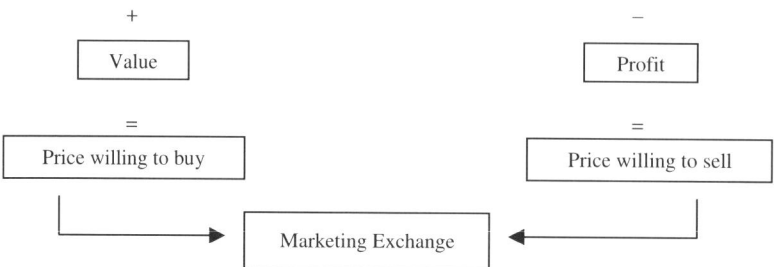

Figure 12.1: Marketing exchange model. Adapted from Peter and Olson (1999, p. 431).

as well as a higher propensity to use computer technologies and the Internet (Kaye & Johnson, 1999; Schillewaert, Langerak, & Duhamel, 1998; Tasci & Knutson, 2003). Although there are sophisticated tools of online research, the e-mail plain text was chosen for the purposes of this study. A group of 40 hotel managers from different touristic cities of Turkey were identified and reached via a mass e-mail distributed all at once. Six questions were defined to clarify the subject of this study: (1) respondents' years of experience in the tourism industry (this question aimed to provide a frame of reference in terms of respondents' proficiency and entitlement in commenting on the next questions), (2) a yes/no type, asking if generally, in Turkey, there is price differentiation for Turkish and foreign tourists, (3) for those who answered 'yes', who pays more (Turkish or foreigners), (4) the reasons of this differentiation and potential implications of this practice, (5) for those who said 'no' to the second question, the potential results of such price differentiation. The question about the potential results of both cases was asked to assess how conscious these managers were about the positive and negative consequences of such segmented pricing. Subjects were contacted four times between October 8 and 19, 2004. In 13 days, a total of 11 managers responded. Respondents answered all questions; thus, a total of 11 responses were used in the content analysis for this rather preliminary study that aims to set the basis for further investigation of the articulated problem.

Discussion of Findings

The respondents had experience in the industry ranging between 5 and 28 years, averaging 12 years. All of these respondents agreed that there is price differentiation between Turkish and foreign tourists in Turkey, in disadvantage to the Turkish tourist. Nine of them thought that, in general, Turkish tourists pay more while two others believe that it changes between different periods and different markets. As for the reasons for the price differentiation in disadvantage of domestic tourists, managers provided multiple reasons, some of which were postulated in the literature review section above. Table 12.1 summarizes the reasons articulated by the managers and number of managers mentioning these reasons.

As can be seen in Table 12.1, responses provided by the managers as the reasons of the seemingly unfair pricing can be allocated to four general categories: domestic tourists, foreign tourists, travel agencies and Turkish tourism industry in general. Responses with

Table 12.1: The reasons and number of managers mentioning these reasons.

Reasons provided for price differentiation in the disadvantage of domestic tourists		# of managers mentioned
Domestic tourists	Start planning just before their vacations	2
	Have tendency to take vacations during high seasons when prices are already high	2
	Do not use travel agencies	2
	Plan for accommodation independently	1
	Don't have other choices	1
	Vacation habits are not well-established	1
	Use hotels 1 or 2 times a year	1
	Are less in number due to low income per capita	1
Foreign tourists	Are organized in vacation planning	1
	Plan and purchase vacations in advance	1
	Are frequent users	1
	Have more demand than that of domestic	1
	Have a wider vacation time span	
Travel agencies	Foreign travel agencies get low prices	2
	Domestic travel agencies do not have competitive advantage	1
	Domestic travel agencies cannot purchase high volumes	1
	Both domestic and foreign travel agencies sell for low prices	1
Turkish tourism industry	Tourism is still a luxury items for the majority of Turkish	1
	Domestic tourism is not developed enough	1
	There is more supply than demand	1
Neutral	Prices are high for all nationalities during important holidays	1

specific references to domestic tourists travel habits are the most common followed by those with references to foreign tourists and travel agencies. Managers think that foreign tourists, who have a higher demand than domestic tourists, pay lower prices because they use travel agencies for reservations, they take vacations at a wider time horizon, they take longer vacations and they stay longer. Domestic tourists, who are less in number and plan their trips independently, plan later, have a shorter vacation period, and stay shorter periods of time. One manager specifically commented that, "Turkish vacation span is about 90 days, when it is high season already; if they traveled over a 150–180 day period they could have lower prices too." Managers also attribute the seemingly unfair pricing to travel agencies who acquire lower prices by reserving in bulk. However, one manager remarked that, "during high seasons, namely July–August, the prices of the foreign travel agencies become higher than those of domestic agencies when flight costs are added."

Some managers attribute the seemingly unfair pricing to the Turkish tourism industry in general. They postulate that domestic tourism is not yet fully developed because tourism is still a luxury item for Turkish people, who have relatively less discretionary income than residents in other countries. One manager asserted that hotel supply is more than necessary in Turkey: "The supply side works without market intelligence and feasibility studies, hotels are built in a way incongruent with the demand and unnecessarily big. To fill these hotels and pay for the fixed costs, they have to accept price offers by the foreign travel agencies. This leads to a constant price pressure in foreign markets. It is impossible to keep the quality high for long periods of time at low prices, which leads to a vicious circle of low prices to low quality in products and services, which in return, hurts the image of Turkey in total. Even with low quality products and services, domestic tourists still pay higher prices and cannot get the value in return." Also, the all-inclusive aspect of the Turkish tourism industry is criticized due to its being an impediment for spreading economic benefits to other sectors in the area. Foreign tourists stay in the hotel with all-inclusive packages and do not spend much outside of the hotel. In fact, all but one response appear to indicate that the Turkish tourism industry is not developed enough, with a lack of a well-established travel culture among domestic tourists and adolescent travel agencies.

The managers were asked what could happen if both domestic and foreign markets received the same price; their responses are summarized in Table 12.2. Several managers did not have any opinion about whether this adjustment would lead toward pricing equality. Still they believed an increase in both supply and demand might result. One manager stated that "same prices for both markets could increase domestic tourism and all inclusive establishments throughout the country; but I don't how British market, an important segment for Turkish tourism, would react to this since, they prefer room and breakfast or room only." Few managers had assumptions about the direction of the price adjustment basically

Table 12.2: Potential results of equal pricing for domestic and foreign markets.

Potential results of equal pricing for domestic and foreign markets	**# of managers mentioned**
Domestic market would develop	2
Tourism industry would develop accordingly	1
Quality would increase	1
More Turks would take vacations	2
Turkey would get out of travel agency monopoly	1
There would be increase in supply	1
All-inclusive deals would spread for the benefit of more Turkish tourists	1
There would be differences between tourist segments from different origins	1
Lower prices for domestic -quality would not increase at all	1
Higher prices for foreign-market would slow down the business but quality would increase	1
Higher prices for foreign-market would slow down the business	1
Prices can't be the same	2
There would be no difference	1

favoring higher prices for foreign tourists rather than lower prices for domestic markets. They felt that potentially of increasing tourism revenues would provide more funds for promotion and opening of luxury facilities. One manager elaborated on his answer by stating "if domestic tourists get the low prices foreigners get, there would be more tourism traffic but the quality would not increase a bit, if the foreigners get the higher prices domestic tourists pay, then the market would slow down in both short and long run but the quality would increase. The problem could be solved with establishing small facilities entailing the historic and natural properties and the uniqueness of Turkey with good quality, receiving fewer but better tourists rather than going for large volumes of tourists with limited budgets."

A couple of managers asserted that prices cannot be the same due to unique properties of tourism supply and demand (i.e. products cannot be stored and tourism demand is rather elastic). They purported that one cannot define a fixed price for all markets as managers conduct yield management and revenue management during slow times by lowering their prices. One manager asserted that, "it is wrong to look at it from foreign-domestic perspective. The most important factor in vacation decision-making is discretionary time. If they don't have it, it doesn't matter if the prices are the same for a Turkish or German tourist with no time to spare for vacation. Except for the parity differences between different currencies, when the exchange rates are considered, the prices would be the same ceteris paribus." One manager mentioned that Turkish tourists prefer traveling abroad due to lower prices they get in other countries. He also suggested that there could be price differences but it should not be as big as it currently is. "Turkish tourists cannot benefit from their own country. All-inclusive deals should be abolished and the prices should be higher." Another manager commented that charging the same price to all markets would change the tourist mix between tourist segments from different origins, which, unfortunately, would lead to the perception of low quality and unsatisfying service among some customers.

Conclusions and Implications

The survey of 11 managers with a fair amount of experiences in the Turkish tourism industry revealed that prices are lower for foreign tourists due to the fact that they use travel agencies for reservation, they take vacations at a wider time horizon, they take longer vacations and they stay longer. Conversely domestic tourists, who plan their trips independently, plan later, have a shorter vacation period, and stay shorter periods of time. Some of these managers attribute this to the undeveloped nature of domestic tourism citing a lack of an established travel culture among domestic tourists. One can easily justify this price differentiation for the Turkish tourism industry as a normal management strategy. However, this would overlook and jeopardize some sociocultural dynamics as well as support for tourism development. This study revealed that managers are aware of the negative impacts of this type of pricing. Managers recognized the fact that domestic tourists complain about it and demand the same prices or attempt to switch to alternatives. In addition, they are aware that lower prices for foreign tourists sends the low-quality message to the foreign tour agencies, which in turn, attracts low or middle income foreign tourists, which leaves lower profits for the industry. One of the determinants of the economic impact of tourism is defined as the type of tourist a destination gets; "larger numbers of tourists generate higher social costs in terms of their impingement upon the life styles of the host community" (Ryan, 1996, p. 70) as well as worse ecological and sociocultural deterioration due to impingement on the cultural and ecological carrying capacity of an area (Chambers, 1997; Crandall, 1987; de Kadt, E. 1979; Lanfant, Allcock, & Bruner, 1995; Oppermann & Chon, 1997; Sharpley, 1994; Williams, 1987).

In her article discussing the fairness of differential (discriminating) pricing, Cox (2001) states that, "price-setting decisions, or decision-making processes, should be free of unacceptable bias or prejudice, and should not offend against the fairness judgment of those involved in the procedures" (p. 274). An outcome that fails to meet the expectation of any party involved in an exchange process would create "tension and perception of unfairness, and "the person receiving the inequitable outcome will feel angry" (p. 274). This is what happens in this case too. Domestic tourists, who know about the differential pricing feel resentment about this treatment. In the case of Amazon.com Company, Cox (2001) argues that customers felt resentment not merely due to price differentiation but because of the policy that was viewed as being 'unfair'. She argues that loyal customers deserve lower prices, while the Company did exactly the opposite of it by breaking the laws of 'distributive and procedural justice' (p. 265). The laws of 'distributive and procedural justice' can be considered as broken in the case of domestic tourists receiving higher prices, since they would claim more rights in using their own land cheaper than an outsider and would feel resentment from being unable to use their own land (Chambers, 1997), considered a common good.

Several tactics can be used to avoid domestic tourists' resentment and anger due to segmented pricing. The easiest one is keeping the pricing strategies of the company as secret. When consumers don't know about segmented pricing, there is no problem. However, in today's increased communication age through mass media and computer technologies, it is almost impossible to keep such a secret. Therefore, more productive and socially responsible ways need to be utilized. Researchers postulate that 'short-changed' consumers would not feel resentment when another group of less fortunate consumers, such as students and pensioners, receive products at cheaper prices; however, they also caution that this would not be the case when the product of concern is a luxury item (Cox, 2001; Martins & Monroe, 1993, 1994; Galston, 1980). Tourism products are luxury items *per se*, even more so for domestic tourists than for foreign in this case as stated by managers surveyed in this study.

Cox (2001) also recommends providing explanations for such segmented pricing, in ways that consumers find their motives acceptable, to avoid the perception of unfairness and resentment. She also recommends harnessing consumers' perception of a company's goodwill through use of charitable acts. For example, if the motive of Turkish hospitality establishments' segmented pricing is expanding market share for Turkey in the international tourism arena and/ or betterment of the image of Turkey through visitation, then these need to be explained to Turkish consumers to gain their support rather than their resentment and anger. Cox also suggests that, "if higher prices are accompanied with added services or product features, customers may be more accepting of these prices" (2001, p. 271). This could be a useful strategy when dealing with domestic tourists most of whom are commonly observed to be more demanding than most foreign tourists. In the short run domestic tourists could be charged the same price with foreign tourists to avoid resentment and extra for added services when necessary.

Higher prices for foreign tourists and increasing the quality of tourism products may be a better solution in the long run. Consumers will be less sensitive to product price if they (1) believe that they are buying a unique product, (2) are unaware of substitute products, (3) receive high end benefits compared to the total expenditure, and (4) receive high quality (Kotler, Bowen, & Makens, 2003). Consumers are believed to be willing to pay higher prices for higher quality products. Thus, lower price ranges of Turkish tourism products could diminish Turkey to a low-end tourism product destination for foreign markets in the long run. A small change in prices might direct these foreign markets to switch to a substitute destination if the Turkish tourism industry does not find a way of increasing their loyalty. Turkey would continue to be a high-end brand for its own residents, most of who do not have any substitutes and thus, would remain loyal *per se*. Therefore, the prices for foreign markets should be increased along with the quality of tourism products, eventually moving the brand to better quality and a higher price position (Kotler & Armstrong, 1996, p. 381).

Tactics such as long-term payment plans on vacations by travel agencies need to be used to increase domestic tourism since it is as important as inbound tourism due to its benefits of (1) slowing down economic leakage by being an alternative to outbound tourism, (2) being less dependent on international fluctuations in financial, social and political conditions, (3) increasing the social consciousness among residents, (4) increasing economic activity within and between regions, and (5) diminishing economic differences among regions by allowing better distribution of economic gains (Erdogan, 1995, p. 140) to name a few. Defending domestic tourism as a chance for regional development in Turkey, Seckelmann (2002) suggests diversion of domestic tourists to destinations in the less-developed and less-popular East and South-east Anatolia while keeping the prices more stable for them.

With a limited sampling frame of managers, this study is more preliminary than conclusive in studying this subject matter. Hence, future studies can conduct large-scale surveys of managers from different regions of Turkey with different level of tourism development in an effort to reveal regional differences. Also, studies of pricing applications in other countries would help benchmark policies to fully understand the pros and cons of segmented pricing. There is a need for developing and underdeveloped destinations to balance their economic gain against the potential for socio-cultural and environmental losses due to tourism development. Pricing may be one way to help achieve this balance.

References

Akerlof, G. (1970). The market for lemons: Quality uncertainty and the market mechanism. *Quarterly Journal of Economics, 84*, 485–500.

Association of Turkish Travel Agencies (Turkiye Seyahat Acentaları Birligi). (1999). "Arastırma: Yurtici Seyahat Pazarı Raporu." *TURSAB Aylık Dergi, 185*, 33–56.

Baloglu, S., & McCleary, K. W. (1999). U.S. International travelers' images of four Mediterranean destinations: A comparison of visitors and nonvisitors. *Journal of Travel Research, 38*(2), 144–152.

Chambers, E. (Ed.) (1997). *Tourism and culture, an applied perspective.* State University of New York Press, Albany.

Cox, J. L. (2001). Can differential prices be fair? *Journal of Product and Brand Management, 10*(5), 264–275.

Crandall, L. (1987). The social impact of tourism on developing regions and its measurement. In: J. R. B. Ritchie, & C. R. Goeldner, (Eds), *Travel, tourism, and hospitality research — A handbook for managers and researchers* (pp. 373–383). Wiley and Sons. NY: Wiley and Sons.

Dann, G. M. S. (1996). Tourists' images of a destination — An alternative analysis. *Recent Advances in Tourism Marketing Research, 5*(1/2), 41–55.

Dinler, Z. (1993). *Mikroekonomi,* Bursa: Ekin Kitabevi Yayinlari.

Erdogan, H. (1995). *Ekonomik, Sosyal, Cevresel Yonleriyle uluslararasi Turizm.* Ankara.

Fakeye, P. C., & Crompton, J. L. (1991). Image differences between prospective, first-time, and repeat visitors to the Lower Rio Grande Valley. *Journal of Travel Research, 30*(2), 10–16.

Galston, W. (1980). *Justice and the human good.* Chicago: The University of Chicago Press.

Gartner, W. C. (1993). Image formation process. *Journal of Travel and Tourism Marketing, 2*(2/3), 191–215.

Kadt, E. D. (Ed.) (1979). *Tourism — passport to development?: Perspectives on the social and cultural effects of tourism in developing countries.* New York: Oxford University Press.

Kaye, B. K., & Johnson, T. J. (1999). Research methodology: Taming the cyber frontier. *Social Science Computer Review, 17*(3), 323–337.

Kotler, P. (1997). *Marketing management-analysis, planning, implementation, and control* (9th ed.). Upper Saddle River, NJ: Prentice-Hall, Inc.

Kotler, P. & Armstrong G. (1996). Principles of *marketing* (7th ed.). Upper Saddle River, NJ: Prentice-Hall, Inc.

Kotler, P., Bowen, J. & Makens J. (2003). *Marketing for hospitality and tourism,* (3rd ed.). Upper Saddle River, NJ: Pearson Education, Inc.

Lanfant, M. F., Allcock, J. B., & Bruner, E. M. (Eds). (1995). *International tourism — identity and change,* London: Sage Publications Ltd.

Liebermann, Y. (1995). Behavioral aspects of product line pricing: An actual marketplace perspective. *Pricing Strategy and Practice, 3*(1), 14–221.

Litvin, S. W., Crotts, J. C., & Hefner, F. L. (2004). Cross-cultural tourist behaviour: A replication and extension involving Hofstede's uncertainty avoidance dimension. *The International Journal of Tourism Research, 6*(1), 29–37.

Loomis, J. B. & Walsh, R. G. (1997). Recreation economic decisions: Comparing benefits and costs. Venture Publishing, Inc, State College, PA.

Martins, M. and& Monroe, K. B. (1994). Perceived price fairness: A new look at an old construct. In: C. T. Allen, & D. R. John, Provo, UT *Advances in consumer research,* (Vol. 21, pp. 75–78). Deborah Roedder John, Provo, UT: Association for Consumer Research.

Morgan, J., Orzen, H., & Sefton, M. (2003). An experimental study of price dispersion. Retrieved on 01/09/2004 from the WWW: http://www.nottingham.ac.uk/economics/cedex/papers/mos3.pdf

Oppermann, M. & Chon, K.S. (1997). *Tourism in developing countries.* International Thomson Business Press, London.

Ozsoy, O. (1999). Dunu, Bugunu, Yariniyla Turkiye'yi Dunya'ya Acmak. Ziya Ofset, Istanbul.

Peter, J. P., & Olson, C. O. (1999). *Consumer behavior and marketing strategy.* New York: Irwin McGraw-Hill.

Pizam, A., & Reichel, A. (1996). The effect of nationality on tourist behavior: Israeli tour guides' perceptions. *Journal of Hospitality and Leisure Marketing, 4*(1), 23–49.

Reisinger, Y., & Turner, L. W. (2002). Cultural differences between Asian tourist markets and Australian hosts, part 1. *Journal of travel Research, 40*(3), 295–315.

Rotschild, M., & Stiglitz, J. (1976). Equilibrium in competitive insurance markets: An essay on the economics of imperfect information. *Quarterly Journal of Economics, 90*, 629–649.

Ryan, C. (1996). *Recreational tourism: A social science perspective.* International Thomson Business Press, London.

Schillewaert, N., F. Langerak, & Duhamel, T. (1998). Non-probability sampling for WWW surveys: A comparison of methods. *Journal of the Market Research Society, 40*(4), 307–322.

Seckelmann, A. (2002). Domestic tourism — a chance for regional development in Turkey?" *Tourism Management, 23*(1), 85–92.

Sharpley, R. (1994). *Tourism, tourists and society.* St. Edmundsbury Press, Cambridgeshire.

Sonmez, S., & Sirakaya, E. (2002). A distorted destination image? The case of Turkey. *Journal of Travel Research, 41*(2), 185–196.

Spence, M. (1974). *Market signaling*, (Cambridge, MA): Harvard University Press.

State Institute of Statistics (Devlet Istatistik Enstitusu). (2004). Hanehalki Bilisim Teknolojileri 2004 Kullanim Anketi." (Release date: 10/15/2004). Retrieved November 20, 2004 at WWW: http://www.die.gov.tr/TURKISH/SONIST/HHBilisim/hhbilisim.html

Suh, Y. K., & Gartner, W. C. (2004). Preferences and trip expenditures — a conjoint analysis of visitors to Seoul, Korea. *Tourism Management, 25*(1), 127–137.

Tasci, A. D. A., & Knutson, B. J. (2003). Online research modes: Waiting for leisure, hospitality and tourism researchers. *Journal of Hospitality and Leisure Marketing, 10*(3/4), 57–83.

Tran, H. (2004) *American tourists image of Vietnam.* MS Thesis. Department of Forest Resources, University of Minnesota, St. Paul, Minnesota.

Weiermair, K. (2000). Tourists' perceptions toward and satisfaction with service quality in the cross-cultural service encounter: Implications for hospitality and tourism management. *Managing Service Quality, 10*(6), 397–406.

Williams, P. W. (1987). Evaluating environmental impact and physical carrying capacity in tourism. In: J. R. B. Ritchie, & C. R. Goeldner, (Eds), *Travel, tourism, and hospitality research — A handbook for managers and researchers* (pp. 385–397). New York: Wiley.

PART IV:
CONSUMER BEHAVIOR

Introduction

Metin Kozak and Luisa Andreu

The most common consumer (buyer or end-user) behavior model consists of three stages: pre-purchase, consumption and post-consumption. In the first stage, potential tourists search for information about various destinations and choose one destination to vacation. A variety of supply- and demand-based factors influence the choice of destinations or the decision to go on holidays: psychological, economic, social, political, geographical and demographic. In the second stage, tourists are expected to have their own experiences with products or services in order to make a judgment about the level of their satisfaction or attitude. They need physically to be in the destination owing to the inseparability of production and consumption of tourism products and services. In the last stage, after having completed their holiday experiences, tourists are expected to evaluate these experiences by matching the outcome not only with information sought from various sources but also with their expectations, evaluate their holidays within the context of satisfaction or dissatisfaction, prefer to come back or switch to other domestic or international destinations and tell others about favorable or unfavorable parts of their experiences.

Given this, it is obvious that, as consumer behavior, the term tourist behavior is also made up of various study subjects: image, attitude, perception, satisfaction, choice, motivations, decision making and so on. As a result of its proposed close relationship with the repeat purchase or the repeat visit behavior, customer satisfaction plays a vital role in the structure of consumer behavior models (e.g. Mountinho, 1987; Yi, 1990). Past empirical studies in the fields of both marketing and tourism confirmed the existence of a strong relationship between overall customer satisfaction and the intention to return (Anderson, Fornell, & Lehmann, 1994; Baker & Crompton, 2000; Bloemer & Ruyter, 1998; Halstead & Page, 1992) and between overall customer satisfaction and the intention to recommend (Sivadas & Baker-Prewitt, 2000; Zeithaml, Berry, & Parasuraman, 1996). Thus, greater customer satisfaction might result in a greater intention to repurchase or return and recommend. This part presents the findings of several research studies to be considered as an example for each stage of the consumer behavior model (i.e. motivations, satisfaction and behavioral intention).

The first chapter is based upon the discussion of motivations of pleasure visitors. The approach-avoidance distinction is not only an appealing bipolar conception of motivation, but also a central concept in many psychological theories, as it posits that individuals are permanently avoiding the undesirable and seeking the desirable. Based on this framework, this chapter analyzes data on the motivations of Portuguese domestic pleasure travelers, showing the prevalence of avoidance (escape) motivation. Considering this result and building up on Iso-Ahola's theory of approach-avoidance dialectics, the chapter concludes by suggesting that avoidance motivation is present on every travel market segment and that positioning decisions should take into account the different forms how tourists seek to escape.

The term "tourist satisfaction" is one of the concepts that has been widely discussed in consumer behavior. The concept most likely has been discussed in a national context. The published research concentrates mostly on the satisfaction of tourists from a certain country/nation; however, there are some comparative cross/cultural tourist satisfaction studies in the tourism literature. Therefore, the scope of the next chapter is a comparison of satisfaction levels of respondents from different nationalities. In this context, it is hypothesized that cultural approximation, especially linguistic approximation is one of the important factors that impacts tourist satisfaction. The variation of satisfaction levels of tourists by different nationalities depends upon their cultural (linguistic) approximation to the host community. Tourists who are culturally (linguistically) more approximated to the host community that they are more satisfied than that of tourists who are culturally (linguistically) less approximated to the host community. Basic findings support hypothesized model that the British have the highest satisfaction levels for all satisfaction dimensions and other nationalities have lower levels than that of the British respondents.

The third chapter tests the role of non-monetary costs in an integrated model of leisure travel value. Despite the fact that services marketing literature has been improving on the theories of value, it lacks sufficient research on the role of non-monetary costs in service evaluations. It is well established in the services marketing literature that the total costs of a service transaction include not only monetary costs, but also non-monetary costs. Non-monetary costs in leisure travel experiences are important because these experiences involve greater risk-taking and more time consumption than most other service experiences. Therefore, it can be expected that the non-monetary costs of leisure travel experiences are a significant factor in determining leisure travel value. Research results revealed that the perceived non-monetary price mediated the relationships between perceived price, perceived monetary benefit and perceived overall tour value. Furthermore, results indicated that the perceived non-monetary price was a significant indicator of behavioral intentions, while the perceived monetary price was not. The chapter, on the basis of the findings, also discusses the managerial implications for leisure travel marketers.

The next chapter aims at identifying factors determining the intention to come back to a rural tourist destination, based on a survey of tourists in North Portugal. In a binary logistic regression analysis the dependent variable was defined as the respondent's belonging to a group with more versus less probability to return. Those variables used as the independent include the respondent's destination image, familiarity with the destination, season and duration of stay, gender, age and education. Apart from a global model, models for the domestic and foreign tourist market were analyzed separately. The research findings suggest that there are significant differences for domestic versus foreign respondents as long as such variables as image, length of stay and age are concerned as the determinants influencing the tendency of respondents to keep their loyalty to the rural tourist destination.

This is followed by another chapter primarily focused upon customer satisfaction and loyalty. It investigates how likely the visitors' perception of waiting time could improve their overall customer satisfaction and loyalty. The aim of this chapter is to extend an affective model of satisfaction and loyalty, with the integration of waiting time effects and the leisure experience. Undertaking a comparative analysis, this chapter analyzes visitor's experiences in leisure and tourism services, i.e. interactive museum and theme park. First, the chapter offers a conceptual framework and research hypotheses that support the research model. This chapter shows that measuring the emotional experience with the length of waiting time for museums and theme parks gives meaningful insights into how differing types of activities impact overall visitor experiences, and their impact on satisfaction and loyalty.

The last chapter of this part is based upon the discussion of the effect of price promotions on the formation of consumer loyalty toward a travel agency. Therefore, an empirical study was carried out, which was directed at consumers who traveled to South America, Central America and the Caribbean through the purchase of a tour package, and the promotional effect was analyzed through the application of structural equation models (SEM). The results indicate that price promotions indirectly affect consumer loyalty toward a travel agency and that this effect is positive when promotions are directed at consumers who give considerable importance to price when acquiring a product. As a practical implication, the authors emphasize that supporting and offering an excellent quality service than in reducing prices is the key for travel agencies to obtain loyal consumers through their commercial policy. This may result in obtaining a high level of consumer satisfaction.

References

Anderson, E. W., Fornell, C., & Lehmann, D. R. (1994). Customer satisfaction, market share and profitability: Findings from Sweden. *Journal of Marketing, 58*(July), 53–66.

Baker, D. A., & Crompton, J. L. (2000). Quality, satisfaction and behavioral intentions. *Annals of Tourism Research, 27*(3), 785–803.

Bloemer, J., & Ruyter, K. (1998). On the relationship between store image, store satisfaction and store loyalty. *European Journal of Marketing, 32*(5–6), 499–513.

Halstead, D., & Page, T. J. (1992). The effects of satisfaction and complaining behavior on consumer repurchase intentions. *Journal of Satisfaction Dissatisfaction and Complaining Behavior, 5*, 1–11.

Moutinho, L. (1987). Consumer behaviour in tourism. *European Journal of Marketing, 21*(1), 5–44.

Sivadas, E., & Baker-Prewitt, J. L. (2000). An examination of the relationship between service quality, customer satisfaction and store loyalty. *International Journal of Retail and Distribution Management, 28*(2), 73–82.

Yi, Y. (1990). A critical review of consumer satisfaction. In: V. A. Zeithaml (Ed.), *Review of marketing* (pp. 68–123). USA: American Marketing Association.

Zeithaml, V. A., Berry, L. L., & Parasuraman, A. (1996). The behavioral consequences of service quality. *Journal of Marketing, 60*(April), 31–46.

Chapter 13

Seeking to Escape: Sights over Approach-Avoidance Dialectics

Carlos Peixeira Marques

Introduction

According to Elliot and Covington (2001) "in approach motivation, behavior is instigated or directed by a positive/desirable event or possibility; in avoidance motivation, behavior is instigated or directed by a negative/undesirable event or possibility". Conceptualizing negative and positive motivation factors is not only highly intuitive, but is also easily related to many theories of motivation, emotion and attitude formation. Numerous studies in psychology and neurosciences have given empirical support to this intuitive framework (Elliot & Thrash, 2002). Central to the social-cognitive perspective of approach-avoidance motivation is the context-specific concept of goal: while "motives" are affectively (positive or negative) based dispositions to act, "goals" are adopted under the influence of those dispositions, but also taking into account expectancies regarding a specific end state (Elliot & Church, 1997). At least in the educational dominion, it has been suggested that approach goals, namely interpersonal, may be instrumental to avoidance motivations, i.e. "approach to avoid" has been identified as a coping strategy in achievement settings (Elliot & Thrash, 2002).

The main purpose of this chapter is to extend this idea to the domain of travel and tourism, suggesting that the different ways by which travellers "seek to escape" are key elements to take into account in destination positioning. This idea resulted from factor analysis of Portuguese domestic pleasure travel motivations, theoretically based on an approach-avoidance consumer motivation framework, conceptualized by Fennell (1975, 1978) and Rossiter and Percy (1987, 1991). The principal difference to the socio-psychological model of motivation developed by Iso-Ahola (1980, 1982, 1983) is the definition of "escape" and "seeking" — a narrower definition, focusing on changes on tourists' arousal, will be proposed. The structure of the chapter is as follows: after literature review and methodological framing, findings from analysis will be discussed with regard to dimensionality and factor salience, then this salience will be related to travellers' background variables assumed to influence the different ways they "seek to escape"; finally, theoretical and practical implications, with particular focus on positioning of tourism "brands", will be considered.

Literature Review

In the field of market research, Geraldine Fennell (1975) presented a generalized typology of consumer motivating situations that may be affiliated to the valence dimension of approach-avoidance motivation. At the negative extreme, the situation is primarily defined by aversive elements from which the consumer escapes by the act of consumption; there are also situations where aversive elements are anticipated, so consumer behaviour is preventive. On the positive side, she places those motives at the top of Maslow's hierarchy, turning consumption into an opportunity to seek novelty, complexity, sensory and aesthetic gratification. Fennell's typology was later refined and presented as "a conceptual framework for identifying consumer wants and formulating positioning options" (Fennell, 1978). The positive appetitive elements of motivation are now divided into two separate classes: an interest opportunity, embodying the needs to explore and to master, and a sensory pleasure opportunity related to enjoyable experiences.

Building on Fennell's work, Rossiter and colleagues (Rossiter & Percy, 1987, 1991) added an interpersonal dimension to the positive motivations, the seeking of social rewards, pursuing the goals of social approval and/or conformity. The positive motivations identified by Fennell were relabelled into intellectual stimulation and mastery, when consumers seek excitement and competence, and sensory gratification, when consumers anticipate enjoyment. On the negative side, besides problem removal and problem avoidance, new motives were also added, namely incomplete satisfaction, normal depletion and mixed approach-avoidance. Rossiter and colleagues (Rossiter & Percy, 1987; Rossiter, Percy, & Donovan, 1991) hypothesize an emotional sequence to guide the creative strategy in order to position a brand with regard to relevant motivations of the target audience. They explicitly account for emotions to be associated with antecedents as well as with end states in the motivational process. Adopting the pleasure and arousal framework of emotions (Russell & Pratt, 1980), they posit that avoidance motivation is characterized by the change from high arousal and unpleasant emotions to low arousal and pleasant (relief) emotions, whereas approach motivation seeks pleasant emotions in high arousal states. In the field of travel and tourism, emotions and moods have also been suggested as antecedents to the dominance of approach or avoidance motivation (Gnoth, Zins, Lengmueller, & Boshoff, 2000).

The approach-avoidance dichotomy seems to be implicit in several models of travel and tourism motivation. For example, Dann (1977) states that tourists are pushed to travel in order to avoid anomie and/or to seek "status", being interpersonal goals prevalent to satisfy both needs. But it was explicitly modelled by Iso-Ahola (1980, 1983) to be applied to any leisure activity, including recreational travel. In this model, avoidance forces are instrumental to satisfaction, in the sense that travel (as leisure in general) helps people "leave the routine environment behind themselves", whereas approach forces lead to "intrinsic rewards, such as feelings of mastery and competence" (Iso-Ahola, 1982). Iso-Ahola gives a leading role to the needs for competence and for relatedness, although relatedness is further regulated by the need to "shut oneself off from others at one time and to open oneself up to interpersonal contacts at another time" (1983). Leisure activities also lead to optimum stimulation level (OSL) by solving the contradiction between the needs for novelty and for familiarity. Optimization of both arousal and relatedness may be attained on any (or both) of the approach or avoidance motivational forces. Goals are thus defined in a two-dimensional framework–tourists are avoiding personal and/or interpersonal situations and are approaching personal and/or interpersonal rewards.

Iso-Ahola repeatedly stresses that tourists usually are motivated by both seeking (approach) and escape (avoidance): "tourism is a dialectical process because it provides an outlet for avoiding something *and* for simultaneously seeking something" (Iso-Ahola 1982, emphasis in the original). He theorizes that tourism is more an avoidance than an approach-oriented activity, but also hypothesises some interaction effects between both forces–meeting intrinsic goals may be a means of better responding to the need for escape and the escape component may be necessary to trigger the pursuit of intrinsic goals. The relative importance of approach and avoidance motivations is due to the experience of contradictions and conflicts within the individual and between him or her and others, thus when setting goals for travelling, tourists tend to optimize or compensate their levels of arousal. In sum, motivating conditions are defined by person-activity occasions, resulting from the intersection of personal and environmental systems (Fennell, 1988).

This rationale was empirically assessed by Wahlers and Etzel (1985) by splitting a sample of potential travellers into two classes: Seekers (15%), having a level of stimulation in their daily lives below their OSL and Avoiders (85%), who are experiencing a level of stimulation above the OSL. Given that the two classes are so disproportionate, avoiders are indistinguishable from the whole population, while seekers distinguish themselves by preferring adventure, excitement and uniqueness in a vacation, showing less preference for familiar and planned holidays as well as for a cultural, educational or intellectual vacation. There was no difference between seekers and avoiders in respect to the preference for rest and relaxation. The authors were able to demonstrate that the explicative power of OSL (actually, sensation seeking) to predict travel preferences improves when the conditions of life people are experiencing at "home" — including "work", which generally is more important than "home" for these matters — are included in the model.

Methodology

This chapter is part of a research project on motivation, attitudes and behaviour of Portuguese domestic travellers. Data for this analysis were collected from telephone interviews conducted during July 2004 with a stratified sample of households from mainland Portugal (i.e. NUTS I Continente). The strata were formed by grouping municipalities on the bases of geographical location and of some demographic variables known to be linked to the probability of engaging in domestic pleasure travel — age and education. Municipalities were selected at random in each stratum, household telephone numbers at random in each municipality and respondents at random in each household, provided they were aged between 18 and 84. Total sample size was 1700, but only one third of interviewees were identified as pleasure travellers and given all questions, including travel behaviour and motivation to participate in recreational activities and pleasure travel; the remaining two thirds answered only the common questions on attitudes to particular destinations and some psychographic and demographic variables. The sub-sample analysed is composed of respondents who answered all motivation items ($n = 558$). In the research project respondents were weighted, but the analysis reported here was done on the unweighted sample, since it acceptably matches the characteristics of Portuguese domestic travellers in all variables, according to data from the National Bureau of Statistics (Portugal, 2004).

The motivation items were assessed on a 7-point scale with poles labelled "not at all important" and "fully important" and the points in between unlabelled. Based on a literature review and personal interviews, 33 items were developed and tested in 100 telephone interviews with pleasure travellers. The data from this test were factor analysed and items that had less common variance and/or most extreme positive or negative skewness were eliminated, with the aim to have about 20 items in the final questionnaire. The actual number of items included in the study was 19, but two of them — "do nothing at all" and "seek solitude" — were further removed from the analysis because they showed poor correlations with other items on the respective factors, thus degrading scale reliability. The final solution presented is a four-factor analysis resulting from principal axis factoring (PAF) extraction and oblimin rotation.

The use of common factor analysis instead of the widely used principal component analysis (PCA) is justified for theoretical reasons, viz. the purpose of measuring latent variables that "cause" the common variance of the observed variables (Ford, MacCallum, & Tait, 1986; Bartholomew, Steele, Moustaki, & Galbraith, 2002; Preacher & MacCallum, 2003) and oblique rotation is justifiable since there is no reason to sustain an orthogonality assumption (Ford et al., 1986). Multivariate analysis of variance (MANOVA) modelled the influence of background variables — as proxies for the routine environment experienced by respondents — on travel motivations, expressed by standardized noncentred factor scores (Thompson, 1993) as dependent variables.

Discussion of Findings

To uncover the structure of domestic pleasure travel motivations, a PAF analysis was executed by using squared multiple correlations as initial communalities estimates. The number of factors to retain was determined by parallel analysis (PA) via a Monte Carlo simulation with 1000 matrices of the same size of the data matrix and composed of random generated numbers; the eingenvalues of the data analysis were compared with the 95th percentile of the values from the PA (O'Connor, 2000) and so the four factors with values greater than the 95th percentile were retained. The decision on the number of factors based on PA is the same regardless of the number of items being the final 17 or the initial 19; the item "do nothing at all" loaded on the 2nd factor and "seek solitude" loaded on the 4th factor, but both had inter-item correlations lower than 0.35 with each of the other items on the same factors, and Cronbach's α on the respective factors improved substantially after their removal.

The Structure of Approach-Avoidance Motivation

Table 13.1 presents the pattern matrix of the final PAF solution after direct oblimin rotation, done with SPSS 12. One may classify the solution as a simple one, in the sense that all items have a considerable loading in one and only one of the factors. Note that loadings from PAF extractions are lower than those that would be reported from PCA, because only common variance is of interest and thus initial communalities estimates are the squared multiple correlation coefficients, while in PCA all item variance is accounted for and initial communalities are equal to 1. Factors are interpretable on the basis of the pattern matrix, so the first factor, being related to items expressing the need for relatedness and ego-enhancement, is labelled *social* factor. The second factor relates to the items expressing avoidance motivation and, to a lesser extent, the need to have fun, being labelled *escape*. Intellectual needs are linked to the third factor, labelled *knowledge*, while in the fourth the highest loadings are from items related to the need to experience something new and different, so the label *novelty* was chosen. In the approach-avoidance conception of motivation, this structure is defined by one avoidance dimension and three different approach dimensions, denoting psychological needs to develop socially and intellectually

Table 13.1: Factor analysis solution of pleasure travel motives.

	Social	**Escape**	**Knowledge**	**Novelty**
Meet people with similar interests	*0.685*	−0.057	0.074	−0.052
Go to places friends have not been to	*0.640*	−0.051	−0.014	0.038
Tell friends about my travel experiences	*0.634*	−0.046	0.012	0.028
Spend more time with friends	*0.521*	0.114	−0.094	0.006
Meet different people	*0.469*	−0.011	0.137	0.171
Relive good memories	*0.466*	0.107	0.098	0.010
Get rid of stress	0.064	*0.857*	−0.001	−0.118
Get away from routine	−0.109	*0.689*	−0.079	0.109
Escape the demanding everyday life	−0.004	*0.667*	0.126	−0.036
Have fun	0.204	*0.393*	−0.066	0.108
Know history better	0.048	−0.044	*0.823*	−0.070
Know nature better	0.121	−0.011	*0.600*	0.042
Go to places with a different culture	−0.036	0.190	*0.520*	0.262
Seek adventure	0.059	−0.038	−0.142	*0.854*
Seek new experiences	0.079	0.004	−0.041	*0.776*
Learn new things	−0.043	0.043	0.261	*0.522*
Experience the unknown	0.040	0.054	0.155	*0.451*
Original eigen values	4.930	1.988	1.599	1.329
Cronbach's Alpha	0.770	0.752	0.731	0.775
Mean noncentered factor scores	5.535	6.915	5.071	5.346
Percentage of respondents with highest score	5.9	87.5	3.4	3.2

and also a need to face thrills or to increase excitement. The results are quite consistent with the formulation of Rossiter and Percy (1987) and with the Leisure Motivation Scale (LMS) (Beard & Ragheb, 1983), already applied to international travel (Ryan & Glendon, 1998; Correia & Crouch, 2004).

In line with the LMS, both the items expressing the need for friendship and the need for esteem or ego-enhancement (Dann, 1977) loaded on the same factor (and continued to load even when the number of factors is increased), suggesting that seeking interpersonal rewards (Iso-Ahola, 1980) may be conceptualized as a single dimension. Even though this finding is conceptually attractive, some authors have reported contradictory results, e.g. Wolfe and Hsu (2004) report a component formed by the 1st, 4th and 5th items of our social factor, while the 2nd and 3rd, related to ego-enhancement, loaded in a different factor. Baloglu and McCleary (1999) also report two separate components, one named social and another named prestige. Several studies on data from the North American Pleasure Travel Market Surveys (e.g. Cha, McCleary, & Uysal, 1995; Lehto, O'Leary, & Morrison, 2002) also found the items related to prestige loading on one component and items expressing need for relatedness loading in another component, but the comparison is not straightforward in these studies, because the items of relatedness in those surveys focus more on kinship than they do on friendship. The same applies to the work of Sirakaya, Uysal, and Yoshioka (2003).

Regarding the knowledge factor, the results are much more consensual. Not only is the conceptual foundation of this factor in the works of Rossiter and Percy (1987) or Beard and Ragheb (1983) straightforward, in both cases identified as an intellectual motivation, but there is also strong empirical evidence on this factor on multiple studies (Dunn Ross & Iso-Ahola, 1991; Figler, Weinstein, Sollers, & Devan, 1992; Fodness, 1994; Cha et al., 1995; Crompton & McKay, 1997; Baloglu & McCleary, 1999). The last approach motivation factor is adventure or novelty seeking, manifested by the concepts of "adventure", "new" and "unknown", and represents the opportunity for unusual experiences, for behaviours very different from the ordinary (Ryan, 2002a), as empirically shown in several studies (Figler et al., 1992; Loker & Perdue, 1992; Cha et al., 1995; Moscardo, Morrison, Pearce, Lang, & O'Leary, 1996; Lang & O'Leary, 1997; Baloglu & McCleary, 1999; C. Kim & S. Lee, 2000; E. Kim & D. Lee, 2000). Adventure seeking may be the pleasure travel equivalent of sensory gratification for consumer goods or the (mostly physical) challenge for leisure, but admittedly there may be place for a factor involving the concepts of hedonism and indulgence (Sirakaya et al., 2003; Wolfe & Hsu, 2004).

Relative Strength of Motivation Factors

This study clearly shows that escape is the main motivator of (domestic, at least) pleasure travel, in accordance to Iso-Ahola's (1982) assumption. After all, getting away is the most obvious reason for taking a holiday (Ryan, 2002b) and the escapade concept is dominant in the increasing short-break market (Mannell & Iso-Ahola, 1987). Table 13.1 reports the means of Thompson's (1993) standardized noncentred factor scores (higher values denote higher importance), allowing for direct comparison between factors and showing that the importance of escape is clearly above the other factors. Most significant is the fact that seven out of eight respondents have escape as their highest score, much in line with the findings from Wahlers and Etzel (1985) who also report such high odds between avoiders and seekers. One could then hypothesize that the prevalence of escape motives is related to the prevalence of overstimulation in the daily lives of pleasure travellers, an issue dealt with below, but first this prevalence is discussed in the light of some published work.

In a survey reported by Krippendorf (1987) the three most frequent answers to the question "What were the main reasons for your holiday journey" are indicators of escape motivation. In the same line, surveying English holidaymakers, Ryan and Glendon (1998) found that respondents gave highest ratings to the items of escape (stimulus avoidance) scale and further accounted that this factor had high importance for most of the clusters they elicited (85% of the sample). On the other hand, Jamrozy and Uysal (1994) found that novelty was the main motivation of German long-haul holiday travellers, escape being the second, generally with scores of the same magnitude, for all traveller types except the organized tour groups (3.4% of their sample). In other studies with long-haul holiday travellers, but this time Japanese (Cha et al., 1995) and British (Jang & Cai, 2002), the knowledge factor was found to be the most important, followed again by escape. In another study (Baloglu & McCleary, 1999) knowledge was definitely the main motivator, but the sample was composed of potential travellers who actively searched for information at the Turkish Tourism Office in New York, so it is probably a segment of knowledge seekers. Comparison with results from other studies reviewed is made difficult because in some cases factors are composed of different manifest variables and in other cases authors only report factor scores centred at zero mean, making inter-factor comparisons useless.

One may conclude then that there is mixed empirical evidence on the relative importance of motivation factors: while our analysis and the study from Ryan and Glendon (1998) note a prevalence for escape, surveys on long-haul vacationers tend to place more importance on knowledge and exploration. Awaritefe (2004) reports that, in Nigeria, domestic tourists are more concerned with tension reduction, while foreign tourists place more value on learning experiences. On the other hand, Jang and Cai (2002) successfully linked the relative strength of some motivation factors with particular long-haul destinations of British travellers (e.g. escape has greatest importance for travellers to Caribbean, being travellers to Central and South America more knowledge seekers). It may then be accepted that escape is a general motive for pleasure travel, but the seeking dimensions are also important and may be more important when tourists are choosing specific destinations, notably unfamiliar destinations and/or destinations having a good position relative to the benefits associated to those dimensions. Consistently with this assumption, in Kozak's (2002) comparative study, British and German tourists taking package holidays to Turkey attribute more importance to the "culture" motivation than their counterparts travelling to Mallorca, but "relaxation" is the most important motivation factor, regardless of destination.

Regarding the relative strength of "escape" and "knowledge" dimensions, an opportune comment on an article by Dunn Ross and Iso-Ahola (1991) is due. It is frequently cited for evincing the prevalence of knowledge motivation among sightseeing tourists, but, although it may be conceptually appealing to assume that people who engage in (guided) city tours score high in intellectual motivation, the authors by no means proved the assumption and only refer to the fact that knowledge should be more important "because two knowledge factors emerged" or that "it should be noted, however, that the escape factor explained only 7.1% of the total variance" (Dunn Ross & Iso-Ahola, 1991).

None of the arguments is tenable and one of the authors himself, in a reference work about 10 years earlier, criticizing the work of Hollender, put it very clearly: "That 'escape' was an important theme (three of seven factors were escape-related) in the study was not surprising, because the number of motivational escape-oriented statements to which subjects responded was considerably greater than the number of other motivational dimensions. Such a bias is undesirable, since factor analysis as a statistical tool can only produce 'factors' (motives) which are based upon the items included" (Iso-Ahola, 1980). The same should be said about knowledge-oriented statements in Dunn Ross and Iso-Ahola's work. And of course eigenvalues (or variance, as the authors report) have nothing to do with relative importance of factors as motivators, as may be seen by our own results: greater variance is accounted for by the social factor, but the escape factor is significantly more important (Table 13.1). A similar pattern may be found in Kozak's (2002, Table 2) study, where "culture" accounts for the greatest variance, but the most important factor is "relaxation".

Relationship between Background Variables and Motivation Factors

Taking into account the approach-avoidance conception of consumer motivation, as expressed by Rossiter and Percy (1987), one should expect the prevalence of escape motivation to occur when the dominant experiences are stressful, i.e. when people experience unpleasant high levels of arousal, in the terms of environmental psychology (Russell & Pratt, 1980). On the other hand, approach motivation forces arise *either* from a sense of unpleasant low levels of arousal or from a neutral state. In reversal theory (Smith & Apter, 1975) one would say that escape is a telic mode of need satisfying, by "relaxing", while the increase in excitement sought by approach motivation dimensions is the paratelic mode of need satisfying. Note that what matters is the level of arousal felt and, for instance, in a telic state a (physically or intellectually) demanding leisure activity may be felt as "relaxing" (Crompton, 1979), which is an additional theoretical support for the fact that some people give such high ratings to escape items even when they are seeking something out there.

Background variables such as level of urbanization, occupation and family life cycle influence the relative importance of motivation factors, because they may be linked with different levels of felt arousal and different roles of psychological needs over the life cycle (Ryff, 1995; Lee & Norman, 1996). The multivariate effects of age, education, urbanization and employment status on the noncentred scores of the four motivation dimensions are all statistically significant, but since there are considerable correlations between those factors, their relative effects were controlled via a MANOVA fixed-effects model. Results of the most parsimonious model are presented in Table 13.2, where it may be seen that age affects the scores of all motivation dimensions, while employment status impacts on escape and, to a lesser extent, on knowledge. No interaction effect was found to be significant.

Notwithstanding the high levels of statistical significance, one must note that the size of the effects (η^2) is small in every case. Estimates of the effects for each level of age (Young = 18–34, $n = 207$; Midlife = 35–54, $n = 204$; Mature (reference level) = 55–84, $n = 147$) and employment (Employed, $n = 324$; Non-employed (reference level),

$n = 234$) are shown in Table 13.3. Both escape and novelty decrease with aging, and the effect of being young in novelty is the largest in the model. Compared to other age groups, young adults tend to score higher on social motivation, while mature adults present the highest knowledge scores. Regardless of age, those employed have a stronger need to escape.

The mean scores estimated from the MANOVA model are shown in Figure 13.1 (the midlife level is omitted for the sake of readability, because their means are usually between the extreme age levels). As expected, escape was estimated to be the main motivator for all combinations of factor levels, despite being considerably higher for young employed than for mature non-employed (mostly retired). Young non-employed (mostly students) have relatively higher social needs and relatively lower knowledge needs, while mature employed show the opposite trend. The largest difference in motivation importance,

Table 13.2: MANOVA results for the fixed effects of age and employment on motivation dimensions.

		Tests of between-subjects effects					
Source	Dimension	Type III sum of squares	df	Mean square	F	Sig.	Partial η^2
Corrected model	Social	8.82	3	4.89	6.37	0.000	0.033
	Escape	29.21	3	10.24	13.20	0.000	0.067
	Knowledge	14.80	3	3.27	4.23	0.006	0.022
	Novelty	50.46	3	15.81	20.65	0.000	0.101
Intercept	Social	11853.77	1	16468.59	21436.30	0.000	0.975
	Escape	25203.46	1	25313.17	32637.13	0.000	0.983
	Knowledge	16490.64	1	13833.49	17886.62	0.000	0.970
	Novelty	14665.98	1	15109.80	19739.18	0.000	0.973
Age	Social	7.97	2	4.48	5.83	0.003	0.021
	Escape	16.50	2	8.40	10.83	0.000	0.038
	Knowledge	8.84	2	4.41	5.71	0.004	0.020
	Novelty	48.43	2	23.12	30.20	0.000	0.098
Employed	Social	3.13	1	2.45	3.18	0.075	0.006
	Escape	5.36	1	6.33	8.17	0.004	0.015
	Knowledge	2.61	1	3.35	4.33	0.038	0.008
	Novelty	1.05	1	0.77	1.01	0.315	0.002
Error	Social	417.72	554	0.77			
	Escape	425.67	554	0.78			
	Knowledge	425.38	554	0.77			
	Novelty	420.94	554	0.77			

Table 13.3: Estimates of the fixed effects of age and employment on motivation dimensions.

Dimension	Parameter	B	Standard error	t	Sig.	Partial η^2
Social	Intercept	5.562	0.076	73.022	0.000	0.906
	Young	0.228	0.097	2.360	0.019	0.010
	Midlife	−0.060	0.108	−0.561	0.575	0.001
	Mature	0.000				
	Employed	−0.153	0.086	−1.784	0.075	0.006
	Non-employed	0.000				
Escape	Intercept	6.502	0.077	84.960	0.000	0.929
	Young	0.451	0.097	4.650	0.000	0.038
	Midlife	0.282	0.108	2.606	0.009	0.012
	Mature	0.000				
	Employed	0.247	0.086	2.858	0.004	0.015
	Non-employed	0.000				
Knowledge	Intercept	5.191	0.076	67.932	0.000	0.893
	Young	−0.313	0.097	−3.226	0.001	0.018
	Midlife	−0.296	0.108	−2.737	0.006	0.013
	Mature	0.000				
	Employed	0.179	0.086	2.080	0.038	0.008
	Non-employed	0.000				
Novelty	Intercept	4.971	0.076	65.388	0.000	0.885
	Young	0.687	0.096	7.127	0.000	0.084
	Midlife	0.192	0.107	1.787	0.074	0.006
	Mature	0.000				
	Employed	0.086	0.086	1.005	0.315	0.002
	Non-employed	0.000				

however, is between young and mature, in the need for novelty. A similar pattern of differences across life stages regarding the escape motive was found by Lee and Norman (1996). As to the effects of age on novelty and knowledge, they are largely in accordance with a study of variations in needs and tourist roles over the life course (Gibson & Yiannakis, 2002), where it is shown that, with aging, roles related to novelty needs, viz. the action seeker, the thrill seeker and the explorer, tend to decrease in preference, while roles related to knowledge needs, viz. the archaeologist and the educational tourist, tend to increase in preference.

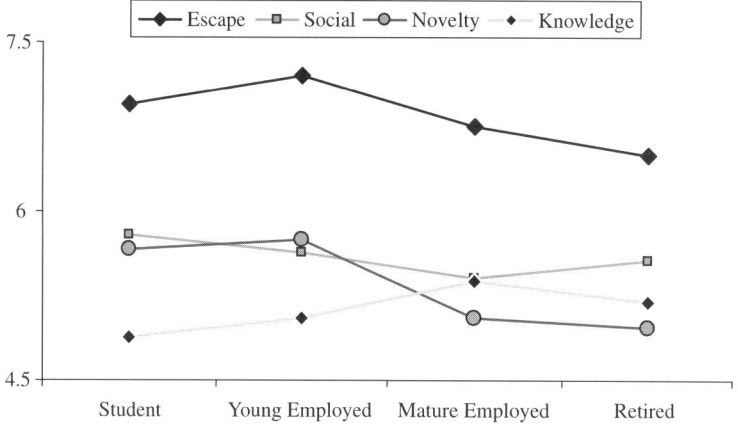

Figure 13.1: Estimated means of motivation scores by age and employment status.

Conclusions and Implications

The factorial structure of motivations to pleasure travel, as analysed in this chapter, fits the idea that an approach-avoidance valence is a fundamental antecedent to travel behaviour. To accommodate the results here presented with previous theory, a critical difference to Iso-Ahola's model (1982) needs to be avowed, which is the position that arousal is a crucial component in the concepts of escape and seeking– escape is a form of motivation through reduction of tension or anxiety, i.e. satisfying travellers in a relaxation state, and seeking is a form of motivation by increasing exploration, i.e. satisfying travellers in an excitement state. This position is in line with the emotional sequence proposed by Rossiter and Percy (1987, 1991) and consistent with the concept of motivation in reversal theory (Smith & Apter, 1975). It is a departure from Iso-Ahola's theory (1982), as avoiding "the routine environment behind oneself" implies a change in arousal but the direction of that change is not determined, since routine may be stressful or it may be dull. The same may be said regarding the seeking "force", as Iso-Ahola includes in this category rest and relaxation as well as learning or interaction with natives.

Arousal avoidance has been correlated with the avoidance mode of need for achievement (fear of failure), while arousal seeking was correlated with the approaching mode (hope of success) (Morgatroyd, Rushton, Apter, & Ray, 1978), so imposing a direction in arousal change appears to be theoretically sound. Furthermore, it facilitates the integration of emotions into the motivational dynamics, as it has been suggested that negative emotions are associated with escape holiday expectations, whereas positive emotions are associated with holiday expectations of curiosity, openness and challenging situations (Gnoth et al., 2000).

It is generally accepted that destination management would either promote benefits that best match tourist motivations, or concentrate on markets whose motivations may be best satisfied by destination attributes (e.g. Kozak, 2002). But not all motivation dimensions are equally actionable for purposes of destination positioning. Crompton (1979) notes that "socio-psychological motives", such as escape, relaxation and enhancement of kinship relationships, are not destination specific and "thousands of destinations" could be "direct substitutes". Gnoth (1997) maintains that, in case of self-directed motivation dominance, destinations are substitutable, whereas destinations targeted by outer-directed motivation are more difficult to substitute, because the beliefs of tourists about the probability of meeting their goals at a particular destination play a prominent role in this case. The chief practical proposition of this chapter is that different motivation factors may be linked to different elements of the communication strategy and that approach factors are best suited to positioning decisions.

Assuming that both avoidance and approach "forces" are present in the decision to travel to a particular destination, salience of one or the other in a given situation is of vital importance for the marketing (mainly, positioning) of that destination (Fennell, 1978; Rossiter & Percy, 1987). If avoidance is more salient, the benefits should be linked to tension-reduction; on the other hand, if approach is "stronger", benefits should reinforce the hope or desire of a positive outcome. But there are two facets of high-involvement buying decisions adding some more complexity to the approach-avoidance dialectics. First, in many high-involvement choice processes, the product-category purchase motives are different from the brand-choice motives (Rossiter & Percy, 1987). Consequently, travelling for pleasure is generally due to the escape problem-solving motivation, whereas choice of brands (e.g. destinations) depends on attitudes formed in relation to relevant seeking motivation dimensions.

Second, because of the risk, high-involvement brand-choice may follow a two-stage process. In the first stage, a favourable attitude develops as the potential buyer anticipates the satisfaction of approach (positive) motives, but then new avoidance (negative) motives arise and the decision maker must be convinced of his or her choice prior to a purchase (Percy, Rossiter, & Elliott, 2001). Rossiter and Percy (1987) refer to these kind of negative motives as *mixed approach-avoidance motivation* when the consumer has to overcome the guilt of indulging in a purchase with potential negative outcomes or risks, and as *incomplete satisfaction* when the consumer has to overcome the disappointment of perceiving available brands far from the ideal.

Consequently, a large spectrum of motivational dimensions may be involved in pleasure travel decisions (Crompton, 1979) and marketing managers have to consider which communication effects should be linked to which motivational dimensions (see Percy et al., 2001 for a detailed discussion of communication effects). The prevalence of the escape motivation and the differences observed for the seeking dimensions in specific targets, combined with theory and findings from Rossiter and colleagues, suggest that escape relates to category need, seeking relates to brand attitude and the mixed approach-avoidance motivation relates mainly to purchase intention and/or facilitation. Approach dimensions are therefore the relevant motivations to position a destination, so market segmentation should focus not on separating seekers and avoiders, but on the way travellers *seek to avoid*, i.e. which (or which combination of) approach dimension they use to increase excitement (i.e. pleasant stimulation) in order to avoid unpleasant states. According to the results presented above, if the target is students, for example, marketing efforts should accentuate benefits linked to opportunities to socialize and adventure; if the target is the young employed, emphasis on adventure should surpass contact occasions; for the mature segments, on the other hand, efforts may be directed to the opportunity to gain knowledge on established sights.

Acknowledgement

This research was funded by the project INTERREG III A North Portugal/Castile and Leon SP2 P11 — Douro-Duero Sec. XXI.

References

Awaritefe, O. D. (2004). Motivation and other considerations in tourist destination choice: A case study of Nigeria. *Tourism Geographies, 6*(3), 303–330.

Baloglu, S., & McCleary, K. W. (1999). A model of destination image formation. *Annals of Tourism Research, 26*(4), 868–897.

Bartholomew, D. J., Steele, F., Moustaki, I., & Galbraith, J. I. (2002). *The analysis and interpretation of multivariate data for social scientists*. Boca Raton, FL: Chapman & Hall/CRC.

Beard, J. G., & Ragheb, M. G. (1983). Measuring leisure motivation. *Journal of Leisure Research, 15*(3), 219–228.

Cha, S., McCleary, K. W., & Uysal, M. (1995). Travel motivations of Japanese overseas travelers: A factor cluster segmentation approach. *Journal of Travel Research, 34*(1), 33–39.

Correia, A., & Crouch, G. I. (2004). A study of tourist decision processes: Algarve, Portugal. In: G. I. Crouch, R. R. Perdue, H. J. P. Timmermans, & M. Uysal (Eds), *Consumer psychology of tourism, hospitality and leisure* (Vol. 3, pp. 121–134). Wallingford: CABI.

Crompton, J. L. (1979). Motivations for pleasure vacation. *Annals of Tourism Research, 6*(4), 408–424.

Crompton, J. L., & McKay, S. L. (1997). Motives of visitors attending festival events. *Annals of Tourism Research, 24*(2), 425–439.

Dann, G. M. S. (1977). Anomie, ego-enhancement and tourism. *Annals of Tourism Research, 4*(4), 184–194.

Dunn Ross, E. L., & Iso-Ahola, S. E. (1991). Sightseeing tourists' motivation and satisfaction. *Annals of Tourism Research, 18*(2), 226–237.

Elliot, A. J., & Church, M. A. (1997). A hierarchical model of approach and avoidance achievement motivation. *Journal of Personality and Social Psychology, 72*(1), 218–232.

Elliot, A. J., & Covington, M. V. (2001). Approach and avoidance motivation. *Educational Psychology Review, 13*(2), 73–92.

Elliot, A. J., & Thrash, T. M. (2002). Approach-avoidance motivation in personality: Approach and avoidance temperaments and goals. *Journal of Personality and Social Psychology, 82*(5), 804–818.

Fennell, G. (1975). Motivation research revisited. *Journal of Advertising Research, 15*(3), 23–28.

Fennell, G. (1978). Consumers' perceptions of the product-use situation. *Journal of Marketing, 42*(2), 38–47.

Fennell, G. (1988). Action as counterchange: Identifying antecedents of the domain and goal of action. Paper presented at the annual convention of the American Psychological Association, 95, New York, August, 1987.

Figler, M. H., Weinstein, A. R., Sollers, J. J., & Devan, B. D. (1992). Pleasure travel (tourist) motivation: A factor analytic approach. *Bulletin of the Psychonomic Society, 30*(2), 113–116.

Fodness, D. (1994). Measuring tourist motivation. *Annals of Tourism Research, 21*(3), 555–581.

Ford, J. K., MacCallum, R. C., & Tait, M. (1986). The application of exploratory factor analysis in applied psychology: A critical review and analysis. *Personnel Psychology, 39*(2), 291–314.

Gibson, H., & Yiannakis, A. (2002). Tourist roles – Needs and the lifecourse. *Annals of Tourism Research, 29*(2), 26.

Gnoth, J. (1997). Tourism motivation and expectation formation. *Annals of Tourism Research, 24*(2), 283–304.

Gnoth, J., Zins, A. H., Lengmueller, R., & Boshoff, C. (2000). Emotions, mood, flow and motivations to travel. *Journal of Travel & Tourism Marketing, 9*(3), 23–34.

Iso-Ahola, S. E. (1980). *The social psychology of leisure and recreation*. Dubuque, Iowa: W.C. Brown.

Iso-Ahola, S. E. (1982). Toward a social psychological theory of tourism motivation: A rejoinder. *Annals of Tourism Research, 9*(2), 256–262.

Iso-Ahola, S. E. (1983). Towards a social psychology of recreational travel. *Leisure Studies, 2*(1), 45–56.

Jamrozy, U., & Uysal, M. (1994). Travel motivation variations of overseas German visitors. *Journal of International Consumer Marketing, 6*(3,4), 135–160.

Jang, S., & Cai, L. A. (2002). Travel motivations and destination choice: A study of British outbound market. *Journal of Travel and Tourism Marketing, 13*(3), 111–133.

Kim, C., & Lee, S. (2000). Understanding the cultural differences in tourist motivation between Anglo-American and Japanese tourists. *Journal of Travel and Tourism Marketing, 9*(1/2), 153–170.

Kim, E., & Lee, D. (2000). Japanese tourists' experience of the natural environments in North QLD region – Great barrier reef experience. *Journal of Travel and Tourism Marketing, 9*(1/2), 93–113.

Kozak, M. (2002). Comparative analysis of tourist motivations by nationality and destinations. *Tourism Management, 23*(3), 221–232.

Krippendorf, J. (1987). *The holiday makers: Understanding the impact of leisure and travel*. (V. Andrassy, Trans.). London: Heinemann.

Lang, C.-T., & O'Leary, J. T. (1997). Motivation, participation, and preference: A multi-segmentation approach of the Australian nature travel market. *Journal of Travel and Tourism Marketing, 6*(3/4), 159–180.

Lee, C., & Norman, W. C. (1996). An application of the family life cycle to understanding tourism behavior and attitudes. Paper presented at the Leisure Research Symposium, Kansas City, MO, October 23–27

Lehto, X. Y., O'Leary, J. T., & Morrison, A. M. (2002). Do psychographics influence vacation destination choices? A comparison of British travellers to North America, Asia and Oceania. *Journal of Vacation Marketing, 8*(2), 109–125.

Loker, L. E., & Perdue, R. R. (1992). A benefit based segmentation of a nonresident summer travel. *Journal of Travel Research, 31*(1), 30–35.

Mannell, R. C., & Iso-Ahola, S. E. (1987). Psychological nature of leisure and tourism experience. *Annals of Tourism Research, 14*(3), 314–331.

Morgatroyd, S., Rushton, C., Apter, M., & Ray, C. (1978). The development of the telic dominance scale. *Journal of Personality Assessment, 42*(5), 519–528.

Moscardo, G., Morrison, A. M., Pearce, P. L., Lang, C.-T., & O'Leary, J. T. (1996). Understanding vacation destination choice through travel motivation and activities. *Journal of Vacation Marketing, 2*(2), 109–122.

O'Connor, B. P. (2000). SPSS and SAS programs for determining the number of components using parallel analysis and Velicer's MAP test. *Behavior Research Methods, Instruments, & Computers, 32*(3), 396–402.

Percy, L., Rossiter, J. R., & Elliott, R. H. (2001). *Strategic advertising management*. Oxford, NY: Oxford University Press.

Portugal, I. N. E. (2004). *Estatísticas do turismo 2003*. Lisboa: I.N.E.

Preacher, K. J., & MacCallum, R. C. (2003). Repairing Tom Swift's electric factor analysis machine. *Understanding Statistics, 2*(1), 13–43.

Rossiter, J. R., & Percy, L. (1987). *Advertising and promotion management* (International ed.). Singapore: McGraw-Hill Book Co.

Rossiter, J. R., & Percy, L. (1991). Emotions and motivations in advertising. Paper presented at the Advances in Consumer Research, 21, New York, October 4–7, 1990

Rossiter, J. R., Percy, L., & Donovan, R. J. (1991). A better advertising planning grid. *Journal of Advertising Research, 31*(5), 11–21.

Russell, J. A., & Pratt, G. (1980). A description of the affective quality attributed to environments. *Journal of Personality and Social Psychology, 38*(2), 311–322.

Ryan, C. (2002a). From motivation to assessment. In: C. Ryan (Ed.), *The tourist experience* (2nd ed., pp. 58–77). London: Continuum.

Ryan, C. (2002b). Motives, behaviours, body and mind. In: C. Ryan (Ed.), *The tourist experience* (2nd ed., pp. 27–57). London: Continuum.

Ryan, C., & Glendon, I. (1998). Application of leisure motivation scale to tourism. *Annals of Tourism Research, 25*(1), 169–184.

Ryff, C. D. (1995). Psychological well-being in adult life. *Psychological Inquiry, 11*(4), 99–104.

Sirakaya, E., Uysal, M., & Yoshioka, C. (2003). Segmenting the Japanese tour market to Turkey. *Journal of Travel Research, 41*(3), 293–304.

Smith, K. C. P., & Apter, M. J. (1975). *A theory of psychological reversals*. Chippenham: Picton.

Thompson, B. (1993). Calculation of standardized, noncentered factor scores: An alternative to conventional factor scores. *Perceptual and Motor Skills, 77*(3), 1128–1130.

Wahlers, R. G., & Etzel, M. J. (1985). A consumer response to incongruity between optimal stimulation and life style satisfaction. Paper presented at the Advances in Consumer Research, 15, Washington, DC, October 11–14, 1984.

Wolfe, K., & Hsu, C. (2004). An application of the social psychological model of tourism motivation. *International Journal of Hospitality & Tourism Administration, 5*(1), 29–47.

Chapter 14

Cultural Approximation and Tourist Satisfaction

Muammer Tuna

Introduction

'Tourist satisfaction' is one of the most discussed concepts in the fields of tourism marketing and the sociology of tourism (Schofield, 2000, p. 269). This is hardly surprising, as so much in the tourism industry depends on the satisfaction levels of tourists. A formal sociological analysis of 'tourist satisfaction' can help policymakers in 'destination areas' and 'provider countries' construct more creative marketing policies, as well as tourism structures and infrastructures that will be stronger and more competitive. While tourist satisfaction has been discussed primarily in a national context, there are also some comparative cross-cultural studies in the tourism literature. This chapter uses these studies as it compares the tourist satisfaction levels of survey respondents from different nationalities.

The studies suggest that one of the important factors impacting tourist satisfaction is 'cultural approximation' — that is, the extent to which the cultures and, especially, the languages, of visiting tourists and host countries are similar. The basic assumption is that different nationalities have different satisfaction levels: the more similar the languages and cultures, the higher the satisfaction levels. Marmaris, Turkey (Tavmergen & Oral, 1996) is the case study 'destination area' for this research. Survey responses of tourists are analyzed, and 'tourist satisfaction' levels are computed. Broader theoretical implications are also discussed, as well as possible practical policies for the tourism community, and for local and national policymakers.

Literature Review

In the sociology of tourism, tourism is viewed primarily as a social phenomenon (Apostolopoulos, 1996; Dann, 1996a; Cohen, 1996), with the consumption and social behavior of tourists being legitimate areas of research and study (Swarbrooke & Horner, 2001; Baudrillard, 1998). There are many theoretical approaches in the sociology of tourism literature, most of which are related to the major sociological theories. The main perspectives are: the evolutionary perspective; the Neo-Durkheimian perspective; the conflict perspective; the functionalist perspective; the Weberian perspective; phenomenology; ethnomethodology; symbolic interactionism; and sociolinguistic. Dann and Cohen (1996) suggest that a study of tourism and tourist behavior using only one theoretical perspective is limiting, and recommend a more pluralistic, integrative, and multi-dimensional approach to these subjects (pp. 312–313).

The sociolinguistic approach defines tourism as a 'language'. Touristic language is language that facilitates communication between the host and guest (Huisman & Moore, 1999; Cohen & Cooper, 1996; Dann, 1996a, 1996b; Nash, 1996; Nield et al, 2000; Ryan, 2002; Singh, 1994; Stefanou, 1992; Gursoy & Rutherford, 2004; Gnoth et al, 2000). Most simply, touristic language takes the many factors of a tourist destination into account and promotes it as being a good and preferable place to visit (Reisinger & Turner, 1998, p. 84). Touristic language can take many forms (such as power, cliché, formulae, vocabularies, speech, talk, voices, idiom, semantics, grammar, text, advertising, publicity, promotion, propaganda, etc.), and is probably the most important cultural code that is shared between the two parties (Dann, 1996a, p. 1). It is also an important factor in determining the level of tourist satisfaction (Huisman & Moore, 1999).

There are three good reasons to pay so much attention to 'tourist satisfaction:' first, high tourist satisfaction provides word-of-mouth recommendations of products and services to family and friends, which in turn brings in new customers; second, it creates repeat customers by satisfying them the first time around, and so provides a steady source of income without the need for additional marketing expenditures; and, third, it limits complaints and compensation payments which are expensive, time-consuming, and bad for an organization's reputation (Swarbrooke & Horner, 2001, p. 238).

Figure 14.1 presents a tourist satisfaction process that has three stages: a 'tourist product,' a 'satisfaction factor,' and an 'outcome' defined as 'satisfaction,' 'partial satisfaction,' or 'dissatisfaction,' and reflecting what tourists think and feel about both their overall experience and their received goods and services (Kozak, 2001b, p. 304; Haber & Lerner, 1999). Since satisfaction is largely a subjective quality, the self-evaluations of their own experiences by tourists themselves are the most commonly used measurement tools (Kozak, 2001b; Schiffman & Kanuk, 2000; Swarbrooke & Horner, 2001).

Cross-cultural comparative research is one of the most important of many different research methodologies and approaches in tourist satisfaction research (Swarbrooke & Horner, 2001; Baker & Crompton, 2000; Todd, 1999; Choi & Chu, 2000; Reisinger & Turner, 1998; Kozak & Rimmington, 2000; Kozak, 2001a, 2000; Pizam & Sussman,

The tourist product	The satisfaction factor	The outcome
*Tangible element *Service element *Role of intermediaries and agents	*Perception of the tourist experience *Tourist attitudes and expectations *Uncontrollable factors	*Tourist satisfaction *Tourist partial satisfaction *Tourist dissatisfaction

Figure 14.1: The tourist satisfaction process.
Source: Swarbrooke and Horner (2001, p. 239).

1995; Richards & Hall, 2000; Kim, 1999; Groburn, 1993). This research compares the tourist satisfaction levels of different nationalities by using either a *direct* or *indirect* method. The *direct* method directly asks the tourists themselves about their experience, perceptions, and satisfaction levels; the *indirect* method asks local residents, business owners, tour guides, etc., for their perceptions of how the tourists are enjoying (or not) their experience (Kozak, 2001a, p. 391). This study has employed the direct method, with respondents being asked, through formal surveys, to answer questions about their holidays.

While the majority of the relevant literature on tourist satisfaction is from national-level studies that are dependent on national-level data, there are numerous cross-national comparative studies. These studies follow the methodology of comparative studies in general and, basically, look at the different factors comprising 'tourist satisfaction' and how they differ from nation to nation (Kim, 1999; Groburn, 1993; Kozak, 2001a; Kozak, Bigne, Gonzales, & Andreu, 2004). Most of these studies employ quantitative rather than qualitative research methodology, and use a factor analyses model to identify the criteria, or factors, that are then used to compare the satisfaction levels of the various nationalities.

Kim (1999), looking at tourist motivation cross-culturally, identified four factors of comparison: level of power distance, collectivism–individualism, level of uncertainty, and masculinity–femininity. Choi and Chu (2000), comparing the satisfaction levels of Asian and Western tourists, identified seven levels of comparison. They suggested that cultural differentiation is a main factor in determining how tourists perceive their hotel experience, and demonstrated that the satisfaction priorities of Asian and Western travelers are different.

Kozak (2001a) also carried out cross-cultural research on consumer satisfaction, comparing British and German consumers' satisfaction levels in Spain (Mallorca) and Turkey. He found that the British were generally more satisfied with their experience than their German counterparts because they viewed a foreign holiday as a luxury, while Germans viewed foreign vacations as a necessity. In another study, Kozak et al. (2004) compared Spanish, British, French, German, and other tourists as to the images they held of their holiday destinations. They discovered that every nationality had a different image of the same destination, and attributed this to 'cultural differentiation.' Reisinger and Turner (1998, p. 84) compared the satisfaction priorities of Korean tourists and their Australian hosts, and found a number of differences, which they, too, attributed to socio-cultural differentiation.

Similarities and differences of tourist and host interaction can be compared using three different form backgrounds: (1) the same of similar; (2) different, but the differences are small and supplementary; and (3) different, with the differences being large and incompatible. Satisfaction levels tend to be higher in the first two forms of interaction, due to the closer cultural approximation between the guest and host, and lower in the third instance where the cultural approximation is more distant. Again, this research proposes that there is a significant relationship between cultural (especially linguistic) approximation and tourist satisfaction — that there is a definite correlation between the quality of verbal and written communication between host and guest and the satisfaction level of the guest (Huisman & Moore, 1999; Cohen & Cooper, 1996; Dann, 1996a). It is further proposed that tourists from different nationalities have different satisfaction levels due to differences in their cultural approximation to various host destinations. In Turkey, the British, have the highest satisfaction levels, because British culture and the English language are the most familiar foreign culture and language to the Turkish people. This means that Marmaris will, therefore, appeal more to British tourists than to tourists of other nationalities.

Methodology

Respondents, through formal questionnaires, are asked about their satisfaction levels in areas such as hosting place, hosting facilities, recreational and historic sites, facilities for children, etc. Quantitative tourist satisfaction research generally uses scale measurements (Baker & Crompton, 2000; Ekinci & Sirakaya, 2004; Fallon and Schofield, 2004; Driscal et al, 1994; Van Raaij, 1986; Weiler, 2002; Geva & Goldman, 1991). Therefore, a 7-category Likert-type scale provides for responses ranging from (1) 'terrible' and (7) 'delighted'. Thirty-seven questionnaire items are analyzed. The first eight questions are general demographic questions; others the remainder address of tourist satisfaction.

The research was a cross-national comparative study conducted at the Dalaman Airport in the summer of 2002 (Tuna, 2002). British, German, Danish, Dutch, Estonian, Spanish, Finnish, Arabic, Australian, Norwegian, and Swedish tourists participated, in the percentages indicated in Table 14.1. Tourists were surveyed randomly just prior to their leaving the airport, the assumption being that this random sample reflected accurately the general tourist population visiting Marmaris. Marmaris is located at the southwestern corner of Turkey, in the Mugla Province, and is a popular tourist destination for mostly Western

Table 14.1: Demographic distribution of the sample.

Nationalities	Frequency	Percent (%)
British	96	29.5
German	84	25.8
Dutch	39	12.0
Russian	37	11.4
Others	69	22.3
Total	325	100.0
Age	**Number**	**Percent**
15–24	94	28.9
25–34	64	20.0
35–44	95	29.2
45–54	54	16.6
55–64	9	2.8
65 <	6	1.8
Unanswered	2	0.6
Total	325	100.0
Gender	**Frequency**	**Percent (%)**
Women	150	46.2
Men	170	52.3
Unanswered	5	1.5
Total	325	100.0

Table 14.1: (*Continued*)

Job situation	Frequency	Percent (%)
Unemployed	15	4.6
Retired	17	5.2
Employed	219	67.4
Student	69	21.2
Unanswered	5	1.5
Total	325	100.0
Type of accommodation	**Frequency**	**Percent (%)**
Hotel	204	62.8
Holiday village	39	12.0
Apartment	64	19.7
Other	10	3.2
Unanswered	8	2.5
Total	325	100.0
Party in the group	**Frequency**	**Percent (%)**
Alone	9	2.8
Family with children	137	42.2
With partner	124	38.2
With friends	55	16.9
Total	325	100.0

tourists. Tourism is the main economic activity in this area. The study, conducted during July and August of 2002, shows that most of the tourists visiting Marmaris — roughly 75% — are from England, Germany, and the Netherlands.

Discussion of Findings

The demographic data shows that most of the respondents — about 80% — are younger. Almost half are below 35 years of age; an additional 30% are between the age of 35 and 45. Gender was evenly distributed — 52% male to 48% female. Two-thirds of the respondents were employed; one-fifth was students. Most of the respondents — 63% — stayed in a hotel, with 20% staying in an apartment, and 12% staying in a holiday village. More than 80% of respondents came either as a family with children or with a partner (42.2% families with children; 38.8% traveling with partner). Almost 17% traveled with friends; only 2.8% traveled alone. Most tourists visiting Marmaris are, therefore, young to middle-aged, employed and with their families or partners.

Table 14.2 indicates that tourists in Marmaris gave the highest satisfaction rating (5.65) to the 'natural environment in the destination area', indicating that they were more than 'mostly

Table 14.2: Descriptive statistics.

Symbol	Name of variable	N	Mean	Std. Deviation
V9	Quality standard of accommodation?	319	5.3386	1.4936
V10	Level of service at your accommodation?	319	5.5486	1.3952
V11	Safety and security in your holiday?	316	5.4430	1.3093
V12	Natural environment in your destination?	315	5.6571	1.3602
V13	Value for money?	310	5.2645	1.5932
V14	General atmosphere in the resort overall?	314	5.5764	1.3526
V15	Attitude of staff toward foreign tourists?	314	5.3981	1.5492
V16	Quality and variety of food?	316	5.2373	1.4835
V17	Responsiveness to customer complaints?	246	4.9187	1.5654
V18	Cleanliness of beaches in the destination?	301	5.0133	1.6020
V19	General hygiene and sanitation?	305	4.5311	1.6201
V20	Availability of sport facilities?	221	4.8959	1.3860
V21	Availability of nightlife and entertainment?	259	5.5598	1.2542
V22	Attractions for children?	182	4.7473	1.4798
V23	Facilities for children?	188	4.9468	1.3071
V24	Facilities on beaches?	277	5.0000	1.4793
V25	Availability of shopping facilities?	302	5.2517	1.5259
V26	Availability of daily tours to other resorts?	274	5.6131	1.1435
V27	Getting to museums and historical places?	236	5.1653	1.3567
V28	Written materials in museums?	131	4.9084	1.4489
V29	Brochures in about the resort overall?	235	4.9447	1.4940
V30	Menu in foreign lang. in restaurants?	277	5.3574	1.4715

Table 14.2: (*Continued*)

Symbol	Name of variable	N	Mean	Std. Deviation
V31	Menu in foreign lang. in accommodation?	275	5.2000	1.4748
V32	Signposts in foreign lang. at the airport?	261	5.0498	1.4120
V33	Level of foreign lang. communication?	306	4.7876	1.6901
V34	Cleanliness of the airport?	305	5.2426	1.2928
V35	Speed of check-in/check-out at the airport?	303	4.9175	1.5894
V36	Time/distance between resort and airport?	300	4.4033	1.5966
V37	Traveling between airport and resort	305	5.0459	1.4772

satisfied' in this area. The item 'daily tour to other resort' was almost as high, and received the second highest satisfaction rating (5.62), indicating that 'the accessibility of public transport' also is viewed as mostly satisfactory. Also receiving high satisfaction marks were 'general atmosphere in the resort area' (5.57), 'level of service' (5.54), and 'nightlife' (5.51).

Several satisfaction items scored below 5.0, indicating that respondents were *not* 'mostly satisfied' with that area. 'Time/distance of resort area to airport' received the lowest score (4.4); other low satisfaction items were: 'speed of check in-check out at the airport' (4.91); 'language of communication' (4.78); 'written materials in foreign language in museums' (4.90); 'responsiveness to consumer complaints' (4.91); 'facilities for children' (4.94); and 'attractions for children' (4.74). So, tourists generally like the natural environment and the general atmosphere of Marmaris — once they get there! They are not mostly satisfied with the airport experience, with the time it takes to get from the airport to their destination, with the lack of 'language-friendly' materials in museums, and with the lack of facilities and activities for children. Respondents also mentioned other satisfaction items (with which they were mostly satisfied) that were not mentioned here; these responses were also taken into account and inform the overall research.

After looking at the individual items, an explanatory factor analyses test was conducted to identify different dimensions of tourist satisfaction. Table 14.3 shows four resulting dimensions: 'General character,' 'Accommodations/Facilities,' 'Museum/Airport,' and 'Children Facilities.' Most of the item correlation scores are over 0.5, with these results having being further tested for internal reliability test. Internal reliability test scores for most items are 0.6 or 0.7; these are also shown in Table 14.3. Confirming the four factors, or dimensions, of the analysis alpha test scores are over 0.8.

Table 14.3: Factor analysis (rotated* component matrix) internal reliability.

	Component							
	General Characteristics		Accommodation/ facilities		Museum/ airport		Children facilities	
	Correlation	Internal Reliable	Correlation	Internal Reliable	Correlation	Internal Reliable	Correlation	Internal Reliable
V9	0.566	0.6073						
V10	0.697	0.7376						
V11	0.705	0.6685						
V12	0.684	0.6237						
V13	0.435	0.4313						
V14	0.672	0.6909						
V15	0.681	0.6884						
V16					0.460	0.4229		
V17	0.504	0.6593						
V18	0.582	0.5535						
V19			0.401	0.5926				
V20	0.508	0.4295						
V21	0.401	0.4406						
V22							0.787	0.7148
V23							0.847	0.7148
V24	0.447	0.5503						
V25					0.562	0.5454		
V26			0.406	0.5503				
V27			0.694	0.7018				
V28			0.721	0.6078				
V29			0.494	0.4851				
V30					0.778	0.6886		
V31					0.737	0.6761		
V32			0.628	0.5719				
V33					0.684	0.6063		
V34			0.601	0.5822				
V35			0.509	0.4816				
V36			0.516	0.5662				
V37			0.606	0.7106				
	Alpha: 0.8777		Alpha: 0.8773		Alpha: 0.8005		Alpha: 0.8320	
	St. Alpha: 0.8819		St. Alpha: 0.8483		St. Alpha: 0.8020		St. Alpha: 0.8337	

Note: Extraction method: Principal component analysis; rotation method: Varimax with Kaiser normalization.
*Rotation converged in 13 iterations.

Table 14.4: Comparison of tourist satisfaction by nationalities.

	1. General characteristics of destination place	2. Facilities using by tourists	3. Airport museums, verbal communication	4. Facility and activity about children
General	5.4007	5.1053	5.2152	4.8406
N=325	(0.9131)	(0.9053)	(1.1170)	(1.2951)
British	5.6750	5.4746	5.5867	4.9306
N=96	(0.9515)	(0.6194)	(0.6732)	(1.2346)
German	5.1909	4.5215	4.4857	4.9697
N=84	(0.9033)	(1.0574)	(1.3386)	(1.3972)
Dutch	5.2769	4.7778	5.1871	4.6000
N=39	(0.7772)	(0.7608)	(0.8516)	(1.1765)
Russian	4.8970	4.9074	4.4769	4.0952
N=37	(0.9739)	(0.5055)	(0.6508)	(1.1249)
Other	5.4618	5.4737	5.4256	4.1682
N=47(Aus, Yug., Est., Fin., Av., İsv., Nor., Lüb., Dan) (22=Un. Ans. Tur)	(0.8097)	(0.7916)	(0.7301)	(1.4083)
F test (ANOVA)	2.171*	7.028***	17.919***	2.115*

*$p<0.10$.
**$p<0.05$.
***$p<0.01$.

The first dimension of tourist satisfaction, 'General Character,' describes 'satisfaction with the general characteristics of the destination place,' and considers questions such as quality and standard of accommodations, quality of services, security, natural environment, value of money, general atmosphere of the accommodation facility, motivation of personnel, handling of complaints, cleanliness of beaches, sports facilities and entertainment. 'Accommodations/Facilities,' the second dimension, describes tourists' 'satisfaction with the various facilities,' and looks at questions such as the quality and variability of food, accessibility of shopping facilities, foreign language menus at restaurants and hotels, and verbal communication. 'Museum/Airport,' the third dimension, describes 'satisfaction with museums, airports and verbal communication,' and considers questions relating to general hygiene, accessibility to museums, information about the museums, enough written information, road and traffic signs, cleanliness of airport, accessibility of services at airport, distance between accommodation facility and airport, and quality and comfort of the journey between the airport and accommodation facility. The fourth dimension describes 'satisfaction with the facilities and activities for children,' and addresses questions related to the quality and availability of services and activities for children.

No significant relationship between the demographic characteristics of the tourists and their satisfaction levels found; rather, different social groups have *similar*, not different satisfaction levels. Differences in age, gender, job situation, family conditions, etc., do not indicate differences in how long tourists stay at a destination, for example, or in how far ahead they make travel and hotel reservations, or in how satisfied they are with their overall travel experience. Older and younger respondents, women and men, short-term visitors and long-term visitors, those who make early reservations and those who do not, first-time as well as repeat visitors — all are equally satisfied. Different satisfaction levels *are* seen, however, in a cross-national test, conducted using an ANOVA test, and represented in Table 14.4. The mean satisfaction levels of the different nationalities are represented by the upper-case numbers; the numbers in parentheses show the standard deviation of means.

Overall, the satisfaction levels of tourists visiting Marmaris are high, with scores above 5.0 in three of the four dimensions of tourist satisfaction. On the 7-category scale, most respondents were somewhere between 'mostly satisfied' and 'pleased.' The fourth dimension of satisfaction, however, relating to children's facilities, received mostly unfavorable responses, indicating that most of the accommodation facilities do not have adequate activities or facilities for children. Different nationalities do have different satisfaction levels, and these differences are statistically significant. Hoteliers and policymakers who pay attention to these statistics, and who address the issue of children's facilities in particular, can realistically expect to meet with success in the form of increased business. Table 14.4 shows that British tourists have the highest satisfaction levels in all the four dimensions, while Russian tourists post the lowest levels. Identifying themselves as the second most satisfied group, just behind the British, is the group defined as 'Other' (tourists from the Scandinavian countries and Estonia). Dutch tourists are next, followed by German tourists.

Conclusions and Implications

The concept of tourist satisfaction has been discussed as a social and cross-cultural phenomenon in this chapter. The applied field research shows that different nationalities have different satisfaction levels, the differences being due primarily to socio-cultural differentiation. The mean satisfaction levels range from 4.5 to 5.5, and indicate that guests visiting Marmaris/Turkey are generally 'mostly satisfied' or 'delighted.' Tourists with closer cultural (linguistic) approximation to the host are generally more satisfied than tourists who are culturally (linguistically) less approximated to the host community (Huisman & Moore, 1999; Cohen & Cooper, 1986; Dann, 1996a).

British tourists have the highest satisfaction levels for all satisfaction dimensions. They are followed by German, Dutch, and 'Other' tourists, which have moderate satisfaction levels, and Russians tourists, who have the lowest levels of satisfaction in all dimensions. The British rank highest primarily because English is the most well-known foreign language in Turkey, and because British (Anglo-Saxon) culture is also a well-known culture in Turkey, especially within the Turkish tourist industry. There is a greater ease of communication between British guests and their Turkish hosts than exists with other nationalities, and this leads to higher satisfaction levels for the British. The Russian language and culture is not as well-known in Turkey, which leads to more strained communication and lower satisfaction levels.

Most other research on 'tourist satisfaction' also shows the British having the highest satisfaction levels of all nationalities. This supports the research of this study, which attributes that high satisfaction to a greater familiarity, in Turkey, with British language and culture. British language and culture also dominate beyond Turkey. English is the most common language in many parts of the world, and the Anglo-Saxon culture is the most well known and dominant culture worldwide (Mowforth & Munt, 1998, pp. 12–15; Huisman & Moore, 1999), creating a world, according to Müller (2002), that is culturally and linguistically uniform and looks alike (p. 62). The main theoretical implication of this study is that, while there are numerous cross-cultural comparative studies on 'tourist satisfaction,' more research is needed to better understand the dominance of British language and culture. Lessons learned from this research could help to increase the influence of other nationalities, raise the satisfaction levels of their tourists, and increase the general level of tourism in Turkey.

The research findings also suggest some practical steps for hoteliers, policymakers, and others in the tourist industry. Providing quality children's activities and facilities will raise satisfaction levels and, likely, bring a monetary benefit. Attention to airport services and to transportation between the airport and tourist destination will, also, raise satisfaction levels. Improving the written and verbal communication between tourists and those working in the tourism industry is perhaps the most glaring need suggested by the research.

Finally, the research shows that Turkey's marketing policy targets primarily Western societies, mainly the British, German, and Dutch, and neglects growing potential markets such as Russia, India, Korea, China, and Japan. The economies of these countries are already strong or swiftly improving. Becoming oriented and trained to serve these potential markets is a task that the Turkish marketing and tourist industries can undertake with confidence, knowing that their efforts will create higher 'tourist satisfaction', which will bring monetary benefits, which will, in turn, create higher Turkish satisfaction!

References

Apostolopoulos, Y. (1996). Introduction: Reinventing the sociology of tourism. In: Y. Apostolopoulos, S. Leivadi, & A. Yiannakis (Eds), *The sociology of tourism: Theoretical and empirical investigations.* London: Routledge.

Baker, D., & Crompton, J. L. (2000). Quality satisfaction and behavioral intentions. *Annals of Tourism Research, 26*(4), 1004–1021.

Baudrillard, J. (1998). *The consumer society: Myths & structures.* London: Sage Publications.

Choi, T. Y., & Chu, R. (2000). Levels of satisfaction among Asian and Western travelers *International Journal of Quality & Reliability Management, 17*(2), 116–131.

Cohen, E. (1996). A phenomenology of tourist experiences. In: Y. Apostolopoulos, S. Leivadi, & A. Yiannakis (Eds), *The sociology of tourism: Theoretical and empirical investigations.* London: Routledge.

Cohen, E., & Cooper, R. L. (1996). Language and tourism. *Annals of Tourism Research, 13*(4), 533–563.

Dann, G. M. S. (1996a). *The language of tourism: A sociolinguistic perspective*. Oxon: Cab International.

Dann, G. (1996b). The people of tourism brochures. In: T. S. Wyn (Ed.), *The tourism image myths and mythmaking in tourism*. New York: Wiley.

Dann, G., & Cohen, E. (1996). Sociology and tourism. In: Y. Apostolopoulos, S. Leivadi, & A. Yiannakis (Eds), *The sociology of tourism: Theoretical and empirical investigations*. Routledge: London.

Driscal, A. et al. (1994). Measuring tourists' destination perceptions. *Annals of Tourism Research, 21*(3), 499–511.

Ekinci, Y., & Sirakaya, E. (2004). An examination of the antecedents and consequences of customer satisfaction. In: G. I. Crouch, R. R. Perdue, H. J. P. Timmermans, M. Uysal (Eds), *Consumer psychology of tourism, hospitality and leisure* (Vol. 3, pp. 189–202). Oxfordshire: Cabi Publishing.

Fallon, P., & Schofield, P. (2004). First-time and repeat visitors to Orlando, Florida: A comparative analysis of destination satisfaction. In: G. I. Crouch et al. (Eds), *Consumer psychology of tourism, hospitality and leisure* (Vol. 3, pp. 203–214). Oxfordshire: Cabi Publishing.

Geva, A., & Goldman, A. (1991). Satisfaction measurement in guided tours. *Annals of Tourism Research, 18*(2), 177–185.

Gnoth, J., Zins, A., Lengmuellrand, R., & Bshoff, C. (2000). The relationship between emotions, mood and motivation to travel: Towards a cross-cultural measurement of flow. In: A. G. Woodside, G. I. Crouch, J. A. Mazanec, M. Oppermann,, M. Y. Sakai (Eds), *Consumer psychology of tourism, hospitality and leisure*. Oxon, NY: Cabi Publishing.

Groburn, N. H. H. (1993). Tourism in cross cultural perspective. *Annals of Tourism Research, 20*(2), 367–368.

Gursoy, D., & Rutherford, D. G. (2004). Host attitudes toward tourism. An improved structural model. *Annals of Tourism Research, 31*(39), 495–516.

Haber, S., & Lerner, M. (1999). Correlates of tourist satisfaction. *Annals of Tourism Research, 26*(1), 197–207.

Huisman, S., & Moore, K. (1999). Natural language and that of tourism. *Annals of Tourism Research, 26*(2), 445–449.

Kim, C. (1999). Cross-cultural perspectives on motivation. *Annals of Tourism Research, 26*(1), 201–204.

Kozak, M. (2001a). Comparative assessment of tourist satisfaction with destinations across two nationalities. *Tourism Management, 22*(2001), 391–401.

Kozak, M. (2001b). A critical review of approaches to measure satisfaction with tourist. In: G. I. Crouch, J. A. Mazanec, J. R. Brent Ritchie, A. G. Woodside (Eds), *Consumer psychology of tourism, hospitality and leisure* (Vol. 2, pp. 303–321). Oxfordshire: Cabi Publishing.

Kozak, M., Bigne, E., Gonzales, A., & Andreu, L. (2004). Cross-cultural behaviour in tourism research: A case study on destination image. In: G. I. Crouch, R. R. Perdue, H. J. P. Timmermans, M. Usyal (Eds), *Consumer psychology of tourism, hospitality and leisure* (Vol. 3, pp. 303–312). Oxfordshire: Cabi Publishing.

Kozak, M., & Rimmington, M. (2000). Tourist satisfaction with Mallarco, Spain as an off-season holiday destination. *Journal of Travel Research, 38*(3), 200–269.

Lanquar, R. (1991). *Turizm ve Seyahat Sosyolojisi. [Sociology of Tourism and Travel.]* İstanbul: İletişim Yayınları.

Mowforth, M., & Munt, I. (1998). *Tourism and sustainability: New tourism in the third world*. London: Routledge.

Müller, H. (2002). Tourism and hospitality into 21st century. In: A. Lockwood, & S. Medlik (Eds), *Tourism and hospitality in the 21st century.* Butterworth Heinemann: Oxford.

Nash, D. (1996). *Anthropology of tourism.* New York: Pergamon.

Nield, K., Kozak, M., & LeGrys, G. (2000). The role of food service in tourist satisfaction. *International Journal of Hospitality Management, 19*(2), 375–384.

Pizam, A., & Sussmann, S. (1995). Does nationality affect tourist behavior? *Annals of Tourism Research, 22*(4), 901–917.

Reisinger, Y., & Turner, L. (1998). Cross-cultural differences in tourism: A strategy for tourism marketers. *Journal of Travel & Tourism Marketing, 7*(4), 79–105.

Richards, G., & Hall, D. (2000). *Tourism and sustainable development.* Routledge: London.

Ryan, C. (2002). Tourism and cultural proximity: Examples from New Zealand. *Annals of Tourism Research, 29*(4), 952–971.

Schiffman, L. G., & Kanuk, L. L. (2000). *Consumer behavior.* New Jersey: Prentice-Hall.

Schofield, P. (2000). Deciphering day-trip destination choice using a tourist expectation/satisfaction construct. In: A. G. Woodside et al. (Eds), *Consumer psychology of tourism, hospitality and leisure.* Oxon, NY: Cabi Publishing.

Singh, S. (1994). *Cultural tourism and heritage management.* New Delhi: Rawet Publications.

Stefanou, J. (1992). Experimental iconology — a tool for analysis for the qualitative improvement and touristic development of places. In: H. Briassoulis, & J. van der Straaten (Eds), *Tourism and the environment.* Dordrecht: Kluwer Academic Publishing.

Swarbrooke, J., & Horner, S. (2001). *Consumer behavior in tourism.* Oxford: Butterworth Heinemann.

Tavmergen, I. P., & Oral, S. (1996). Tourism development in Turkey. *Annals of Tourism Research, 26*(2), 449–451.

Todd, S. (1999). Examining tourist motivation methodologies. *Annals of Tourism Research, 26*(4), 1022–1024.

Tuna, M. (2002). *Marmaris Kentinde Turizm, Çevre ve Toplumsal Eğilimler Araştırması.* Martav Yayını: Marmaris.

Van Raaij, W. F. (1986). Consumer research on tourism mental and behavioral constructs. *Annals of Tourism Research, 13*(1), 1–9.

Weiler, B. (2002). Tourism research and theories: A review. In: A. Lockwood, & S. Medlik (Eds), *Tourism and hospitality in the 21st century.* Oxford: Butterworth Heinemann.

Chapter 15

The Role of Non-Monetary Costs in a Model of Leisure Travel Value

Teoman Duman, Goknil Nur Kocak and Ozkan Tutuncu

Introduction

Zeithaml's (1988) well-known model of perceived value proposes that perceived quality and perceived sacrifice are the two main drivers of consumers' value perceptions. In general, these two constructs represent the "give and get" parts of value composition, which set the bases of perceived value theory in marketing (Zeithaml & Bitner, 2000). A number of service studies later showed that service value perceptions are largely determined by service quality and sacrifice perceptions (Cronin, Brady, & Hult, 2000). Although the importance of the sacrifice component of service value is recognized in services marketing literature, most research on services value focused on the "get" part of perceived value and attempted to demonstrate how quality and satisfaction determine value and behavioural intentions (Cronin et al., 2000). As for the "give" part of perceived value, past research has generally focused on monetary cost perceptions among service customers leaving non-monetary cost perceptions largely unanalyzed. A few research studies analyzed the roles of the sacrifice perceptions of service customers in value models (i.e. Cronin, Brady, Brand, Hightower, & Shemwell, 1997; Petrick, 2002), but the findings in these studies about the specific roles of monetary and non-monetary price perceptions on service value were unclear. Furthermore, the role of sacrifice perceptions in service value for different service industries was largely unclear. This point is important because the effects of the monetary and non-monetary costs of service purchases on service value might differ greatly for different service evaluations. For example, the role of the non-monetary costs in value cannot be expected to be the same for fast food services and package tour services. In other words, the time and effort spent on fast food purchases are not comparable to the time and effort spent on a one-week package of leisure travel. Accordingly, non-monetary cost perceptions in package travel evaluations might have significant effects on the perceptions of overall value of the tour.

Progress in Tourism Marketing
Copyright © 2006 by Elsevier Ltd.
All rights of reproduction in any form reserved.
ISBN: 0-08-045040-7

The purpose of this chapter is to test the role of non-monetary price perceptions on value perceptions and behavioural intentions for organized leisure travel services in a cost-based value model. For this purpose, the sacrifice component was separated into monetary and non-monetary price perceptions, and the effects of these perceptions on value and behavioural intentions were tested in a model. A conceptual cost-based model of value for package tour evaluations was developed and tested to determine if non-monetary price perceptions influence value perceptions and behavioural intentions. With the finding of this research it is hoped to extend leisure travel value literature by showing that the value perceptions of leisure travellers are determined also by non-monetary cost evaluations in addition to monetary cost, service quality, emotional response, and reputation. With respect to its effect on behavioural intentions, non-monetary costs are likely to be a crucial determination of future intentions. Additionally, monetary gains of package travel are likely to be an important consideration for travellers. As these expectations are supported by the research findings, it is suggested that package tour marketers give careful attention to the way in which they manage the tour and use cost comparisons between alternative ways of travelling in advertising.

Research Model and Related Literature

The proposed research model is presented in Figure 15.1. The model consists of five factors and 10 relationships. It builds on Thaler's (1985) transaction utility theory, Oliver's (1999) value theory, and the value models of Monroe and Chapman (1987), Grewal, Monroe, and Krishnan (1998), and Zeithaml (1988). According to the proposed model, the monetary price perceptions of package tour participants influence their evaluations of the monetary benefits, non-monetary costs, perceived value, and behavioural intentions. Also, perceived monetary benefit evaluations affect the non-monetary price, value, and behavioural intentions. As shown in the model, value perceptions mediate the relationship between non-monetary price perceptions and behavioural intentions. Each of the 10 proposed relationships in the model makes up one of the research hypotheses in this study.

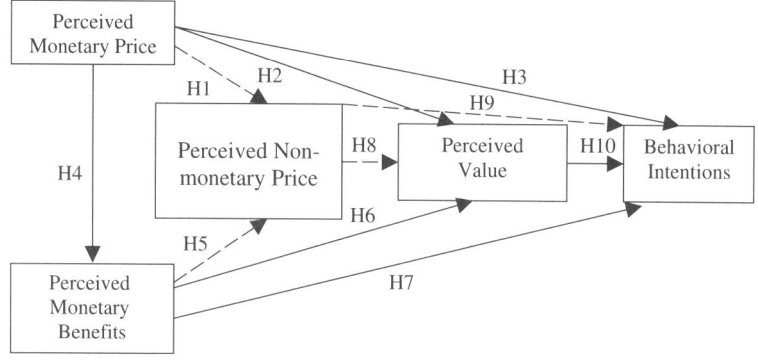

Figure 15.1: Proposed cost-based model of leisure travel value.

Perceived Sacrifice Concept

By definition, "perceived sacrifice includes all that the consumer perceives has to be given up to obtain a service" (Zeithaml & Bitner, 1996, p. 501). Therefore, the actual price paid is not the only purchase cost for consumers (Bender, 1964; Peterson & Wilson, 1985; Monroe, 1990; Zeithaml & Bitner, 2000). Other costs include time costs, search costs (i.e. effort spent on search and selection of the product), convenience costs, and, psychic costs (Zeithaml & Bitner, 2000). Bender (1964) categorizes purchase costs into two groups: prime cost (i.e. the price paid) and secondary costs. Bender argues that there are three kinds of secondary purchase costs including price-type costs, time-type costs, and psychological-type factors. For example, in a retailing environment, parking fees, installation charges, credit charges, sales taxes, etc., could be considered as price-type secondary purchase costs, while waiting time, travel time, and searching time can be considered as time-type secondary purchase costs (Bender, 1964). Psychological factors include inner conflict, frustration, depression, discomfort, anxiety, tension, annoyance, mental fatigue, and the like (Bender, 1964).

Non-monetary costs might differ significantly among different product categories. Zeithaml and Bitner (2000) argue that even though non-monetary costs may not be a serious consideration for many goods purchases, they may be an important part of many service evaluations. For example, waiting time; appointment time; time and effort spent on searching and selecting the product; time and effort spent preparing to receive the service (e.g., preparing home for a repair service); and the fear of uncertainty, rejection or not understanding the services can become very important considerations for service purchase decisions and evaluations (Zeithaml & Bitner, 2000). Similarly and to a greater extent, non-monetary costs of package tour experiences may be an important part of participant evaluations because travellers pass through a number of stages in these travel experiences from the search for the type of travel to the return home. The actual experience on a typical package tour starts with a pre-tour briefing and continues with travel to destination, accommodation, dining, excursions, shopping, and return (Wang, Hsieh, & Huan, 2000). The time and effort spent on the search for information and travelling during this process make up an important part of the overall experience. Generally, package tours offer most of these services at a single price. Therefore, the sacrifice perceptions for a package tour can be separated into the perceptions of the package tour price (perceived monetary price) and of the relevant psychological factors (perceived non-monetary price).

In the research model, it is proposed that an important indicator of non-monetary price perceptions is monetary price perceptions. Typically, package tours are paid before the traveller sets off and the price paid serves as the reference point for further evaluations. Monroe and Chapman (1987) argue that perceptions about the actual price of a product are an indicator of further sacrifice evaluations. In a similar vein, throughout the tour experience, the perceptions of the package price may influence tour experience evaluations. For example, those travellers who have negative perceptions about the tour price may be more sensitive about the way in which the travel services are offered. These travellers may have higher expectations than others who think that they got a bargain on the package tour price. During and after the experience, the evaluations of travellers can therefore differ greatly on the basis of their perceptions of package tour price compared with their budget. More positive price perceptions can be expected to result in more positive non-monetary price perceptions. This forms the first research hypothesis.

H1: Monetary price perceptions are positively related to perceived non-monetary price perceptions.

Hypotheses 2 and 3 concern the effects of monetary price perceptions on value perceptions and behavioural intentions. In a number of studies, the perceived monetary price has been shown to have a direct influence on perceived value directly (Bojanic, 1996; Bolton & Drew, 1991; Chang & Wildt, 1994; Cronin et al., 2000; Dodds, Monroe, & Grewal, 1991; Kashyap & Bojanic, 2000; Monroe, 1990; Oh, 2000; Zeithaml, 1988). It has been well established in the marketing literature that perceived monetary price and perceived value are negatively related. As the price of a product is perceived to rise, the value perception in consumer's (single) mind deteriorates. Furthermore, recent research shows that price perceptions can also influence behavioural intentions directly (Varki & Colgate, 2001). Higher comparative price perceptions can be a cause of lower value perceptions and behavioural intentions. Therefore, hypotheses 2 and 3 propose that:

H2: Monetary price perceptions are negatively related to value perceptions.

H3: Monetary price perceptions are negatively related to behavioural intentions.

Perceived Monetary Benefits

One of the important factors that influence perceived value is the perceived monetary benefits (Darke & Chung, 2005). In the marketing literature, perceptions of the monetary benefits were conceptualized as the perceived transaction value (Grewal, Monroe, & Krishnan, 1998). According to Grewal et al. (1998), the perceived transaction value is "psychological satisfaction or pleasure obtained from taking advantage of the financial terms of the price deal" (p. 48). All of the monetary benefits in a purchase transaction, such as price-cuts, promotions, group discounts etc. form consumer's (single) transaction value perceptions. In an organized travel context, attractiveness of the package price itself can be considered as a monetary benefit because a tour package with a single price is much less costly than an independent travel in most cases (Cruise Lines International Association (CLIA), 2004).

Previous research on the monetary benefits showed that consumer's (single) price perceptions influence perceptions of the transaction value directly (Grewal et al., 1998; Lichtenstein, Netemeyer, & Burton, 1990). Grewal et al. (1998) finds out that the actual selling price of a product affects transaction value negatively. An overall price perception can be expected to influence transaction value negatively because as the perceived price increases, consumer's (single) satisfaction from price deals will decrease. Similarly, for package tour purchases, if the travellers perceive package price as high or expensive, their satisfaction from price benefits will decrease. Therefore,

H4: Monetary price perceptions are negatively related to monetary benefit perceptions.

Cost-based value perceptions (i.e. transaction value) may have significant effects on satisfaction or dissatisfaction from a service (Oliver, 1999). In other words, positive perceptions about the monetary benefits in a package tour may result in the perceptions of lower non-monetary price because these benefits might lead to more tolerable evaluations of travel experience. For example, travellers benefiting from group or seasonal discounts might be more tolerable about problems during the tour compared to those who do not benefit from such discounts. Therefore, a negative relationship between monetary benefit perceptions and non-monetary price perceptions seems likely. Accordingly:

H5: Monetary benefit perceptions are negatively related to perceived non-monetary price perceptions.

Grewal et al. (1998) detects that higher satisfaction received from the financial gains results in higher value perceptions. Similarly, in package tour evaluations, more favourable evaluations of price benefits may lead to more positive evaluations of value and behavioural intentions. According to the previous research, higher value is associated with price benefits and promotions (Hardesty & Bearden, 2003). Therefore, it is proposed that the monetary benefits (discounts etc.) can be the direct causes of value perceptions and behavioural intentions.

H6: Monetary benefit perceptions are positively related to value perceptions.
H7: Monetary benefit perceptions are positively related to behavioural intentions.

Perceived Non-monetary Price — Value — Behavioural Intentions Relationships

Higher discomfort levels resulting from factors related with time and psychological factors will add up to the total cost of the vacation and they will be used in the vacationer's value equation (Zeithaml, 1988). The more the dissatisfying experience is, the less the value of the vacation should be. Disorganization and crowding in a package tour vacation, for example, may very well influence vacationers' value perceptions negatively because those dissatisfying factors contribute to the total cost of the vacation. Similarly, troublesome vacations can affect vacationers' future behaviours negatively. Two studies have addressed these relationships in the service value literature. Cronin et al. (1997, 2000) test the relationships between sacrifice, value perceptions and behavioural intentions. They conclude that overall value mediates the relationship between sacrifice and behavioural intentions. Hypotheses 8 and 9 concern the relationships between non-monetary price, value perceptions, and behavioural intentions.

H8: Non-monetary price perceptions are negatively related to value perceptions.
H9: Non-monetary price perceptions are negatively related to behavioural intentions.

In the final hypothesis, the relationship between value perceptions and behavioural intentions are tested. Previous services and marketing research show that value is one of the strongest indicators of behavioural intentions (Cronin et al., 1997, 2000; Chang & Wildt, 1994; Bolton & Drew, 1991). Cronin et al. (1997) tested the role of value perceptions on behavioural intentions for six service industries (i.e. spectator sports, participation sports, entertainment, health care, long distance carriers, fast food) and concluded that service value is a strong indicator of repeat purchase and recommending intentions. Furthermore, they found support for their model that value mediates the relationships between service quality, sacrifice, and behavioural intentions. Furthermore, package tour value research reveals similar findings that tour participants' value perceptions are influential on repurchase and recommending intentions (Duman & Mattila, 2005). Accordingly, hypothesis 10 in this research proposes that,

   H10: Value perceptions are positively related to behavioural intentions.

Methodology

The design of this research is based upon a two-page questionnaire survey. In the first page, a number of questions regarding the tour and the participants were included. Second page of the questionnaire contained 18 questions measuring five model constructs. Non-monetary price scale was composed of eight items that included time, convenience, psychological, and effort costs that may be experienced in package tour experiences. Kocak, Yagci, and Duman (2004) developed this scale based on Cronin et al. (1997) and Petrick (2002) conducting personal interviews with package tour participants and travel agents, expert consultation, and pilot tests (DeVellis, 1991). In their study, Cronin et al. (1997) use a nine-item scale that measured price, effort, time, financial risk, physical risk, performance risk, social risk, psychological risk, and overall risk components of sacrifice associated with the purchase of a number of services. Also, Petrick (2002) develops an overall value scale in which non-monetary cost of the cruise travel is named "the behavioural price" which is measured with a six-item scale. These six items questioned whether cruise participants perceived that their vacation was easy to buy, required little energy to purchase, was easy to shop for, required little effort to buy, and was easily bought.

Measurement items for four other constructs in the proposed research model were adapted from the previous studies on the value in marketing. The perceived monetary price was measured with two items, which were previously used (Sweeney, Soutar, & Johnson, 1999; Sirohi, McLaughlin, & Wittink, 1998). The perceived monetary benefit was also measured with two items and the perceived overall value was measured with three items. These scales were adopted from previous studies (Grewal et al., 1998, Duman, 2002; Varki & Colgate, 2001; Brady & Cronin, 2001). Finally, behavioural intentions were measured with three items (Cronin et al., 2000; Brady & Cronin, 2001; Varki & Colgate, 2001). All the items used in the questionnaire were measured with a five-point Likert scale that ranged from "strongly disagree" to "strongly agree" (see Table 15.1).

To collect data, a number of travel agencies were contacted in four big cities in Turkey, namely, Istanbul, Ankara, Izmir, and Mersin. One of the reasons for selecting these four cities is that most of the travel agencies operate in these major cities in Turkey. A total of 500 questionnaires were distributed to the travel agencies using a snowball format. Tour guides were briefly informed about the purpose and significance of the research and requested to distribute and collect the questionnaires at the end of the tours. The data collection was completed during June, July, and August of 2003. Researchers had visited

Table 15.1: Final measurement items.

Construct and reliability	Item
Perceived monetary price (PMP) $\alpha = 0.71$	PMP1: In general, the price I paid for this tour is expensive PMP2: The price I paid for this tour is more expensive than the price of similar tours
Perceived monetary benefit (PMB) $\alpha = 0.77$	PMB1: Benefiting from price advantages (price-cuts, installments etc.) made me feel good PMB2: I had pleasure to know that I saved money compared to a similar independent vacation
Perceived non-monetary price (PNMP) $\alpha = 0.87$	PNMP1: I had difficulties in conveying my needs and desires to the guide PNMP2: It was quite bothersome to reach gathering spots during the tour PNMP3: It was a waste of time to join this tour PNMP4: Travelling time during the tour was so boring that I thought it would never end PNMP5: Travelling time during the tour was like a torture PNMP6: I got bored during free times PNMP7: I was worried that the food would upset my stomach during the tour
Perceived overall value (POV) $\alpha = 0.86$	POV1: Compared to the price I paid, my vacation was quite economical POV2: I feel that my vacation was worth the money and time I spent POV3: Overall, my vacation was a good buy
Behavioural intentions (BI) $\alpha = 0.89$	BI1: The probability that I will choose the same travel agency for my next vacation is high BI2: The likelihood that I will recommend this travel agency to a friend is high BI3: I will tell all positive things about my last vacation

engaged agencies in a routine to receive the completed questionnaires. At the end of the data collection period, 429 questionnaires were received. Of the 429 questionnaires, 15 were eliminated from the analysis for various reasons, and a total of 414 questionnaires were used in the final analysis. Data analysis was accomplished through the use of two statistical programs, SPSS 10.0 (Norusis, 2000) and AMOS 4.0 (Arbuckle, 1997). Exploratory phase of the data analysis was performed using SPSS, while structural analysis was conducted with the AMOS, structural equations modelling program. Before testing the structural model, validity, and reliability of the scales were analyzed. Initially, to check whether 8 non-monetary price items load on a single factor, a principal component analysis with varimax rotation was run. The principal component analysis resulted in a two-factor solution. As seen in Table 15.2, the item that reads, "I had spent a lot of time for searching before I decided on this tour" was loaded on a second factor. Therefore, this item was eliminated from further analysis.

Discussion of Findings

Following the principal component analysis, the reliability of the scales was analyzed. Table 15.1 presents Cronbach's coefficient alpha scores for each model construct along with relevant items. As seen in the table, reliability coefficients are above the suggested level of 0.70, supporting their internal consistency levels (Nunnally, 1978). One of the issues that needed to be resolved before the analysis of structural model was to check for the discriminant validity of model constructs. For this purpose, correlation matrix was analyzed, and two multiple regression analysis were conducted. The means, standard deviations and correlation coefficients of the model constructs are reported in Table 15.3.

As shown in Table 15.3, correlation coefficients range between 0.58 and 0.79. As a rule of thumb, a correlation coefficient less than 0.85 is a sign of discriminant validity (Kline, 1998). However, to further examine the redundancy of the constructs, two other regression analyses were conducted, and multicollinearity statistics were analyzed. In the first regression analysis, perceived overall value was used as a dependent variable, and it was regressed on perceived monetary benefit, perceived non-monetary price, and perceived monetary price (see Table 15.4). After three modelling steps, all three independent variables

Table 15.2: Principal component analysis of perceived non-monetary price scale items.

Item	Factor loading	
1. I had difficulties in conveying my needs and desires to the guide.	.76	
2. It was quite bothersome to reach gathering spots during the tour.	.68	
3. It was a waste of time to join this tour.	.85	
4. Traveling time during the tour was so boring that I thought it would never end.	.63	
5. Traveling time during the tour was like a torture.	.82	
6. I got bored during free times.	.81	
7. I was worried that the food would upset my stomach during the tour.	.68	
8. I had spent a lot of time for collecting information before I decided on this tour.		.93
Eigenvalue	3.96	
Total variance explained	56.6 %	

Table 15.3: Correlations between constructs in the research model.

Constructs	Mean (Standard deviation)	PMP	PTV	PNMP	POV	BI
PMP	2.42 (1.02)	1				
PMB	3.65 (1.10)	−0.70	1			
PNMP	2.21 (0.94)	0.58	−0.62	1		
POV	3.71 (1.04)	−0.73	0.79	−0.72	1	
BI	3.76 (1.03)	−0.63	0.70	−0.72	0.77	1
N		413	413	414	414	414

Table 15.4: Multiple regression analysis on perceived overall value.

Model	Variables	R-square	Coefficients	t-value	p-value	VIF*
1	PMB	0.62	0.742	25.73	0.00	1
2	PMB	0.71	0.518	16.04	0.00	1.63
	PNMP		−0.421	−11.15	0.00	1.63
3	PMB	0.74	0.378	10.59	0.00	2.26
	PNMP		−0.350	−9.51	0.00	1.75
	PMP		−0.274	−7.42	0.00	2.08

*Variance inflation factor

remained in the model explaining certain unique portion of the variance in overall value. As a general rule, a variance inflation factor value above 10 is a sign of multicollinearity. The variance inflation factor values suggest that the three independent variables explain certain unique portion of the variance in overall value, therefore suggesting no sign of multicollinearity. In the second regression analysis, behavioural intentions were regressed on perceived overall value, perceived monetary benefit, perceived non-monetary price, and perceived monetary price (see Table 15.5). Similar to the results found in first regression analysis, each independent variable explained a unique portion of variance in behavioural intentions suggesting no sign of multicollinearity. In sum, preliminary analyses support the reliability and validity of constructs that can be used for further analysis in the structural analysis.

Frequencies of demographic and travel profile variables are presented in Table 15.6. As shown in the table, gender and marital status percentages are approximately equal in the sample. Majority of the respondents are under 40 years of age with high school or higher education levels. About 65% of the sample indicated that their monthly household income was above 750 US dollars. As for the travel profiles, latest package tour experiences of the 60% of the research participants were overnight tours while the rests' were daily tours. 17% of the respondents joined their latest package tour experience single whereas 83% of the respondents participated their last tour experience as couples, family, or with friends. Finally, 73% of the respondents indicated that they joined package tours once a year or more.

Table 15.5: Multiple regression analysis on behavioural intentions.

Model	Variables	R-square	Coefficients	t-value	p-value	VIF*
1	POV	0.60	0.77	24.72	0.00	1.00
2	POV	0.65	0.53	12.61	0.00	2.09
	PNMP		−0.37	−7.95	0.00	2.09
3	POV	0.67	0.38	7.38	0.00	3.40
	PNMP		−0.34	−7.41	0.00	2.12
	PMB		0.20	4.53	0.00	2.65
	PMP		−0.06	−1.31	0.19	2.36

*Variance inflation factor.

The structural model was analyzed using single-scale scores, which represented average scores for each scale. Analysis using single indicators is common in behavioural research to overcome sample size related problems (Chaudhuri & Holbrook, 2001; Grewal et al., 1998; Gruen & Shah, 2000). Before the test of research model, plots of residuals and predicted values were analyzed to check if there was a significant sign of normality, linearity, or homoscedasticity in the data. These analyses showed no digression from normal signs of these tests. Analysis of the final model was accomplished in two stages. In the first stage, the research model with 10 proposed links was run with Amos 4 (Arbuckle, 1997). This model was a saturated model with perfect fit measures (i.e. chi-square: 0, df: 0) since it comprehended all possible links in the model. At this stage, the relationships between model constructs were analyzed, and nine of the relationships in the model were found significant ($p < 0.05$). In the second stage, non-significant relationship between perceived monetary price and behavioural intentions was fixed at zero and the model was rerun. In the second run, all the remaining relationships in the model were significant and the model showed acceptable fit values. Therefore, the revised model was retained for further analysis. Figure 15.2 and Table 15.7 show revised model relationships, model coefficients, and fit values. As seen in Table 15.7, this model exhibits a good fit to the data with chi-square = 1.73 (df = 1), RMSEA = 0.04, GFI = 0.99, and CFI = 1.00.

Table 15.7 shows tested model coefficients and explained variance values in the dependent variables. Perceived monetary price, perceived monetary benefit, and perceived non-monetary price perceptions explain 74% of the variance in value perceptions. Furthermore, 67% of variance in behavioural intentions is explained by other model constructs. Nine of the 10 research hypotheses were supported by data, and all the proposed relationships were on the proposed direction (see Figure 15.2). The only relationship that could not be supported by the data was the relationship between monetary price and behavioural intentions (H3; CR: −1.32; p = 0.19). In Hypothesis 1, a positive relationship between monetary price perceptions and non-monetary price perceptions was proposed. This hypothesis was supported (CR = 5.48, p = 0.000). Furthermore, the second hypothesis is positing that monetary price was negatively related to value perception (H2; CR: −7.44; p = 0.000), and fourth hypothesis is positing that monetary price was

Table 15.6: Demographic and travelling profile of the respondents.

Variables	N	%
Gender		
Female	211	51
Male	203	49
Total	414	100
Age		
18–29	161	38.9
30–40	132	31.9
41–54	87	21
55 and above	34	8.2
Total	414	100
Approximate monthly household income (US dollars)		
Under $750	138	34.8
$751 – $1200	110	27.7
$1201 – $1750	30	7.6
$1750 – $2200	54	13.6
$2201 – $2750	30	7.6
$2751 and above	35	8.8
Total	397	100
Education		
Middle school	38	9.2
High school	96	23.2
College	231	55.9
Masters	48	11.6
Total	413	100
Marital status		
Married	198	47.9
Single	215	52.1
Total	413	100
Tour type		
Daily tour	171	41.3
Overnight tour	243	58.7
Total	414	100

(*Continued*)

Table 15.6: (Continued)

Variables	N	%
Tour composition		
Single	71	17.3
Couple	150	36.5
Family	84	20.4
Friends	106	25.8
Total	411	100
Annual frequency of package tour travel		
Less than one	110	26.6
Once a year	149	36.1
More than once	154	37.3
Total	413	100

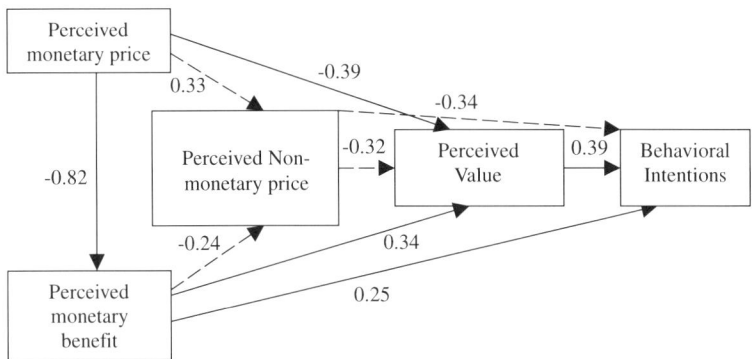

Figure 15.2: Tested cost-based model of leisure travel value.

negatively related to perceived monetary benefit (H4; CR: -19.7; $p = 0.000$) and both were supported. The hypothesized direct relationships between monetary benefit and non-monetary price (H5; CR: -8.18; $p = 0.000$), value (H6; CR: 10.63; $p = 0.000$), and behavioural intentions (H7; CR: 4.01; $p = 0.000$) were also supported by the data. These results suggest that higher monetary benefit perceptions result in lower non-monetary price perceptions, higher value perceptions, and behavioural intentions. In Hypotheses 8, 9, and 10, the direct relationships between non-monetary price, value perception, and behavioural intentions were tested. As expected, non-monetary price perceptions had negative relationships between value perception (H8; CR: -9.55; $p = 0.000$) and behavioural intentions (H9; CR: -7.40; $p = 0.000$). Finally, value perception had a positive relationship with behavioural intentions (H10; CR: 6.46; $p = 0.000$).

Table 15.7: Path estimates for the proposed links in the research model.

Paths in the model	Unstandardized relationship estimate			Critical ratio (CR)	p-value	SMC
	Direct	Indirect	Total			
PMP → PMB	−0.75	—	−0.75	−19.73	0.000	PMB = 0.49
PMP → PNMP	0.26	0.27	0.53	5.48	0.000	PNMP = 0.43
PMP → POV	−0.27	−0.47	−0.74	−7.44	0.000	POV = 0.74
PMP → BI	−0.06	−0.59	−0.65	−1.32	0.188	BI = 0.67
PMB → PNMP	−0.36	—	−0.36	−8.18	0.000	
PMB → POV	0.38	0.13	0.51	10.63	0.000	
PMB → BI	0.18	0.30	0.48	4.01	0.000	
PNMP → POV	−0.35	—	−0.35	−9.55	0.000	
PNMP → BI	−0.34	−0.12	−0.46	−7.40	0.000	
POV → BI	0.36	—	0.36	6.46	0.000	

Absolute fit measures	
Chi-square	1.73 (df: 1)
GFI	0.99
RMSEA	0.04
Incremental fit measures	
Null chi-square	1518.4 (df: 10)
AGFI	0.98
NNFI (TLI)	0.99
Parsimonious fit measures	
CFI	1.00
IFI	1.00
RFI	0.99

Note
1. N: 414, critical ratio and p values in the table correspond to direct effects.
2. SMC: Squared Multiple Correlations.
3. GFI: Goodness of fit index, RMSEA: Root mean square error of approximation, AGFI: Adjusted goodness of fit, NNFI: Non-normed fit index, CFI: Comparative fit index, IFI: Incremental fit index, RFI: R

Conclusions and Implications

The purpose of this chapter was to test the role of the perceived non-monetary costs of package tour services in a cost-based value model. In the conceptual model, non-monetary price factor was hypothesized to mediate the relationships between the perceived price, the perceived benefits, value, and behavioural intentions. The results of the study suggested that the non-monetary price factor partially mediates the relationships between the price, the perceived benefits, and the value perceptions. Therefore, it seems that the non-monetary price is an important indicator of the value in organized leisure travel contexts. Findings about the relationships between the perceived price, the perceived benefits, and the value perceptions are consistent with the findings in the literature on these relationships (Bojanic, 1996; Bolton & Drew, 1991; Chang & Wildt, 1994; Oh, 2000). In other words, the perceived price and benefits seem to be the two main predictors of value with respect to cost-based indicators of value perception (Duman, 2002; Grewal et al., 1998).

In terms of the relative influences of price, benefits, and non-monetary price on the value perception, it seems that the strongest predictor of the value perception is the perceived price followed by the perceived benefits and the non-monetary price (i.e. respective total effects = $-0.74, 0.51, -0.35$). As for the behavioural intentions of package tour participants, the perceived benefits, the perceived non-monetary price, and the value perceptions seem to be the significant predictors of this construct. Perceived price does not have a significant direct effect on behavioural intentions. Accordingly, it seems that the future intentions of package tour participants are significantly influenced by their evaluations of value, price-benefits, and non-monetary costs.

The findings are also congruent with the organized leisure travel literature. One of the important aspects of leisure travel value is "whether the time invested in a visit (experience) was worthwhile" (Murphy, Pritchard, & Smith, 2000, p. 46). In other words, the way in which the time spent on a leisure trip (i.e. quality of experience) is an important indicator of value perceptions of leisure travellers. This aspect of value becomes even more important for package tour experiences because the trip is pre-organized and traveller expectations are at the maximum (Atherton, 1994). To this end, current research findings show that non-monetary cost of package tour experiences is an important indicator of trip value.

One of the important reasons for the rise of package travel is its being more economical compared to independent travel (Phillips & Webster, 1983). Package tour seekers are known to apt to a value price for a convenient travel. This calls for the importance of monetary benefits received from participating in an organized vacation. Therefore, the perceptions of the overall value of a package tour can significantly be determined by the level of monetary benefits received. Research findings support this argument that the monetary benefits of package travel are an important aspect of trip value evaluations. Current research findings extend leisure travel value literature in the way that value perceptions of leisure travellers are largely determined by monetary and non-monetary cost evaluations in addition to service quality, emotional response, and reputation (Petrick, 2002). The findings also provide support for the argument that experiential quality perceptions enhance value perceptions of leisure travellers (Duman & Mattila, 2005; Otto & Ritchie, 1996). Those experiences that are perceived to be hassle-free and full of enjoyment can be expected to create better value.

An overall implication of the research findings for package tour organizers is that the perceptions of package price are not the primary evaluation for traveller's (single) future decisions. Whether or not the actual package price is perceived as low or high value, the monetary benefit and the non-monetary cost evaluations take precedent in repurchase and in recommending intentions. Furthermore, with respect to its effect on behavioural intentions, non-monetary costs seem to be a crucial determination of future intentions. In other words, while determining what to tell others about the tour and considering taking another tour from the same travel agent, traveller's focus on the smoothness of the tour as planned initially. Package tour participants give significant attention on the way in which their vacation time is managed by their tour organizers. Additionally, monetary gains of package travel seem to be an important consideration for travellers. From this point, it is suggested that package tour marketers use cost comparisons between alternative travel types in advertising. A good example to this point is that CLIA makes item by item comparisons of the cost between package cruise travel and independent travel in their web site and this is very likely to have effect on cruise vacationers' decisions (Cruise Lines International Association (CLIA), 2004).

The final discussion is about the future research and limitations of this study. In this study, it was attempted to develop a more comprehensive scale for the perceived non-monetary price and the study tested its role in a value model. The non-monetary price scale of this study only measures the during and after experience evaluations. However, the value theory suggests that the pre-purchase non-monetary costs should also be included in the measurement of non-monetary costs. For example, time and effort spent for searching and purchasing the product is also a part of the non-monetary costs of purchase (Zeithaml & Bitner, 2000). Additionally, the concept of perceived risk (Cronin et al., 1997; Sweeney et al., 1999) should also be included in the non-monetary price measurement. The findings of this research are limited to daily and overnight package tours taken by Turkish travellers. Therefore, future studies that employ different types of leisure travel and samples from different national origins will enhance the generalizability of the results. Finally, as with any other empirical research, limitations about the statistical analysis apply to this study. For example, one time test of causal relationships and lack of testing reversal causal effects limit the findings of this research. Replication of the findings is necessary for a more grounded theoretical analysis.

References

Arbuckle, J. (1997). *Amos user's guide, version 3.6*, Smallwaters Corporation, Chicago.
Atherton, T. (1994). Package holidays: Legal aspects. *Tourism Management, 15*(3), 193–199.
Bender, W. (1964). Consumer purchase costs. *Journal of Retailing, 40*(52), 1–8.
Bojanic, D. C. (1996). Consumer perceptions of price, value and satisfaction in the hotel industry: An exploratory study. *Journal of Hospitality and Leisure Marketing, 4*(1), 5–22.
Bolton, R. N., & Drew, J. H. (1991). A multistage model of customers' assessments of service quality and value. *Journal of Consumer Research, 17*(March), 375–384.
Brady, M. K., & Cronin, J. J. (2001). Customer orientation: Effects on customer service perceptions and outcome behaviors. *Journal of Service Research, 3*(3), 241–251.
Chang, T. Z., & Wildt, A. R. (1994). Price, product information, and purchase intention: An empirical study. *Journal of the Academy of Marketing Science, 22*(1), 16–27.
Chaudhuri, A., & Holbrook, M. B. (2001). The chain of effects from brand trust and brand affect to brand performance: The role of brand loyalty. *Journal of Marketing, 65*(April), 81–93.
Cronin, J. J., Brady, M. K., Brand, R. R., Hightower, R., & Shemwell, D. J. (1997). A cross-sectional test of the effect and conceptualization of service value. *Journal of Services Marketing, 11*(6), 375–391.
Cronin, J. J., Brady M. K., and Hult, G. T. M. (2000). "Assessing the effects of quality, value and customer satisfaction on consumer behavioral intentions in service environments". *Journal of Retailing, 76*(2), 193–218.
Cruise Lines International Association (CLIA). (2004). Retrieved April 02, 2004, from http://www.cruising.org/index0.htm

Darke, P. R., & Chung, C. M. Y. (2005). Effects of pricing and promotion on consumer perceptions: It depends on how you frame it. *Journal of Retailing, 81*(1), 35–47.

DeVellis, R. F. (1991). *Scale development theory and applications*. Applied Social Research Methods Series (Vol. 26). Sage Publications, Thousand Oaks, CA, USA.

Dodds, W. B., Monroe, K. B., & Grewal, D. (1991). The effects of price, brand and store information on buyers' product evaluations. *Journal of Marketing Research, 28*(August), 307–319.

Duman, T. (2002). *A model of perceived value for leisure travel products*. Unpublished dissertation. The Pennsylvania State University. The Graduate School College of Health and Human Development.

Duman, T., & Mattila, A. S. M. (2005). The role of affective factors on perceived cruise vacation value, *Tourism Management, 26*(3), 311–323.

Grewal, D., Monroe, K. B., & Krishnan, R. (1998). The effects of price-comparison advertising on buyers' perceptions of acquisition value, transaction value and behavioral intentions. *Journal of Marketing, 62*(April), 46–59.

Gruen, T. W., & Shah, R. H. (2000). Determinants and outcomes of plan objectivity and implementation in category management relationships. *Journal of Retailing, 76*(4), 483–510.

Hardesty, D. M., & Bearden, W. O. (2003). Consumer evaluations of different promotion types and price presentations: The moderating role of promotional benefit level. *Journal of Retailing, 79*(1), 17–25.

Kashyap, R., & Bojanic, D. C. (2000). A structural analysis of value, quality, and price perceptions of business and leisure travelers. *Journal of Travel Research, 39*(August), 45–51.

Kline, R. B. (1998). *Principles and practice of structural equation modeling*. NY: The Guilford Press.

Kocak, G., Yagci, M. I., & Duman, T. (2004). Seyahat edenlerin katıldıkları tur süresince algıladıkları parasal olmayan bedellere ilişkin bir ölçek geliştirme çalışması. *Anatolia, 15*(2), 105–112.

Lichtenstein, D. R., Netemeyer, R.G., & Burton, S. (1990). Distinguishing coupon proneness from value consciousness: An acquisition-transaction utility theory perspective. *Journal of Marketing, 54*(July), 54–67.

Monroe, K. B. (1990). *Pricing: Making profitable decisions*. NY: McGraw-Hill.

Monroe, K. B., & Chapman, J. D. (1987). Framing effects on buyers' subjective product evaluations. In: M. Wallendorf, & P. Anderson (Eds), *Advances in consumer research* (Vol. 14, pp. 193–197). Provo, UT: Association for Consumer Research.

Murphy, P., Pritchard, M. P., & Smith, B. (2000). The destination product and its impact on traveler perceptions. *Tourism Management, 21*(1), 43–52.

Norusis, M. J. (2000). *SPSS 10.0 guide to data analysis*, Upper Saddle River: Prentice Hall.

Nunnally, J. C. (1978). *Psychometric theory* (2nd ed.). NY: McGraw-Hill.

Oh, H. (2000). The effect of brand class, brand awareness, and price on customer value and behavioral intentions. *Journal of Hospitality and Tourism Research, 24*(2), 136–162.

Oliver, R. L. (1999). Value as excellence in the consumption experience. In: M. B. Holbrook (Ed.), *Consumer value: A framework for analysis and research* (pp. 1–29). New York, NY: Routledge.

Otto, J. E., & Ritchie, J. R. B. (1996). The service experience in tourism. *Tourism Management, 17*(3), 165–174.

Peterson, R. A., & Wilson, W. R. (1985). *Perceived risk and price reliance schema as price-perceived quality mediators*. Lexington, MA: Lexington books.

Petrick, J. F. (2002). Development of a multi-dimensional scale for measuring the perceived value of a service. *Journal of Leisure Research, 34*(2), 119–134.

Phillips, R. G., & Webster, S. (1983). *Group travel: Operating procedures*, Van Nostrand Reinhold Company: NY.

Sirohi, N., Mclaughlin, E. D., & Wittink, D. R. (1998). A model of consumer perceptions and store loyalty intentions for a supermarket retailer. *Journal of Retailing, 74*(2), 223–245.

Sweeney, J. C., Soutar, G. N., & Johnson, L. W. (1999). The role of perceived risk in the quality-value relationship: A study in a retail environment. *Journal of Retailing, 75*(1), 77–105.

Thaler, R. (1985). Mental accounting and consumer choice. *Marketing Science,* 4 (Summer), 199–214.

Varki, S., & Colgate, M. (2001). The role of price perceptions in an integrated model of behavioral intentions. *Journal of Service Research, 3*(3), 232–240.

Wang, K., Hsieh, A., & Huan, T. (2000). Critical service features in group package tour: An exploratory research. *Tourism Management, 21*(2), 177–189.

Zeithaml, V. A. (1988) Consumer perceptions of price, quality and value: A means-end model and synthesis of evidence. *Journal of Marketing, 52*(July), 2–22.

Zeithaml, V. A., & Bitner M. J. (1996). *Services marketing,* NY: McGraw-Hill.

Zeithaml, V. A., & Bitner, M. J. (2000), *Services marketing : Integrating customer focus across the firm,* Boston: Irwin/McGraw-Hill.

Chapter 16

Studying Visitor Loyalty to Rural Tourist Destinations

Elisabeth Kastenholz, Maria João Carneiro and Celeste Eusébio

Introduction

High levels of competition nowadays registered within the tourism industry lead to an increased interest, among those responsible for tourist destination marketing, in creating and sustaining destination loyalty among visitors. This paper focuses first on the concept of destination loyalty, then on its potential relevance in the rural tourism context and finally presents an analysis of the determinants of destination loyalty for a rural tourist destination in Portugal, applying binary logistic regression analysis. The analysis was undertaken based on the responses to a survey undertaken in North Portugal between summer 1998 and summer 1999. Results reveal the applicability of the binary regression models, with most relevant determinants of likelihood to come back being prior visits, as well as dimensions of the destination image. However, there are differences identifiable for the domestic versus international tourist market encountered in the region, particularly as far as the role of image determinants is concerned.

These results confirm some of the assumptions suggested in consumer behavior research in general, as far as habit formation is concerned, and in tourism theory, in particular, where this habit formation is closely related to a particular type of tourist, designed as "psycho-centric". Also the relevance of destination image is confirmed by this study, with different contents valued by different nationality groups, though, which is also frequently suggested in tourism literature. For these groups also other variables assume a differential determinant role, such as age and duration of stay, which may be related to different travel contexts and levels of involvement. Understanding these differences and the most important factors in enhancing destination loyalty should help destinations in directing specific marketing efforts to the potentially more loyal clients. This should be beneficial both from an economic and a social point of view, enhancing sustainable destination development.

Literature Review

Today's tourist destinations need a new philosophy centered on keeping loyal visitors in order to guarantee long-run success and enhance the destination's sustainability. It is more desirable, and less expensive, to retain tourists than to conquer new ones. Kotler (1997) explains that it is five times more expensive to attract a new customer than to retain a loyal one. In consumer research, the term "customer loyalty" is often measured by three different indicators, namely intention to continue buying the same product, intention to buy more of the same product and willingness to recommend the product to others. According to Chen and Gursoy (2001), the measure most used in tourism consumer behavior studies to assess tourist's destination loyalty has been repeat visitation (Oppermann, 1998; Pritchard & Howard, 1997). Repeat visitation is conceptually similar to intention to continue buying and intention to buy more, but does not include the willingness to recommend the product to others. In this context, some researchers (e.g. Chen & Gursoy 2001) defined this variable as the degree to which a tourist perceives the destination as a recommendable place. It may thus be concluded that destination loyalty is not easy to assess.

Taylor (1998) suggested that "likelihood to recommend a product or service to others" and "likelihood to purchase a product or service again" were good indicators to assess customer loyalty (cited by Chen, 2001). In this paper, rural destination loyalty was operationally defined as "likelihood to come back to a rural tourist destination". Even though it may be an interesting goal in rural destination marketing to make visitors loyal, it is still not clear what factors lead to tourist loyalty. According to Skogland and Siguaw (2004), our knowledge of customer loyalty and its determinants is replete with ambiguities. Actually, in the tourism context, novelty seeking has been suggested as a major tourist motivation (Poon, 1993). This should make it theoretically more difficult to achieve a loyal visitor market. However, studies like the one undertaken by Plog (1974) show that there are different tourist types, with some being more likely to seek familiarity. These tourists have been designed as "psychocentrics", contrasting with "allocentrics" that seek novelty. Correspondingly, it should be easier to make "psychocentrics" loyal destination visitors than "allocentrics".

Apart from this, a literature review on destination loyalty reveals that familiarity with the destination, overall satisfaction with the visit, the socio-demographic profile of the visitor and the motivations of visitors are potential determinants of a tourist's increased willingness to come back (Ross, 1993; Schroeder, 1996; Baloglu, 1996; Chen & Gursoy 2001; Lee & Cunningham, 2001; Skogland & Siguaw, 2004). Skogland and Siguaw (2004), for example, analyzed the relationship between guest satisfaction of two similar big-city hotels and repeat-purchase behavior, showing only a weak connection between these variables. However, Petrick and Sirakaya (2004) segmented cruisers by loyalty and observed that loyal travelers were more satisfied with their past cruise. Chen and Gursoy (2001) investigated the link between the tourist's destination loyalty and preferences, with results revealing that three benefit types sought at the destination, including different culture experiences, safety and convenient transportation, impact positively on tourists' loyalty to the destination.

Rural Tourism

Definitions of rural tourism are diverse, ranging from the inclusion of "the entire tourism activity in a rural area" (EC, 1987, cited by Keane, 1992, p. 44) to very specialized tourism products closely related to "rurality", such as "agro-tourism" (Leite, 1990). Definitions vary from country to country, as do manifestations of rural tourism (Davidson, 1992). A comparison of the Portuguese situation with other European countries shows that the legally defined Portuguese product of rural accommodation (TER) is relatively recent, not as thematically developed as elsewhere, and still of minor importance in most rural areas. TER stands for "turismo no espaço rural" and refers to family-owned country-houses which serve as tourist accommodation, which are specially regulated, registered and classified by the national tourism entity DGT (Direcção Geral de Turismo). TER combines heritage concerns with the ideal of personalized, high-quality tourism supply. DGT distinguishes: TH (turismo de habitação), the most "noble" form of accommodation in manor houses with high architectonic value and quality decoration and equipment; TR (turismo rural), good quality accommodation in typical rustic family houses located in a rural setting; and AT (agro-turismo), accommodation in country or manor houses integrated in a functioning farm.

According to Lane (1994), rural tourism units should ideally fulfill the following criteria: they should be located in rural areas; be functionally rural (based on the rural world's special features, such as open space, natural resources and traditional practices); be rural in scale (small scale) and traditional in character, organically and slowly growing and controlled by local people. If the last condition is fulfilled, Keane (1992) suggests the term "*rural community tourism*", where tourism development takes place in an integrated and coordinated manner at the local level, permitting maximum benefits for long-term local development. Even if the importance of rural tourism is minor in absolute terms, its significance for the development of single rural areas may be outstanding. The multiplier effect may be more important in rural areas, where the entire rural lifestyle is of interest, leading to a typical increase of demand for local products. Additionally, tourists visiting these areas may increase the areas' attractiveness in the eyes of the local population, enhancing their pride and self-esteem. That is why rural tourism, if carefully planned, managed and marketed may significantly enhance economic, social and cultural development goals (Page & Getz, 1997), although it should not be considered a panacea for all problems of all kinds of rural areas (Ribeiro, 2004).

The attractiveness of rural areas for tourism and recreation is partly due to the *image of "rurality"*, the *traditional* and *authentic*, standing for some romantic idea of "the good old days", pure and simple lifestyle, intact nature and perfect integration of Man in his natural environment (Clary, 1993). Sometimes this motive is further associated with effective family origins and an interest in visiting friends and relatives still living in rural areas, while visitors migrated, frequently for economic and professional reasons, to the more developed urban areas. There seems to be a high degree of identification of this type of tourists with the visited rural areas, which may induce these visitors to correspondingly increased destination loyalty.

Other motivations are linked to recreational activities, which require large open spaces and are nature-based. Also the need of closeness to nature for health reasons and furthering psychological balance is an important driving force for urban populations visiting the countryside. In this context, the esthetic value of landscape as an attraction must be stressed (Burton, 1995). Last, but not the least, the interest in discovering something new, in respect to rural life and nature, as well as by experimenting new, exciting activities, may drive people to visit rural areas. An increased level of education, information, time and resources available to travel nourishes all these motives, as well as the increased tendency to split holidays, combined with a general trend toward "widening horizons" and diversifying holiday practices (Poon, 1993). If novelty is the main motive for visiting a rural destination, the likelihood to become a loyal visitor should be relatively low.

Some studies confirmed this diversity of motivations within the rural tourist market (Davidson, 1992; Kastenholz, Davis, & Paul, 1999). These motives are responded to by a variety of resources, such as nature, history, cultural manifestations, special facilities etc., resulting in different tourism forms and products. In this context it is of strategic importance to know both the region's tourism resource base and the potential tourist (Page & Getz, 1997). A professional marketing approach, permitting the identification of the most appropriate target market and of ways to attract and satisfy it, combined with a concern about sustainability, is therefore defended as most appropriate for rural tourism development (Gilbert, 1989; Dolli & Pinfold, 1997; Kastenholz, 2004). In this context, a focus on more loyal destination visitors may be an interesting option, improving perspectives of long-term destination success, reducing costs, creating relationships that may enhance mutual understanding and reduce potential conflict.

Methodology

The data used for studying determinants of destination loyalty was collected in a one-year survey undertaken between 1998 and 1999, directed at tourists staying in rural areas in North Portugal, which yielded a total of 2280 valid responses (Kastenholz, 2000). The main objective of the survey was the identification of the tourists' profile, their tourist behavior and their image of North Portugal as a rural tourist destination. The questionnaire was developed, based on a literature review on rural tourism and destination image studies as well as on an exploratory study with students who had already been on holidays in the countryside. A pre-test at a rural area in North Portugal ($N = 185$) further permitted refinement of the instrument. The questionnaire was translated into five languages (Portuguese, English, French, German and Spanish), with the help of native speakers, fluent in two languages, and partly refined during the process, considering the tourists' comments.

Specifically, field trips were organized every 1–2 months, with a duration of 4–5 days, in which the main author of this study and 2–3 carefully selected and instructed students were present as interviewers. The sites for interviewing were selected, based on the knowledge of the most relevant attraction sites and most popular facilities in the rural areas studied and included rural tourism establishments, small hotels, camping sites, tourist offices, restaurants, cafés, museums, castles, churches and other monuments, nature and archeological parks. All tourists that were encountered at a specific time at a specific site were approached to identify those who actually spent holidays in the countryside, with at least a complementary leisure motive, and asked to participate. Apart from this, the Oporto airport as the main entrance of international tourists was visited on a regular basis, leading to 21% of total valid responses. Here tourists were approached after their holidays. The response rate of the interview approach can be estimated as close to 90%, based on a counting of persons approached and responses obtained on several days. However, when leaving questionnaires with intermediaries at tourist posts and accommodation units, response rates were considerably lower (hardly achieving 20%). The latter approach led to 12% of valid responses collected.

Data collection was planned to lead to an approximately representative sample of leisure tourists staying in rural areas in Northern Portugal for holiday purposes. The carefully chosen cluster-sampling procedure, at diverse tourist attraction sites in the region at different points in time, the very assertive approach of directly interviewing about 88% of the tourists encountered in these circumstances, and the global number of valid responses obtained sustains this assumption. The sample was controlled for a balanced spread between rural subregions, high and low season and the national versus foreign tourist market. The most important foreign nationalities were the German, British, French, Dutch and Spanish markets. Respondents tended slightly to the younger age ranges and higher educational levels. They revealed a high propensity of traveling and visiting the countryside for a holiday.

Discussion of Findings

Considering the objective of the present research, respondents were divided into two groups: those manifesting highest likelihood to come back to the destination (most loyal tourists) and those revealing the least likelihood to do so (least loyal tourists), with these groups being defined based on the identification of the most extreme responses on a scale ranging from 1 (not likely at all) to 7 (very likely). Only the most extreme responses were considered in order to clearly separate likelihood tendencies and better identify corresponding determinants, ignoring for this study the medium values, resulting in a number of 718 responses usable for the model (being 80% classified as most likely to come back). The so-created binary variable is considered to be the dependent variable in a logistic regression model that aims at identifying those factors that most determine the likelihood to return to a destination.

In this context, the impact of a series of independent variables, related with previous destination experience, behavior at the destination, destination perception and socio-demographics, was analyzed, as explained below. Prior destination experience or familiarity with the destination was assessed by dividing the tourists into two groups — those who had never visited the region before and those who repeated their visit. As far as tourist behavior on site is concerned, two binary variables conditioning the holiday experience were considered — duration of stay (up to four days/short-break versus superior to four days) and season of stay (high versus low season). The socio-demographic variables analyzed were the binary variable gender, as well as two ordinal variables, grouped into three categories and treated in the logistic regression analysis as nominal variables — age range and level of education.

Finally, the impact of five components of cognitive destination image was analyzed. These resulted from a *Principal Components Analysis* of perceptive ratings of 25 destination attributes, assessed through 5-point Likert-type scales, revealing reasonable values of internal consistency (Hair, Anderson, Tatham, & Black, 1998, p. 118). The resulting factor structure can be described as follows: the KMO value of 0.852 confirms the adequacy of PCA. The Bartlett test indicates a chi-square value of 4310.064 with a significance of 0.000, i.e. the null hypothesis of the correlation matrix being an identity matrix can be rejected. Communalities are all above 0.32, which is not very high, but 60% are above 0.5. All factor-loadings are above 0.52. The measures of sampling adequacy (MSA) of all variables are above 0.77. A substantial amount of residuals (73%) between observed and reproduced correlations have an absolute value of below 0.05. The extraction of five principle components, based on the Kaiser criterion (eigenvalue > 1), leads to the explanation of about 51.1% of the variance, which can be considered acceptable in the domain of social sciences. After a "*Varimax*" rotation, which facilitates the distinction between principle components, the data structure presented in Table 16.1 becomes visible.

Table 16.1: PCA of cognitive images.

Components	"Loadings" of components	Cronbach alpha	Accumulated explained variance (%)
I. Nature			
1. Nature	0.73	0.75	11.7
2. Peace and quiet	0.70		
3. Walking	0.63		
4. Rural life	0.62		
5. Unpolluted environment	0.59		
6. Isolation	0.52		
7. Scenery	0.44		
II. Basics (Welcoming Atmosphere)			
1. Accommodation	0.65	0.69	23.1
2. Sympathy of population	0.62		
3. Climate	0.61		
4. Infrastructures	0.53		
5. Price	0.52		
6. Gastronomy	0.49		
7. Ease of communication	0.45		
III. Action/socializing			
1. Sports and Recreation	0.81	0.75	33.5
2. Nightlife	0.72		
3. Opportunities for children	0.71		
4. Socializing	0.52		
5. Variety of activities, opportunities	0.42		
IV. Information and Access			
1. Sign-posting	0.77	0.66	43.4
2. Tourist Information	0.62		
3. Accessibility	0.57		
4. Professional Service	0.55		
V. Culture			
1. Architecture, monuments	0.79	0.68	51.1
2. History and Culture	0.77		

A binary logistic regression analysis was used to identify the impact of the above-described independent variables on the likelihood to come back to the destination (0, low likelihood of coming back; 1, high likelihood of coming back). Apart from the identification of a global model, specific models for the domestic and foreign markets were analyzed. The model used in this research can be specified in the following way (Figure 16.1).

In these logistic regressions the *backward* estimation method was selected, in the sense of highlighting the most significant independent variables. This method was based on the *maximum likelihood ratio*, which was considered superior to the Wald statistic for evaluating the contribution of each independent variable (Tabachnick & Fidell, 1996, pp. 598–599; SPSS Inc., 1999, p. 51). *Outliers* were identified by analyzing studentized residuals, being cases with absolute values superior to 2 excluded from the model. In order to evaluate the appropriateness of the model, classification tables were analyzed, as well as the chi-square statistic for the model, the *Nagelkerke R^2* value and the *Hosmer–Lemeshow* test.

As far as socio-demographics are concerned, the sample used for this model ($N = 718$) was quite balanced in terms of gender (51% of respondents were male) as well as in terms of foreign versus domestic market (52% were Portuguese). There was a slight predominance of people with lower educational levels (slightly more than 55% of the sample) and

$$PROB(event) = \frac{1}{1+e^{-Z}}$$

Where:

PROB(event) = likelihood to come back to the North of Portugal;
e = is the base of the natural logarithms, approximately 2.718

And Z is the following linear combination:

$$Z = B_0 + B_1 PV + B_2 DS + B_3 G + B_4 SS + B_5 AGE_{\leq 25} + B_6 AGE_{\geq 55} + B_7 LE_{low} + B_8 LE_{high} + B_9 DA_{nature} + B_{10} DA_{basics} + B_{11} DA_{action/socializing} + B_{12} DA_{information\ \&\ access} + B_{13} DA_{culture}$$

Where:
- $B_0 \ldots B_{13}$ = Coefficients estimated from the data;
- PV = dummy for previous visit to the North of Portugal: 0 for newcomer and 1 for repeat visitor;
- DS = dummy for duration of stay in the North of Portugal: 0 for duration of stay ≤ 4 days and 1 for duration of stay >4 days;
- G = dummy for gender of visitors: 0 for male and 1 to female;
- SS = dummy for season of stay in the North of Portugal: 0 for high season and 1 for low season;
- $AGE_{\leq 25}$ = dummy for age of visitors: 1 for age ≤ 25 and 0 for otherwise;
- $AGE_{\geq 55}$ = dummy for age of visitors: 1 for age ≥ 55 and 0 for otherwise;
- LE_{low} = dummy for level of education of visitors: 1 for low education and 0 for otherwise;
- LE_{high} = dummy for level of education of visitors: 1 for high education and 0 for otherwise;
- DA_{nature} = factor score of principal component of cognitive imaging relating to nature;
- DA_{basics} = factor score of principal component of cognitive image relating to basics (welcoming atmosphere);
- $DA_{action/socializing}$ = factor score of principal component of cognitive image relating to action/socializing;
- $DA_{information\ \&\ access}$ = factor score of principal component of cognitive image relating to information/access;
- $DA_{culture}$ = factor score of principal component of cognitive image relating to culture.

Figure 16.1: Model specification.

relatively young tourists (respondents below 25 years represented about 75% of the sample). About 60% of the subjects in the sample had already visited the North of Portugal before (repeat visitors). As far as the visit was concerned, about half of the sample (51%) was visiting the Northern Region in the high season (between June and September) and the majority (about 56%) was staying more than four days at the destination.

The global regression model, corresponding to all the respondents included in this study, presented very reasonable values in terms of *goodness-of-fit*, with *Nagelkerke R^2* presenting the value of 0.38. The model permitted the correct classification of a considerable number of cases (83.3%). The cases corresponding to those very likely to come back were easier to classify (more than 90% were classified correctly) than those who were unlikely to come back, representing also the majority of the sample (about 80%). The results of the binary logistic regression clearly show that the likelihood to come back to North Portugal was strongly associated with the familiarity visitors have with this destination, with some destination image components and with level of education of visitors (Table 16.2).

Repeat visitors show a higher probability to return than those who never visited this region before. The odds (ratio of the probability that an event will occur to the probability it will not) of visiting North Portugal of those who had visited the destination before are 6–7 times higher than the odds of those who were visiting it for the first time. The image

Table 16.2: Determinants of the likelihood to come back to North Portugal. (Results of the binary logistic regression for all the visitors analyzed in the study.)

Independent variables (predictors)	Global model				
	B	S.E.	Wald	Sig.	Exp(B)
Level of education					
otherwise	X				
high	0.684	0.236	8.398	0.004	1.981
Gender					
male	X				
female	−0.759	0.230	10.941	0.001	0.468
Previous visit to the North of Portugal					
newcomer	X				
repeat visitor	2.015	0.244	68.039	0.000	7.497
Nature	0.888	0.174	26.035	0.000	2.430
Basics (welcoming atmosphere)	0.829	0.200	17.166	0.000	2.291
Action/socializing	0.485	0.165	8.694	0.003	1.625
Constant	−7.024	0.940	55.875	0.000	0.001

X, category of reference; Nagelkerke $R^2 = 0.38$; Hosmer and Lemeshow test $X^2 = 13.91$ (sig. 0.084)

visitors have of the region in terms of nature and welcoming atmosphere is also one of the factors that impact most on the decision of whether or not to return to the region. Hence, the characteristics of the area's life, its quiet and peaceful environment and the beauty of its scenery seem to be important factors in motivating people to visit this region again. However, also the destination's image as providing a welcoming atmosphere, such as the sympathy of local people, the infrastructure, the climate and the level of prices at the destination are important in the decision to come back (Figure 16.2).

Also the image people had of the destination in terms of opportunities for entertainment, the level of education of visitors and their gender were significant in determining the intention to come back. Those who recognized the destination as having more opportunities for entertainment (e.g. sports and recreation facilities, nightlife, opportunities/activities for children) were most likely to return to the region than those who did not perceive these opportunities. People with higher levels of education seemed more interested in coming back to the destination. Significant differences were only noticed between the visitors with the highest level of education and the other visitors (this last group represented the category of reference in the regression). Male respondents also showed a slightly higher likelihood of returning than female visitors (Figure 16.2).

In order to determine whether the reasons that motivated Portuguese to return to the North of Portugal were different from those that encouraged foreigners to come back, a binary logistic regression analysis was undertaken separately for each of the two groups. The independent and dependent variables in the regressions corresponded to those used in the global model. Hence, in both models the dependent variable was the binary variable representing the likelihood to come back. As in the global model, the independent variables included in these models were: visitors' familiarity with the destination; the five image components associated with the destination image (nature, welcoming atmosphere,

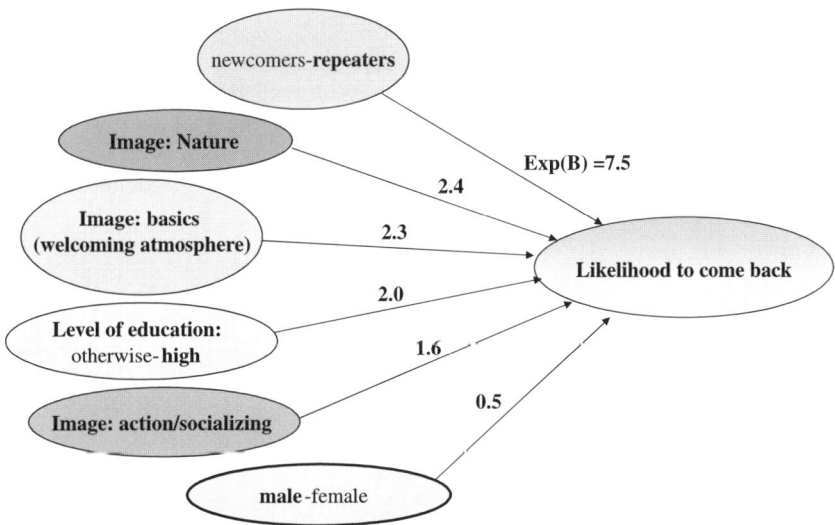

Figure 16.2: Global Model of likelihood to come back.

action/socializing, information and access, and culture); duration and season of stay; and some socio-demographic characteristics of respondents — gender, age and educational level. These variables were operationalized as in the global model (Figure 16.1).

Both the models for Portuguese and for foreigners had a considerable *goodness-of-fit*, with *Nagelkerke R^2* yielding values of 0.41 and 0.38, respectively (Table 16.3). Similar to what happened in the global model, it was easier to classify those very likely to come back (90% or more being correctly classified in each sample). Although in both samples, the number of people willing to return to the destination was superior to those who did not want to return, there was a larger percentage of Portuguese wanting to come back (87%) than of foreigners (73%).

In the two models, similar to what was found in the global model, repeat visitors show a greater interest in coming back than newcomers. However, some differences may be detected in the factors that motivate Portuguese and foreigners to come back. Whereas foreigners seem to be more motivated by nature, scenery and features of rural life that can be found in the region (factor I of PCA), Portuguese seem to be more interested in returning because of the region's welcoming atmosphere, that is, the tourist infrastructure existing within the region, the sympathy of the population, the climate and the level of prices (factor II of the PCA). Portuguese also seem to be willing to return to North Portugal because of the cultural heritage of this region. In contrast, this feature does not seem to play a very important role in foreigners' decision to come back. For foreigners, an additional feature that determines their willingness to return is the perception they have about the accessibility to the North of Portugal and about the existence of tourist information.

In the case of Portuguese, those who stay for longer periods of time at the destination show a higher interest to come back. Nevertheless, the duration of stay did not have a significant influence in the foreigners' decision. In terms of socio-demographics, it is interesting to notice that younger foreigners were more likely to return than the other age ranges. The level of education and gender also had a significant influence in the willingness to come back, although the impact of these variables was much lower than that of the other variables mentioned above. In both models, male visitors and people with the highest level of education were those more interested in coming back. In the regression for the Portuguese sample, differences were only found between those with the lowest education and the other respondents (reference category), whereas in the regression for the foreigners' sample differences were only found between those with the highest education and the other visitors (Figure 16.3).

Conclusions and Implications

Although novelty seeking is generally considered a major driving force of tourist behavior, destination loyalty was suggested as an interesting factor in increasing the destination's long-run success, being particularly helpful in a sustainable destination development strategy for rural tourist destinations. The study, based on survey data of tourists staying in rural areas in North Portugal, revealed the possibility of distinguishing tourists with high and low likelihood to come back to the destination. Binary regression analysis helped to identify factors determining this likelihood to return to the destination, for the overall sample, as well

Table 16.3: Determinants of the likelihood to come back to North Portugal (Results of the binary logistic regressions for Portuguese and foreigners).

Independent variables (predictors)		B	S.E.	Wald	Sig.	Exp(B)
Model for Portuguese	Level of education					
	low	−1.005	0.434	5.355	0.021	0.366
	otherwise	X				
	Gender					
	male	X				
	female	−0.956	0.385	6.157	0.013	0.384
	Duration of stay					
	< 4 days	X				
	> 4 days	1.474	0.545	7.306	0.007	4.367
	Previous visit to the North of Portugal					
	newcomer	X				
	repeat visitor	1.963	0.411	22.788	0.000	7.118
	Basics (welcoming atmosphere)	1.833	0.364	25.376	0.000	6.252
	Culture	0.713	0.262	7.408	0.006	2.040
	Constant	−5.930	1.538	14.862	0.000	0.003
Model for foreigners	Level of education					
	otherwise	X				
	high	0.571	0.305	3.497	0.061	1.770
	Gender					
	male	X				
	female	−1.122	0.303	13.708	0.000	0.326
	Age					
	< 25	1.172	0.426	7.551	0.006	3.227
	otherwise	X				
	Previous visit to the North of Portugal					
	newcomer	X				
	repeat visitor	1.822	0.380	22.962	0.000	6.187
	Nature	1.323	0.239	30.655	0.000	3.756
	Information and access	0.826	0.210	15.454	0.000	2.285
	Constant	−6.650	1.087	37.450	0.000	0.001

X, category of reference.
Model for Portuguese: Nagelkerke $R^2 = 0.41$; Hosmer and Lemeshow test $X^2 = 9.76$ (sig. 0.28).
Model for foreigners: Nagelkerke $R^2 = 0.38$; Hosmer and Lemeshow test $X^2 = 10.54$ (sig. 0.23).

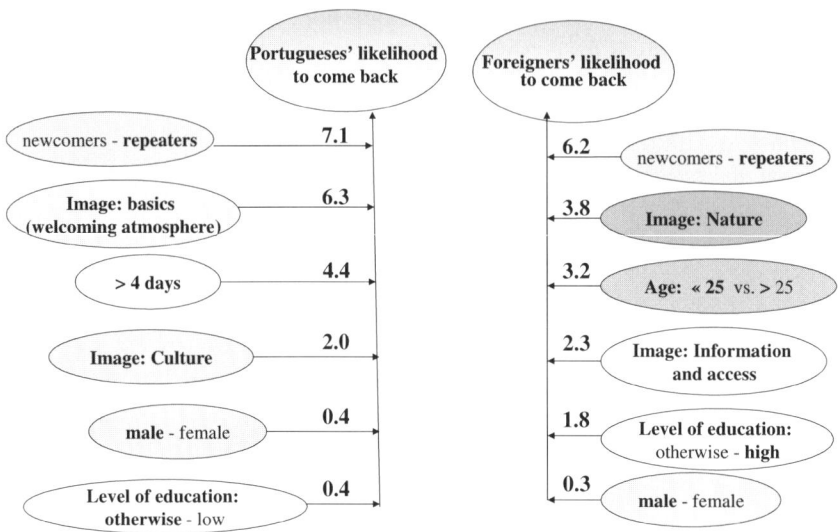

Figure 16.3: Separate models of likelihood to come back for Portuguese and foreign tourists.

as for the Portuguese and the foreign visitor groups separately. All models analyzed presented very reasonable *goodness-of-fit* values and permitted the correct classification of a high number of cases.

In the global model, the variables that revealed a significant impact on likelihood to come back were, in this order: familiarity with the destination (playing the overall most important role), components of destination image, level of education and gender. The outstanding relevance of prior experience for explaining future travel behavior has already been identified by a series of authors (e.g. Woodside & Lysonski, 1989; Chon, 1990; Milman & Pizam, 1995). This is also true for the relevance of destination image (Hunt, 1975; Fakeye & Crompton, 1991; Gartner, 1993; Fesenmaier & MacKay, 1996; Kastenholz, 2002a).

As far as destination image is concerned, determinant image factors differ for Portuguese versus foreign respondents, though. Specifically, Portuguese attribute a higher value to their perception of a welcoming, comfortable atmosphere at the destination, being also positively influenced by culture in their intention to come back. Foreign visitors, on the other hand, seem to value relatively more the natural and rural features of the destination, as well as the destination's accessibility and ease of obtaining quality tourist information. These differences may be related to different benefits sought typical for distinct nationality groups, with nationality frequently functioning as a proxy for cultural differences (Berry, 1979). On the other hand, the perception of accessibility may be more relevant for those traveling longer distances and overcoming more obstacles to get to the destination than for the domestic market. Spending a holiday in a foreign country further naturally increases their perception of strangeness and need for information (Kastenholz, 2002b). These factors should be taken into account when developing a destination, not only to attract tourists for the first time, but also to eventually make them loyal tourists.

Additionally, Portuguese visitors staying longer tend to be more willing to come back, which is not visible for the foreign sample. For the domestic market, length of stay may be another indicator for involvement, typical for the loyal market. Portuguese short-break visitors may only come "by accident", which would occur to a lesser degree in the case of international tourists, for whom a rural holiday abroad would naturally imply higher degrees of involvement and typically longer stays. For the destination this may suggest that domestic tourists coming for longer stays should be catered to with particular care, since they show a relatively higher level of involvement and interest in rural areas and may further become loyal clients. On the other hand, younger foreign visitors tend to be more likely to return, which does not occur within the Portuguese sample. This result may be surprising, but might be related to the fact that younger foreign tourists may expect to return to the destination more easily than those of an older age, or that this younger group may identify more with the destination, perhaps feeling less "frightened" in a less familiar environment (Kastenholz, 2002b).

These results provide relevant contributions to the definition of marketing strategies and appropriate destination development, when aiming at attracting and satisfying more loyal visitors. A well-designed and targeted *Customer Relationship Management* would be a valuable tool in inducing repeat visitors to ever-increasing destination loyalty. There is a need to differentiate strategies to retain the domestic and foreign tourist markets of North Portugal, which reveal in part distinct profiles and preferences most associated with likelihood to come back. Thus, destination development and the corresponding creation and projection of an appealing destination image, specifically targeted to each group might improve a destination's success. From a sustainability point of view, this success should be aimed at for the long run, with the loyal visitor market presenting a most valuable asset, permitting repeated and stable economic benefits, the reduction of costs, as well as the creation of relationships that may enhance mutual understanding and reduce potential conflict.

References

Baloglu, S. (1996). *An empirical investigation of determinants of tourist destination image*. Published doctoral dissertation. Virginia Polytechnic Institute and State University, UMI dissertation Services.

Berry, J. W. (1979). A cultural ecology of social behaviour. In: L. Berkowitz (Ed.), *Advances in experimental social psychology* (Vol. 12, pp. 177–206). New York: Academic Press.

Burton, R. (1995). *Travel geography*. London: Pitman Publishing.

Chen, J. S., & Gursoy, D. (2001). An investigation of tourist's destination loyalty and preferences. *International Journal of Contemporary Hospitality, 13*(12), 79.

Chon, K. S. (1990). *Consumer satisfaction and dissatisfaction as related to destination image perception*. Published doctoral dissertation. Virginia Polytechnic Institute and State University, UMI dissertation Services.

Clary, D. (1993). *Le tourisme dans l'espace français*. Paris: Masson Géographie.

Davidson, R. (1992). *Tourism in Europe*. London: Pitman Publishing.

Dolli, N., & Pinfold, J. F. (1997). Managing rural tourism businesses: Financing, development and marketing issues. In: S. J. Page, & D. Getz (Eds), *The business of rural tourism: International perspectives* (pp. 38–58). London, Boston: International Thomson Business.

Fakeye, P. C., & Crompton, J. L. (1991). Image differences between prospective, first-time, and repeat visitors to the lower Rio Grande Valley. *Journal of Travel Research, 30*(2), 10–16.

Fesenmaier, D., & MacKay, K. (1996). Deconstructing destination image construction. *Revue de Tourisme*, *51*(2), 37–43.

Gartner, W. C. (1993). Image formation process. *Communication and Channel Systems in Tourism Marketing*, *2*(2/3), 191–215.

Gilbert, D. (1989). Rural tourism and marketing: Synthesis and new ways of working. *Tourism Management*, *10*(1), 39–50.

Hair, J. F., Anderson, R. E., Tatham, R. L., &. Black, W.C. (1998). Multivariate data analysis. *Englewood Cliff, NJ: Prentice-Hall. (original work published 1984)*

Hunt, J. (1975). Image as a factor in tourism development. *Journal of Travel Research*, *13*(3), 1–7.

Kastenholz, E. (2000). *O Mercado do Turismo em Espaço Rural no Norte de Portugal – Relatório Final*. Unpublished document. Porto, ISEE/ CCRN.

Kastenholz, E. (2002a). The role and marketing implications of destination images on tourist behavior: The case of northern Portugal. Published doctoral dissertation. Universidade de Aveiro, UMI dissertation Services.

Kastenholz, E. (2002b). The impact of 'Cultural proximity' on how tourists view a holiday destination, *Proceedings of the 2002 multicultural marketing conference of the academy of marketing science*, Valencia, Espanha.

Kastenholz, E. (2004). 'Management of Demand' as a tool in sustainable tourist destination development. *Journal of Sustainable Tourism*, *12*(5), 388–408.

Kastenholz, E., Davis, D., & Paul, G. W. (1999). Segmenting tourism in rural areas: The case of North and Central Portugal. *Journal of Travel Research*, *37*(4), 353–363.

Keane, M. (1992). Rural tourism and rural development. In: H. Briassoulis, & J. van der Straaten (Eds), *Tourism and the environment*. Dordrecht, NL: Kluwer Academic Publishers.

Kotler, P. (1997). *Marketing management – Analysis, planning, implementation and control*. Englewood Cliff, NJ: Prentice-Hall. (original work published 1980).

Lane, B. (1994). What is rural tourism? *Journal of Sustainable Tourism*, *2*(1/2), 7–21.

Lee, M., & Cunningham, L. F. (2001). A cost/benefit approach to understanding service loyalty. *The Journal of Services Marketing*, *15*(2), 113.

Leite, A. (1990). Que turismo rural no Alto Minho? In: *1º Encontro: Minho-Identidade e Mudança*. Braga: Escola de Economia e Gestão. Universidade do Minho: 396–402.

Milman, A., & Pizam, A. (1995). The role of awareness and familiarity with a destination. *Journal of Travel Research*, *33*(3), 21–27.

Oppermann, M. (1998) Destination threshold potential and the Law of Repeat Visitation. *Journal of Travel Research*, *37*(2), 131–137.

Page, S. J., & Getz, D. (1997). The business of rural tourism: International perspectives. In: S. J. Page, & D. Getz (Eds), *The business of rural tourism: International perspectives* (pp. 4–37). London, Boston: International Thomson Business Press.

Petrick, J. F., & Sirakaya, E. (2004). Segmenting Cruisers by Loyalty. *Annals of Tourism Research*, *31*(2), 472–475.

Plog, D. (1974). Why destination areas rise and fall in popularity. *Cornell Hotel and Restaurant Quarterly*, *14*(4), 55–58.

Poon, A. (1993). *Tourism, technology and competitive strategies*. Wallingford: CAB International.

Pritchard, M., & Howard, D. (1997). The loyal traveler: Examining a typology of service patronage. *Journal of Travel Research*, *35*(4), 2–10.

Ribeiro, M. (2004). Pelo Turismo é que vamos/ podemos ir (?). Sobre as representações e as visões dos responsáveis das administrações públicas de âmbito local, acerca do turismo para o desenvolvimento rural. In: O. Simões, & A. Cristóvão (Eds), *TERN — Turismo em Espaços Rurais e Naturais* (pp. 41–56). Coimbra: Instituto Politécnico de Coimbra.

Ross, G. (1993). Ideal and actual images of backpacker visitors to northern America. *Journal of Travel Research, 32*(2), 54–59.

Schroeder, T. (1996). The relationship of residents' image of their state as a tourist destination and their support for tourism. *Journal of Travel Research, 35*(3), 71–73.

Skogland, I., & Siguaw, J. D. (2004). Are your satisfied customers loyal? *Cornell Hotel and Restaurant Administration Quarterly, 45*(3), 221–234.

SPSS Inc. (1999). *SPSS regression models 9.0.* Chicago, IL: Marketing Department SPSS Inc.

Tabachnick, B. G., & Fidell, L. S. (1996). *Using multivariate statistics.* (3rd ed.) New York: Harper Collins College Publishers.

Taylor, T. (1998). Better loyalty measurement leads to business solutions. Marketing News, *32*(22), 41. In: Chen, J. S., & Gursoy, D. (2001). An investigation of tourist's destination loyalty and preferences. International Journal of Contemporary Hospitality, *13*(2), 79.

Woodside, A.G., & Lysonski, S. (1989). A general model of traveler destination choice. *Journal of Travel Research, 27*(4), 8–14.

Chapter 17

Waiting Time Effects on the Leisure Experience and Visitor Emotions

Juergen Gnoth, J. Enrique Bigné and Luisa Andreu

Introduction

Emotions are an important component of the leisure experience (Tinsley & Tinsley, 1986). The emotional component in the service experience brings together a central construct from the discipline of tourism marketing: consumer satisfaction (Kozak, 2001; Zins, 2002). The affective side of the experience in hedonic consumption has become important and worthy of study as it adds to our understanding of satisfaction which appears to be the predictor of loyalty. The aim of this research is to extend an affective model of emotions and satisfaction (Bigné, Andreu, & Gnoth, 2005) by adding waiting-time effects and the active/relaxing visitor experience. Even though the relationship between waiting time and service evaluations has received research attention (see, for instance, Baker & Cameron, 1996; Houston, Bettencourt, & Wenger, 1998), the existing conceptualizations fail to capture the interrelated visitor experience.

This chapter focuses on Leisure and Tourism Services (LTS) as hedonic and experience services in which the consumer seeks pleasure, fun or fantasy (Gnoth, 1997; Holbrook & Hirschman, 1982), and consumers can evaluate after some purchase consumption (Ostrom & Iacobucci, 1995). In particular, this chapter analyses the leisure experience and visitor emotions at two man-made tourist attractions, a museum and a theme park. As sources of income and target of investment, such attractions are increasingly man-made. While this improves the number of opportunities for investors and tourists alike, such venues also offer the opportunity (and challenge) of increased managerial control over natural attractions. Despite some notable exceptions (e.g. Goulding, 1999; Jansen-Verbeke & van Rekom, 1996; Milman, 2001; Rowley, 1999; Stevens, 2000; Swarbrooke, 1995), however, the visitor attraction sector has tended to receive relatively little attention in the tourism literature. Recognizing the interest of analysing visitor emotions in tourist attractions, this chapter begins with a review of the relevant literature. An overview of the model and study hypotheses is then presented followed by the methodology and results sections. The paper concludes with a discussion of the study's results and its limitations.

Literature Review

The starting point of this study requires the conceptualization of the main constructs that forms the basis of the research model as well as the foundations of the affective model of satisfaction and loyalty. With regard to emotions, the most frequently encountered approaches suggest that the emotional space is made up of a limited number of underlying dimensions, such as pleasure–arousal (Mehrabian & Russell, 1974; Russell, 1980) or negative–positive affect (Mano & Oliver, 1993; Watson & Tellegen, 1985). In the proposed framework of this study, consumers' two types of emotional responses are considered: valence and arousal. Valence (pleasantness) is a subjective feeling of pleasantness or unpleasantness, and arousal is an activated or deactivated subjective feeling (Russell, 1980).

As mentioned beforehand, this chapter analyses visitor emotions at two man-made tourist attractions, a museum and a theme park. Amusement parks are man-made tourist attractions that emphasize a major theme on which man-made, natural, and human resources are coordinated in order to offer a unique visitation experience (Formica & Olsen, 1998). While they usually attract an entrance fee, further spending often depends on the length of time tourists are motivated to attend, as well as on how absorbing the experiences are. As such, theme parks do not differ from museums and they are thus clearly related forms of tourist attractions. Where these two types do differ, however, is in the way the visitor interacts with the facilities. Whereas a museum often relies on contemplative interactions between visitor and exhibition that induces reflection and education, theme parks tend to involve visitors physically and learning tends to be more a matter of skill and the experience of thrill. Such differences appear to be vanishing, however, as, in recent years, particularly museums have permitted visitors to become more interactive with exhibitions (Kotler & Kotler, 1998). Motivated by the apparent contrasts among museums and theme parks, this research develops a number of hypotheses that highlight differences in emotional experience, satisfaction formation and loyalty intentions, taking into account the waiting time effects and leisure experience.

The generation of consumer emotions affects consumer satisfaction and this, in fact, influence consumers' loyalty. The complexity of emotions as a broad concept suggests the importance to analyse their dimensions, i.e. pleasure and arousal. While the experience of arousal over pleasure may be either positive or negative (Chebat & Michon, 2003), for example, in moments of panic in a risky adventure situation, when assuming an amusing or enjoyable LTS, the effect of arousal on pleasure should be positive. In using the said services of a museum and a theme park, it can be assumed that the different levels of opportunity they offer tourists to become active, makes for stronger relationships between positive arousal and visitor pleasure for a theme park in comparison to a museum. More formally,

> **Hypothesis 1** Positive arousal should positively influence visitor pleasure in LTS, and this effect is stronger in the theme park environment than in the museum study.

Previous studies emphasize the relationship between the pleasure experienced during the consumption experience and post-consumption satisfaction (see, for instance, Wirtz & Bateson, 1999). These studies have mainly used the Izard (1977) DES scale for measuring emotions. Exceptions are Mano and Oliver (1993) who used Watson and Tellegen's (1985) PANAS scale, and Wirtz and Bateson's (1999) study, which is based on Russell's (1980) two-dimensional model of pleasure and arousal. In relation to the latter model, further research is needed to confirm this relationship in an LTS environment, from a comparative perspective. Hence, satisfaction contains an affective response in the hypothesized affective model of satisfaction. Based on both emotional dimensions, we assume the following hypotheses in both LTS.

Hypothesis 2a The pleasure dimension of emotions positively influences visitor satisfaction both in the context of a museum and a theme park environment.

Hypothesis 2b The arousal dimension of emotions positively influences visitor satisfaction both in the context of a museum and a theme park environment.

The relationship between satisfaction and loyalty has been investigated in numerous previous studies (e.g. Cronin & Taylor, 1992; Fornell, 1992; Sirakaya & Petrick, 2004). The concept and degree of loyalty is one of the critical indicators used to measure the success of marketing strategy (Flavián, Martínez, & Polo, 2001). A satisfactory experience appears to be an important predictor of a consumers' likelihood for participating in future events (Madrigal, 1995). Similar to travel destinations, tourist attractions can be considered as products, and tourists may revisit or recommend these attractions to other potential visitors, such as friends or relatives (Yoon & Uysal, 2005). Retesting this relationship in LTS (interactive museums and theme parks) will help consolidate this body of knowledge.

Hypothesis 3 The greater the consumer's satisfaction, the greater is his/her loyalty to the LTS, both in the context of a museum and a theme park environment.

An emerging stream of research has looked at the influence of affective reactions to consumption experiences on post-purchase satisfaction judgments (Madrigal, 1995). Some marketing scholars have examined the influence of positive emotions as a moderating variable between satisfaction and brand loyalty (Bloemer & de Ruyter, 1999; Oliver, Rust, & Varki, 1997). To date, only a few empirical studies include affect as mediators in the evaluation-behaviour link. Notable exceptions to these are studies undertaken by several pure marketing and tourism researchers (Oliver et al., 1997; Sirakaya & Petrick, 2004; Zins, 2002). Consistent with Mehrabian and Russell's approach-avoidance model (e.g. Mehrabian & Russell, 1974), it is proposed that

Hypothesis 4 The pleasure dimension positively influences visitors' loyalty behaviour, both in the context of a museum and a theme park environment.

Together with the emotions–satisfaction–loyalty sequence, the present study extends previous research by introducing the impact of consumers' experiences in consumption emotions and by doing a comparative analysis in two LTS. Regarding the study of consumers' experiences, it is important to highlight the findings of Gyimóthy (1999) study.

She introduces the *depth-acquisition* construct as an interesting indicator to analyse how tourists experience holidays. It contains two orthogonally positioned axes in the following.

- The horizontal axis describes the quantity at which attractions are used. A horizontally oriented visitor is considered to be active and aspiring to use as many attractions as possible. Applied to the LTS context, this dimension refers to the "active experience" of the visitors when enjoying the LTS.
- The vertical axis describes the depth of the experience the visitor seeks. Such depth is expressed in the manner, rather than the number of which exhibitions and attractions are consumed. In the context of LTS, this dimension refers to the "passive experience" of the visitors when enjoying the LTS.

Previous studies (Swarbrooke & Horner, 1999) have pointed out the more active nature of certain services (for example, theme parks) in relation to other LTS (for example, museums). In view of this, in the theme park environment, we assume that the *active experience* influences the emotional dimensions of arousal and pleasure significantly (Russell, 1980). Conversely, in the museum environment, it is assumed that the *relaxing experience* influences consumer emotions significantly. Therefore, it is suggested that the type of tourist attraction has a moderator role in the relationship between service experience and consumption emotions. Specifically,

Hypothesis 5 (a) For theme park visitors, an active experience has a positive influence on arousal, while (b) for museum visitors, it is the relaxing experience that has a positive influence on arousal.

Hypothesis 6 (a) For theme park visitors, the active experience has a positive influence on pleasure, while (b) for museum visitors, it is the relaxing experience that has a positive influence on pleasure.

Together with the analysis of leisure experience, the management of consumers' perceptions of waiting time by service businesses may be critical to customer satisfaction (Baker & Cameron, 1996; Houston et al., 1998). Waiting for the service is by no means foreign to the consumers' experience in LTS (Dawes & Rowley, 1996) and has been discussed as being of particular importance to entertainment practitioners (Hightower, Brady, & Baker, 2002). Experience tells us that perceived extended delays can negate an otherwise enjoyable service encounter, regardless of perceptions of the service product, the interaction with employees, or the physical environment. The other way round, i.e. the "perception of *no* waiting time" is a positive experience for consumers. Visitor management uses different marketing strategies in order to avoid consumers' waiting time. The perception of no waiting time could increase the consumer feelings of being active (i.e. enjoying an active experience) or more relaxed (as they do not have to run to avoid queues, or experience congestion). Simultaneously, it may influence the arousal dimension positively. Based on the support garnered in the literature, as well as its practitioner relevance, the perception of no waiting time is included in the affective research model (see Figure 17.1). This leads to the final research hypotheses.

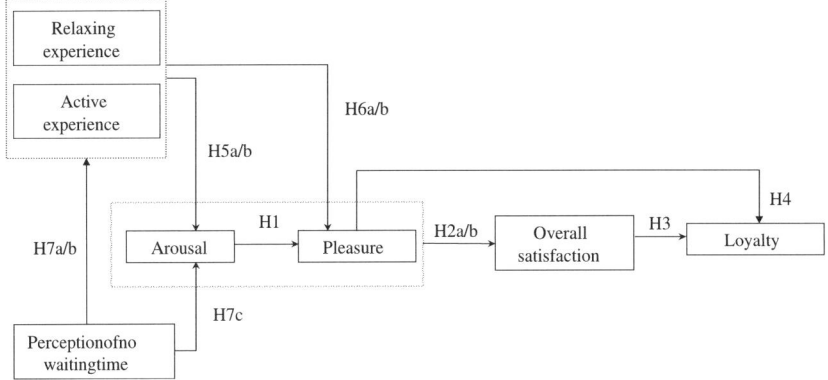

Figure 17.1: A model of visitors' experience in LTS.

Hypothesis 7a For LTS visitors, the perception of no waiting time has a positive influence on active experience.

Hypothesis 7b For LTS visitors, the perception of no waiting time has a positive influence on a relaxing experience.

Hypothesis 7c For LTS visitors, the perception of no waiting time has a positive influence on arousal.

Methodology

As mentioned above, the empirical research is applied to two LTS: an interactive museum (M-study) and a theme park (TP-study). The choice of these service settings is justified for two main reasons: firstly, they are products which *a priori* represent a source of stimulation for the activation of emotions (Goulding, 2000; Oliver et al., 1997; Otto & Ritchie, 1996) and, secondly, such service settings are gaining increasing importance in the leisure and tourism industry (Kotler & Kotler, 1998; Stevens, 2000).

The M-study is applied to the visitors of an interactive museum, where the intention is to transmit different facets of the world of science in an entertaining, attractive and involving fashion. Through interactive modules, the museum manages to awaken curiosity in the visitor, thus provoking his/her reflection and his/her immersion in the exhibits, and the surrounding museum environment in general. In the TP-study, we encounter a multitude of attractions for children and grown-ups, shows, restaurants and shops. With the objective of providing a greater sense of reality, immediacy and impact, designers used modern technology, i.e. special effects, animated robots, three-dimensional images and related features, in the creation of this modern venture. Additionally, the atmosphere and the bustling activity in the park contribute, in general, to an active participation of the visitors. The museum and the theme park are both very popular among tourists traveling to Spain, and are situated in a Northern city (A Coruña) and on the Mediterranean coast, respectively.

The utilization of questionnaires for gathering information on consumption emotions is based on the principle of retrieval (Solomon, Bamossy, & Askegaard, 1999), i.e. the identification and evaluation of perceptions by the tourist interviewed during his/her visit to the museum or to the theme park. In research on satisfaction, consumption emotions are generally evaluated in a retrospective, global way, and once the service transaction has been carried out. As Dubé and Menon (2000) point out, at the end of the service transaction, the different emotions can be measured by means of a questionnaire, together with the measurements of satisfaction.

Sample Selection

The definitive version of the questionnaire used for gathering information was obtained following a pre-test ($n=20$) of the questionnaire in its two versions (museum and theme park) to assess and purify the measures. Duly trained interviewers collected data during the 2001 summer season. An interviewer was stationed outside the entrance to the hall, show or attraction, and the interviewees were selected at random, and included 400 consumers over the age of 18 (48% male, 52% female) of LTS. With the objective of getting close up to the stimuli that triggered the emotions that a visitor experiences during his/her enjoyment of the attractions, the interviews were carried out *in situ*, right after the interviewee visited the hall, left the show or had got off the park attraction. An analysis of the respondent's socio-demographic characteristics is presented in Table 17.1.

Research Instrument

A structured questionnaire contained socio-demographic variables, variables concerning the affective sequence of satisfaction and loyalty, as well as statements related to the consumer experience (waiting time, active and relaxing experience). The measurement of the selected emotions is based on Russell's (1980) model. This measure consists of 12 items, representing the bipolar dimensions of pleasure and arousal. Satisfaction was measured on a five-item, five-point Likert-type scale based on Oliver's (1997) scale. With regard to loyalty, Zeithaml, Berry, and Parasuraman's (1996) scale was taken as a reference, and adapted to the context of the two studies. The perception of no waiting time was measured on a single item (Pruyn & Smidts, 1998), five-point Likert scale: "I didn't have to wait very long to try or go on any of the modules/attractions". Based on Gyimóthy (1999) study, an active experience is measured by means of the following item: "I have seen all areas of the museum/theme-park, and some of them I have visited several times", and the "relaxing experience" by "I preferred to take it easy, even though this meant leaving some things unseen".

Discussion of Findings

Prior to investigating how structural paths of interest compare across groups, a test for configural invariance across the two contexts was undertaken (cf. Steenkamp & Baumgartner,

Table 17.1: Socio-demographic characteristics.

Socio-demographic variable	M-study	TP-study	% of total	χ^2
Age (years)				
18–24	11.50	19.50	15.50	
25–34	27.50	21.50	24.50	
35–44	22.00	39.50	30.75	49.44*
45–54	14.50	16.50	15.50	
55–64	12.00	1.50	6.75	
65 years and above	12.50	1.50	7.00	
Gender				
Male	47.50	48.50	48.00	0.04
Female	52.50	51.50	52.00	
Social status				
High	20.50	15.50	18.00	
Middle-high	35.50	22.00	28.75	
Middle	39.50	55.00	47.25	14.61*
Middle-low	4.00	6.00	5.00	
Low	0.50	1.50	1.00	
Monthly income (euros)				
Below 1082	26.53	25.64	26.09	
Similar to 1082	31.63	32.82	32.23	0.07
Above 1082	41.84	41.54	41.69	
Place of origin				
Domestic	84.50	98.00	91.25	22.83*
International	15.50	2.00	8.75	

*$p<0.01$.

1998). In each sample separately, therefore, a four-construct confirmatory factor model was estimated using EQS 5.7b (Bentler, 1995; Byrne, 1994) to assess the measurement properties of the constructs with more than two items. In both samples, the results indicate that the overall confirmatory factor model fits the data well. Once the fit of the four-factor measurement model was verified, the construct reliability and construct validity were estimated. Discriminant validity was assessed based on confidence intervals (Anderson & Gerbing, 1988). All possible correlations between the seven factors represented in the scales were calculated, as well as the confidence interval ±2 standard errors. The condition that there can be no values of 1 within the interval was met in the present research, thus confirming the discriminant validity of the scales analysed. Composite scores of each set of items (sums of scores divided by the number of items) were used for the path model in Figure 17.1.

To test the research model, consistent with Bettencourt and Brown (2003), a fully restricted theoretical model was tested, in which all estimated structural path coefficients were constrained to be invariant across the museum and theme park samples. A review of the univariate LM χ^2 statistics (Byrne, 1994) revealed five paths to be significantly different ($p < 0.05$) across museum and theme park studies (no waiting time and active experience, arousal and pleasure, active experience and arousal, no waiting time and arousal, pleasure and satisfaction). The final multi-group structural model with partial metric invariance constraints (liberating the five above-mentioned relationships) fits the data well. The fit indices for this multi-group model were: χ^2 (25, $N = 200, N = 200$) = 34.59, $p = 0.10$; comparative fit index (CFI) = 0.98; Tucker–Lewis index (TLI) = 0.98; root mean square error of approximation (RMSEA) = 0.03. Table 17.2 shows the standardized and unstandardized estimates corresponding to each of the hypothesized effects.

Overall, it can be stated that, directly, satisfaction is significantly impacted ($p < 0.01$) by the feeling of pleasure and arousal visitors' experience in the two analyses scenarios (museum and theme parks), confirming H2a and H2b. However, pleasure and arousal are of similar strength for museum visitors, it is particularly the experience of pleasure that contributes to the satisfaction of theme park visitors (H2a: 0.45 and H2b: 0.14). The multi-group analyses reveal significant differences in the relationship between pleasure and satisfaction (see Table 17.2). When checking for what helps determine pleasure and arousal, it turns out that both groups of visitors experience both variables differently, in terms of their strength, and in terms of mediators. It is particularly interesting to see that the active experience impacts positively both arousal and pleasure for theme park visitors (H5a: 0.17 and H6a: 0.11), and however it influences negatively on arousal for museum visitors (H5a: −0.31). Even though unexpected, active experience influence positively on pleasure for museum visitors (H6: 0.13).

In addition, unexpectedly, relaxing experience influences arousal and pleasure of museum and theme park visitors, with no significant differences between both tourist attractions. It confirms partially H5b and H6b. No waiting time influences both the perceptions of relaxing and active experience for museum and theme park visitors. However, theme park visitors find that no waiting time significantly impacts their arousal (H7c: 0.20), whereas there is no such influence for museum visitors (H7c: 0.12). Lastly, loyalty is influenced by satisfaction and pleasure for both visitor groups directly. Both these variables thus mediate the impact of all other variables in the design. As to the mediating influences of variables, it is noteworthy that arousal impacts pleasure for both samples while being comparatively stronger for theme park visitors (see Table 17.2). Previous studies evidence the relationship between the perceived duration of a wait and negative affect (Houston et al., 1998). In this research, arousal mediates the impact of no waiting time for theme park visitors, while in the case of the M-study, arousal mediates the relaxing experience on satisfaction and loyalty somewhat, and the perception of active experience negatively.

Conclusions and Implications

The main contribution of this chapter is to extend an affective model developed in previous studies (cf. Bigné et al., 2005), with the integration of waiting time effects and the leisure experience by adding the comparative analysis among museums and theme parks. Using consumption emotions in relation to satisfaction and loyalty, the analysis of tourist behaviour in LTS is enriched by integrating critical issues regarding participants' experiences during services. Perceived waiting time is an experience that is dominant in most of

Table 17.2: Final multi-group structural equation model results with partial metric invariance constraints[a].

Structural path[b]		M-study			TP-study		
		Unstandardized estimates		Standardized estimates	Unstandardized estimates		Standardized estimates
Arousal → pleasure	H1	0.35	(8.21)	0.51	0.76	(16.85)	0.74
Pleasure → satisfaction	H2a	0.31	(4.53)	0.32	0.52	(7.69)	0.45
Arousal → satisfaction	*H2b*	*0.15*	*(3.47)*	*0.22*	*0.15*	*(3.47)*	*0.14*
Satisfaction → loyalty	*H3*	*0.32*	*(7.37)*	*0.31*	*0.32*	*(7.37)*	*0.38*
Pleasure → loyalty	*H4*	*0.30*	*(6.68)*	*0.29*	*0.30*	*(6.68)*	*0.34*
Active experience → arousal	H5a	0.20	(−4.09)	−0.31	0.10	(2.55)	0.17
Relaxing experience → arousal	*H5b*	*0.09*	*(2.44)*	*0.11*	*0.09*	*(2.44)*	*0.13*
Active experience → pleasure	*H6a*	*0.06*	*(3.22)*	*0.13*	*0.06*	*(3.22)*	*0.11*
Relaxing experience → pleasure	*H6b*	*0.06*	*(2.54)*	*0.10*	*0.06*	*(2.54)*	*0.08*
No waiting time → active experience	H7a	0.44	(6.94)	0.44	0.15	(2.06)	0.15
No waiting time → relaxing experience	*H7b*	*0.11*	*(2.60)*	*0.13*	*0.11*	*(2.60)*	*0.13*
No waiting time → arousal	H7c	0.08	(1.58)	0.12 (ns)	0.12	(2.96)	0.20

[a]Fit indices are as follows: $x^2(25, N=200, N=200) = 34.59$; CFI = 0.98; TLI = 0.98; AGFI = 0.95; CAIC = −140.19; RMSEA = 0.03; RMR = 0.04.
[b]The structural estimates reported are from a multi-group analysis in which the structural model was estimated simultaneously with partial metric invariance constraints for the museum and theme park samples using EQS 5.7b. t-values are shown in parentheses. Coefficients that do not differ significantly ($p < 0.05$) across the two samples are in italics.
*$p < 0.05$.
**$p < 0.01$.

the services, and it is inevitable for customers, influencing to a high extent, and negatively, on the overall satisfaction and customer loyalty (Hui & Tse, 1996; Pruyn & Smidts, 1998). Although reducing actual waiting time is important, what managers' view as a short time to wait may feel too long to customers (Baker & Cameron, 1996). Another factor related to perceived waiting time concerns to how the visitor manages the time in his/her LTS experience. For example, holidaymakers arrive to an LTS and intend to see everything in the short time they have. This experience can be characterized as "active experience". On the contrary, holidaymakers who expend two weeks in a tourist resort can enjoy the LTS in a "relaxing experience" (Gyimóthy, 1999). The integration of the waiting time effects and leisure experience to explain the relationships between emotions, satisfaction and loyalty provides interesting implications for museum and theme park managers.

For museum visitors, the impact of active experience, i.e. the number and frequency with which activities can be enjoyed, has a negative influence on arousal. This means that the inner state, the poise or quality of the energy with which visitors approach activities is determined not by the number but by the depth of experiences. The more the quality of that experience can be enhanced, the stronger is the perception of pleasure as arousal completely mediates the impact of active experience. In the case of museum visitors, no waiting time adds to the perception that the museum offers a relaxing experience. The moderate impacts of waiting time and relaxing experience on arousal, versus the much stronger impact of no waiting time on active experience demonstrate that waiting times play a different role in the experience than for theme park visitors. Not having to wait while visitors amble through the exhibitions and activities on offer mediated in the relaxing atmosphere and indirectly impacts satisfaction. In contrast, no waiting time impacts strongly on the perception as to how much museum visitors perceive that they can participate in interactive exhibitions or contemplate other presentations. Yet, this is only of importance to satisfaction if their experience has depth, as the negative path means that the less respondents agreed to the statement that they have seen all areas and done a few activities or seen exhibitions more than once, the more arousal is generated, totally mediating the impact of active experience onto pleasure.

For the museum management, it is thus also important to manage waiting times but not so that visitors can experience more exhibitions in number, but experience them in depth. While the time visitors can spend on an attraction at a theme park is usually limited by the time it takes to go on the various rides, standing in front of a work of art or a pageant is a much more contemplative, cognitive and aesthetic, rather than a physical experience that creates pleasure directly. In the absence of any other variables in the model, arousal completely determines pleasure. The activity in a museum thus works on people's receptivity and response to an exhibition as an end in itself, the perception of which creates pleasure, while also being the reason for satisfaction. And as with theme park visitors, both pleasure and satisfaction impact loyalty. We can appreciate now, however, that it is not only the nature of the attraction that differs between the two venues but also the type of response. In the case of the theme park, the experience is much more physical, whereas for the museum it is more physiological.

The perception of pleasure is determined by the response to inner stimuli, whereas in the case of theme parks it is also caused by direct physical experiences. For theme park visitors, the managerial tool of managing waiting time has a direct influence on arousal, as well as a somewhat weaker impact on the perception of active and relaxing experiences. In other words, while not having to wait is a considerable impact on the perception that visitors can see all they want, it also impacts arousal directly. When adding that active experience also influences arousal, further mediating some of the no waiting time experience, we can conclude that no waiting time is of high importance for theme park management. As pleasure for theme parks visitors explains a large amount of the occurring variance of both satisfaction and loyalty, waiting time becomes an important variable within the overall management mix. Arousal constitutes a person's emotional attitude towards an experience. It describes the focus and level of energy with which the person is poised towards an object of contemplation or activity. Managing waiting times is thus of utmost importance as the thrill theme park visitors experience is the balance between the time visitors have to prepare for the experience as well as the actual experience the activity renders.

This chapter has shown that measuring the emotional experience gives meaningful insights into how differing types of activities impact overall visitor experiences, and their impact on satisfaction and loyalty. In building towards a clearer understanding of consumer experiences in LTS, the authors would like to suggest new variables to take into account for future enquiries. Pertinent goals for future research are to study attitudes, personal involvement and consumer interest shown towards an attraction and their influence on the affective responses on LTS. Additionally, the study findings can be generalized in reference to other experience services (Klemz & Boshoff, 2001; Ostrom & Iacobucci, 1995), where the consumer who is involved in the service delivery, will experience emotions that influence in the service evaluation and, consequently, in his/her satisfaction and future purchase behaviour. It is important to note the limitation inherent to focus only in two studies. Given the existence of other LTS formats, this leads the authors to envisage that a further application of the framework represented in Figure 17.1 would be to extend to other man-made attractions. More in-depth studies are needed to explore techniques and effects of arousal management (i.e. both its generation and alleviation) in areas, such as visitor management in waiting situations and expectation formation (Gnoth, 1997), as this study shows a significant and possibly even more complex effect of waiting times on visitor satisfaction and loyalty, as well as management opportunities than hitherto realized. Finally, it is noteworthy to consider the dynamic nature of leisure experience (Lee & Shafer, 2002), which could be approached in further research.

References

Anderson, J. C., & Gerbing, D. W. (1988). Structural equation modelling in practice: A review and recommended two-step approach. *Psychological Bulletin, 103*(3), 411–423.

Baker, J., & Cameron, M. (1996). The effects of the service environment on affect and consumer perception of waiting time. An integrative review and research propositions. *Journal of the Academy of Marketing Science, 24*(4), 338–349.

Bentler, P. M. (1995). *EQS structural equations program manual.* Encino, CA: Multivariate Software, Inc.

Bettencourt, L. A., & Brown, S. W. (2003). Role stressors and customer-oriented boundary-spanning behaviors in service organizations. *Journal of the Academy of Marketing Science, 31*(4), 394–408.

Bigné, J. E., Andreu, L., & Gnoth, J. (2006). The theme park experience: An analysis of pleasure, arousal and satisfaction. *Tourism Management, 26*(6), 833–844.

Bloemer, J. M. M., & de Ruyter, K. (1999). Customer loyalty in high and low involvement service settings: The moderating impact of positive emotions. *Journal of Marketing Management, 15*(4), 315–330.

Byrne, B. M. (1994). *Structural equation modeling with EQS and EQS/Windows. Basic concepts, applications, and programming.* Thousand Oaks, CA: Sage.

Chebat, J.-C., & Michon, R. (2003). Impact of ambient odors on mall shoppers' emotions, cognition, and spending. *Journal of Business Research, 56*, 529–539.

Cronin, J. J., & Taylor, S. A. (1992). Measuring service quality: A reexamination and extension. *Journal of Marketing, 56*, 55–68.

Dawes, J., & Rowley, J. (1996). The waiting experience: Towards service quality in the leisure industry. *International Journal of Contemporary Hospitality Management, 8*(1), 16–21.

Dubé, L., & Menon, K. (2000). Multiple roles of consumption emotions in post-purchase satisfaction with extended service transactions. *International Journal of Service Industry Management, 11*(3), 287–304.

Flavián, C., Martínez, E., & Polo, Y. (2001). Loyalty to grocery stores in the Spanish market of the 1990s. *Journal of Retailing and Consumer Services, 8*, 85–93.

Formica, S., & Olsen, M. D. (1998). Trends in the amusement park industry. *International Journal of Contemporary Hospitality Management, 10*(7), 297–308.

Fornell, C. (1992). A national satisfaction barometer: The Swedish experience. *Journal of Marketing, 56*, 1–21.

Gnoth, J. (1997). Tourism motivation and expectation formation. *Annals of Tourism Research, 24*(2), 283–304.

Goulding, C. (1999). Contemporary museum culture and consumer behaviour. *Journal of Marketing Management, 15*(7), 647–671.

Goulding, C. (2000). The museum environment and the visitor experience. *European Journal of Marketing, 34*(3/4), 261–278.

Gyimóthy, S. (1999). Visitor's perceptions of holiday experiences and service providers: An exploratory study. *Journal of Travel and Tourism Marketing, 8*(2), 57–74.

Hightower, R., Brady, M. K., & Baker, T. L. (2002). Investigating the role of the physical environment in hedonic service consumption: An exploratory study of sporting events. *Journal of Business Research, 55*, 697–707.

Holbrook, M. B., & Hirschman, E. C. (1982). The experiential aspects of consumption: Consumer fantasies, feelings and fun. *Journal of Consumer Research, 9*, 132–140.

Houston, M. B., Bettencourt, L. A., & Wenger, S. (1998). The relationship between waiting in a service queue and evaluations of service quality: A field theory perspective. *Psychology and Marketing, 15*(8), 735–753.

Hui, M. K., & Tse, D. K. (1996). What to tell consumers in waits of different lengths: An integrative model of service evaluation. *Journal of Marketing, 60*, 81–90.

Izard, C. E. (1977). *Human emotions*. New York: Plenum Press.

Jansen-Verbeke, M., & van Rekom, J. (1996). Scanning museum visitors. Urban tourism marketing. *Annals of Tourism Research, 23*(2), 364–375.

Kotler, N. G., & Kotler, P. (1998). *Museum strategy and marketing: Designing missions, building audiences, generating revenue and resources*. Jossey-Bass, New York.

Kozak, M. (2001). A critical review of approaches to measure satisfaction with destinations. In: J. A. Mazanec, G. I. Crouch, J. R. B. Ritchie, & A. G. Woodside (Eds), *Consumer psychology of tourism, hospitality and leisure* (Vol. II, pp. 303–320). Oxon: CABI.

Klemz, B. R., & Boshoff, C. (2001). Environmental and emotional influences on willingness-to-buy in small and large retailers. *European Journal of Marketing, 35*(1/2), 70–91.

Lee, B., & Shafer, C. S. (2002). The dynamic nature of leisure experience: An application of affect control theory. *Journal of Leisure Research, 34*(3), 290–310.

Madrigal, R. (1995). Cognitive and affective determinants of fan satisfaction with sporting event attendance. *Journal of Leisure Research, 27*(3), 205–227.

Mano, H., & Oliver, R. L. (1993). Assessing the dimensionality and structure of the consumption experience: Evaluation, feeling, and satisfaction. *Journal of Consumer Research, 20*(3), 451–466.

Mehrabian, A., & Russell, J. (1974). *An approach to environmental psychology*. Cambridge: MIT Press.

Milman, A. (2001). The future of the theme park and attraction industry: A management perspective. *Journal of Travel Research, 40*, 139–147.

Oliver, R. L. (1997). *Satisfaction. A behavioral perspective on the consumer.* Singapore: McGraw-Hill.

Oliver, R. L., Rust, R. T., & Varki, S. (1997). Customer delight: Foundations, findings, and managerial insight. *Journal of Retailing, 73*(3), 311–336.

Ostrom, A., & Iacobucci, D. (1995). Consumer trade-offs and the evaluation of services. *Journal of Marketing, 59*(1), 17–28.

Otto, J. E., & Ritchie, J. R. B. (1996). The service experience in tourism. *Tourism Management, 17*(3), 165–174.

Pruyn, A., & Smidts, A. (1998). Effects of waiting on the satisfaction with the service: Beyond objective time measures. *International Journal of Research in Marketing, 15*(4), 321–334.

Rowley, J. (1999). Measuring total customer experience in museums. *International Journal of Contemporary Hospitality Management, 11*(6), 303–308.

Russell, J. A. (1980). A circumplex model of affect. *Journal of Personality and Social Psychology, 39*, 1161–1178.

Sirakaya, E., & Petrick, J. (2004). The role of mood on tourism product evaluations. *Annals of Tourism Research, 31*(3), 517–539.

Solomon, M., Bamossy, G., & Askegaard, S. (1999). *Consumer behaviour — a European perspective.* New Jersey: Prentice-Hall.

Steenkamp, J. E. M., & Baumgartner, H. (1998). Assessing measurement invariance in cross-national consumer research. *Journal of Consumer Research, 25*, 78–90.

Stevens, T. (2000). The future of visitor attractions. *Travel and Tourism Analyst, 1*, 61–85.

Swarbrooke, J. (1995). *The development and management of visitor attractions.* Oxford: Butterworth-Heinemann.

Swarbrooke, J., & Horner, S. (1999). *Consumer behaviour in tourism.* Oxford: Butterworth-Heinemann.

Tinsley, H. E. A., & Tinsley, D. J. (1986). A theory of the attributes, benefits, and causes of leisure experience. *Leisure Sciences, 8*, 1–45.

Watson, D., & Tellegen, A. (1985). Toward a consensual structure of mood. *Psychological Bulletin, 98*(2), 219–235.

Wirtz, J., & Bateson, J. E. G. (1999). Consumer satisfaction with services: Integrating the environment perspective in services marketing into the traditional disconfirmation paradigm. *Journal of Business Research, 44*, 55–66.

Yoon, Y., & Uysal, M. (2005). An examination of the effects of motivation and satisfaction on destination loyalty: A structural model. *Tourism Management, 26*(1), 45–56.

Zeithaml, V. A., Berry, L. L., & Parasuraman, A. (1996). The behavioral consequences of service quality. *Journal of Marketing, 60*(2), 31–46.

Zins, A. (2002). Consumption emotions, experience quality and satisfaction: A structural analysis for complainers versus non-complainers. *Journal of Travel and Tourism Marketing, 12*(2/3), 3–18.

Chapter 18

Effects of Price Promotions on Consumer Loyalty towards Travel Agencies

S. Campo Martínez and M. J. Yagüe Guillén

Introduction

In the tourism market, price promotions are frequently used in order to stimulate the short-term sales of tourist trips. However, if these sales are made at the expense of future sales, or if they turn consumers into offer seekers, agents would be sacrificing future returns for short-term sales. It is therefore, especially, important in such a highly competitive industry that the study of promotional effects is not limited solely to the short-term effects and that the effects be analysed beyond the promotional period. Specifically, the agents responsible for setting up tour packages must be aware of the capacity of these packages to retain customers.

As its main objective, this chapter proposes the study of the effect of price promotions on the variables that make up consumer loyalty. Therefore, based on contributions provided in academic literature, a theoretical model of the formation of tourist loyalty is configured and the hypotheses of the study are set forth. Subsequently, with the data obtained from the initial research directed at consumers, structural equation models are applied, and the results allow the formulated hypotheses to be verified. Finally, the main conclusions, limitations and implications of the study are presented.

Literature Review

Academic definitions of the term, loyalty, include a positive attitude towards a product, brand or commercial establishment, and the consumer's promise to repurchase the product. This attitude and intent are the result of a consumer's satisfaction with a product, and they will positively influence the profitability of a firm (Berné, Múgica, & Yagüe, 1996). Academic literature shows the existence of a positive relationship between consumer satisfaction and loyalty, and the former is a predecessor of the latter, which is usually measured as the intent of post-purchase behaviour (Bearden & Teel, 1983; Szymanski & Henard, 2001, quoted by Andreu, 2001). Nevertheless, in recent years this relationship has been enriched by new research coming from the relationship marketing approach (Baker & Crompton, 2000; Berné et al., 1996, 2001; Bigné, Sánchez, & Sánchez, 2000).

The effect of promotions on prices in this relationship has given rise to constant debates and contradictory results in literature. Some authors, based on the theories of *Self-Acceptance* or *Behavioral Learning*, affirm that price promotions cause a decrease in consumer loyalty when the promotions are withdrawn (Shoemaker & Shoaf, 1977; Dodson, Tybout, & Sternthal, 1978; Jones & Zufryden, 1980; Klein, 1981; Guadagni & Little, 1983; Kopalle, Mela, & Marsh, 1999). A second group of research performed over the final two decades of last century (Neslin & Shoemaker, 1989; Davis, Inman, & McAlister, 1992; Ehrenberg, Hammond, & Goodhardt, 1994) affirm that there is no relationship between the price promotions of a brand and repeat purchases, and they sustain that the results obtained in other research are due to methodological measurement problems or the omission of variables that influence the long-term promotional results.

Finally, a third group finds a positive relationship between promotion and consumer loyalty when the study of the same is extended to the attitude component of this variable (Cotton & Babb, 1978; Rothschild & Gaidis, 1981; Bawa & Shoemaker, 1987; Lattin & Bucklin, 1989). These authors affirm that if a consumer has a high preference towards a brand, and if he feels a promotion as a reward for his loyalty, the image of quality and satisfaction will be reinforced. This leads to an increase in the probability that the brand will be chosen, even after the promotion is withdrawn, thereby successfully increasing/reinforcing consumer loyalty.

These contradictory results lead to the affirmation that there is no direct relationship between price promotions and consumer loyalty (Neslin & Shoemaker, 1989; Davis et al., 1992; Ehrenberg et al., 1994). Conversely, it is expected that price promotions would indirectly affect loyalty and this effect would depend on the variables that intervene in the process of loyalty formation. Specifically, the sign of the indirect effect depends on the effect exercised on satisfaction. If price promotions directly affect satisfaction through the price–value relationship (Davis et al., 1992), the indirect effect on loyalty has a positive sign. Conversely, if price promotions negatively affect satisfaction through the price–quality relationship (Shoemaker & Shoaf, 1977; Dodson et al., 1978; Jones & Zufryden, 1980; Guadagni & Little, 1983; Kopalle et al., 1999), the sign of the indirect effect of price promotions on loyalty towards the travel agency is negative (Figure 18.1). These affirmations lead to the formulation of the following hypothesis of the study.

H$_1$ The degree to which price promotions are used indirectly affects consumer loyalty towards a travel agency through the effect of the price promotions on satisfaction.

The main effects of a price promotion on loyalty can be intensified or weakened according to the characteristics of the goal segments. Several researchers affirm that the promotional effect is moderated by consumer sensitivity towards price and their level of response to promotions (Blattberg & Sen, 1976; Eskin & Baron, 1977; Guadagni & Little, 1983). Therefore, it seems reasonable to think that if a consumer assigns great importance to price when acquiring a product, and if he positively appraises the trip sold in the promotion,

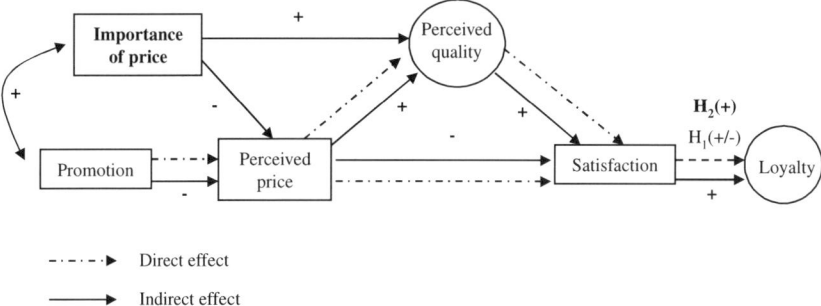

Figure 18.1: Theoretical model of price promotions on consumer loyalty towards a commercial establishment.

there will be a greater probability that that consumer will become a loyal consumer. These affirmations lead to the postulation of the following hypothesis:

H$_2$ The greater the importance that consumers assign to price in their purchase decisions, the greater the indirect and positive effect of the degree of use of price promotions on a consumer's loyalty towards a travel agency.

In the theoretical model showed in Figure 18.1, and following the conceptual approach generally accepted in the literature that considers the perceived quality as an antecedent of the satisfaction (Cronin & Taylor, 1992), it has been decided not to include a direct relationship between the perceived quality and the consumer loyalty. Nevertheless, since the model is applied to the tourist market, it is expected to find a direct relationship between the perceived quality and the loyalty (Baker & Crompton, 2000; Bigné et al., 2000; Zins, 2001). In this case, the indirect and negative effect of the price promotion on the consumer loyalty towards a travel agency would increase its magnitude, and also it would increase the probability that the result of the price promotions on loyalty — H$_1$ — has a negative sign.

Methodology

In order to compare the proposed theoretical model and the formulated hypotheses, empirical research was carried, which was applied to a study of the purchase behaviour of a tour package. The information came from a personal survey of tourists who travelled in the last two years to destinations of Central America, South America or the Caribbean through the acquisition of a tour package. Additionally, the information obtained is enriched and corrected with additional data coming from travel brochures published by tour operators and available at travel agencies. The fieldwork was carried out at collective places, where there is access to a high number of individuals belonging to the researched population. These places were Barajas Airport (Madrid, Spain) and at various malls that are representative of the city of Madrid. The survey was carried out during the months of November and December 2003. The size of the sample, after cleaning up the questionnaires, amounts to

358, whereby the sample error increases to 5.2% and the confidence level is 95%. The size of the population used for extracting the sample size is calculated based on information published by the Institute of Tourism Studies about the number of Spanish tourists who had travelled to destinations cited above during 2000. It amounts to 77,484 individuals.

The theoretical model set forth is empirically validated through an application of the structural equations methodology, thereby using the EQS (Structural Equation Modelling Software) statistical programme. In order to analyse the theoretical model presented above, six variables were used: four observable variables (namely, degree of purchase in promotions, perceived monetary price, satisfaction, importance assigned to price) and two latent variables (perceived quality of the travel, consumer's loyalty to the travel agency). The reliability and validity indicators of the latent variables ("perceived quality" and "travel agency loyalty") are presented in Table 18.1.

A reading of the coefficients indicates that, first, the latent variable "perceived quality" reach levels of acceptability in all the measures of reliability and convergent validity, except in the measure corresponding to the variance extracted, which does not reach the value (0.50) recommended by Fornell and Larcker (1981). Nevertheless, the latent variable is accepted, given that the value of the test approaches the recommended minimum, and there is certain consensus in accepting that this indicator is conservative (Hatcher, 1998). Secondly, the latent variable "travel agency loyalty" fully complies with the conditions of reliability and validity of the construct recommended by Hatcher (1998) (Cronbach's alpha and composite reliability > 0.7; variance extracted > 0.50), which qualifies it to be accepted as the measurement of the consumer's loyalty to the travel agency.

Table 18.2 presents the details of the variables that are included in the model, as well as the main descriptive statistics. In order to measure the perceived quality, we decided to perform two measurements: the first one is a weighted scoring related to the importance assigned by the customer to each component of the travel. The second scoring is related to the awareness and reputation of the tour operator. The measure of the consumer's loyalty to the travel agency comprises indicators related to two aspects of the loyalty: behavioural (intention of the tourist to travel again with the same travel agency) and attitudinal (positive intention of recommending the travel agency to some other person).

Discussion of Findings

The effect of promotions on the level of consumer loyalty towards a travel agency is presented in the estimated relationship model (Figure 18.2). Prior to configuring the relationship model, a confirmatory factor analysis was performed, which allowed verifying the overall fitness of the model to the analysed information. The results obtained regarding the goodness-of-fit indicators recommended by Hatcher (1998) allow affirming that the estimated models, both the measurement model and the relationship model, provide an excellent statistical fit of the data. On the one hand, the value of χ^2 is not significant, and on the other, the indicators of Bentler (1989) and Bentler and Bonett (1980) take on values between 0.95 and 1.

The results obtained in the relationship model show a high, positive, significant ($p<0.001$) and direct relationship between the quality perceived by the consumer and the level of consumer loyalty towards a travel agency. This direct effect of perceived quality

Table 18.1: Reliability and validity of "perceived quality" and "travel agency loyalty".

Latent variable	Observable variable	L_i[a]	E_i[b]	Reliability		Validity	
				Indicator reliability (R^2)	Composite reliability	Variance extracted (VE[e])	Convergent validity (t)
Perceived quality	AQ (Airline Quality)	0.59	0.65	0.35			9.57
	HQ (Hotel Quality)	0.58	0.66	0.34			9.28
	ORQ (Organization Quality)	0.57	0.68	0.32	CA[c] = 0.77		9.15
	GQ (Guaranties Quality)	0.62	0.62	0.38			9.95
	TOQ (Tour Operator Quality)	0.75	0.44	0.56		0.33	–
	TAQ (Travel Agency Quality)	0.57	0.68	0.32	CR[d] = 0.79		12.54
	KWN (Knowledge of the Tour Operator)	0.31	0.90	0.10			5.10
	REP (Travel Agency Reputation)	0.53	0.72	0.28			8.64
Travel agency loyalty	TA1 (Travel Agency Loyalty1)	0.88	0.22	0.78	CA[c] = 0.89	0.70	16.95
	TA2 (Travel Agency Loyalty2)	0.73	0.46	0.54	CR[d] = 0.87		13.45
	TA3 (Travel Agency Loyalty3)	0.89	0.21	0.79			–

[a]Standardized loading.
[b]Error variance $E_i = (1-R^2)$.
[c]Cronbach's alpha.
[d]$CR = \dfrac{\left(\sum L_i\right)^2}{\left(\sum L_i\right)^2 + \sum \mathrm{var}(E_i)}$
[e]$VE = \dfrac{\sum L_i^2}{\sum L_i^2 + \sum \mathrm{var}(E_i)}$

Table 18.2: The effect of price promotions on the formation of brand loyalty.

Latent variable	Observable variable	Variable number	Descriptor	Measurement	Mean	SD
Promotion	Promotion	V_{14}	Degree of purchase of the tourist packages supplied	Scale of 1–10	6.6	2.2
Perceived monetary price	Perceived monetary price	V_{13}	Price that the consumer states having paid for a trip	€	1179	549
Perceived quality	AQ	V_4	Importance * score of the quality of the airline	Scale of 1–10	5.27	2.51
	HQ	V_5	Importance * score of the quality of the hotel service	Scale of 1–10	7.32	2.12
	ORQ	V_6	Importance * score of the organization	Scale of 1–10	6.09	2.59
	GQ	V_7	Importance * score of the guarantees included	Scale of 1–10	6.48	2.47
	TOQ	V_8	Importance * score of the quality offered by the tour operator	Scale of 1–10	5.05	2.71
	TAQ	V_9	Importance * score of the quality offered by the travel agency	Scale of 1–10	5.91	2.78

	KWN	V_{10}	Degree of agreement with the following affirmation: "The tour operator with whom I travelled is known in the market"	Scale of 1–10	8.06	2.10
	REP	V_{11}	Degree of agreement with the following affirmation: "The tour operator with whom I travelled has a good reputation in the market"	Scale of 1–10	7.77	1.76
Satisfaction	Satisfaction	V_{12}	Degree of satisfaction with the trip taken	Scale of 1–10	8.33	1.49
Loyalty towards the travel agency	TA_1	V_1	Degree of agreement with the following affirmation: "I would feel completely comfortable travelling again with the same travel agency"	Scale of 1–10	8.17	1.82
	TA_2	V_2	Degree of agreement with the following affirmation: "I would travel again with the same travel agency even though they changed tour operators"	Scale of 1–10	7.82	2.05
	TA_3	V_3	Degree of agreement with the following affirmation: "If anyone asks for a recommendation, I would recommend travelling with this travel agency"	Scale of 1–10	7.93	1.93
Importance of price	IMP P	V_{15}	Indicate the importance that the price paid has for you when choosing a tour package	Scale of 1–10	8.09	1.78

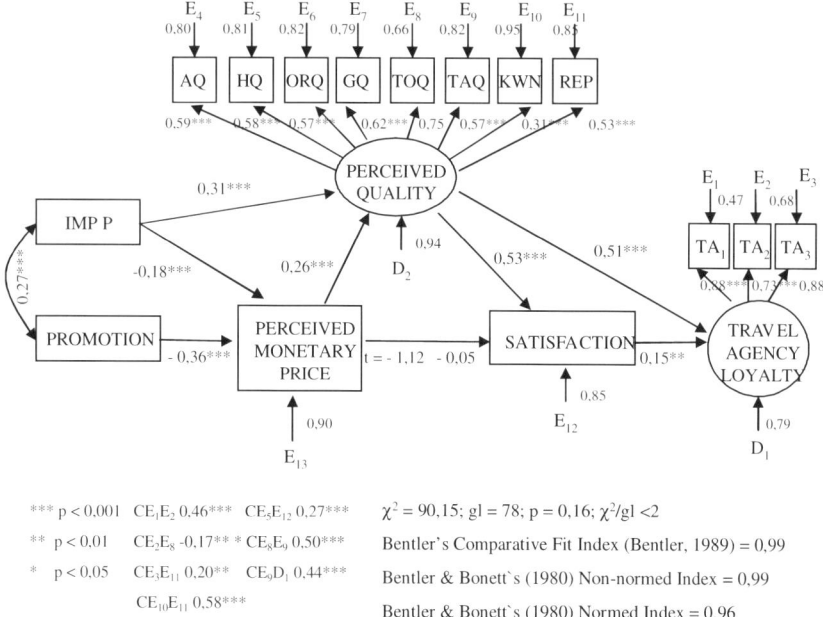

Figure 18.2: A model of the effect of promotions on consumer loyalty towards a travel agency.

on loyalty towards a travel agency had not been proposed in the formulated theoretical model, given that most of the specialized literature had found that the impact by perceived quality on loyalty occurs indirectly through satisfaction. The relationship between satisfaction and loyalty is likewise direct, significant and positive ($p<0.01$), but with a lower coefficient than the preceding relationship. Therefore, it can be affirmed that the key to achieving both satisfaction with a tour package and consumer loyalty towards a travel agency is achieved by providing high levels of perceived quality in the service.

The effect of price and the degree to which promotions are used in the formation of loyalty towards a travel agency is indirect, its importance is low, and it depends on the variables that comprise loyalty, which thus allows the formulated hypothesis, H_1, to be confirmed. Specifically, there is a negative and significant effect between promotions and loyalty through the price–quality relationship, such that an increase of one point in the degree of use of promotions decreases the probability that a consumer will remain loyal to a travel agency by 0.05 points. Conversely, the indirect effect of promotions on consumer loyalty towards a travel agency through the direct relationship between perceived price and satisfaction is not significant ($t = -1.12$), although it does have the expected sign.

Nevertheless, the results indicate that the indirect effect of promotions differs between consumer groups. The positive relationship existing between the degree of use of price promotions and the importance given to price by a consumer indicates that, when price promotions are used by those consumers who assign considerable importance to price, the effect of price promotions is the following. On the one hand, the appraisal of the quality of a tour package acquired under a promotion improves, and therefore so does the satisfaction with the same and the probability of remaining loyal to a travel agency. On the other hand, the perceived monetary price decreases, and as a result, satisfaction with and loyalty towards a travel agency through the price–quality relationship likewise decreases. Both effects, positive and negative, cause a reduction in the negative and indirect effect that price promotions exercise on loyalty towards a travel agency, such that the increase of one point in the degree of use of promotions decreases the probability of remaining loyal towards a travel agency by 0.01 points. These results allow the formulated hypothesis, H_2, to be confirmed.

Conclusions and Implications

This chapter analyses the effect of promotions on the scheme of how consumer loyalty towards a travel agency is formed. The results obtained have important implications from the theoretical and management points of view. First, the study of the effect of promotions has been incorporated to the model of consumer's behaviour (which has been extensively studied in the tourist market). Such analysis is of great importance in order to better understand the effect of price promotions in the long term, and their influence over the consumer's perceived quality, satisfaction and degree of loyalty. Specifically, the results obtained with respect to the influence of price promotions also contribute to confirm the results provided in the literature, which leads to the affirmation that price promotions do not directly erode consumer loyalty. This effect is indirect, with low intensity and it has a negative sign. It also depends on the variables that constitute loyalty.

Second, the present work suggests the incorporation of moderating variables that help to understand the dynamic effect of promotions. In particular, the indicator variables about the consumer's sensitivity to the price allow us to explain the positive effect of promotions over the customer's behaviour after the purchase. The results of the estimated relationship model are useful for the agencies to decide on their commercial policies. These indicate that the key for travel agencies to obtain loyal consumers through their commercial policy is based more on supporting and offering an excellent quality service than in reducing prices, given that such a policy thus guarantees obtaining a high level of consumer satisfaction.

However, if the travel agencies offer price promotions, they must be aware of the effect on the formation of loyalty differs according to the analysed consumer group. The results of the study confirm that when price promotions are used by consumers who assign considerable importance to price in their purchase decisions, these promotions increase the probability that a consumer who positively values product quality and who was satisfied with the purchase will remain loyal to the travel agency. For those agencies that currently design undifferentiated price promotions, this work suggests to them that they should plan their promotions in a differentiated manner according to the importance that consumers give to advantageous prices.

This study is not without limitations, which should be taken into account in future research. Specifically, the positive effect by price promotions could not be confirmed through the price–value relationship due to the existence of a non-significant relationship between the variables of perceived monetary price and satisfaction. This result indicates the need to delve deeper into a study of this relationship. Moreover, it would be necessary for future research to extend this work by incorporating variables that allow quantifying the effect that price promotions have on changes to long-term financial results. Finally, it would be necessary to incorporate additional variables that moderate the effect of price promotions, such as socio-demographic or behavioural variables, and it is necessary to expand the analysis to other agents of tourism marketing and to other categories of products and/or markets.

References

Andreu, L. (2001). *Emociones y satisfacción del consumidor: propuesta de un modelo Cognitivo-Afectivo en servicios de ocio y turismo.* Tesis Doctoral, Facultad de Economía, Universidad de Valencia.

Baker, D. A., & Crompton, J. L. (2000). Quality, satisfaction and behavioural intentions. *Annals of Tourism Research, 27*(3), 785–804.

Bawa, K., & Shoemaker, R. W. (1987). The effects of a direct mail coupon on brand choice behaviour. *Journal of Marketing Research, 24*(4), 370–376.

Bearden, W. O., & Teel, J. E. (1983). Selected determinants of consumer satisfaction and complaint reports. *Journal of Marketing Research, 20*(1), 21–28.

Bentler, P. M. (1989). *EQS structural equations program.* Los Angeles: BMDP Statistical Software.

Bentler, P. M., & Bonett, D. G. (1980). Significance tests and goodness-of-fit in the analysis of covariance structures. *Psychological Bulletin, 88*(4), 588–606.

Berné, C., Múgica, J. M., & Yagüe, Mª. J. (1996). La gestión estratégica y los conceptos de calidad percibida, satisfacción del cliente y lealtad. *Economía Industrial, 307*(1), 63–74.

Berné, C., Múgica, J. M., & Yagüe, Mª. J. (2001). The effect of variety-seeking on customer retention in services. *Journal of Retailing and Consumer Services, 8*(6), 335–345.

Bigné, J. E., Sánchez, M. I., & Sánchez, J. (2000). Tourism image, evaluation variables and alter purchase behaviour: Inter-relationship. *Tourism Management, 22*(6), 607–616.

Blattberg, R. C., & Sen, S. K. (1976). Market segments and stochastic brand choice models. *Journal of Marketing Research, 13*(1), 17–28.

Cotton, B. C., & Babb, E. M. (1978) Consumer response to promotional deals. *Journal of Marketing, 42*(3), 109–113.

Cronin, J. J., & Taylor, S.A. (1992). Measuring service quality: A reexamination and extension. *Journal of Marketing, 56*(3), 55–68.

Davis, S., Inman, J. J., & McAlister, L. (1992). Promotion has a negative effect on brand evaluations — or does it? Additional disconfirming evidence. *Journal of Marketing Research, 29*(1), 143–148.

Dodson, J. A., Tybout, A. M., & Sternthal, B. (1978). Impact of deals and deal retractions on brand switching. *Journal of Marketing Research, 15*(1), 72–81.

Ehrenberg, A. S. C., Hammond, K., & Goodhardt, G. J. (1994). The after-effects of price-related consumer promotions. *Journal of Advertising Research, 34*(4), 11–21.

Eskin, G. J., & Baron, P. H. (1977). Effects of price and advertising in test — market experiments. *Journal of Marketing Research, 14*(4), 499–508.

Fornell, C., & Larcker, D. F (1981). Evaluating structural equation models with unobservable variables and measurement error. *Journal of Marketing Research, 18*(1), 39–50.

Guadagni, P. M., & Little, D. C. (1983). A Logit model of brand choice calibrated on scanner data. *Marketing Science, 2*(3), 203–238.

Hatcher, L. (1998). *A step-by-step approach to using the SAS system for factor analysis and structural equation modelling.* Cary, NC: SAS Institute Inc.

Jones, M., & Zufryden, F. (1980). Adding explanatory variables to a consumer purchase behaviour model: An exploratory study. *Journal of Marketing Research, 17*(3), 323–334.

Klein, R. L. (1981). Using supermarket scanner panels to measure the effectiveness of coupon promotions. In: J. W. Keon (Ed.), *Proceedings: Third ORSA/TIMS special interest conference on market measurement and analysis* (pp. 118–126). Providence, RI: Institute of Management Sciences.

Kopalle, P. K., Mela, C. F., & Marsh, L. (1999). The dynamic effect of discounting on sales: Empirical analysis and normative pricing implications. *Marketing Science, 18*(3), 317–332.

Lattin, J. M., & Bucklin, R. E. (1989). Reference effects of price and promotion on brand choice behaviour. *Journal of Marketing Research, 26*(3), 299–310.

Neslin, S. A., & Shoemaker, R. W. (1989). An alternative explanation for lower repeat rates after promotion purchases. *Journal of Marketing Research, 26*(2), 205–213.

Rothschild, M. L., & Gaidis, W. C. (1981). Behavioural learning theory: Its relevance to marketing and promotions. *Journal of Marketing, 45*(2), 70–78.

Shoemaker, R. W., & Shoaf, F. R. (1977). Repeat rate of deal purchases. *Journal of Advertising Research, 17*(2), 47–53.

Szymanski, D. M., & Henard, D. H. (2001). Customer satisfaction: A meta-analysis of the empirical evidence. *Journal of the Academy of Marketing Science, 29*(1), 16–35.

Zins, A. H. (2001). Relative attitudes and commitment in customer loyalty models. *International Journal of Service Industry Management, 12*(3), 269–294.

Author Index

Abbey, J.R., 150
Achrol, R.S., 87
Agrusa, J., 81
Airey, D., 133–134, 136, 141
Akama, J.S., 11
Akerlof, G., 173
Akin, B., 35
Allcock, J.B., 180
Allen, J., 150
Andereck, K.L., 14
Anderson, J.C., 88, 261
Anderson, R.E., 62–64, 66, 187
Andreu, L., 209, 255, 262, 270
Andsager, J.L., 16
Apostolakis, A., 133, 144
Apostolopoulos, Y., 122, 207
Apter, A., 136
Apter, M.J., 199, 201
Apter, M., 201
Arbuckle, J., 227, 230
Armoo, A.K., 16
Ashworth, G.J., 133
Askegaard, S., 260
Asplund, C., 120
Assael, H., 161
Ataman, B.K., 47
Atherton, T., 234
Avraham, E., 116, 117, 121
Awaritefe, O.D., 197

Babb, E.M., 270
Back, K., 12
Backman, K.F., 151
Backman, S.J., 11, 151
Baillie, J., 45
Baker, D.A., 187, 208, 270–271

Baker, D., 208, 210
Baker, J., 255, 258, 263
Baker, T.L., 258
Baker–Prewitt, J.L., 187
Ballantyne, R., 134, 144
Baloglu, S., 12, 174, 196–197, 240
Bamossy, G., 260
Baral, A., 78, 119, 122
Baral, S., 78, 119, 122
Baron, P.H., 270
Barsky, J., 10, 12
Bartholomew, D.J., 194
Bateson, J.E.G., 256–257
Baudrillard, J., 207
Baumgartner, H., 260
Bawa, K., 270
Beaman, J., 13
Beard, J.G., 196
Bearden, W.O., 225, 270
Beeho, A.J., 141, 144
Beirman, D., 78, 119
Beirne, M., 57
Bejou, D., 83
Bel, J.L., 13
Bellenger, D., 11
Bello Acebrón, L., 148–149
Bender, W., 223
Bennett, O., 75, 83
Bensghir, T.K., 33
Bentler, P.M., 261, 273, 276
Berce, J., 38
Beriatos E., 117, 122
Berné, C., 270
Berry, J.W., 250
Berry, L. L., 14, 36, 187, 260
Bettencourt, L. A., 255, 258, 261–262

Bieger, T.a.L., 88
Bigne, E., 209
Bigné, J.E., 255, 262, 271
Birks, F.D., 139
Bitner, M.J., 221, 223, 235
Black, W.C., 62–64, 66
Blackwell, R., 161
Blake, A., 16, 117
Blattberg, R.C., 270
Bloemer, J.M.M., 257
Bloemer, J., 187
Bojanic, D.C., 224, 234
Bojanic, D., 14
Bolton, R.N., 224–225, 234
Bonett, D.G., 273, 276
Bordas, E., 102
Borgers, A., 14
Boshoff, C., 192, 201, 265
Bowen, D., 10, 15
Bowen, J., 79
Bowen, J.T., 1–3, 10, 12
Boxer, S., 121
Boyd, S.W., 134–135, 144
Brady M.K., 221, 224, 225–227, 235, 258
Brand, R.R., 221, 225–226, 235
Breitbach, S., 116
Brown, J.R., 12
Brown, S.W., 261
Brownell, J., 13
Bruner, E.M., 135
Bucklin, R.E., 270
Buckman, S., 116
Buhalis, D., 13, 33, 36, 38–42, 77, 79, 82–83
Burton, R., 241
Burton, S., 224
Butler, P., 68
Butler, R.W., 87–88
Butler, R., 133–134, 136, 141
Byrne, B.M., 261–262

Cai, L.A., 197
Calantone, R., 151
Caldwell, N., 14, 81
Callod, C., 13, 75, 79

Caltabiano, M.L., 150
Cameron, M., 255, 258, 263
Canfield, B.R., 120
Cannon, D.F., 14
Carroll, B., 13
Cha, S., 196–197
Chambers, E., 180
Chang, T.Z., 224–225, 234
Chapman, J.D., 222–223
Chaudhuri, A., 230
Chavez, D., 88
Chebat, J.C., 256
Chen, J.S., 11–12, 240
Cheung, C., 16
Cho, Y., 13
Choi, T.Y., 208–209
Chon, K.S., 250
Christou, E., 12–13
Chu, R., 208–209
Chung, C.M.Y., 224
Church, M.A., 191
Churchill, A.G., 57
Clary, D., 241
Cohen, E., 207–208
Colgate, M., 224, 227
Cooper, C., 82–83
Cooper, R.L., 216
Cosenzā, R.M., 150
Correia, A., 196
Coshall, J., 14
Cotton, B.C., 270
Covington, M.V., 191
Cox, J.L., 173, 180
Crandall, L., 180
Crask, M.R., 150
Crocker, K., 15
Crompton, J.L., 151, 174, 187, 196, 199, 201–202, 208, 210, 270–271
Cronin, J.J., 221, 224–227, 235, 257, 271
Cross, J.A., 46
Crotts, J.C., 16, 78, 172
Crouch, G.I., 81, 196
Crouch, G., 101–102, 110
Cunningham, L.F., 240

Curasi, C.F., 11
Curran, C., 81

Dann, G.M.S., 174, 192, 196, 207–209, 216
Dann, G., 208
Darden, D.K., 150
Darden, W.R., 150
Darke, P.R., 224
Darnton, G., 36
Davidson, R., 241–242
Davis, D., 242
Davis, S., 270
Dawes, J., 258
Day, G.S., 2
de Ruyter, K., 257
Dean, A., 14
Devan, B.D., 196
DeVellis, R.F., 226
Devlin, P.J., 135
Dewald, B., 16
Dierking, L.D., 134
Dinler, Z., 172, 174
Dodds, W.B., 224
Dodson, J.A., 270
Dolli, N., 242
Dolnicar, S., 11–12
Donlon, J., 81
Dore, L., 81
Drew, J.H., 224–225, 234
Drzewiecka, J.A., 16
Dubé, L., 260
Dubs, L., 13
Duman, T., 226–227, 234
Dunn Ross, E.L., 197
Dwyer, L., 15, 102, 109, 111

Edwards, A., 109
Edwards, B., 13, 79
Efrati, B., 118
Ehrenberg, A.S.C., 270
Ekinci, Y., 14, 68
Elizur, J., 116
Elliot, A.J., 191
Elliott, R.H., 202

Engel, J., 161
Enz, C.A., 39
Erdogan, H., 181
Eskin, G.J., 270
Essex, J., 116
Etzel, M.J., 151, 193, 197

Fahy, J., 81
Fakeye, P.C., 174, 250
Faulkner, B., 117
Feldman, L., 149
Fennell, G., 191–193, 202
Fesenmaier, D.R., 13, 162
Fidell, L.S., 139, 245
Figler, M.H., 196
Fisher, A.B., 148
Flavián, C., 257
Fodness, D., 196
Foley, A., 81
Ford, D., 88
Ford, J.K., 194
Formica, S., 15, 256
Fornell, C., 187, 257, 272
Forsyth, P., 15, 102, 109
Frank, R.E., 148
Freire, J.R., 81
Frisby, E., 119
Fuchs, G., 163
Fyall, A., 13, 79, 83

Gaidis, W.C., 270
Galbraith, J.I., 194
Gallarza, M.G., 16
Galston, W., 180
Ganapathy, S., 56
García, H.C., 16
Garrod, B., 83
Gartner, W.C., 172, 174, 250
George, R., 14, 16
George, R.T., 14
Gerbing, D.W., 261
Gertler, M.S., 87–88
Getz, D., 241–242
Geva, A., 210
Gibson, H., 16, 200

Gilbert, D., 14, 242
Glendon, I., 196–197
Gnoth, J., 89–90, 95, 97, 192, 201–202, 255, 262, 265
Godbey, G., 33
Goeldner, C.R., 148
Goeldner, R., 101–102
Goh, C., 15
Goh, H.K., 16
Goldman, A., 210
Gonzales, A., 209
González Fernández, A.M., 148–149
Goodall, B., 129
Goodhardt, G. J., 270
Gospodini, A., 117, 122
Goulding, C., 133–134, 255, 259
Graefe, A., 162
Graham, L., 57
Granovetter, M., 87
Grazer, W.F., 11
Greenspan, R., 40
Gregoire, M., 13
Grewal, D., 222, 224–225, 227, 230, 234
Groburn, N.H.H., 208–209
Gruen, T.W., 230
Guadagni, P.M., 270
Guerin. S., 141
Gummesson, E., 88
Gursoy, D., 16, 240
Gyimóthy, S., 257, 260, 263

Haber, S., 208
Haider, D.H., 116–118, 120–121
Hair, J.F., 62–64, 66
Hakansson, H., 88
Hall, C.M., 122
Halstead, D., 187
Hammond, K., 270
Hancer, M., 14
Hankinson, G., 83
Hardesty, D.M., 225
Hardine, M.D., 14
Harper, R.H.R., 45
Harris, K.J., 14
Hatab, J., 136

Hatcher, L., 139, 272–273
Hawes, D.K., 150
Hayward, B.M., 135
Heath, E., 129
Hefner, F.L., 172
Hemphill, B., 46
Henard, D.H., 270
Henderson, J.C., 16
Heresniak, E.J., 45
Heung, V.C.S., 14
Hiemstra, S., 15
Higham, J., 15
Highlander., 119
Hightower, R., 221, 225–226, 235, 258
Hilgen, D., 45
Hinch, T., 15
Hinkin, T.R., 10
Hippler, H.J., 136
Hirschman, E. C., 255
Holbrook, M.B., 230, 255
Hooper, P., 77, 119
Horner, S., 207–208, 258
Hornik, J., 149
Houston, M.B., 255, 258, 262
Howard, D., 240
Hsieh, A., 223
Hsu, C., 196
Hsu, C.H.C., 11
Huan, T., 223
Huan, T.C., 13
Hui, M.K., 263
Huisman, S., 208–209, 216–217
Hustad, P., 149
Hwang, J., 56

Iacobucci, D., 255, 265
Icoz, O., 48
Inman, J.J., 270
Isaacs, L., 46
Iso–Ahola, S.E., 191–193, 196–198
Israeli, A.A., 16
Izard, C.E., 256

Jackson, J., 88
Jacoby, J., 161

Jamrozy, U., 197
Jang, S., 197
Jansen–Verbeke, M., 255
Jarillo, J.C., 97
Jarvenpaa, S.L., 55
Jaworski, B.J., 89
Jeong, M., 13
Jogaratnam, G., 14
Johanson, J., 88
Johnson, L., 14
Johnson, L.W., 235
Johnson, T.J., 176
Johnston, R.J., 15
Jones, D.L., 11
Jones, K.C., 14
Jones, M., 270
Jurowski, C., 11

Kadt, E.D., 180
Kaiser, H.F., 62, 64
Kandampully, J., 12
Kanuk, L.L., 208
Kaplan, L., 161
Kaplanseren, E., 46–47
Kasavana, M.L., 13, 15
Kashyap, R., 224
Kassianidis, P., 13
Kastenholz, E., 242, 250–251
Kaye, B.K., 176
Keane, M., 240–241
Keaveney, S.J., 55
Kerin, R.A., 2
Khan, M., 14
Kieti, D.M., 11
Kim, C., 111, 208–209
Kim, E., 196
Kim, H., 1, 16
Kim, K., 14
Kim, S., 1, 16
Kim, W.G., 15
King, J., 75–76, 81, 83
Kirby, V.G., 135
Kirkova, I., 41
Klein, R.L., 270
Klein, S., 39

Klemz, B.R., 265
Klenosky, D.B., 14
Kline, R.B., 228
Knutson, B.J., 176
Kocak, G., 226
Kohli, A.J., 89
Konecnik, M., 81
Kopalle, P.K., 270
Kotler, N.G., 256, 259
Kotler, P., 12, 87, 116–118, 120–121, 171, 173–175, 240, 256, 259
Kozak, M., 10, 13–14, 33, 41–42, 79, 201, 208–209, 255
Krippendorf, J., 197
Krishnan, R., 222, 224–225, 227, 230, 234

Lagacherie, F., 56
Lam, T., 11
Lanfant, M.F., 180
Lane, B., 241
Lang, C.T., 196
Larcker, D.F 272
Lattin, J.M., 270
Law, R., 10, 12–13, 15–16
Laws, E., 77
Lawson, R., 150
Lazer, W., 148
Lee, B., 265
Lee, C., 199–200
Lee, M., 240
Lehmann, D.R., 187
Leite, A., 241
LeMay, S.A., 153
Lengmuellerand, R., 192, 201
Lepisto, L.R., 11
Lepp, A., 16
Lerner, M., 208
Levine, M.S., 153
Licata, M.C., 13, 40
Lichtenstein, D.R., 224
Liebermann, Y., 172
Light, D., 134–135
Little, D.C., 270
Litvin, S.W., 16, 172
Livaic, Z., 111

Lo, A., 16
Loker, L.E., 196
Long–Tolbert, S., 15
Louviere, J.J., 14
Lovelock, C., 56
Lucas, A.F., 15
Lynn, M., 16
Lysonski, S., 250

MacCallum, R.C., 194
Macintosh, G., 12
Mack, R., 11
Maddison, R., 36
Madrigal, R., 257
Makens, J., 12, 171, 181
Malhotra, N.K., 139
Mannell, R.C., 196
Mano, H., 256–257
Mansfeld Y., 119, 163
Marsh, L., 270
Martínez, E., 257
Mäser, B., 162
Massy, W.F., 148
Matovic, D., 17, 19
Matthews, A., 56
Mattila, A.S.M., 226, 234
Mattila, A., 11
Mattila, A.S., 11
Mayo, E., 150
Mazanec, J.A., 15
McAlister, L., 270
McCahon, C., 12, 15
McCain, G., 134, 144
McCarthy, 107
McCleary, K.W., 11, 17, 19, 174, 196–197
McCleary, K., 15
McGugan, S., 141
McIntosh, R., 101–102
McKay, S.L., 196
Mclaughlin, E.D., 227
McMillian, S.J., 56
McMullan, R., 11
Mehrabian, A., 256–257
Mela, C.F., 270
Mellor, R., 111

Menon, K., 260
Michael, E., 104
Michon, R., 256
Middelkoop, M.V., 14
Miller, A.R., 11
Miller, J., 12, 15
Milman, A., 10, 250, 255
Miniard, P., 161
Minor, M., 161–162
Mitchell V.W., 162
Money, R.B., 16, 78
Mongknonvanit, C., 14
Mongomery, D.B., 2
Monroe, K.B., 222–225, 227, 230, 234
Monty, B., 15
Moore, E.S., 17
Moore, H.F., 120
Moore, K., 208–209, 216–217
Moorman, C., 89
Morais, D.B., 12
Morgan, D., 14
Morgan, J., 173–174
Morgan, N.J., 81
Morgan, N., 78, 119, 122
Morgatroyd, S., 201
Morrison, A.M., 16, 33, 40, 111, 196
Moscardo, G., 134–135, 196
Moscardo, G.M., 16
Moschis, G., 11
Mount, D.J., 11
Moustaki, I., 194
Moutinho, L., 148
Mowen, J., 161–162
Mowforth, M., 217
Mueller, R.D., 11
Múgica, J.M., 270
Müller, H., 217
Munt, I., 217
Murphy, J., 13
Murphy, P., 88, 234

Namasivayam, K., 10
Nash, L., 10, 12
Neslin, S. A., 270
Netemeyer, R.G., 224

Nielsen, C., 122
Niininen, O., 79
Norman, W.C., 199–200
Norusis, M.J., 227
Nunnally, J.C., 227
Nworah, U., 117

O'Conner, 42
O'Connor, B.P., 194
O'Connor, P., 37–38, 42
O'Leary, J.T., 196
O'Sullivan V., 122
Odabas, H., 45, 47
Oh, H., 10–13, 224, 234
Oliver, R.L., 14, 73, 225, 256–257, 259
Olsen, M.D., 256
Olson, C.O., 175–176
Oppermann, M., 79, 240
Orzen, H., 173–174
Ostrom, A., 255, 265
Otto, J.E., 234, 259
Ozsoy, O., 174

Page, S.J., 241–242
Page, T.J., 187
Palmer, A., 11, 83
Pan, G.W., 13
Parasuraman, A., 14, 36, 187, 260
Parfitt, N., 77
Parks, S.C., 10, 12
Parthasarathy, M., 55
Paul, G.W., 242
Pavlovich, K., 88
Pearce, D.G., 13
Pearce, P.L., 16, 196
Pearch, P.L., 150
Pedhazur, E.J., 57
Pellinen, J., 15
Peppard, J., 68
Percy, L., 191–192, 196, 199, 202
Perdue, R.R., 196
Perreault, W.D., 150
Pessemier, E., 149
Peter, J.P., 175–176
Peter, P., 161

Peterson, C., 107
Petrick, J.F., 11, 16, 221, 226, 234
Petrick, J., 257
Phelan, S.E., 45
Phillips, R.G., 234
Piggott, R., 81
Pike, S., 14, 73
Pinfold, J.F., 242
Pink, D., 117, 121
Pitts, R.E., 151
Pizam, A., 16, 119, 172, 250
Plaschka, G., 14
Plog, D., 240
Polo, Y., 257
Poon, A., 36, 101–102, 104–105, 240, 242
Poria, Y., 134, 136, 141
Porter, M.E., 73, 87
Porter, M., 102–104, 106, 113
Portugal, I. N.E., 194
Pratt, G., 192, 199
Preacher, K.J., 194
Prentice, R.C., 141, 144
Prentice, R., 134–135, 141
Pride, R., 117
Prideaux, B., 81, 83
Pritchard, A., 81
Pritchard, M.P., 234
Pritchard, M., 240
Pruyn, A., 260, 263
Pullman, M.E., 15

Qu, H., 14–15

Ranchhod, 56
Raaij, F. van., 151
Ragheb, M.G., 196
Ragsdale, C.T., 12
Ranganathan, G., 56
Rao, P., 15, 102, 109
Ray, C., 201
Ray, N.M., 134, 144
Reichel, A., 16, 163, 172
Rein, I., 116–118, 120–121
Reisinger, Y., 172, 208–209

Reynolds, D., 13
Rhee, S., 56
Ribeiro, M., 241
Richard, M.D., 153
Richardson, S.L., 1, 16
Riggins, F., 56
Riley, M., 79
Rimmington, M., 41–42, 208
Ritchie, B.W., 115, 117
Ritchie, J.R.B., 77, 148, 234, 259
Ritchie, J., 101–102
Ritchie, J.R.B., 101–102
Ritchie, R.J.B., 77
Rittichainuwat, B.N., 14
Roehl W., 56
Roehl, W.S., 56, 162
Roselius, T., 162
Ross, G., 240
Rossiter, J.R., 191–192, 196, 199, 202
Rothschild, M.L., 270
Rotschild, M., 173
Rowley, J., 255, 258
Rushton, C., 201
Russell, J.A., 192, 199, 256, 258
Russell, J., 256–257
Rust, H., 11
Rust, R.T., 89, 257, 259
Ruyter, K., 187
Ryan, C., 180, 196–197
Ryan, M., 161
Ryff, C.D., 199

Sánchez, J., 271
Sánchez, M.I., 271
Santana, G., 119
Sari, Y., 33
Saura, I.G., 16
Schall, M., 10
Schewe, C., 151
Schiffman, L.G., 208
Schofield, P., 207
Schroeder, T., 240
Schul, P., 151
Schuster, A.G., 31, 43
Schwarz, N., 136

Scott, N., 77
Sears, D., 13
Seckelmann, A., 174, 181
Seddighi, H.R., 14
Sefton, M., 173–174
Selin, S., 88
Sellen, A.J., 45
Sen, S.K., 270
Senn, J.A., 33, 36
Sessa, A., 88
Sheldon, P.J., 33, 40
Shafer, C.S., 265
Shah, R.H., 230
Sharpley, R., 180
Sheldon, P.J., 33, 40
Shemwell, D.J., 221, 225–226, 235
Sherrell, D., 73
Shifflet, D.K., 58
Shoaf, F.R., 270
Shoemaker, R.W., 270
Shoemaker, S., 12, 79
Short, J.R., 116
Shostack, G.L., 95
Sigala, M., 13
Siguaw, J.D., 39, 240
Siguaw, J., 13
Silberberg, T., 134
Silverberg, K.E., 151
Sin, L., 56
Sinclair, M.T., 16, 117
Singer, M., 121
Singh, A.J., 15
Sirakaya, E., 11, 174, 196, 257
Sirohi, N., 227
Sivadas, E., 187
Skayannis, P., 34
Skidmore, M., 15
Skogland, I., 240
Smeral, E., 103
Smidts, A., 260, 263
Smith, B., 234
Smith, K.C. P., 199, 201
Snehota, I., 88
Sollers, J.J., 196
Solomon, M., 260

Song, H., 15
Sonmez, S.F., 122
Sönmez, S., 174
Soutar, G.N., 235
Sparks, B.A., 1–3, 10
Spence, M., 173
Stafford, G., 16
Stamboulis, Y., 34
Steenkamp, J.E., 260
Steele, F., 194
Sternthal, B., 270
Stevens, T., 255, 259
Stewart, E.J., 135
Stiglitz, J., 173
Strauss, A.L., 121
Sturman, M.C., 16
Suh, Y.K., 172
Suhartanto, D., 12
Sui, J.J., 12
Sundaram, D.S., 11
Swarbrooke, J., 134, 207–208, 255, 258
Sweeney, J.C., 235
Szivas, E., 79
Szymanski, D.M., 270

Tabachnick, B.G., 139, 245
Tait, M., 194
Tan, A.Y.F., 15
Tan, I., 13
Tan, T.E., 14
Tang, V., 11
Tarlow, P., 122
Tasci, A.D.A., 176
Tatham, R.L., 62–64, 66
Taylor, G.S., 153
Taylor, G.A., 15
Taylor, S.A., 257, 271
Teel, J.E., 270
Telfer, D., 83
Tellegen, A., 256–257
Theocharous, A.L., 14
Thompson, B., 194
Thompson, G.M., 15
Thrash, T.M., 191
Timmermans, H., 14

Timothy, D.J., 134–135
Timothy, J.D., 134–135, 144
Tinsley, D.J., 255
Tinsley, H.E. A., 255
Todd, P.A., 15
Todd, S., 208
Tran, H., 173
Travelmole., 56
Tremblay, P., 87
Triandis, H., 149
Tsaur, S., Chang 13
Tsaur, S., Chiu 14
Tsaur, S.H., 162
Tse, A., 56
Tse, A.C., 16
Tse, D. K., 263
Turner, G.B., 153
Turner, L.W., 172
Turner, L., 208–209
Tyano, S., 136
Tybout, A.M., 270
Tyrrell, T.J., 15
Tzeng, G.H., 162

Um, S., 129
Uriely, N., 16
Uysal, M., 11–12, 196–197, 257
Uzzell, D., 134, 144

van Rekom, J., 255
Vanhove, N., 103–104
Varki, S., 224, 227, 257, 259
Vassos, V., 162
Verma, R., 14
Vogt, C.A., 14
Von Friedrichs Grängsjö, Y., 83, 88
Vyncke, P., 151

Wahab, S., 82, 122
Wahlers, R.G., 151, 193, 197
Wall, G., 129
Walsh, K., 14
Wan, H.A., 55
Wang, D., 79
Wang, K.C., 162

Wang, K., 223
Wang, Y., 13
Watson, D., 256–257
Webber, K., 56
Webster, C., 11
Webster, S., 234
Wei, S., 10–11
Weiermair, K., 162
Weilbaker, D.C., 15
Weinstein, A.R., 196
Weiziman, A., 136
Wenger, S., 255, 258, 262
Werthner, H., 39
White, C.J., 81
Wildt, A.R., 224–225, 234
Wilkie, W.L., 17
Williams, P.W., 180
Willis, T., 79
Wind, Y., 148
Wirtz, J., 256–257
Witt, S.F., 148
Wittink, D.R., 227
Wolfe, D.A., 87–88
Wolfe, K., 196
Wong, J., 10, 13
Wong, K.K.F., 15
Wong, M.Y., 14
Wong, R.K.C., 14
Woodside, A.G., 73, 151, 250
Wooldridge, B.R., 14

Yagci, M. I., 226
Yagüe, M.J., 269
Yarcan, S., 35, 37
Yi, Y., 187
Yiannakis, A., 200
Yolal, M., 36
Yoon, T., 14
Yoon, Y., 16, 257
Yoshioka, C., 196
Yoshioka, C.F., 11
Yu, L., 16
Yu, Q., 13
Yuksel, A., 79

Zeithaml, V.A., 14, 36, 187, 221–225, 235, 260
Zillifro, T., 12
Zins, A.H., 10, 192, 201, 271
Zins, A., 255, 257
Zufryden, F., 270

Subject Index

Advertising, 3, 5, 116–119
Agricultural revolution, 34, 35
Agriculture economy, 42
Agro-tourism, 241
Airline reservation systems, 38
Allocentrics, 240
Amadeus, 39
American Defence Ministry, 40
Amplifying determinants, 110, 111, 112
Approach-avoidance model, 187, 257
Arousal theory, 11, 191, 256–259, 262–264
Artifical agents, 31, 43
Artifical intelligence applications, 42
Atmospheric pollution, 47
Attitudes, 4, 149, 187, 191, 193
Attitudinal loyalty, 10

B2B, 13, 41
B2C, 12, 13, 41
B2G, 41
Behavioral intentions, 32, 187–189, 221, 222, 224–226, 229, 230, 232–234, 239, 240, 245–251, 257, 265, 269, 270, 275
Benchmarking, 19, 175, 181
Brand extension, 5, 17, 18
Brand image, 81
Brand positioning, 12, 192, 202
Branding, 5, 17, 18, 117
Business relationship management, 5
Buying behavior, 36

C2B, 41
C2C, 41
C2G, 41

Choice behavior, 17
Choice theory, 4
City image, 122
Commercial networks, 42
Communication networks, 41
Communication strategies, 117, 123, 202
Communication technology, 45
Comparative advantage, 74
Competitive advantage, 33, 36, 37, 87, 97, 102–104, 110, 112, 129
Competitive edge, 38, 73
Competitive environment, 103, 110
Competitive forces, 103, 113
Competitive identity, 117
Competitive models, 101
Competitive performance, 108
Competitive position, 107
Competitive rivalry, 103
Competitive strategy, 103, 105, 107, 113
Competitive success, 105
Competitiveness, 73, 74, 101, 105–108, 111
Complaint behavior, 2, 4, 10, 11, 192, 239, 240, 242, 248
Complaint handling, 11
Computer technology, 35, 45
Consumer activated network, 90, 96, 97
Consumer behavior, 2, 4, 16, 36, 57, 73, 130, 148, 161, 164, 172, 173, 185, 187, 188, 262, 277
Consumer costs, 175
Consumer perceptions, 13, 130, 133, 136, 138, 139, 141, 144, 188, 221, 258
Corporate image, 12
Cost leadership, 103
Country branding, 117

Country image, 74, 116, 117, 122–124
Crisis management, 5, 16, 17, 78
Cross-cultural research, 188, 207–209, 215, 217
CRSs, 38, 39, 82
Culinary tourism, 19
Cultural approximation, 188, 207, 209, 216
Cultural differentiation, 209
Cultural tourism, 18
Customer database development, 37
Customer feedback, 49, 52
Customer loyalty, 4, 12, 13, 39, 189, 240, 269–273, 265–277
Customer relationship management, 4, 12, 18, 251
  marketing, 4, 12, 17, 18
  strategies, 77
Customer satisfaction, 2, 4, 10, 11, 12, 16, 17, 18, 19, 134, 187–189, 207–211, 213, 215–217, 224, 225, 255–260, 262–265, 269–271, 276, 277
Cyber market, 55
Cyber marketing, 31, 55
Cyber positioning, 55
Cyber tourism, 43
Cybermediaries, 31, 43
Cyberspace, 13, 82, 84

Data mining, 38, 42
Databanks, 42
Decision making, 18, 36, 39, 179, 180, 188, 202
Decision theory, 14
Demand conditions, 104–106, 111
Demand factors, 108, 112, 113
Demand generation, 17
Destination branding, 17, 18, 77, 81, 89
Destination choice, 13, 14, 16, 188
Destination competition, 71, 73, 80, 101, 102, 109–111, 113
Destination development, 97, 251
Destination image, 17, 111, 112, 120, 121, 188, 239, 242, 243, 246, 247, 250, 251
Destination logos, 120, 121
Destination loyalty, 188, 239–242, 248, 251

Destination management, 73, 97, 102, 110–113
  organisations, 76–78, 83
  systems, 76, 77, 82, 84
Destination marketing organisations, 3, 13, 16
Destination networks, 87–89, 98
Destination positioning, 118, 191, 201
Destination products, 75, 80, 82
Destination risk, 162
Destination slogans, 120, 121
Destination symbols, 120
Differential pricing, 130, 171, 180
Digital currency, 33
Digital environment, 31
Digital office, 52
Digital TV, 13
Discrete choice analysis, 14
Discriminatory pricing, 130, 171, 180
Distribution channels, 13, 18, 33, 36, 84
Distribution systems, 42
Dutch heritage, 138, 141, 143

Eating behavior, 16, 18, 19
E-brochures, 31, 32, 47, 48, 49, 50, 51, 52
E-business, 56, 41
E-channels, 13
E-commerce, 13, 33, 40, 56
E-communications, 32, 55
Economic costs, 109
ECOSERV, 14
Ecotourism, 134
E-data, 47
E-devices, 39
E-distribution, 5, 13
E-distribution channels, 33
E-documents, 31, 32, 47, 48, 49, 50, 51, 52
E-environment, 47
Ego-enhancement, 196
Electrical signals, 47
E-mail, 38, 47, 56
E-marketing, 5, 13, 17, 38, 41
E-mediaries, 13, 17
Emotions, 191, 192, 255–258, 260, 264, 265
Empowerment, 3, 5, 106

Equal pricing, 178
Equipment risk, 162
Equity theory, 11
E-shopping, 13
Ethics, 4
E-trade, 51
Euro pricing, 15
European heritage, 138, 141, 142
Expectancy disconfirmation model, 10
Extranet, 37, 38, 41, 42

Factor conditions, 104–106
Financial risk, 161, 162, 165–169, 226
Food quality, 19
Food safety, 18

G2B, 41
G2C, 41
G2G, 41
Galileo, 39
GDSs, 38, 39, 40, 82
Geographical information systems, 38, 42
German Culture Bureau, 119
Global economy, 115
Global TV networks, 115
Goods production, 35
Gross domestic production, 89
Guest satisfaction, 10, 240

Hard storage devices, 37, 38
Hardware technology, 34
Hedonic consumption, 255
Hedonic pricing, 15
Heritage management, 133, 144, 145
Heritage sites, 133–135, 137, 144, 145
Heritage tourism, 129, 130, 133, 141
Homeshopping, 37, 38
Hospitality-oriented journals, 1, 2, 3, 16, 17

Image, 4, 17, 73, 116, 117, 121, 187, 241, 270
   crisis, 74, 115–124
Importance-performance analysis, 10
Indian Tourist Bureau, 118
Industrial economy, 42
Industrial revolution, 34, 35

Information era, 35, 42
Information industry, 35
Information processing, 4
Information search, 4, 16
Information storage, 46
Information technology, 5, 17, 18, 31–39, 42, 45, 47, 51, 52
Information transfer process, 45
Innovation, 18, 105, 106, 112, 113, 158
Intelligent agents, 37, 38
Intelligent cards, 37, 42, 38
Inter destination solutions, 84
Interactive TV, 37, 38
Intermediaries, 43, 76
Internal marketing, 5
Internet, 5, 17, 31–33, 40, 41, 46, 48, 50, 51, 52, 55, 56, 57, 60, 82
Intra destination networks, 83
Intra-firm information, 49
Intra organisational systems, 38
Intranet, 37, 38, 41, 42
Inventory systems, 38
Isolation strategy, 119

Jewish heritage, 138, 139, 141, 143
Justice theory, 11

Labour management, 17
Leisure experience, 188, 255, 256, 258, 260, 265
Lifestyles, 130, 147–155, 158, 180, 241
Linguistic approximation, 188
Local heritage sites, 129, 135, 136, 138, 141,
London Tourist Board, 119

Macro economic factors, 108, 109, 112, 113
Market orientation, 12, 89
Market positioning, 3, 4,10, 11, 12, 188
Market segmentation, 3 , 4, 11, 12, 20, 127, 129–131, 133–135, 139, 141, 144, 147, 148, 150, 151, 153–155, 158, 169, 170, 175, 188, 197, 202
Market targeting, 3, 4, 11, 12

Marketing environment, 4, 5
Marketing exchange model, 175, 176
Marketing functions, 4, 89
Marketing strategies, 79
Maslow's hierarchy theory, 192
Mass customisation marketing, 81
Mass tourism products, 76
Media strategies, 74, 115
Mega events, 122
Menu engineering, 17
Menu labeling, 18
Menu planning, 18
Microelectronics, 35, 38, 45
Monetary (prices) costs, 188, 221–228, 230, 232, 234, 274, 276, 277
Monetary values, 175
Multi-branding, 18
Multimedia kiosks, 37, 38, 41
Multiple access systems, 38

National heritage sites, 129, 135, 136, 138, 141,
National image, 115
National income, 34
Negative image, 115–124
Nepal Tourist Board, 119
Network economy, 83
Network technologies, 46
Network theory, 87, 88, 98
Niche marketing, 81
Niche strategy, 103
Non-monetary (prices) costs, 175, 188, 221–228, 230, 232–235
Novelty seeking, 4, 16, 192, 195–197, 199–202, 242, 248

Olympic games, 122
Online consumer benefits, 55
Online consumer incentives, 55
Online distribution channels, 3
Online marketing activities, 56
  tools, 56
Online purchasing behavior, 61
  decisions, 56
Online reservation, 49

Online shopping, 56
Online travel agencies, 32, 55, 57, 61, 65, 66, 67, 68
Opportunity loss risk, 162
Optical devices, 45

Paper consumption, 32, 45, 46, 47, 48, 50, 52
Paperless environment, 32, 51, 52
Paperless office, 32, 45, 46, 52
Perceived cost, 109, 113
Perceived price, 188, 271
Perceived quality, 221, 271–274, 276, 277
Perceived risk, 4, 18, 130, 161, 162, 169, 235
Perceived sacrifice, 221, 223, 226
Perceived value, 4, 109, 113, 188, 221, 222, 224, 225, 227, 232–234
Performance evaluation, 2, 4, 13, 14
Performance risk, 161, 226
Personal heritage sites, 129, 135–138, 141, 142, 144
Personal selling, 3, 5, 15
Persuasion, 4
Physical distribution, 5
Physical efforts, 109
Physical market, 55
Physical risk, 161, 162, 166, 226
Place branding, 74
Place image, 122
Place marketing, 116
Place promotion, 116
Polish Tourism Bureau, 122
Positive image, 116, 118–121, 124
Post-industrial societies, 35
Price, 112
  competitiveness, 15, 102, 109
  differentiation, 130, 171–177, 179, 180
  elasticity, 109, 174, 175
  Pricing, 5, 15, 17, 18, 181
  models, 15
  strategies, 130, 180, 181
Prime promotions, 189, 269–271, 274, 276–278
Printing quality, 46

Prior knowledge, 16
Problem handling, 11
Product development, 17, 107
Product differentiation, 37, 103
Product promotion, 49
Product quality, 36, 181
Production economy, 42
Psychocentrics, 240
Psychological costs, 109
Psychological risk, 162, 166–168, 226
Public relations, 116–118
Pull factors, 4, 13
Push factors, 4, 13

Qualifying determinants, 110, 111, 112
Quality management, 107
Quality plans, 107

Regional development agencies, 77
Regional tourism strategies, 77
Relationship marketing, 79, 81
Repeat visitation, 240
Reservation agents, 39
Resource exchange theory, 12
Revenue management, 5, 179
Reversal theory, 198, 201
Risk factors, 166, 169
Risk perception, 161–164, 166, 167, 169, 170
Risk reduction strategies, 130, 161–163, 166–170
Romanian Tourist Office, 120
Rural tourism, 188, 239, 241, 242, 248

Sales promotion, 5, 15, 18, 112, 116
Satisfaction benchmarking, 10
Satisfaction theory, 11
Segmented pricing, 130, 171–173, 180, 181
Self-esteem, 196
Sensation seeking, 16
Service delivery, 4, 14, 95, 265
Service failure, 2, 10, 11
Service production, 35
Service promotion, 49

Service quality, 2, 4, 14, 19, 36, 37, 222, 226, 234
Service recovery, 2, 4, 10, 11
Service value, 221
Services branding, 117
SERVQUAL, 14
Social responsibility, 4
Social risk, 162, 226
Sociolinguistic approach, 208
Sociological theories, 208
Sociology of tourism, 207, 208
Software programs, 46
Sound recognition systems, 42
Space technologies, 37, 38
Special interest tourism, 134
Stereotypes, 74, 115, 116, 120–122
Strategic alliance, 112
Strategic marketing, 78
Strategic planning, 112, 113
Strategy formulation, 105
Strategy implementation, 105
Supply factors, 108, 112, 113
Systems theory, 87, 88, 98

Technological change, 35
Techological devices, 47
Teleconference, 33
Terrorism, 4, 18, 118, 162, 165
Time risk, 162
Tipping behavior, 4, 15, 16
Tourism characteristic industries, 90–98
  operations, 95
Tourism clusters, 87, 88, 102–104
Tourism crisis, 74, 115, 117, 123
Tourism demand, 15, 31, 33, 179
Tourism development, 179, 181
Tourism market, 31, 147–151, 242
Tourism policy, 108, 112, 113
Tourism products, 33, 35, 42, 74, 89, 90, 95, 97, 98, 104, 108, 129, 163, 171, 175, 180, 181
Tourism related industries, 90–98
Tourism satellite systems, 74, 89, 90, 95, 97, 98
Tourism supermarket, 80

Tourism system, 88, 110
Tourism-oriented journals, 1, 2, 3, 16, 17
Tourist activated network, 95
Tourist behavior, 133, 134, 144, 148, 194, 201, 207, 208
Tourist choice, 13
Tourist complaints, 179
Touristic language, 208
Traditional distribution channels, 76
Traditional intermediaries, 31, 40, 43
Transaction utility theory, 222
Transport factors, 108
Travel intermediaries, 40
Travel motivations, 4, 13, 18, 130, 147–150, 152–155, 158, 188, 191–202, 209, 240–242, 248
Travel portals, 38
Travel value, 188, 221, 222, 232, 234

Utility model, 4
Utility theory, 14

Vacation choice, 18
Vacation risk, 162
Value composition, 221
Value model, 222, 233, 235
Value theory, 222
Variety seeking, 4, 16
Virtual intermediaries, 82
Virtual market, 31
Virtual reality, 33, 37, 38, 41, 42, 46, 52
Visitor loyalty, 239, 240, 243, 247, 248, 251, 256, 257, 259, 260, 262–265

Water pollution, 47
Web site quality, 65
Website development, 3
Website evaluation, 18
World heritage sites, 129, 135, 136, 138, 141, 142, 144
World Tourism Organisation, 41, 89

Yield management, 5, 15, 179